Internet Telephony

Internet Telephony

edited by *Lee W. McKnight, William Lehr,* and *David D. Clark*

The MIT Press
Cambridge, Massachusetts
London, England

© 2001 Massachusetts Institute of Technology

All rights reserved. No part of this book may be reproduced in any form by any electronic or mechanical means (including photocopying, recording, or information storage and retrieval) without permission in writing from the publisher.

This book was set in Baskerville by Best-set Typesetter Ltd., Hong Kong and printed and bound in the United States of America.

Library of Congress Cataloging-in-Publication Data

Internet telephony / edited by Lee W. McKnight, William Lehr, and David D. Clark.
p. cm.
Includes bibliographical references and index.
ISBN 0-262-13385-7 (hc. : alk. paper)
1. Internet telephony. I. McKnight, Lee W. II. Lehr, William, 1958– III. Clark, David D.

TK5105.8865 .I57   2001
004.6—dc21
00-050012

Contents

Foreword

Sharon Eisner Gillett

The publication of this book marks a remarkable transformation taking place in telecommunications. In February 1995—ancient history by Internet time—VocalTec introduced the first commercial software to enable telephone conversations over the Internet. The traditional telecommunications industry greeted this harbinger of Internet telephony with widespread skepticism. At that time, the conventional wisdom held that only "hobbyists"—a euphemism for computer geeks—would use the Internet for phone calls.

Now, a large number of companies have incorporated Internet technology into a wide variety of voice and data service offerings. These companies include not just new entrants, ranging from garage start-ups to Wall Street darlings, but the established giants of the industry. It is clearly evident that the world of telecommunications is changing from one in which the Internet runs as a specialized application on top of a voice-oriented telephone network, to one in which telephony is but one of many applications running on top of a network of digital networks built from that Internet technology.

Back in the "hobbyist" days, a few visionary individuals anticipated the profound impact that Internet technology would have on telecommunications. They did not know exactly what form this impact would take, but they felt a deep conviction that it would arrive. To help give shape to their vision, they created a forum in which selected participants from industry, academia, and government could meet to charter research, discuss the results of rigorous analysis of industry fundamentals, exchange knowledge, brainstorm ideas, and challenge each others' views. Originally named the MIT Internet Telephony Interoperability Consortium (ITC), the forum consisted of sixteen forward-looking member companies working with an interdisciplinary group of academic researchers at the Massachusetts Institute of Technology and elsewhere, with participation from policymakers.

No one is better suited to present the work in this book than the moving forces behind ITC's beginnings: Lee McKnight, David Clark, and Bill Lehr. Lee, a political scientist, founded the consortium and served as its first principal investigator (PI). David, a computer scientist, has chaired the consortium's advisory board since its inception and has served as PI since 1998. Bill, an economist, has been a leading researcher for ITC and has also served as its executive director. The quality of the work presented here, much of it developed within the framework of ITC, is a testament to their thoughtfulness, leadership, and vision.

As the industry has evolved, so has the consortium. In the winter of 1999, ITC changed its name (but not its acronym) to the Internet and Telecoms Convergence Consortium. The new name reflects the blurring of distinctions between the voice and data industries, as well as the impact of the Internet on industries and applications beyond telephony, such as music and television. It also reflects the broadening of the consortium's research agenda to encompass issues of broadband local access, Internet appliances and applications, and Internet industry and market structures.

Much of the analytic work on Internet telephony presented in this book would not have been possible without the support of current and former ITC member companies: British Telecom, Broadband Access Systems, Delta Three, Hewlett-Packard, Lucent Technologies, MediaOne, Mediatrix Peripherals, Motorola, Natural Microsystems, Netspeak, Nokia, Nortel, Sprint, Telecom Italia, Telefonica, Telenor, Telia, VocalTec, and Zephyr Telecommunications. We thank them not only for their financial sponsorship but also for their constructive engagement in the research process, ensuring that ITC work is of the highest quality and relevance. We look forward to continuing this collaborative process in this millennium—the age of the Internet.

Acknowledgments

We thank the many, many colleagues, friends, and sponsors who have contributed to this book. Our faithful friends at The MIT Press, including Bob Prior, Victoria Warneck, and Katherine Innis, patiently shepherded this book to its completion. Annalee Babb, Merrick Berman, Lupita Ervin, and Greg Czarnecki provided able assistance without which this book would not have been completed. Past and current members or the Internet Telephony Consortium, now the renamed Internet and Telecoms Convergence Consortium, provided invaluable feedback and made innumerable contributions and suggestions that made this work possible. Our faculty colleagues and students at The Fletcher School of Law and Diplomacy at Tufts University and at MIT have been understanding and supportive as we labored to complete this work.

Special thanks go to John Wroclawski, Russ Neuman, Shawn O'Donnell, John Tsitsiklis, Petros Kavassalis, Yannis Paschalidis, Ritva Siren, Raj Bansal, Stephen Hinde, John Heiman, and Pedro Chas for their helpful comments and suggestions. The ITC's student research assistants, some of whom graduated to chapter authorship in this book and all of whom made critical contributions to our understanding of what is, and what is not, Internet telephony, and why we should care, are acknowledged here. Much of this work was first presented outside the Consortium at the Annual Telecommunications Policy Research Conference, and we gratefully acknowledge the helpful feedback from our colleagues and friends there.

Acknowledgments

Any errors of fact or by omission are the editors' or authors' responsibility. The views expressed are those of the authors and should not be taken as the views of Tufts University, The Fletcher School of Law and Diplomacy, the Massachusetts Institute of Technology, or ITC sponsors.

Acronyms

ADSL	asymmetric digital subscriber lines
ATM	asynchronous transfer mode
CO	central office
CSU	channel service unit
DNS	domain name service
DSU	data service unit
FCC	Federal Communications Commission
IAP	Internet access provider
IP	Internet protocol
IP-PBX	Internet protocol private branch exchange
ISDN	integrated services digital network
ISP	Internet service provider
IT	Internet telephony
ITXC	Internet telephony interexchange carrier
IXC	interexchange carrier
LAN	local area network
LATA	local access and transport area
LEC	local exchange carrier
NAP	network access point

PSTN	public switched telephone network
POP	point of presence
POTS	plain old telephone service
VoIP	voice over Internet protocol

Internet Telephony

1

An Introduction to Internet Telephony

Lee W. McKnight, William Lehr, and David D. Clark

Human-mediated communication is being transformed. Not long ago, people were generally happy with the telephone and television systems as they then existed. Few could imagine a need for anything different. The telephone was just not something worth thinking about. Frankly, telephone systems, and telecommunications generally, were boring. Very boring. No longer: enter the Internet.[1]

As technologies augmenting human expression continue to advance, the intended and unintended consequences for business as well as social interaction and information exchange are vast. It is incumbent on all of us to understand the technologies and the related application, architecture, business, cost, economic, industry structure, market, media, network, policy, pricing, regulatory, and service issues that may affect business and home users and technology and service providers alike. Understanding the transformation of the underlying converging telecommunications and Internet infrastructure itself is also necessary, whether one is devising business strategies or simply trying to order a pizza. Should you get in your car, dial a phone, click on a web page— or talk to and maybe see the real or simulated pizza person via an Internet "phone" conversation? How should we think about the choices we will all be asked to make as the varieties of human-mediated communication experience increase? This book introduces these issues and considers scenarios of future market and application development for Internet telephony.

Internet telephony first developed to provide interactive voice communications over the existing Internet Protocol–based public Internet. Making an Internet "telephone call" required the use of personal computers with the same telephony application software on both computers.[2] The personal computers needed to be connected to Internet service providers and equipped with a sound card (multimedia enabled), a microphone, and speakers. From this beginning circa 1994–1995, new technologies and business models have emerged that have transformed the telecommunications industry and telecommunications regulation worldwide.

This book presents a variety of analyses of Internet telephony. The implications and opportunities for advanced services, applications, architectures, costs, economics, enterprise networks, industry structures, multimedia, policy models, pricing, regulation, and service providers are analyzed. Our own search for answers to the questions arising from the convergence of the telecommunications and Internet industries motivated us to found The Massachusetts Institute of Technology's Internet and Telecoms Convergence Consortium (previously known as the Internet Telephony Consortium), or ITC, and continue the collaboration from the Edward R. Murrow Center at Tufts University's Fletcher School of Law and Diplomacy.[3] From our prior work on the technologies and pricing challenges of Internet economics, it was evident that real-time voice conversations would be one of the first areas in which the traditional technical operations of the Internet would collide with new user and business demands.[4] To help us explore this challenge to economic theory and business practice, we convened a cross-industry group drawing from the telecommunications and computer industries, attracted some of MIT's and other affiliated universities' best and brightest faculty and students, and established methods for industry to inform the academy, and vice versa—and for both to engage in dialogue on these questions with public officials at the national and international levels.

This book draws together and presents to a broader audience for the first time some of the fruits of this multifaceted collaboration and also includes a few additional chapters by experts that were not originally developed within the context of the consortium. The analyses, authored principally by faculty, staff, (now former) graduate students, and industrial partners of the consortium, are technically grounded in the bleeding edge of Internet protocol development. The opportunity to work at the interdisciplinary frontiers of knowledge was due in large part to the close collaboration with the consortium of researchers from MIT's Laboratory of Computer Science. The ITC has in fact been overseen since its founding by the coauthor of this chapter, and coeditor of this book, David Clark, who leads the Advanced Network Architecture group there.

Given the rate of change of the underlying technologies and their associated costs, these chapters should not be read as a fully accurate description of what the cost structure of Internet telephony would be circa, say, 2005. Rather, the chapters seek to illustrate what the economic considerations, cost elements, and analytic approaches are that may assist business and policy analysts as well as our fellow researchers in developing their own analyses and business plans of the then-current state of the art. The broader readership, which may not wish to undertake such analyses, may still benefit from a deeper understanding of the cost and architectural elements of a converged telecommunications and Internet industry.

What Is Internet Telephony?

Some use the term *Internet telephony* to refer only to first-generation systems for making telephone calls over the public Internet, and hence prefer what they believe is the more precise term *IP telephony* (Internet protocol telephony), which would refer to the use of the Internet protocol for the networking of packetized voice services. Internet telephony is also referred to as next-generation telephony, computer telephony integration, packet telephony, Intranet and/or extranet telephony, voice over IP (VoIP, or VOIP), voice over the network (VON), or voice conferencing.

By *Internet telephony* we mean broadly the transformation of the Internet from an application on the public telephone network to a general communications infrastructure platform capable of supporting telephone service as well as a myriad of other multimedia applications. The traditional public switched telephone networks (PSTN), modified to support IP, will be part of this global infrastructure, but the cast of characters, applications, and types of networks involved will be more diverse, ubiquitous, capable, and global. By this definition, *Internet telephony* stands for all of the multimedia applications that can be supported over IP-derived protocols running on diverse physical media (cable, telephone, wireless, and others). The economics of Internet telephony applied in this sense are the economics of the transformation of our communications infrastructure from one based on circuit-switched networks controlled by a small number of facilities-based telephone companies into a next-generation infrastructure based on packet communication protocols. Realizing this transformation entails the entry of new types of firms and the reform of old ones, the collision and convergence of industries previously regarded as separate (computers and data communications, content and conduit, equipment and services), and the development of new and innovative services. This will require new business models, new network and service architectures, and new policy frameworks. The goal of this book is to elucidate these phenomena.

We acknowledge that in time another term may be accepted—and that for many practitioners, the preferred term even now is *IP telephony*. In any case, we know from historical precedent that the definition will be refined, and the words used to describe what we now call Internet telephony could be quite different. Internet telephony may come to sound to people's ears as *horseless carriage* does to ours. But it is our fate to be writing at the time of transition in communication technologies, and without the benefit of 20/20 (or year 2020) hindsight. Nonetheless, writing as we are in the year 2000, we have not yet heard a term better suited to our meaning, or at least not one that we have recognized as such. Hence we employ the term *Internet telephony* and accept its baggage, including the confusion of those who assume we mean just software for free phone calls across the Internet.

What Is a Telephone Call?

Up to 75 percent of telephone calls are estimated to end as voice mail or are not answered. If this is the case, does it make sense to engineer a "phone system" for telephone calls? What are telephone calls anyway? Many "telephone calls" are actually faxes or data sessions, not voice calls.

And why not substitute low-cost generic technologies of the Internet wherever possible to reduce costs and increase flexibility? This logic leads not just to computer-telephony integration, or CTI, a popular buzzword among the phone geeks, but Internet telephony.

To carry this logic further, why shouldn't e-mail and voice mail and fax be integrated with a common web interface for the "phone" or Internet appliance? And if end users are capable of multimedia voice communication, shouldn't Web sites, including e-commerce sites, chat rooms, and customer service call center sites, be augmented with voice recognition systems and interactive voice response systems for instant two-way or multiparty communications? Technologies and architectures for some of these Internet telephony business opportunities are described in the chapters of this book.

We do not attempt to provide in this book detailed Internet telephony product descriptions (they can be found in the trade or business press), nor is this a how-to manual for those looking to reconfigure their computers to support such services. Similarly, the arcana of technical standards for Internet telephony are not addressed in depth in this book. Although these are admittedly critically important, detailed expositions on such topics, we fear, would drive away those interested in the broader economic, business, and user issues we focus on. Further, the critical standard of the moment is too ephemeral to be worth the effort of including in a publication such as this book, which we hope will have a reasonably long shelf life. If a reader is hoping to unravel the mysteries of, for example, H.323, H.324, G.911, SIP, diffserv, Intserv, RSVP, MGCP, SS7, SGCP, MPLS, VML, IPDR, gateways, and gatekeepers, we suggest that person look elsewhere, including to some of our other publications. The public, private, and nonprofit organizations that set those standards should be the first stop, followed perhaps by a session with one or another of the myriad consulting and training organizations only too happy to assist in this quest for such knowledge. Rather, in this book we focus on the underlying economic forces and technical architectures that will lead to tomorrow's headlines and standards for Internet telephony.

In the past, a person would normally call another person only at his or her telephone number and speak for a few minutes. There are now a wide variety of communication modes. Many people today have several phones, pagers, fax machines, computers, appliances, and boxes that may or may not have associated with them a telephone number or IP address. Further, teleconferences have become increasingly common, whether for business planning or for extended families to plan their summer vacations. Technologies enabling people to reach one or many other people across any media are needed. Internet telephony technology offers potential solutions to these market needs.

The public Internet is not a controlled network environment. The IP technology currently employed on the Internet uses nondeterministic switching (datagrams), which offers little potential for approximating real-time voice connectivity in that environment, except through overprovisioning of bandwidth. As a consequence, Internet telephony over the public Internet is not yet a significant direct competitor in the field of voice telephony. However, using IP networks, conceived as either intranets or virtual private networks, to provide voice services across a well-managed, overprovisioned, best-effort network, is technically feasible today. Entrepreneurs and established businesses large and small are using IP technologies in just this fashion. Typically, the end user or customer may not know or care that her voice was carried across a packet network rather than across a circuit-switched network along a portion of its transmission path.

The traditional core elements of the phone network, including the central office switches and private branch exchanges (PBXs) that route phone calls within large businesses, are being redesigned to accommodate packet-based telephony routing, whether internal to the organization or externally, to take advantage of new least-cost routing options and new service options. Access equipment for small businesses and individual users such as cellular phones is being similarly transformed and made IP capable. The onrush of new technologies and business models has already led to "free" phone and Internet services. That is, rather than viewing phone network resources as a scarce commodity for which a high price is to be charged, it may be given away in the hopes of selling some other good or value-added service.

The extension of PC connectivity from a single network across the Internet was the greatest advantage made possible through the early application of Internet telephony technology. This form of connectivity using personal computers was the primary focus for the first stage of development of Internet telephony technology. Access to advanced integrated services, as well as access to services enabling interworking across the PSTN to and from the Internet, is still at an early stage, due to limited bandwidth, processing power, service development, and interoperability.

The development of voice communication capabilities, using IP over the Internet, has progressed to where these capabilities may be viewed more precisely as IP telephony rather than as Internet telephony. IP telephony capabilities are now becoming widespread. The limitations of the circuit-switching techniques of conventional telephony may now be overcome through integration with IP technologies. The areas that IP telephony address include delivery of incoming calls from the Internet to existing call centers, provision of virtual office capabilities for at-home workers (telecommuters), provision of mobile services for traveling employees, and the multimedia enabling of enterprise wide area networks.

A key element in making effective use of the emerging Internet telephony technology is the development and use of gateways that bridge the IP environment of the Internet and the circuit-switched environment of wired and wireless public telecommunications networks. Such gateways are devices that make it possible to construct application-specific network structures that provide for real-time, two-way communication between circuit-switching and packet-switching technologies to create an integrated, networking fabric. Encouraging interoperability between public telecommunications networks and the Internet, as can be done with gateways, was one of the original objectives, which led to the formation of the ITC.

We define Internet telephony as the services, applications, and equipment for mediated human communication emerging from the convergence of the Internet and telecommunications. That is the subject of this book.

Structure of the Book

Part I, "Applications, Architecture, and Industry Structure," reviews the wide range of potential applications of Internet telephony, the challenges of architecting global networks to support such services spanning the Internet and telecommunications infrastructures globally, and the industrial structure implications of Internet telephony. The wide range of applications, the variety of IP network architectures, and the diversity of industrial structures made possible by Internet telephony are highlighted.

Part II, "Networks and Media," explores diffusion scenarios for Internet telephony and Internet multimedia applications, as well as the repercussions of a converged Internet and telecommunications industrial structure. The growth in data traffic, a critical factor in shifting networks toward the Internet protocol and away from circuit-switched architectures, is highlighted and projected into the future.

Part III, "Economics and Costs," reviews the cost elements and economics of Internet telephony from the diverse perspectives of service providers and home and corporate users. These chapters offer detailed examples of the consequences for users of the new applications, architectures, and vertically disintegrated industrial structures.

Part IV, "Markets, Strategies, and Regulation," analyzes the motivation for and structure of bandwidth markets as a necessary complement to Internet telephony service provision. The chapters describe the services enabled by Internet telephony technologies and highlight the potential for obtaining bandwidth or "minutes" through new market mechanisms. Also, the business strategy options confronting Internet telephony carriers of various types are assessed, as are the regulatory issues raised by Internet telephony.

Applications, Architectures, and Industry Structures

This part of the book is an overview and initial consideration of the applications, architectures, and industry structures made possible by Internet telephony. In "A Taxonomy of Internet Telephony Applications," David Clark identifies three classes of Internet telephony (computer to computer, telephone to telephone, and hybrid, that is, computer to phone and phone to computer) and considers their implications. He then suggests which range of applications and services is best served by which type of Internet telephony and identifies the technical, business, and regulatory difficulties of providing these various types of Internet telephony. He concludes that although many dismiss computer-to-computer Internet telephony as solely the domain of computer geeks and international students seeking to avoid phone charges to "phone home," it is precisely in this arena that Internet telephony has its greatest promise over the long term. When human-mediated communication is freed of the technical and service constraints of the hundred-year legacy of the phone networks, a whole new class of services may arise to enable a broadened and deepened interpersonal experience, unconstrained by geography and bandwidth.

In "Virtually Global Telcos: International Internet Telephony Architectures," Terry McGarty and Lee W. McKnight explore the technical architecture of international IP telephony networks and consider the business logics that may—or may not—support such networks. Drawing on McGarty's practical experience as an entrepreneur building such global networks, the chapter highlights the technical and economic considerations others hoping to follow his virtual footsteps must follow.

In "Vertical Integration, Industry Structure, and Internet Telephony," William Lehr considers the extent to which the traditionally vertically integrated telecommunications industry may become increasingly disaggregated and fragmented. The potential disaggregation of phone services can be seen as a positive or negative development depending on one's point of view. That is, are you employed by a large incumbent telecommunications operator or a new entrant? Are you a customer looking for specialized services or a "plain vanilla" customer looking for the best possible deal from the largest possible provider?

In "Local Loop Technology and Internet Structures," David Clark demonstrates how the unique nature of the Internet is undermining the traditional vertical stovepipe structures of media industries. Television no longer requires a "broadcaster," cable television no longer requires a "cable," and telephony no longer requires either a telephone or a telephone company. In the emerging Internet-centric industry structure, services are decoupled from physical infrastructures. The implication for consumers is that there may be increased competition in the provision of services as well as increased fluidity in the services and in the receivers of Internet-based information communications and entertainment services.

Networks and Media

The chapters in part II consider scenarios for future growth in data traffic and the adoption and diffusion of Internet telephony and multimedia services. In "Internet Telephony and the Datacentric Network," Philip Mutooni and David Tennenhouse show that data traffic is rapidly exceeding traditional circuit-switched telephony in volume terms. The data for their analysis were gathered with the cooperation of leading firms such as AT&T and MCI (née WorldCom) directly from the firms' own switching centers. The implications of this transition for Internet telephony are that even if at the moment the revenue for voice services far exceeds data revenues, the economic basis of the industry must ultimately conform to the value proposition that is driving these dramatic shifts in network usage patterns. Data is dominant, and voice-only networks are rapidly becoming a historical, and high-cost, legacy.

In "After the Web: Diffusion of Internet Media," Lee W. McKnight and Marc Shuster also draw on data on historical trends. The birth and decline of gopher and the rise of the Web are reviewed, as is the problematic case of Internet multicasting. In its first iteration as the MBONE (Internet multicast backbone), the quality and utility of the service was too low for it to be accepted by users. The future trends in the number of Internet hosts, web sites, and future growth in Internet multimedia services are also the subject of speculation. Time will tell whether the authors' fit of S-curves to data on adoption and diffusion of Internet telephony was a gross over- or underestimate but our hunch is that McKnight and Shuster are far too cautious.

Economics and Costs

In an industry characterized by Moore's law and other theorems on the rate of decline in price and increase in capability of digital and optical technologies, the specific cost numbers and figures in the chapters in part III should be accepted, if at all, with a high degree of skepticism. The point of the chapters is not the numbers but the methods by which they are derived.

In "Internet Telephony Service Providers," Lee W. McKnight and Brett Leida review the cost considerations for an Internet service provider in offering Internet telephony services. The application of new pricing models and the potential impact of regulatory changes on the costs seen by an ISP are also briefly addressed. The authors conclude that in the short term, Internet telephony is a threat mainly to ISPs, because it will increase costs and change usage patterns without necessarily a resultant increase in revenues. With the introduction of new pricing and service models, however, Internet telephony can become an opportunity for ISPs to threaten other telecommunications firms.

In "Local Internet Access Network," Marvin Sirbu, Kanchana Wanichkorn, and Daniel Fryxell build on and refine McKnight and Leida's methods and analyses to consider what the costs will be for home users of Internet telephony services. The potential cost savings and benefits of access to new services will be affected by a number of technical choices, the authors conclude.

In "Internet Telephony in the Corporation," Kanchana Wanichkorn and Marvin Sirbu address the same set of questions from the perspective of the corporation. Would an integrated network offering both data and voice services be preferable, in terms of costs, to the provision, maintenance, and operation of two dedicated networks for voice and data services? The authors conclude that the case for an integrated approach relying on Internet technologies is not yet as strong as some of its proponents might allege.

Markets, Strategies, and Regulation

This part addresses the considerations confronting carriers and manufacturers in assessing where the market opportunities will be for Internet telephony. The emergence of new markets for bandwidth and minutes to aggregate the capabilities and service offerings of Internet telephony providers, and the potential strategies of those carriers, are addressed. In "Internet Telephony Markets and Services," Terrence P. McGarty considers how bandwidth markets may be required for the efficient operation of flexible IP–based telephony services. Methods for determining the least-cost routing of phone calls within the Internet telephony framework are also addressed.

In "Internet Telephony Carrier Strategies," Husham Sharifi, drawing on his experience as an owner of an ISP, as an intern with the International Telecommunication Union contributing to its initial report on Internet telephony, analyzes the strategic options facing Internet telephony carriers. Sharifi points to both the risks and the new opportunities that rapidly changing technologies and markets provide to carriers. He concludes that there is no one ideal strategy for Internet telephony carriers, which must instead rely on their wits and rapid response capabilities to the shifting threats and alliance opportunities arising from an easily reconfigurable network architecture for the provision of Internet telephony.

Finally, in "Internet Telephony Regulation," Jonathan Weinberg reviews the legal basis for and regulatory issues arising from Internet telephony. The historical origins of the treatment and separation of data and information services from telecommunications services is explained. Whether that separation is still legally justifiable, and if so how it might be defended, is also addressed. Weinberg concludes that the convergence of the Internet and telecommunications industries offers both new opportunities for a more equitable and logical regulatory environment, as well as the potential for the creation of a new regulatory morass if the opportunities are not well understood by regulators and the courts.

Conclusion: After Convergence, the Data Deluge?

This collection of work on Internet telephony introduces the broad range of economic, technical, business, and policy issues arising from the convergence of the Internet and telecommunications industries. There is as yet little consensus on whether and, if so, when legacy circuit-switched networks present will be wholly or partially superseded by packetized voice communications systems. We hope this book motivates readers to contribute their own perspective, whether as users, entrepeneurs, or authors, to the debate. We hope too that this book has provided some clarity on the often fuzzy debate on the merits and demerits of alternative futures. While we recognize we may have just completed a book on the horseless carriage of the information age, we are comforted by the thought that, with a "search and replace" we can make this book in its second edition about whatever term emerges as the long-term winner to describe the services, applications, and equipment for mediated human communication emerging from the convergence of the Internet and telecommunications.

Notes

1. At least, we don't think so! We admit to being among those few who found even traditional telephony fascinating. We have been delighted to find our peculiar passion shared by many more "normal" people as the Internet and deregulation have opened up the phone systems worldwide to new innovations, new applications, and new uses.

2. In fact, voice "phone calls" have been made across the Internet's precursor packet-switched networks since the early 1970s, but the software to support this application was not commercially available. This introductory chapter draws on the "Comment to the European Commission Concerning the Status of Voice on the Internet under Directive 90/388/EEC," submitted by the Internet Telephony Consortium European Regulatory Task Force, July 1997.

3. The ITC (Internet and Telecoms Convergence Consortium) is chaired by David Clark and directed by Sharon Gillett. William Lehr has been involved with the consortium since its founding, including serving as executive director, 1999–2000. For more information on the ITC, which was founded by Lee McKnight, see http://itel.mit.edu.

4. This work led to an NSF-funded workshop on Internet economics and subsequently to an edited volume of the same name. See Lee W. McKnight and Joseph P. Bailey, eds., *Internet Economics* (Cambridge: MIT Press, 1997, 1998). A subsequent workshop to reassess the state of the field was held in December 1999. For more information on the MIT/ Tufts Internet Service Quality Economics Workshop and subsequent publications, see www.marengoresearch.com/isqe.

I

Applications, Architectures, and Industry Structures

A Taxonomy of Internet Telephony Applications

David D. Clark

Internet telephony can mean the use of Internet technology to replace a long-distance or international provider of traditional telephone service, or an enhanced form of human-to-human communication based on the computer as the user interface rather than the telephone. There are as well a broad range of objectives and opportunities that can be lumped under the heading of Internet telephony. A number of criteria can be used to separate these Internet telephony applications into classes, including the degree of interoperation with the existing telephone system and the extent to which the existing Internet must be augmented to support them. Different Internet telephony applications have very different motivations and very different implications for industry structure, economics, and regulation. The immediate opportunities for Internet telephony involve cost reductions relative to current telephone pricing. The long-term trajectory is for Internet telephony to become a new mode of computer-mediated human communication, which will have profound consequences for the telephone industry. This long-term form of Internet telephony will not necessarily grow directly from the products that are being deployed now, but will come from a number of intermediate developments that can be anticipated over the next several years.

Internet telephony applications can be organized into classes, thereby providing a framework around which to speculate on its broader implications. The different classes of Internet telephony have very different justifications and very different implications for the relevant industrial sectors involved, as well as policymakers and users.

Some applications focus on a short-term cost savings strategy, which may not have strong long-term market viability. However, a possible long-term outcome of the Internet telephony evolution is that people use computers rather than telephones to communicate. This outcome, were it to happen, could trigger a major restructuring of the telephone industry, in which separate firms provide the low-level physical connectivity and Internet service, and the higher-level telephone service itself.

This form of Internet telephony is not practical today, because the necessary supporting features in the Internet are not in place. Nevertheless my hypothesis is that Internet telephony will evolve as a series of incremental steps. Early variants will be identified that can be deployed without requiring as much enhancement of the Internet. These offerings will serve as experiments to prove the market, evaluate demand, explore the desirability of features, and motivate the fuller deployment of enhanced Internet service.

How Much PSTN? The Most Important Question

The most significant distinction between the various Internet telephony applications is the question of how much the public switched telephone network (PSTN) and how much computer-based telephony is in the scheme. There are three important classes of Internet telephony applications:

- Class 1. Proposals with the goal of using the Internet to provide POTS (plain old telephone service) telephony between existing telephone end user equipment. Applications of this class require technology for interconnection between the PSTN and Internet networks, but do not require access to computer-based end nodes and can often operate across dedicated regions of the Internet.

- Class 2. Proposals that require interoperation between the existing telephone and Internet networks and provide communication between users with either computers or existing telephone sets as end nodes. This class requires both the interoperation between Internet and PSTN and the use of computer-based end nodes.

Taxonomy of Internet Telephony Applications

Class 1: POTS over Internet

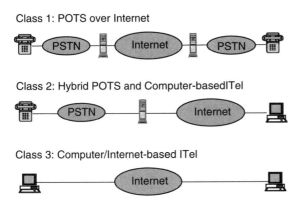

Class 2: Hybrid POTS and Computer-basedITel

Class 3: Computer/Internet-based ITel

Figure 2.1
The three classes of Internet telephony

• Class 3. Proposals that use Internet-attached computers to provide some form of human communication across the packet-switched Internet. This class, the pure form of Internet-based communication, does not involve any aspect of PSTN interaction, or interworking with telephone end nodes. This class is 100 percent Internet and 0 percent PSTN.

These three classes are illustrated in Figure 2.1. This classification seems to provide the most powerful way of articulating the broad categories of Internet telephony.

To illustrate some of the issues, this chapter first considers an example of a class 1 service, before looking at some of the other ways applications can be distinguished.

Class 1: International/Long-Distance POTS Using Internet Technology

This variant of Internet telephony uses Internet technology to connect into the existing telephone infrastructure as an international or long-distance carrier. Customers continue to use their local phone system and telephones and see this just as a long-distance or international alternative. Since the customers continue to use their existing handsets, the service is still essentially POTS. Although some variation in voice quality is possible, the motivation is to deliver a lower-cost variant on traditional POTS telephony by using Internet technology.

There are three ways that a lower cost could be realized. First, some of the costs in existing telephony are artificially high, and Internet telephony may be able to sidestep these artificial costs. Second, by efficient compression of the voice, costs could be reduced at the expense of a somewhat lower sound quality. Third, the Internet technology could deliver a lower intrinsic cost for the same service. I claim that the first factor is actually the only important one.

Although there has been considerable debate about the relative cost of carrying voice over the Internet and the PSTN, there seems to be no intrinsic cost advantage to carrying POTS-style calls of the same audio quality over the two networks. The argument is that the same circuit is used in both cases, the same compression scheme could be used in both cases if the cost reduction warrants, the compression (if done) is implemented in a component of the same complexity in both cases, and both schemes can take advantage of the statistical nature of talk spurts if warranted. In the long run, the use of Internet (or packet switching in general) does not appear to lead to greatly reduced per-minute costs for carrying a call.[1]

Although there may be few long-term intrinsic cost advantages to using Internet technology as a component of the POTS infrastructure, current telephone prices, with regulated rates and high prices sustained by monopoly players in certain countries, appear to provide a number of options for new entrants to offer a much lower-cost alternative to incumbent providers by structuring themselves as Internet providers. In the international market, these options for arbitrage are substantial. In the long-distance market in the United States, prices have already been driven down by competition, so there is less advantage for arbitrage than in the international case. However, the access fees paid by traditional long-distance providers to the local exchange providers currently do not apply to the Internet, so long distance provided over Internet avoids these fees. The motivation for some providers to propose long-distance POTS telephone service over the Internet may be the indirect one of forcing the Federal Communications Commission (FCC) to move on the resolution of the current consideration of local access charges.

Class 3: Long-Term Internet-Based Communication

The first example is a short-term proposition to exploit price distortions. There is also a long-term vision of what Internet telephony might be. The speculative end point of Internet telephony is a general set of applications for computer-mediated human communications. The distinguishing characteristic of these applications is not lower cost but enhanced functions. The computer and the Internet are central to this objective.

The Internet is a natural network for this application (more so than the existing phone system) for several reasons. Packet switching allows these applications to be mixed with others over a common network. Voice can be combined with other modes of communication—text, video, shared workspace, and so on. For telephone-like applications, the Internet can deliver the signaling information all the way to the end node, so the telephone features can be implemented at the edge of the network. It will permit several calls to coexist over one physical copper pair (or other medium), and it supports advanced features such as multicast that permit many-to-many communications.

The computer provides the end node functionality. It can be used as a call manager, keeping track of numbers and unanswered calls, assigning priority to incoming calls and redirecting them as appropriate, and logging and archiving calls. It can personalize the communications service for each user that shares the system—for example, providing a different response for business callers, friends, and strangers calling the same location. The computer can provide a sophisticated user interface to these functions (as opposed to the touch-pad interface obtained with a PBX today) and can implement these functions for a single telephone line. The computer can assist in lowering costs for communications by obtaining network service from the lowest-cost provider at each instant.

Differentiating Characteristics

This form of Internet telephony differs from the class 1 PSTN substitution in a number of important ways. These differences will turn out to be important characteristics that can be used to classify variants of Internet telephony generally.

Divergence Away from POTS Functionality

Any system that includes traditional telephone handsets must interoperate in a way that is consistent with the very limited nature of that device. The richness and flexibility of the user interface envisioned by this long-term form of Internet telephony depends on having no (or very little) need for backward compatibility with the POTS-style service. Only for the class 3 variations (0 percent PSTN) does the application designer have the option of seriously diverging from the POTS-style interface.

Migration of Function Toward End Node

A characteristic that is closely intertwined with divergence away from POTS functionality is the extent to which the location at which functions are implemented has migrated from the center of the network to the edge. The traditional telephone system has very primitive end nodes (the telephone) and much intelligence inside the network. The Internet in general represents a different balance, with intelligent end nodes (the computer) and a simple set of functions inside the switches of the network. To a large extent, this long-term class 3 variant of Internet telephony will be an application implemented in the end nodes rather than inside the network.[2] Features such as call waiting and caller-ID, which today are implemented inside the telephone network, will be implemented as software on the user's computer.

Ease of Use

PSTN telephony is getting more difficult to use, with longer strings of numbers necessary to complete calls, prefix sequences to select long-distance carriers (a concept that many consumers find very confusing), and advanced features such as call waiting or voice mail implemented using the telephone keypad as the user interface. The addition of more features can only make this worse. The use of a computer as an alternative user interface might improve the situation. Also, if the computer were programmed to automate certain steps (such as selecting the long-distance carrier based on the number being called and the current costs from different providers), increased ease of use might be combined with increased value. Ease of use is thus a factor that may get either better or worse, depending on the details of specific offerings.

Augments Needed to the Internet

In order to bring this Internet-based telephony application into existence, it will be necessary for the Internet to evolve in a number of ways, with new protocols and technology. Five significant enhancements to the Internet are necessary to support Internet telephony:

Quality of service. The term *quality of service* (QOS) is used in Internet design to describe the ability to assign specific treatment within the network to certain flows of packets. For example, a specified flow of packets might receive an assured minimum bandwidth or a bound on the delay of the delivery.[3] Work is underway now in the Internet engineering and standards community to add QOS support to the Internet protocols.[4]

Pricing for enhanced services. If the network infrastructure is enhanced with QOS mechanisms to provide different sorts of service, some controls will be required on the selection of these services by the users. In a private network (a corporate intranet, for example) administrative controls may be sufficient to limit the use of enhanced QOS. In the public Internet, pricing seems the obvious mechanism to control the selection of enhanced QOS, since it both limits user consumption and provides increased income to compensate the provider of the service. So pricing mechanisms of some sort seem necessary as a complement to the basic QOS mechanisms.[5]

Reliability. Telephony is traditionally associated with a level of reliability greater than that of the Internet today. Providers of Internet technology, such as routers, may find themselves pressed to meet expectations of greater reliability. Protocols and mechanisms for requirements such as fault detection and recovery may have to be upgraded. Providers of network infrastructure that supports Internet, such as hybrid fiber-coaxial cable facilities and wireless, may be similarly pressed to improve reliability and availability.

"Always-on" connectivity. Today most residential Internet customers are not connected to the Internet at all times, but only when they explicitly dial up. To support general calling patterns among users—for example, receiving a call without prearrangement—users would have to be connected to the Internet constantly, so they could receive a call at any time. This pattern of "always-on" connection would add to the cost of providing modem-based Internet access, since it would require a modem at the central site to be provided for each user, and the modem banks provided by Internet access providers represent a significant part of their overall cost. Continuous connection would also increase the load on the telephone switches and trunks of the local exchange companies that provide the dial-up circuits. The access technology of the cable industry makes it easy to provide this always-on service over cable. Industry is not blind to the advantage that this offers it, in providing both Internet telephony services and other applications.[6]

Ubiquitous deployment. The term *network externality* means that a network is increasingly valuable to any one user as more other users are attached. If only a small percentage of the population is actually online, the appeal of enhanced service Internet telephony will be minimal. General-purpose Internet telephony depends for its appeal on a sufficiently widespread deployment of the service, the Internet itself, and suitable end node equipment such as computers.

All five augments to the Internet are required to support the general form of Internet telephony described in this example. As Table 2.1 illustrates, the short-term application of long-distance POTS and the long-term application of next-generation computer-based human communication differ in almost every one of these key attributes.

In particular, the class 1 variant requires fewer augments to the Internet technology because one can avoid the need for explicit QOS mechanisms in the Internet infrastructure by building a dedicated Internet used only for the long-haul telephony and controlling the load by blocking calls. Using dedicated capacity also avoids the need for billing mechanisms at the Internet level. Finally, since the PSTN is being used to distribute the voice traffic to the end nodes, there is no concern with widespread deployment of Internet or with providing the user with an always-on service model.

Table 2.1
Comparison of class 1 long-distance POTS and class 3 long-term Internet telephony

| Class | Application | Beyond POTS? | End Node Function? | Ease of Use | Internet Augments | | | | |
					Quality of Service	Pricing	Reliability	Always On	Ubiquitous
1	Long-distance POTS	No	None	Same	No	No	Local	No	No
3	General application	Yes	Major	Better?	Yes	Yes	Yes	Yes	Yes

There are concerns about reliability. Within the specific part of the Internet being used for carriage of the voice traffic, this application requires robust equipment capable of telephone-grade reliable operation. However, this requirement applies only to the dedicated region of the Internet being used for the voice. Because few enhancements are needed to existing Internet to implement this application, it is feasible to undertake class 1 Internet telephony today. Indeed, there are already commercial, Internet-based international providers of telephone preparing to offer service.

Trying Class 3 Internet Telephony Now

Internet-only telephony is already being used today by consumers. This short-term version of class 3 telephony represents individuals' attempting to take advantage of the same price distortions as identified in the class 1 discussion. Using only the Internet and their personal computers, they establish packet flows and attempt voice communications.[7]

There is considerable skepticism that this short-term use of class 3 Internet telephony is commercially significant. The following issues apply:

• The use is attractive only because of current price distortions, which (while entrenched) are not fundamental and will be challenged by more organized business undertakings.

• The existing lack of support for explicit voice QOS in the Internet makes the quality of the call unpredictable. There is no evidence that the broad consumer market is interested in dealing with these fluctuations in quality.

• Since most consumers do not have a residential Internet service that allows them to be connected at all times, it requires prearrangement to receive such a call. This limits the utility of the service.

Without these Internet augments (and the others already discussed), this use of Internet is a bit of a "hobby" application, and there is little evidence that it will grow if all it does is emulate simple POTS calling. In the long run, a pure class 3 offering will not survive as a simple

POTS-style telephone replacement, but will be enhanced by new features that advance it away from a POTS equivalent. The simple class 3 Internet telephony will survive only if regulators attempt to suppress the class 1 business, in which case the class 3 variant might persist as a consumer-activist campaign for price reform, keeping pressure on the commercial providers. It must be the case that if this use of Internet starts to become widespread, either it will be regulated to make it relatively less attractive or other prices will shift. So it seems unlikely that this represents a use with long-term widespread benefit, so long as the functionality is simple POTS replacement.

On the other hand, because this class 3 version of Internet telephony more resembles what a long-term Internet telephone service might be, it can be a platform for early market entrants to position themselves while they gain experience. In the first stage of this form of Internet telephony, the major business opportunity is providing software to end users. The major supporting service that is required for telephony is a directory service that allows users to locate each other. Providers may position themselves to be major players in a later, more mature version of class 3 services.

Comparing POTS-Compatible Telephony: Classes 1, 2, and 3

The descriptions of the class 1 and class 3 variants of this service represent end points on a spectrum. There are a number of places between the two that could be realized. This intermediate, which I categorize as class 2, uses the same gateways between Internet and PSTN as the class 1 option, but extends the service so that users directly connected to the Internet can interconnect to PSTN users. Computers and telephones can interoperate.

One way to assess the importance of this sort of proposal is to ask whether it adds appeal to either of the class 1 or 3 end points. Looking at the class 1 variant, with gateways connecting into the PSTN, there is little intrinsic benefit to extending this so that calls can be completed over the Internet. First, almost anyone with a computer also has a phone and can be reached without adding this option. In other words, the network externality represented by the telephone system swamps the externality represented by the Internet today. Second, there are substantial infrastructure implications if one attempts to reach all the way to the end user over the Internet, because the full range of augments to the existing Internet infrastructure to support QOS, billing, and always-on access will eventually be required. For the pure class 1 option, to provide long-distance or international POTS over Internet, one can build a dedicated infrastructure, which removes the necessity of these augments.

Looking instead at the class 3 variant as a starting point, adding the ability to cross-connect to existing PSTN end points burdens the application with the limitation that it must interwork with POTS-style restrictions and can never evolve to new forms of service. Once that restriction is accepted, since the telephone end points so outnumber the Internet end points, the demand for the service will be generated by the telephone end points, which is the class 1 situation. I therefore conclude that in the abstract, the class 2 option of simple POTS replacement does not add much vigor to the simpler class 1 option and imposes a burdensome restriction on the class 3 option.

Nevertheless, there is a specific context in which the class 2 option has benefits. Calling in the direction *from* a computer *to* a telephone provides two specific short-term benefits. Since the charges for a long-distance call are normally charged to the sender, calling *from* a computer over the Internet avoids the charges associated with the telephone system and moves the cost into the Internet context, which is currently flat rate. At the same time, calling *to* a telephone bypasses the always-on Internet requirement and makes it possible to complete a call without prearrangement. Thus, calls from Internet to a telephone have benefit in the short run. Note that this has nothing to do with the power of the computer, only with the current costs and features in the two regimes. This class 2 hybrid is an excellent example of a short-term opportunity with no obvious long-term utility.

The class 2 option of POTS-style interconnection between Internet and PSTN raises interesting business questions. If the Internet were to be connected to the telephone system in a widespread way, it is not clear who would install, operate, and benefit from the gateways. They could be installed by Internet providers, the telephone companies, or third parties. The revenue situation is very different depending on whether the presumed model of calling is from Internet to PSTN or the other direction, and whether the goal is to keep the call in the Internet or in the PSTN for the maximum time. The assumption in most cases is that the Internet will have a lower incremental price for a call, so the goal is to keep the call in the Internet. This implies that the existing telephone service providers will view this service with hostility and will need some further motivation (e.g., defensive offense) to deploy Internet phone gateways. Internet service providers might deploy these boxes if they can justify the cost as a part of their total service offering. This would represent a way to tie the lower-level Internet service to the higher-level Internet telephony service, an example of vertical integration in the Internet industry. Third-party providers will deploy the gateways only if they can derive revenues, which implies that they must bill someone for the use. This billing will add complexity to the basic service.

From the Present to the Future

The examples provide a sufficient context to summarize the high-level assessment of the Internet telephony arena. My thesis is that the goal of the class 1 applications is primarily a cost-savings objective, which may not have strong long-term durability as a business opportunity. The class 2 applications will evolve to provide speech access to a wider variety of network resources, and thus diverge from simple POTS service. The class 3 options represent the important long-term outcome of the Internet telephony evolution. However, the final speculative form of class 3 is not practical today, because the necessary augments to the Internet are not in place, and the utility and usability of the service features to the consumer have not been demonstrated.

I believe that Internet telephony will evolve as a series of incremental steps. Early variants will be identified that can be deployed without requiring all the augments described to be fully in place. These offerings will serve as experiments to prove the market, evaluate demand, explore the desirability of features, and motivate the fuller deployment of enhanced Internet service. The long-term options will evolve to more advanced forms as the demand becomes clearer and the necessary augments come into place.

Descriptions of short-term variants of Internet telephony will illustrate the requirements and potential of each in taking us from today to the speculative future.

Other Class 1 Examples

Bypass of Local Loop by Cable Providers
The goal here is to use Internet infrastructure to deliver telephone service over alternative technology (specifically cable infrastructure), bypassing the local loop and the local telephone provider.

Cable providers currently provide telephone service over cable using customer premise network interface devices dedicated to telephone service. They separately provide Internet service using so-called cable modems that provide high-speed packet transport over cable. If they could provide telephone service over Internet, they could provide both Internet access and telephone service using one device at the customer premise, which would appear to provide substantial cost advantages.

The cable industry is currently speculating on exactly what forms of telephony to offer over their cable plant in the short run. Offering full first-line telephone service raises many regulatory and technical issues for that industry, such as funding of universal service and the need to engineer their infrastructure to the level of reliability of the telephone system (for example, to remain operational when the power is off). A more advantageous short-term alternative might be to offer "second-line" telephone service, which need not be as reliable or as full functioned. This would allow them to "cream-skim" the telephone business, and steal high-profit offerings from the existing local-loop providers. For example, they could offer access to alternative long-distance service and take away the resulting access charges that the local exchange carrier would receive. They can supply second lines for fax (which need not work when the power is off), and so on.

As Table 2.2 illustrates, the only augments required for this application are to provide QOS over the cable infrastructure to mix the voice and data traffic. Cable modems currently do not support explicit QOS, but the current approaches to bandwidth allocation for cable modems could be extended to provide this support.

Table 2.2
Two class 1 applications: Local-loop bypass using cable and voice over private infrastructure

Class	Application	Beyond POTS?	End Node Function?	Ease of Use	Internet Augments				
					Quality of Service	Pricing	Reliability	Always On	Ubiquitous
1	Loop bypass	No	Little	Same	Local	No	Local	Yes	No
1	Voice over	No	None	Same?	Yes	No	Yes	No	No

A significant aspect of this variant is that while it is fully interoperable with the PSTN and uses the existing telephones of the consumer, it begins a push of function toward the edge of the network. A device would be needed at the customer premise to control the connection of the consumer's telephones and house wiring to the two external phone services: the cable and the copper loop. This box then begins to take on functions of call control, selection of provider based on cost, and so on. It represents a small step toward the migration of telephone function out of the network and into the end point.

Shared Use of Private Packet Networks for Voice

Corporations and other users that have procured private Internets, whether built from trunks or switched infrastructure, can carry some of their voice traffic over this infrastructure in order to make use of this investment. Since network capacity typically comes in large chunks, there may be economies of scope that derive from combining voice and data over one infrastructure.[8] This application resembles the class 1 long-distance variant of POTS-style telephony, except that the wide-area infrastructure being used is operated by a private organization rather than as a public offering.

Other Class 2 Examples

Computer Telephony: Use of Computer to Control the Telephone

This application is not strictly Internet telephony but rather computer-mediated telephony. The concept is to connect the computer to the telephone system so that it becomes a more sophisticated user interface for advanced telephony functions. The computer could receive, process, and store voice mail, maintain a log of all incoming calls, store catalogs of called numbers, and so on. The telephone could still be used for the actual communication.

In the home, this opportunity raises several interesting and important issues. The typical home today has several phones, perhaps one in almost every room. This density of computers is not likely in the near future, so any significant use of the computer as part of residential telephony must be a hybrid that permits the telephone to be used when its convenience outweighs the primitive user interface.

In the corporate world, many employees have both a telephone and a computer. These are currently managed separately, and when an employee moves, both must be changed separately. Assuming that the employee will continue to have a computer, the opportunity here is to use the computer and its network infrastructure as a replacement for the telephone and the PBX to which it is attached. This would reduce two systems to one, with presumed cost savings.

As Table 2.3 summarizes, this application moves functions to the edge of the network (a computer or similar consumer device) while continuing to interwork with the existing PSTN and the resulting POTS-style service. It implies high reliability of the computers and networks, and computers that are always on and available to process calls.

Adding Voice to the Web

One of the emerging examples of voice as a component of multimedia computer application is adding voice communication to Web pages. The concept is that a user browsing a Web page can click a button and talk to a representative of the company providing the Web page, thus merging the Web with 800 numbers.

I call this a class 2 application because the client side is a computer, while the current implementation at the server side is to connect the incoming call into the existing call-dispatching equipment that deals with PSTN calls. This is a rather powerful hybrid, because it could be possible for the representative receiving the call to have access to the computer information that the customer is seeing. So this option mixes POTS-style telephony and computer-based multimedia functions.

This application, if mature, will shift 800 traffic onto the Internet, which could cause existing telephone providers to lose revenue. The voice calls are carried as far as possible across the Internet and connected into the existing telephone system only at the premises of the Web provider.

Since this application carries the voice across the Internet as far as possible, connecting into the existing telephone system only at the premises of the server, several Internet augments will be required to make this service real. Wide-scale introduction of QOS and the related pricing mechanisms will be required, but it does not require always-on

Table 2.3
Three class 2 applications: Computer telephony, adding voice to the Web, and voice access to Web information

					Internet Augments				
Class	Application	Beyond POTS?	End Node Function?	Ease of Use	Quality of Service	Pricing	Reliability	Always On	Ubiquitous
2	Computer telephony	Slight	Some	Better?	No	No	PC: yes	PC: yes	No
2	Web voice	Slight	Yes	Better?	Yes	Yes	Yes	No	No
2	Voice access to Web information	Major	No	Better?	No	No	No	No	No

Table 2.4
Three class 3 applications: Teleconferencing, consumer multiperson applications, and telework

					Internet Augments				
Class	Application	Beyond POTS?	End Node Function?	Ease of Use	Quality of Service	Pricing	Reliability	Always On	Ubiquitous
3	Teleconferencing	Yes	Major	Better?	?	No	Yes	No	No
3	Consumer applications	Yes	Major	Better?	Yes	Yes	No	No	No
3	Telework	Yes	Major	Better?	Yes	Yes	Yes	Yes	Yes

operation (the consumer originates the calls), nor does it depend strongly on ubiquitous Internet deployment. Any consumer with the service can fully benefit from it.

Voice Access to Information on the Web

In the long run, the future of the class 2 hybrid (PSTN/Internet interconnection) is not to provide simple voice communication between humans, but to provide voice access, within the POTS paradigm, to a range of new Internet-based services. The use of touch-tone selection to navigate services is a primitive example of this; the mature form will involve computerized voice understanding and conversation between a human on a telephone and a computer, which then reaches out into the Internet to obtain services and information for the user.

Services such as this exploit telephone calls across the PSTN, but do not much resemble a classic phone call, since the device at the other end is not a human but a computer, and the goal of the call is to obtain access to information located within the Internet.

This service requires no augments to the Internet because the voice only passes over the PSTN. These sorts of applications can be deployed as soon as the speech understanding issues have been resolved.[9]

Class 3 Examples

As shown in Table 2.4, the long-term form of class 3 Internet-based telephony involves a major migration away from the assumptions of the traditional telephone system and requires a number of augments to the current Internet. Nevertheless, a number of class 3 applications are more limited in their objectives and thus in the augments that they require. These represent first steps that the industry will take as it explores the space of real Internet-based voice communication.

Teleconferencing
This application exploits the power of the computer to move beyond simple POTS service in support of human communications. The objective is to augment simple voice communications with other modes, such

as video, multiway (many-to-many) communication patterns, and shared workspace and other groupware tools.

There are several patterns of teleconferencing. One is within the corporate campus. Achieving the necessary QOS may be achieved by over-provisioning in the short term, which will permit this application to be initiated without explicit QOS support in the Internet routers. The second pattern is among the sites of a corporation. This will require support from the Internet technology similar to that discussed for shared use of private packet networks for voice. The third mode of teleconferencing is telework, which is sufficiently different that I discuss it separately.

An important aspect of Internet teleconferencing is the many-to-many mode, which is more natural in the Internet but requires special arrangement (a conference call) in the telephone system. Many-to-many communications greatly benefits from Internet multicast, which is only now being deployed and still suffers from concerns about scale and robustness.

Chat Room, Games, and Other On-Line Real-Time Applications

Chat rooms and open group interaction share with teleconferencing the basic objective of linking together a number of people in a common real-time experience. However, the details are very different. First, this application is a leisure activity, and thus targets the consumer at home, not the worker at a place of business. Second, the groupware components might be very different. Third, the open nature of the group will call for a more complex directory and group location service.

This could be considered in the context of a hybrid Internet/PSTN mode (class 2), but is more likely to succeed as a pure class 3 application, where the groupware modalities can be exploited to enhance the experience. The possibility of some user having multimodal participation while others have only voice seems unappealing.

This application requires QOS, pricing, reliability, and reasonable overall bandwidth to the consumer at the residence.

Telework

Telework is a variant of teleconferencing carried out from the home or other remote location.[10] The objective here is to make teleconferencing available at residences. Although corporations can deploy teleconferencing within and among their business sites, it will be the public Internet service providers that provide (at least the infrastructure for) telework. The bandwidth and service requirements for telework may somewhat resemble the requirements for chat rooms and other recreational applications. This application will thus provide an opportunity for the consumer-oriented ISPs to play in the business sector and diversify their revenue base.

Most corporations seem to desire to roll out a telework option only when the infrastructure is widely in place. Thus, there is a requirement for widespread deployment of Internet access.

Conclusions: The Long-Term Implications of Internet Telephony

Internet telephony will evolve from early offerings that can be assembled today into mature forms that have diverged substantially from simple POTS-style telephony.

Implications for Timing

Some options for Internet telephony such as teleconferencing, voice access to information, and computer-mediated telephony, require fewer Internet augments to deploy (Table 2.5). These can happen sooner and will thus serve to explore the demand and position players in the market. Teleconferencing, for example, will explore the utility of other modes of communication, such as video and shared workspace. The end node device supporting the user, whether PC or specialized server, will start to implement a sophisticated user interface to Internet telephony services and will start to act as the user's agent in implementing key Internet telephony functions. In parallel with these first steps, Internet service providers will start to implement augments such as QOS and pricing. These will permit the next applications, such as voice over the Web and leisure activities such as games and chat rooms. With sufficient success in the marketplace, there will be enough penetration of Internet service to make the final form of class 3 computer-mediated communication practical.

Table 2.5
Summary of Internet Telephony Applications

Class	Application	Beyond POTS?	End Node Function?	Ease of Use	Internet Augments				
					Quality of Service	Pricing	Reliability	Always On	Ubiquitous
1	Long-distance POTS	No	None	Same	No	No	Local	No	No
1	Loop bypass	No	Little	Same	Local	No	Local	Yes	No
1	Voice over	No	None	Same?	Yes	No	Yes	No	No
2	Computer telephony	Slight	Some	Better?	No	No	PC: yes	PC: yes	No
2	Web voice	Slight	Yes	Better?	Yes	Yes	Yes	No	No
2	Voice access to Web information	Major	No	Better?	No	No	No	No	No
3	Teleconferencing	Yes	Major	Better?	?	No	Yes	No	No
3	Consumer applications	Yes	Major	Better?	Yes	Yes	No	No	No
3	Telework	Yes	Major	Better?	Yes	Yes	Yes	Yes	Yes
3	General application	Yes	Major	Better?	Yes	Yes	Yes	Yes	Yes

Implications for Industry Structure

The speculative final form of computer-mediated human communications implies a substantial change in the structure of the telephone service and the industry that provides it. The design of the Internet, with open interfaces between different service layers, tends to create an industry structure in which the lower-level service providers (the ISPs) do not have a substantial competitive advantage in supplying higher-level services such as Web hosting.[11] This pattern differs from that of the telephone industry, where the provision of physical facilities has been linked to the higher-level telephone service. Despite that history, if telephony (or more generally, class 3 computer-mediated human communication) were to move to the Internet, there is no reason that it would be immune to this separation of lower- and higher-level services among different players. In that case, local exchange carriers would be shifted into a role where they provide copper loops, and perhaps provide Internet service over those loops, but have no consequential advantage in providing Internet telephony. The ISP participates in the implementation of the higher-level Internet telephony service only to the extent that it provides a selection of QOS and a set of supporting services that exist in the network.

In fact, Internet telephony ceases to be a single unified service at all. As the end node computer, owned and provided by the subscriber, becomes part of the telephone context, it will accentuate the fracturing of the service. The implementation of key functions at the end node removes them from the control of the telephone industry. Internet telephony becomes a service built out of software purchased by the consumer, operating over a general (e.g., Internet) communications infrastructure that is independent of application.

Another aspect of the fragmentation of the industry is the manner in which secondary services are supported. The services that have been mentioned here include directory services such as White and Yellow Pages. Yellow Pages, which is essentially advertising, can be expected to become a very competitive business, whose final form is hard to predict. But Web-based services are already beginning to appear, and there is no longer any telephone company monopoly on directory services.

Policy Considerations

Faced with the prospect of the vertical disintegration of the telephone industry, the incumbent players may reasonably try to create circumstances that forestall or mitigate this potential. One leading indicator for the long-term form of Internet telephony is the standards and interfaces proposed by major industry players. Several examples are obvious. For example, directory services are just emerging, and there is scope for these standards either to encourage or discourage the interworking of different services as a uniform overall directory system.

The form of Internet telephony described here, with major functions implemented in the end nodes, can be realized only if the necessary control information (what the telephone industry calls signaling) is carried end to end across the Internet. This is the natural mode for Internet control protocols, but one could imagine an attempt to close or restrict these protocols in some way. If, for example, the called end node could not determine the number and identity of the calling party, this would help maintain Internet telephony as a centralized application. If a class 2 hybrid form of Internet telephony does succeed in the market, the interconnection of the telephone and Internet telephone service will require some interface to telephone signaling protocols. The two extremes are the use of touch-tone signals and the internal signaling protocols of the telephone system, Signaling System 7 (SS7). These would represent very different modes of access into the existing functions of the PSTN and might cause Internet telephony signaling to grow in different ways.

Regulation of Internet telephony has been proposed, and may again be proposed in the future, based on the observation that in some forms, it is similar to the service of the PSTN.[12] The hypothesis here is that most of the class 1 alternatives in fact exist to exploit pricing distortions, and thus arguments about regulation are germane to class 1 Internet telephony. However, if the hypothesis is true that the final form of Internet telephony will result from the evolution of class 2 and class 3 applications, it seems more difficult to apply a "similar service" criterion. The class 3 application will diverge greatly from the function of existing telephony. The class 2 applications will continue to exploit a "phone call" to access the Internet, but if the person on the telephone is talking to a computer that is reading a Web page as the overall service, it seems difficult to describe the collective event as resembling POTS. This suggests that any attempts to regulate Internet telephony, based on looking at the class 1 variants, will quickly unravel in definitional confusion.

One of the consequences of this predicted evolution may be a gradual loss of reliability, dependability, and utility of the "telephone service." This trend is already visible as a consequence of divestiture; some people are already so confused that they are unable to make long-distance calls from pay phones, rogue pay phones lure the unwary, bills are unpredictable, there is no accountability for disrupted service, and so on. There could be a possible consumer backlash that demands a more predictable, reliable, and usable service. One outcome could be regulation as to the characteristics of a future "telephone service," regulation more akin to safety and consumer protection than pricing and cost recovery.

As the industry becomes more and more fragmented, it will become less and less easy for the various industry players to meet and agree on common objectives and approaches. This will contribute to a further deterioration in the overall utility of the service and a resulting pressure for forces other than those of autonomous private industry to come to bear on the problem. These issues will have to be addressed and resolved in a multinational context.

Notes

I gratefully acknowledge the comments and suggestions of Sharon Gillett, Andrew Sears, Russ Newman, Bill Lehr, John Wroclawski, and Lee McKnight. This work was funded by the MIT Internet Telephony Consortium and its industrial partners.

1. In the short run, the Internet solution might have lower costs, because the telephone provider must deal with the depreciation of capital equipment such as circuit switches that makes less efficient use of the same circuit. An important second-order effect is that because an Internet infrastructure can support the signaling and operations requirements as well as carry the voice traffic, there may be some significant efficiencies in building a single Internet to support all aspects of the telephone application.

2. The counterbalance to this is that for some Internet applications that have dynamic information shared among several parties, such as multiplayer games and multiuser dungeons, there may be pressure to move aspects of the application back into the core of the network. Thus, there are pressures that move function in both directions within the Internet.

3. The term QOS, as used by Internet designers, has nothing to do with what change the user of an application may perceive as a result of using the QOS features of the network. QOS describes network-level mechanisms, not user-perceived quality. As a specific example, if a voice application needs a bounded delay on the packet delivery time, this can be achieved either by adding QOS mechanisms to the Internet or by restricting the offered load (e.g., by blocking voice calls) so that the Internet infrastructure is somewhat underloaded.

4. Internet services to support real-time delivery of audio and similar material are described in Wroclawski (1997) and Braden (1997).

5. A number of approaches to the pricing of services in the Internet are discussed in McKnight and Bailey (1997, 1998).

6. For an alternative discussion of important enhancements to the Internet, including the "always-on" feature and several other related requirements, see Computer Science and Telecommunications Board (CSTB) (1996, chap. 2).

7. There are a number of vendors of PC-based IT software today. For a collection of pointers to product information, see the web site at http://itel.mit.edu.

8. This opportunity applies to Internet and also (and currently more popularly) to lower-level switched technologies such as frame relay, which provide slightly better control of QOS.

9. Early examples of systems that employ computer-based voice understanding are available in the research lab today. For example, the Jupiter system developed by the Spoken Language Systems group at the MIT Lab for Computer Science allows a user to call and have a phone-based conversation with a computer concerning the weather, based on current weather information that the computer retrieves from the Web.

10. More generally, telework could imply only more primitive network access for shared files, but we choose to use the term here to capture the human-to-human communications aspects of remote work.

11. For a discussion of the overall design of the Internet and the role of open interfaces in fragmenting the market segments, see CSTB (1994, chap. 2). For a discussion of some of the specific business consequences, see CSTB (1996).

12. See Werbach (1997) for a recent discussion of options for regulation of the Internet.

3

Virtually Global Telcos: International Internet Telephony Architectures

Terrence P. McGarty and Lee W. McKnight

International Internet protocol (IP) telephony services are built on network architectures that incorporate a number of elements and must be artfully combined for a voice service to function effectively and efficiently. In addition to the technical requirements, any international IP service crosses distinct regulatory domains that must be accounted for in order for a network to be both practical and profitable. This chapter presents a technical architecture for the implementation of the network and provision of international Internet telephony services. It provides sufficient detail on the architecture, operation, and regulation of international Internet Telephony networks so that readers could, if they wished, start their own international "phone" company.

International Internet and Telephony Architectures

The concept of architecture and the use of design elements are critical in understanding the structure of information systems. It is essential to develop a philosophical perspective and understanding of how to view networks, given their central importance to the global and national economies and societies in the coming decades. Architectures for international Internet or Internet-like telecommunications can be analyzed in terms of the users, the uses, the worldview, and the underlying enabling technology. The structural elements of architectures typically have not played a role in the development of policies. In this section the concept of an architecture as a means to understand networks as both market and regulatory entities is presented and provides perspective for viewing networks in terms of new worldviews.[1]

An architecture requires that the underlying system be treated in terms of a set of commonly understood elements that have a clearly demarcated set of functions and interfaces that allow for the basic set of elements to be combined. The way the elements then can be combined, reflected against the ultimate types of services provided, determines the architecture. Architecture is derived from two factors: technology and worldview. Technology places bounds on what is achievable; however, those bounds are typically well beyond the limits self-imposed by the designers. The concept of a paradigm as applied to networks is the collection of current technologies that we have at hand for the network and the ways we put these elements together. New paradigms result from new technologies (Kuhn, 1996), which allow for placing the elements together in new ways. A worldview is an overlying concept that goes to the heart of the arguments made in this chapter. If we view our world as hierarchical, then the network may very well reflect that view. If we add to that view a bias toward voice communications, these two elements will be reflected in all that we do.

Architecture can be defined as the conceptual embodiment of a worldview, using the commonly understood set of structural elements, based on the available set of technologies. The architectural elements for a network are control, transport, interconnect, and interface. Figure 3.1 depicts the overall architecture of the interrelationships of the elements, and the component functions of the individual network elements. Four distinct and separable areas for growth and policy formation are also defined by this architecture. Issues of regulation, due to potential monopolist control, are always a concern. This chapter supports the arguments made in chapter 2 that a new network and service paradigm is emerging and will demonstrate that in all areas, there are now significant economies to be gained through market disaggregation. This implies a correlated need to remove or restructure regulatory barriers worldwide, for the full economic and social benefits of new services and new uses of IP-supporting communication technologies to be realized.

The following elements will be affected from an architectural and regulatory perspective:

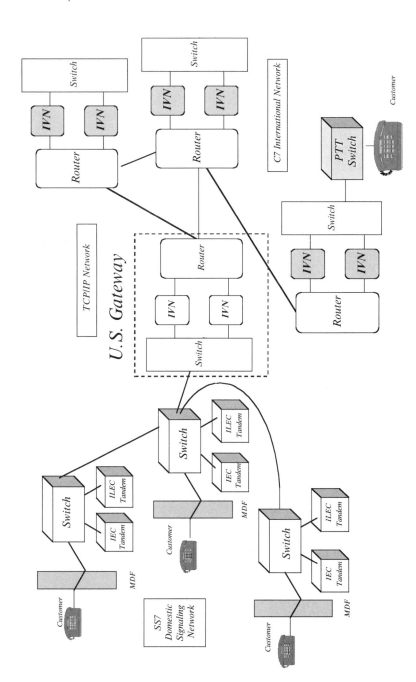

Figure 3.1
International Internet telephony network architecture (Source: McGarty 1999). *Note.* PTT = Post, telephone, and telegraph; IVN = Internet voice node; ILEC = Incumbent local exchange carrier; MDF = ••; IEC = ••.

Control. Control elements in an architecture provide for such functions as network management, error detection, service restoration, billing, inventory management, and diagnostics. In legacy systems, the voice network provides these functions on a centralized basis. Current systems include network management and control schemas and products that allow for the custom control and management of one's own network. Network control providing these functions is an essential element for public and private networks. Thus, as we consider network evolution, this element or set of functions must be included. Control has now been made flexible and movable. The control function is probably the most critical in the changes to be viewed in the context of an architecture.

Transport. Transport is the provision of physical means to move information, in some form such as digital, from one point to another. It is provided by the underlying transport fabric, whether that is a twisted pair of copper, fiber-optic cable, radio, or other means, and is expressed in bits per second or, at best, in bandwidth only. Bandwidth as a transport construct is the most enabling. Transport does not encompass the need to change or to do any other enhancement to the information.

Interconnect. The interconnect element of the architecture is synonymous with switching and describes how the different users are connected to one another or to any of the resources on to the network. Interconnection assumes that there is an addressing scheme, a management scheme for the addresses, and a scheme to allow one user to address, locate, and connect to any other user. Interconnection in the past was provided exclusively by central office switches. This implementation of an architectural element was based on certain limitations of the transport element. With the change in the transport technologies allowing greater bandwidth, switching needs have changed. Scale economies of distributed architectures allow for interconnectivity controlled by the customer premises equipment (CPE) and not the central office. There are three general views of interconnection that are valid today: the telecom, the computer scientist, and the user. The telecom view is based on the assumption of voice-based transport with universal service and the inseparability of interconnects and control. The computer scientist view is based on the assumption that the network, as transport, is unreliable and that computer hardware and software must be used to handle each data packet. Furthermore, this view is one where timeliness is secondary to control. It has been epitomized in the quotation, "Every packet is an adventure." The third view is that of users, who are interested in developing an interconnect capability that meets their needs and minimizes cost.

Interface. The interfaces are the end users' connection to the transport element. The interface element provides for the conversion from the end user information stream and the information streams that are used in the transport form of the network. For example, the telephone interface for voice is the analog conversion device.

Internet Architecture

The essence of the Internet is the set of protocols available to the community to allow access by a wide variety of hosts in a complex and fully distributed fashion. They are the software and system agreements that allow disparate machines and software to talk across equally disparate networks. The current protocols focus on data transactions, with some innovation allowing images and limited multimedia—voice and video. The future challenge will be the development of new and innovative protocols to allow both low-end user accesses to grow while at the same time enriching the capability of the information transferred.

The key underlying protocol structure that makes the Internet function is the transport control protocol/Internet protocol (TCP/IP). TCP/IP protocols have emerged as the standard network interface to the Internet that allows users to send messages from one point to another in a reliable form and embody in those messages certain characteristics that make them more than just a collection of bits.[2] IP gets the packet across the network, and TCP brings the underlying nature of the packet stream into context as a reconstituted entity. This protocol allows for the easy and ready flow of data from one user to another by agreements at various levels of the network to handle, process, manage, and control the underlying data packets. TCP/IP will remain at the heart of the evolution of the Internet and is increasingly applied to multimedia and new access methods. Network architectural and system requirements must be articulated clearly and carefully for each new dimension of the Internet.

The current Internet architecture thus has two main elements: the semihierarchical structure of backbone, regional, campus, and host, and the agreement on a single protocol to talk across the Internet in the TCP/IP suite. These elements reflect a great deal about how the Internet is managed and what its growth potential truly is. Several observations can be made about the Internet in its current embodiment and how this relates to IP telephony:

Host orientation. The Internet is host oriented, that is, it is focused around the host as the terminal entity. This implies that the concept of a host may have to be expanded to include a new and wider variety of electronic entities, some physical and other actually virtual devices. The Internet is not telephone oriented; it does not understand telephone signaling, protocols, and the internalization of intelligence. The Internet externalizes intelligence.

Disaggregation of data. The Internet or IP network assumes a high degree of disaggregation of the data from one location to another. The current assumptions are that data from one location are independent of data from other locations. In a multimedia environment, this will no longer be the case. Data are virtually aggregated into a compound multimedia object, creating a spatially disjoint set of data elements. Specifically, mouse movement at one location will be related to voice at another and a third party's video at a third. The concatenation and orchestration of these disparate entities will be viewed as a single totality. In the world of IP telephony, the telephony parts want to see structure data as may appear in SS7 or C7 databases. Such is not the case in the IP world.

Variable transmission link performance. The underlying structure of IP was built to deal with a poor-quality transmission path, not those found in fiber-optic networks. The new fiber-optic networks are almost error free. In fact, with the processing at higher protocol layers, one may now assume error-free transmission. This means that the latency prevalent from the old analog telephone lines may be eliminated. This is a critical factor for multimedia transactions. On the other hand, wireless communications services may not have higher data rates until we better understand how to deal with multipath and other radio propagation factors. The network must handle error-free fiber and error-prone wireless. The Internet telephony world must work around that problem.

Low intranetwork intelligence. Limitations of processing in the network are due to the simplicity of the routers and the "intelligence" of the host. New network elements are highly intelligent, and even the personal digital assistants (PDAs) and the wireless devices contain dramatically greater intelligence to perform processing. The ability of the network to drive more processing to the periphery and to the new, fully distributed host environment will enable the Internet to add new degrees of access and services flexibility.

Variable-speed transport. The layered structure of the protocol suite allows for flexibility in low- to moderate-speed networks. At higher speeds the protocol suites may break down. Fiber networks will rapidly allow gigabit-per-second transmission, and high-resolution images and video will be integrated in complex multimedia objects. This may require a rethinking of object control and the development of new and innovative protocols.

Single media messaging. The TCP layer focuses on getting a single stream of data through. Modifications can be made for voice or even video streaming, but a full multimedia network is not achievable. An enhanced multimedia TCP/IP type system will be constructed that allows the entire suite of users access to multimedia sessioning with high data rates by means of fully distributed high-end processing devices, albeit at dramatically lower cost. The telephony world has out-of-band signaling, thus imposing multiple paths for communications, again all driven by the voice paradigm.

The Internet was initially intended as a data communications tool across the academic community. No intelligence was built in to the network to guarantee arrival of messages or to mitigate congestion. Issues of security and virus protection are management options left to the discretion of the host configuration.

Applications, Architectures, and Industry Structures

IP Telecommunications Architectures

The U.S. domestic public switched network is the result of an evolutionary process that gave rise to the Bell system in the early 1900s and has resulted in the current structures under the modified final judgment (MFJ) strictures as outlined by the 1996 Telecommunications Act.[3] The network is based on a set of technologies that require very large investments in capital assets to allow for the interconnection of many users to each other. The system requires massive switching infrastructures since the underlying transport facilities, the classic copper cables called twisted pairs, have very limited information-carrying capacity—at least until recently, with, for example, the advent of technologies such as asymmetric digital subscriber lines (ADSL). Nevertheless, to build an IP architecture on top of the existing public-switched telecommunications network, one must first understand the architecture of the underlying, or legacy, network. The public switched telecommunications network is built around a hierarchical architecture that makes several assumptions of its environment and the customer base:

• Bandwidth is a costly commodity. It is necessary to provide for concentration of circuits on trunks and tandem lines. This concentration leads to the need for multilayered switching centers, a class 5 central office being the lowest level.

• Voice is the primary means of communications, and all circuits are to be considered multiples of voice circuits. In addition, the voice is to be sampled at a rate of 8,000 samples per second, and the number of bits per sample may be from 7 to 8.

• Universal service is necessary to meet the needs of federal and state regulatory bodies. Telephone service must serve the rural home and the large corporation.

• Quality of service is to be as high as possible, with overall system availability to exceed 99.95 percent. This implies redundancy, disaster recovery systems, and a trained workforce that will permit as near real-time restoral as possible.

• The focus is on operations, keeping the network service up to the performance standards set. This implies that the workforce must have the capacity to deal with complex operations requirements. All personnel should be cross-trained to meet the level of service that consumers of the service expect.

The local telephone company is an infrastructure entity. As the local operating company, it has a highly redundant, high quality-of-service network, with an integrated workforce. The critical qualities of the architectural elements of this network are:

Control. Control, which is highly centralized, emanates from a set of methods and procedures, flows through the overall control mechanism for the network, and is integrated to the maintenance and restoral efforts.

Interconnect. This is a hierarchical interconnection, based on the central office switch, which is designed to conserve bandwidth at the trunk side. It provides a level of common access based on a single voice channel.

Transport. The basic transport is the twisted-pair copper wire to the end user. There is fiber in the loop and some fiber to the user, specifically those users in the higher data rate category, where much of the new investment and growth is occurring.

Interface. Generally the interface is the telephone handset. More recently, the interface has been expanded to include data sets.

Internet Telephony Architectures

The contrasting worldviews and architectural choices stemming from the Internet and legacy telecommunications system have led designers of Internet telephony networks to confront a number of alternative ways for developing such services. These choices become more complex if the network being planned is assumed to be global in scope. Figure 3.1 depicts an international Internet telephony network. The network must support any form of end user telecommunications and must also handle the signaling that supports network operations, for example, Signaling System 7 (SS7) in the United States. This out-of-band signaling must be interfaced via a gateway-type switch. Figure 3.1 also shows the use of the TCP/IP protocol suite as the backbone for the international transport network. The figure shows a domestic U.S. network using SS7 signaling and a gateway switch that allows for international transport using devices called IP voice nodes (IVNs), which convert between traditional circuit-switched voice to Internet-style packet-switched voice. In the international Internet telephony network architecture shown in Figure 3.1, the approach blends the telecommunications world of standards such as SS7 into the TCP/IP world of the Internet.

Network Elements

The network elements consist of switches, transport, interface, and control. The assumption throughout this chapter is that the IVN is the basic system building block, as shown in Figure 3.2. The specific elements and their functions are as follows:

LCU. The line control unit (LCU) is the interface between the telephone network and the IVN. It provides for call initiation and termination. The initial LCU provides for signaling to and from the local

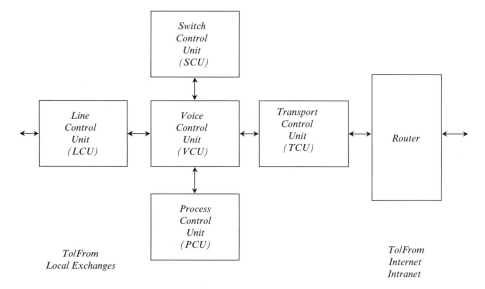

Figure 3.2
Elements of an IP voice node (Source: McGarty 1999)

telephone network. This unit must provide for signaling system 7 (SS7) and control system 7 (C7) interfacing or primary rate interface (PRI) or similar interfacing. One approach may be to front-end the LCU with a PBX or switch to perform these functions.

PCU. The process control unit (PCU) provides the capability of controlling the processes of a general nature, such as network management, billing, and the IVN provisioning capability. The PCU typically has a simple network management protocol (SNMP) agent for network management and a billing control unit (BCU) for the management of calling cards and other similar elements.

SCU. The switch control unit (SCU) provides for the conversion between the telephone number for dialing and the TCP/IP address for Internet/intranet connectivity. On call initiation, the IVN sends the SCU the telephone number to be called. The SCU converts the telephone number into an IP address, and the SCU inserts this in the transmitted packet. On the receive or termination end, the SCU converts the IP address and other header information into the terminating called number. The SCU sends this to the LCU, which then connects this to the local telephone exchange network.

VCU. This voice processor or the voice control unit (VCU) compresses or decompresses the speech, turns it into a packet, and sequences, schedules, and protocol converts it for Internet access. It also converts between a local telephone number and an Internet address. The VCU compresses the analog voice signal into a digital signal. Current systems typically convert the voice into an 8 Kbps signal; 4 Kbps compression can be achieved, as can 2.4 Kbps compression, with minimal loss in voice quality, enabling more subscribers to be supported on the same intranet backbone network. An alternative strategy is to maximize voice quality and forgo compression altogether, to provide for CD-quality or MP3-quality sound—that is, a quality for high-fidelity music and audio. Making this architectural choice to maximize voice quality instead of bandwidth efficiency would imply use of a different, or differently configured, VCU.

TCU. The transport control unit (TCU) provides for packet synchronization between transmit and receive. It is the scheduler of the packets on transmit and the synchronizer of the packets on receive. It also

Applications, Architectures, and Industry Structures

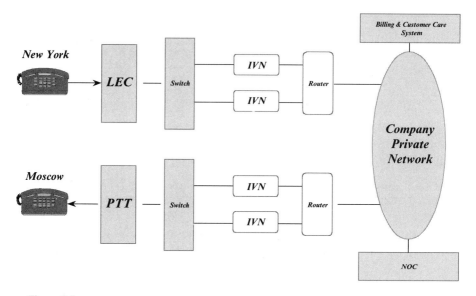

Figure 3.3
Private IP telephony network (Source: McGarty 1999)

provides for the sorting out of the packets on transmit and receive. The TCU interfaces with the router via an ethernet interface.

Router. This is a standard router such as those provided by Cisco or other vendors. Depending on the traffic load, a carrier-class switch or router could be substituted for the more modest devices needed for a less heavily trafficked network.

The IVN is then placed in one of two generic configurations, as shown in Figure 3.3. The configuration shown is for a dedicated network or channel configuration, which uses a private network.

An alternative configuration is the pure Internet approach, which was taken by many of the early Internet telephony start-up companies. It is important to note in the second architecture, relying on the public Internet for transport (Figure 3.4) that there is the same IVN, but now there is no switch, there is no billing system, and there is no network operations center (NOC). Instead, there is the shared network of the public Internet replacing any dedicated IP links. The result is a different architecture, a differing worldview, and different quality

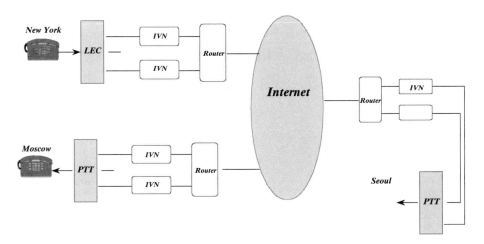

Figure 3.4
A public IP telephony network (Source: McGarty 1999)

expectations and economics. The difference in the architecture is quite evident. The difference in the worldview, however, is not necessarily evident on first glance. But it is possible to deconstruct the worldview from the architecture. The intranet player shown in Figure 3.3 wants to work within the context of the global telephone network. He believes that the change from circuit-switched to packet-switched networks will be slower than some anticipate, and he believes that the user expectations for voice quality must be met. Therefore, the quality of voice provided must be at a nominal threshold, and further, there will be no bifurcation on voice quality. In other words, the end user will demand a voice quality that is at a minimal level and will not pay a differential for poor quality versus good quality. The Internet worldview is one that says that the growth will be significant, that there will be a separate network, and that at best the meet point will remain the cumbersome multiple dial network that is in the Internet approach—dial once for access to the Internet and then dial the ultimate number. The Internet approach also assumes that there will be a "ham radio" voice acceptability at a lower cost. The strengths and weaknesses of these alternatives are summarized in Table 3.1.

Applications, Architectures, and Industry Structures

Table 3.1
IP telephony architectural alternatives

Element	Shared Channel Internet	Dedicated Channel
Security	Highly vulnerable access and control.	Very secure from external attack.
Latency	Unpredictable latency.	Traffic engineered for low latency.
Availability	Uncertain availability since there are multiple elements that cause outages, lost packets, and other failure mechanisms.	High availability due to the controlled environment.
Accessibility	Easily accessible from any location with a telephone line.	Need points of connection or "meet" points for dedicated circuits.
Costs	Low costs since they depend on fixed costs per port per month and may actually be usage independent. Some pricing may have a usage factor.	Low costs depending on amount of traffic. Example: An E1 from New York to Russia, at $32,500 per month, that can carry 2.5 million minutes per month of traffic is $0.0150 per minute.
Control	Little control. May have SNMP access via TCP/IP at end points.	Control via embedded network operations center (NOC), facilities.
Management	Management at best at end points. Otherwise unmanageable.	Controllable at NOC level.
Provisioning	Readily provisioned. Can be implemented in a few days.	Complex provisioning of circuits and at meet points. May take weeks to months.
Speed/data rate	Can use whatever speed the Internet allows at the time controlled by the speed of the end circuit.	Totally under control of bandwidth obtained in the transmission path.
Flexibility	Flexible in the context of an internet connection.	Flexible in the context of a telephone network connection.
Interconnectivity	Limited interconnectivity.	Full interconnectivity to all telecommunication networks.
Speech quality	Very poor due to latency and transmission reliability problems.	Toll-grade quality. Allows for implementation of national as well as international networks.
Signaling compatibility	Has no ability to cross-transfer traffic from IP to SS7/C7	Fully compatible. Allows transfer from C7/SS7 and any IP network.
Standards	Meets Internet standards.	Meets all integrated standards.

Switches

Switches perform the function of allowing multiple users access to each other. The switch may be a stand-alone device separate from the end user, or it may be integral to the end users' equipment. We shall consider both. However, it must be remembered that the network being considered is one where the communications will be between all other networks, including the existing telephony network. That telephony network has evolved over 125 years into one where there are many standards, protocols, agreements, and other elements that make interconnections generally straightforward but also generally less responsive to changes in technology. Thus, one must align with the existing technical structure of the global telephone network if one accepts the point of view of customers of telephony services, who assume they will be able to reach any other telephone user. This constrains network architecture planning, in spite of the further service enhancements likely to come in TCP/IP networks.

Transport

The transport elements allow for interconnection by electronic means between multiple switches and end user devices. Two types are relevant to Internet services: dedicated and shared. In the dedicated form, clear channel circuits most likely will use the TCP/IP protocol. For shared transport, the market focus is on Internet connections. The differences between the two are significant and have led some to state that there is a difference between IP voice and standard voice. However, whatever differences may exist between IP and standard voice services will disappear over time (for reasons explained later in this chapter). The clear channel approach is best for secure channels of known capacity, where control and management are feasible and desired. The Internet approach is best viewed as the ubiquitous expedient. It allows implementers to get a service up and running in short order, but it does not allow much control over the quality of any of the network elements and places control in the hands of multiple and generally unknown third parties. This may change over time as Internet service quality protocols and policies are agreed to, implemented, deployed, and adopted by end users. But it will remain generally true that the extent to which the

Applications, Architectures, and Industry Structures

network is controlled will affect users' experience of that network and its services.

Network Control

For Internet telephony services to function with the quality and reliability assumed to be necessary, the backbone network must be managed and controlled in a real-time fashion. Operating entities at all levels will have the capability of being monitored for operational effectiveness, network performance, and impact on their interconnecting network elements. The NOC manager will be able to determine the locations of any outage or system degradation points in the network or in any other network that a customer may have access to. The NOC combines the interfaces from several subsystems. The vendor equipment provides its own stand-alone network manager. The NOC has important functions for international Internet telephony services.

Fault Management. This allows for the detection, isolation, identification, and repair of any system faults. Fault management assumes that there are subnetwork managers that can generate fault recognition and transmit it in a common format to the NOC, which then takes these fault reports and combines them from all of the subnetwork managers. Fault management must integrate all of the network elements and their subnetwork managers. The IVN system provider may provide a robust manager for the IVN equipment. The backbone service provider may or may not provide those elements. The international Internet telephony NOC must take all of those elements and integrate then into a single network function.

Accounting Management. Accounting functions allow for the provision and sourcing of network elements necessary for an audit trail on the faults in the system. The accounting function provides for managing the capital asset base. It may be integrated into the overall NOC functionality, which is essential if it is to support the configuration database.

Configuration Management. This capability ensures that all elements in the system are properly configured and identified in this process. The configuration management process allows for the updating of the system—a mapping of the overall accounting function for actively deployed parts and system elements. Configuration management is an essential element in the processes of repair dispatching and inventory management. Configuration management requires the critical control of installation as well as operations and maintenance. Any time a unit or object is installed, replaced, modified, or in any other way changed, the configurations system must track it.

Performance Management. This function allows for the optimization of the system. We suggest the inclusion of both "hard" trouble tickets for identifying specific faults and "soft" trouble tickets for measuring performance of international Internet telephony services. NOCs typically do not perform overall performance optimization but do provide reports on performance analysis and trend analysis. Such NOCs are capable of isolating performance factors and can, combined with the fault tree system, help isolate factors affecting overall system performance.

Security Management. The management of the security and integrity of an international Internet telephony system is ensured by means of a fully integrated and protected system design. There are three levels of security that the system will support: physical, software and database, and system access. Physical security management is performed by the communications of alarms on IVNs, buildings, and other secure locations into the NOC and the connection of the NOC to the appropriate security support systems required. Software and database security are security management measures taken by the NOC and other operators to prevent internal compromising of the system. The NOC can manage the overall internal access management role. The third area is external access to the system resources. This is a great concern with access via TCP/IP or Internet connections. This will require firewall protection of the system.

Network Management. The network management function provides interfaces to all other network system elements. The overall philosophy of the service functions of the network infrastructure is one of complete integration and integrity of the data elements. Network management

Applications, Architectures, and Industry Structures

functions to ensure such data integrity. Other interface factors are linked to meeting the overall performance goals of the system.

Network Interconnection Gateways

On the non-U.S. end of an international Internet telephony service, the connection is typically via the local PTT and its switch and the IVN. In the United States or other competitive markets for telecommunications services, the connection is on the router and digital subscriber unit (DSU) side via the international gateway. The network elements of a typical international Internet telephony service are shown in Figure 3.5.

Note that in the configuration shown in Figure 3.6, the IVN connects directly to the local post, telephone, and telegraph (PTT) authorities. In this case, the LCU is required to perform multiple functions, and the PCU must also perform some billing functions. Another approach is to

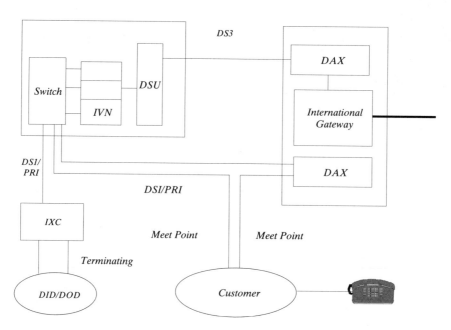

Figure 3.5
IP telephony network interfaces (Source: McGarty 1999)

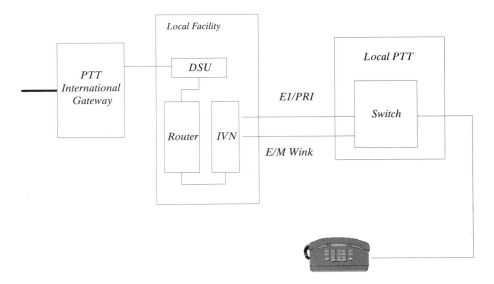

Figure 3.6
National Internet telephony network interconnection (Source: McGarty 1999)

employ a switch adjacent to the IVN for E1 primary rate interface compatibility.[4] This is shown in Figure 3.7. This configuration allows the switch to perform the signaling and offer, via the IVN, a gateway function. The switch also becomes a billing platform as well as a PTT meet point. The latter factor is generally critical in the implementation of these networks with the cooperation of public network operators. As illustrated in Figures 3.5 through 3.7, the IVN in each country in an international Internet telephony network must have access to, at a minimum, the public Internet or, preferably, an intranet backbone via an ISP. The intranet backbone is a compilation of controlled high-speed, dedicated links between countries.

The next issue that must be addressed as the architecture is developed is the capacity and sizing of the network links. The description has presented alternative architectural choices for the placement of the IVN in an international Internet telephony network. The sizing of the network is also a key factor in its overall operational competitiveness. The IVN has three significant financial factors as an operational element: low capital costs per subscriber, an ability to reach full-scale economies with

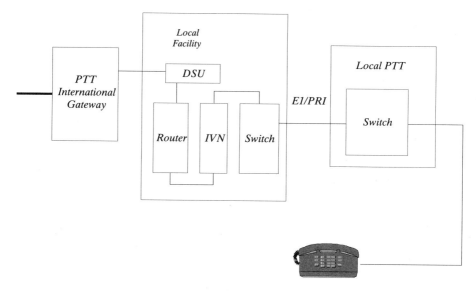

Figure 3.7
International Internet telephony network interconnection (Source: McGarty 1999)

a small amount of loading of traffic (average capital per subscriber equals marginal capital per subscriber), and is highly scalable, that is, it can grow to any arbitrary size.

The sizing is first performed by looking at the capital plant. Although the planning of capital plant involves a multitude of factors, a relatively simple formula may provide sufficient accuracy for most networks.[5] Figure 3.8 is a graphical representation of the network capacity and sizing calculations made by international Internet telephony network operators. Two E1 IVNs are needed for every point-to-point link with 300,000 minutes. The fully loaded cost of the links typically is about $50,000 each (at 1999 telecommunications market prices).

An international Internet telephony carrier must have the ability to interface with the customer either directly or via a third-party reseller, which may obtain the customer and deliver the traffic to the carrier. Figure 3.9 depicts the possible interfaces to customers for resellers, Internet telephony carriers, and PTTs. The reseller may be a facilities-based reseller with a switch that performs the billing function and interfaces with the reseller's customer care system. In this case, the carrier is

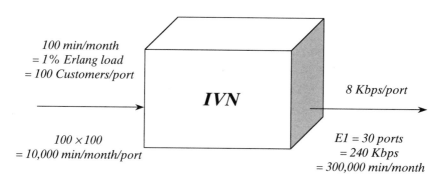

Figure 3.8
Capacity and sizing Internet voice networks (Source: Zephyr 1998)

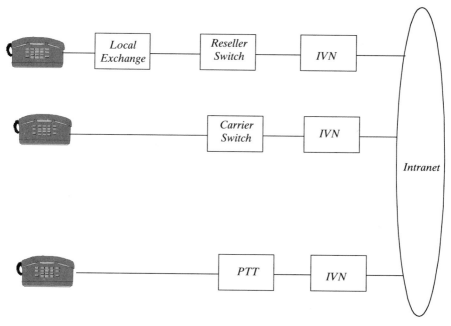

Figure 3.9
Resellers in an international IP telephony network (Source: McGarty 1999)

Applications, Architectures, and Industry Structures

Table 3.2
Call originator and terminator cost relationships

Factor	Originator	Terminator
Sales costs	This is the customer of the originator, and thus sales costs are attributable.	No costs as terminator.
ISP Interconnect costs	Must pay for ISP costs on a per customer basis. Any originating customer must be a "customer" of the business.	Must pay for ISP costs on a per customer basis. Originating customer may not terminate on a "customer" of the business. In fact, it is most likely that they will not.
IVN costs of capital equipment	At both nodes.	At both nodes.
IVN operations	At both nodes.	At both nodes.
Interconnect costs to PTT/LEC	None. Customer effectively pays at originator end.	Must pay for terminating interconnection.

a wholesale provider to the customer via the reseller. Alternatively, the Internet telephony carrier may go directly to the customer, which would require the carrier to have its own switch to provide certain nominal telephone functions.

Figure 3.9 depicts the variety of possible interfaces with customers. The first alternative is for the customer to dial in via a reseller's switch. In this case, the carrier sells the service wholesale to the reseller, which then buys the time in bulk from the carrier. In the second case, the customer is the carrier's customer and dials in directly to the carrier switch. This switch may then support a prepaid card system or may even prepare a bill. The third case shows a PTT configuration, where the customer may call from a foreign country on a call-back basis.

The operator may take two roles in this business: as the originator and the terminator of calls. Table 3.2 depicts the relationship between these factors.

IP Telephony Strategic Alternatives

Three alternatives from an operations perspective of the IP telecommunications architectures are now currently understood and being offered: the clear channel network approach, where a dedicated circuit is used; the Internet backbone approach, using the current Internet transport mechanism; and, for example, the use of an IP "service bureau" for other "carriers" to access a well-managed IP backbone that will provide a quality-of-service (QOS) type of IP transport.

The provision of a global IP network guarantees a QOS at a price point that is matched to the amount of service, its QOS, and possibly its actual usage. The IP service network approach allows the provider to become the network backbone at the IP level, and anyone interested in connecting to it must do so at the IP level and not at the raw bandwidth level, as is typically done today.

There are four possible architectures that may be made available to the IP telecommunications community. Figure 3.10 illustrates these

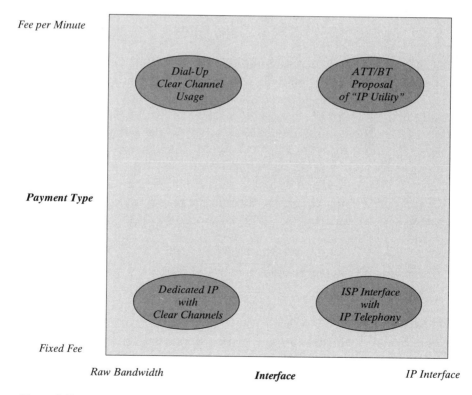

Figure 3.10
IP telephony strategic alternatives (Source: McGarty 1999)

four extremes, depending on what the interface is (clear channel or IP backbone) and what the fee structure is (fixed fee per unit access or fee per transaction, such as bps, packet, or minute). The four alternatives show that standard Internet telephony on the Internet uses an IP interface but has a fixed fee per Internet access to an ISP. The IP service bureau approach is one that uses an IP interface but charges on a per transaction basis. The approach taken by others uses dedicated clear channel circuits. The interface is at the clear channel basis, bit per second, and carriers do the IP processing on their own network equipment. A fourth approach is a clear channel dial-up, where the IP is done independently.

The most important element in the IP service approach is who is the responsible agent for the definition of interfaces and standards as compared to the open Internet environment of today. The offering of a fully open IP network will take a great deal of time to implement and will face significant regulatory and political hurdles. Foremost among them is the issue of who defines IP interfaces and services. The IP community is highly diversified and entrepreneurial, and the last thing they want is a third party trying to tell them how to build the network.

The provision of telecommunications services via IP consists of the utilization of several elements. At one end is raw bandwidth, which is installed in the ground, under the water, or in the skies. The next step leases bandwidth, such as an E1 circuit. Then there is the access to TCP/IP backbone, as may be obtained by accessing the Internet. The next step is the provision of voice carriage. Finally, there is the customer or end user. Figure 3.11 shows the multiple players and where they play within this segmented space (also known as the IP food chain) in the market as of late 1999.

International Regulation and Internet Telephony

From the national regulator's perspective, an individual service provider's network architecture and profit level may be of little interest. Other policy objectives, however, such as protecting domestic incumbent firms, promoting competition, and complying with international trade treaty commitments, may be of utmost concern. Traditionally, PTTs built, owned, and operated national telephony systems. The

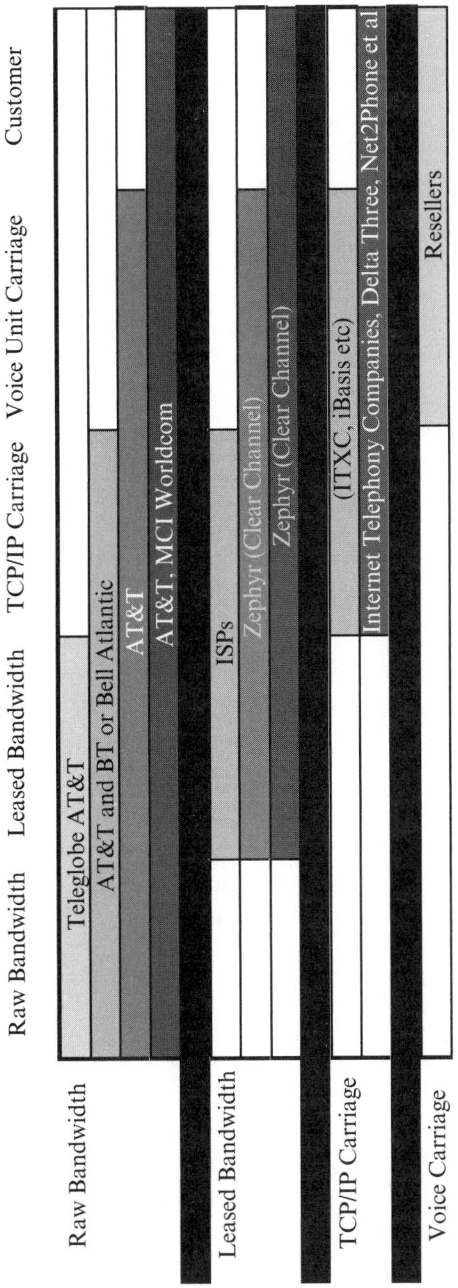

Virtually Global Telcos

Figure 3.11
IP telephony food chain (Source: McGarry 1999)

international interconnection of PTTs was similarly under national control, administered through international agreements on technical standards and tariffs and settlement charges under the auspices of the International Telecommunication Union (ITU). With the emergence of digital technologies as a fundamental driver of the global economy over the past few decades, national governments have generally recognized that telecommunications is too important to leave under the exclusive control of the PTT. In fact, many PTTs have been restructured, corporatized, and privatized out of existence, with a national regulatory authority emerging distinct and independent from the operator of telecommunications facilities.

In this more competitive international system, the World Trade Organization (WTO) has superseded the ITU as the organization setting the terms for international telecommunications services. Just as telecommunications has become too important to leave to the PTTs, it also has become too important to leave to the ITU. The WTO is the principal international body concerned with solving trade problems between countries and with negotiating trade liberalizing agreements. The WTO replaces the General Agreement on Tariffs and Trade (GATT) and is the embodiment of the results of the 1986–1994 Uruguay Round of trade negotiations conducted under the GATT. Understanding the role, rules, and structure of the WTO is therefore an important task for the new operators of international Internet telephony services, as well as their customers. In many cases, national authorities, particularly in developing countries that still have PTTs, generally have entered into WTO agreements that typically place voice in the settlement arena and data in the nonsettlement elements. (Settlement is the term used in the telecommunications arena to describe how revenues are shared across carriers for initiating and completing a telephone call. Regulatory authorities are typically involved in determining their fates. On the other hand, for data communications, rates are solely determined by commercial contracts without regulatory intervention.)

The WTO has a cooperative relationship with the United Nations but is not a UN specialized agency. It was established on January 1, 1995, as a result of the implementation of the Uruguay Round results.[6] The WTO encompasses previous GATT legal instruments as they existed when the Uruguay Round was completed (known as GATT 1994), but also extends new disciplines to economic and trade sectors not covered in the past.

Whereas the GATT's scope was limited to trade in goods, the WTO also covers trade in services, including such sectors as banking, insurance, transport, tourism, and telecommunications sectors, as well as the provision of labor. In addition, the WTO covers all aspects of trade-related intellectual property rights (such as copyrights, patents, and trademarks). Furthermore, while the GATT had a relatively ambiguous status as a multilateral agreement without any institutional provisions, the WTO is an international organization with a stature commensurate with that of the World Bank or International Monetary Fund (IMF).

The GATS (General Agreement for Trade in Services), which is part of the current WTO structure, developed a set of rules and regulations and a schedule of timetables to open up the member markets to trade in telecommunications services. There are three dimensions for such trade in services. The first two are basically for the intracountry markets and represent the local and long-distance telephony market. The third is the international telecommunications market. We can further break up all three cases into voice, data, video, valued-added services, and other types and classes of services. Table 3.3 summarizes the GATS treatment of various telecommunications services.

Table 3.3
GATS and telecommunications services

	International	Long Distance	Local
Switched voice	Generally tightly controlled	Generally controlled by internal ownership	Generally controlled by internal ownership
Switched data (off net to off net)	Generally tightly controlled	Generally controlled by internal ownership	Generally controlled by internal ownership
Nonswitched data (on net to on net)	Generally limited control	Limited to little control	Limited to little control
Video (CATV)	Issue is ownership and content	Not applicable in general	Control limited to any entity having a franchise or similar license
Internet	Generally open and limited by government controls on content	Generally open and limited by government controls on content	Generally open and limited by government controls on content
Value-added services	Generally controlled as an on-net service	Generally controlled as an on-net service	Generally controlled as an on-net service

Table 3.4 summarizes the WTO agreements for telecommunications services. It is for Korea and is typical.

Trade in Settlements

The current international record carriers (IRCs) enter into bilateral agreements with other IRCs, the PTTs of the foreign entities, to agree to mutual settlement or accounting rates. Generally these are bilateral agreements performed one at a time. The main concern from a U.S. policy perspective has been twofold: there may be a significant amount of revenue flowing to countries due to accounting irregularities, and where there is a desire to expand the market for U.S. services in international traffic, the accounting rules act as a barrier to entry.[7]

The system works in the following fashion. One carrier negotiates with another for the right to terminate traffic. For example, Canada negotiates with the Ivory Coast. They agree on a settlement rate of, say, $0.40 per minute. This applies only to voice traffic. At the end of the year, they add the traffic up, and if there is more traffic from Canada to the Ivory Coast, then the difference must be paid by Canada to the Ivory Coast at $0.40 per minute. If someone in Canada wants to place a call to Uganda, the call is placed in transit through the Ivory Coast, which charges a transit fee of perhaps $0.020 per minute, and the Ivory Coast has an agreement with Uganda for terminating at $0.15 per minute. Teleglobe, as the Canadian party to the transaction, gets charged that sum.

The key issue is that a carrier that has an agreement stating that any traffic it terminates is voice and it will pay the Ivory Coast at the agreed-to rate cannot generally go back and say, "This is Internet voice, and I do not want to pay the Ivory Coast." A new entrant can start that way, but an existing entrant places its existing agreements in jeopardy. Thus, there is a general consensus that if there is an existing settlement pact between two parties, the parties shall honor the terms of the agreement and any termination or transit of traffic shall be by the agreement and thus will require the payment of the agreed settlement fees. This places an existing carrier at jeopardy in attempting to get Internet terminations.

Table 3.4
Republic of Korea WTO Telecommunications Agreement

Sector or Subsector	Limitations on Market Access
C. Telecommunications services *Facilities based*: 1. Voice telephone services 2. Packet-switched data transmission services 3. Circuit-switched data transmission services 4. Private leased circuit services	None except that the provision of all services is subject to commercial arrangements with licensed Korean service suppliers. None except that: (i) Each service supplier must be a licensed Korean juridical person. (ii) Until December 31, 1998, a license, including radio station license, may not be granted to a juridical person whose largest shareholder is: (a) Foreign government, (b) Foreign person, or (c) Juridical person 50 percent (15 percent if the largest shareholder of the juridical person is a foreign government or a foreign person) or more of whose voting shares are owned by foreign governments or foreign persons. (iii) Until December 31, 2000, a license, including radio station license, may be granted to a juridical person in whom no more than 33 percent of the aggregate voting shares are owned by entities identified in (a) through (c). From January 1, 2001, a license, including radio station license, may be granted to a juridical person in whom no more than 49 percent of the aggregate voting shares are owned by entities identified in (a) through (c). (iv) A license, including a radio station license, may not be granted to a juridical person more than 33 percent (10 percent, in the case of wireline-based voice telephone services) of whose voting share is owned by a person. (v) The largest shareholder of Korea Telecom (KT) must be the Korean government or a Korean person. While KT's share owned by a person must be no more than 3 percent, the aggregate foreign shareholding in KT must be no more than 20 percent until December 31, 2000, and no more than 33 percent from January 1, 2001. (4) Unbound except as indicated in horizontal commitments.
Resale based: 1. Voice telephone services 2. Packet-switched data transmission services 3. Circuit-switched data transmission services 4. Private leased circuit services	None except that provision of all services is subject to commercial arrangements with licensed Korean service suppliers. Until December 31, 2000, resale of voice telephone services interconnected to the public telecommunications network can be supplied only by companies established in Korea. None except that each service supplier must be a licensed Korean juridical person. Foreign shareholding in suppliers of resale voice telephone services, interconnected to the public telecommunications network, will be permitted only after January 1, 1999. From January 1, 1999, foreign shareholding will be permitted up to 49 percent. As of January 1, 2001, 100 percent foreign shareholding will be permitted.

Source: WTO, 1998.

Applications, Architectures, and Industry Structures

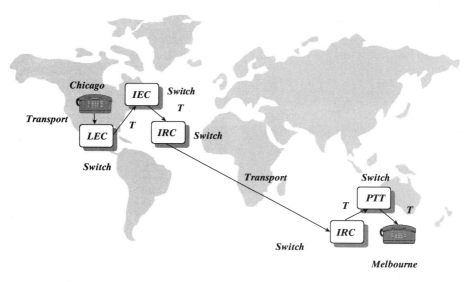

Figure 3.12
Architecture of international accounting rates (Source: McGarty 1999)

Accounting Rates and Settlements

To understand the principles of accounting rates and settlement costs, it is necessary to understand how an international call is made—that is, the call architecture.[8] The accounting rules are to international traffic what the access fees are to domestic.

In the example of the international accounting rate process shown in Figure 3.12, a customer in Chicago wants to place a call to Melbourne, Australia. The customer first uses the transport and switch of Ameritech, which then connects to MCI. MCI provides transport and switching. The international record carrier chosen by the customer is AT&T. MCI then hands the call off to AT&T, and AT&T has an accounting agreement with the Australian IRC to handle all traffic at the net rate of perhaps $0.55 per minute. For that, the Australian PTT then handles the call and places it to the terminating point in Melbourne. The customer is billed $1.55 per minute. The IRC in the United States charges the customer for switching and transport and then adds the costs of MCI and Ameritech, generally via the access fee applied as a local exchange carrier (LEC).

The accounting rate is the rate agreed to by, between, and among international record carriers for the provision of a unit, say, a minute, of telecommunications, generally voice, between two locations or terminations. For example, the U.S. carrier AT&T may agree to a number, say $0.45 per minute, with France Telecom, for all traffic between the United States and France, no matter the direction of the traffic. This fee is the full and complete fee for the delivery of that minute from the midway point of the cable to the end destination point in the called location. The accounting rates are supposed to represent the total cost of carrying the traffic from point of origin to point of destination.

The settlement rate is the mechanism that any pair of carriers selects to divide up the number of minutes from and to each other based on the accounting rate already agreed to. If AT&T provides France Telecom with 500 million minutes and France Telecom provides AT&T with only 400 million minutes and the agreed accounting rate is $0.045, then at the end of a period, AT&T owes France Telecom 500 million less 400 million: 100 million times $0.45, or $45 million.

There is the third factor of why a call is $0.55 from the United States to Israel but $1.90 from Israel to the United States. The U.S. and Israeli carriers have agreed to a settlement fee of, say, $0.35 per minute. The U.S. market is competitive for barriers; thus, there cannot be an excessive distortion in price. The $0.55 represents a fail-demand-based price subject to the $0.35 "subsidy" paid in the accounting rate. However, in Israel, there is a pure monopoly, and thus there is no clearing of the market, and the PTT charges a rate based on a social and fiscal policy that states that this is a means to subsidize those who cannot afford to call internationally. It is social policy, not economic policy, that dictates the actual price.

The FCC states that the accounting rate system has the following characteristics:[9]

The current accounting rate system was developed as part of a regulatory tradition that international telecommunications services were supplied through a bilateral correspondent relationship between national monopoly carriers.[10] An accounting rate is the price an U.S. facility-based carrier negotiates with a foreign carrier for handling one minute of international telephone service. It was originally intended to allow each carrier to recover its costs for terminating an international call.[11] Each carrier's portion of the accounting rate is referred to as the settlement rate. In almost all cases, the settlement rate is equal to one-half of the negotiated accounting rate. At settlement, each carrier nets the minutes of service it originated against the minutes the other carrier originated. The carrier that originated more minutes of service pays the other carrier a net settlement payment calculated by multiplying the settlement rate by the number of imbalanced traffic minutes.[12]

Thus, under the existing settlement agreement, bilateral and multi-lateral, carriers have generally agreed to pay settlements on their voice circuits, and any change they make directly or otherwise would put their agreements in breach and could result in the immediate termination of their traffic from their home locations to the countries with which they have agreements. The existing agreements are in most cases expressly for the provision of voice traffic and have followed the generally accepted terms in existence for the past 130 years.

U.S. Policy and Cost-Based Settlements

The FCC in its IB Docket No. 96-261, adopted December 19, 1997, stated the major policy issue clearly and precisely:

U.S. consumers pay on average 16¢ a minute for a domestic long distance call, but they pay 99¢ a minute for an international call. Yet, the difference in cost between providing domestic long distance and international service is no more than a few cents. As a result of recent technological advances, the underlying costs of providing telephony are becoming virtually distance insensitive. For example, because of new fiber optic technology, the cost of undersea cables on a per circuit basis is only one eighth of what it was seven years ago. We antici-pate that increased competition in international satellite services will bring similar potential benefits to countries that are not now served by undersea cables and comparable land facilities. Differences in underlying costs therefore do not explain why international services are so much more expensive than domestic long distance services. The difference is attributable in part to limited compe-tition in the IMTS market and in part to the inflated settlement rates paid by U.S. carriers to terminate traffic in foreign markets.

The FCC argued in its Notice of Proposed Rule-Making (NPRM) that costs should be the key factor in establishing settlement rates and pro-posed costs be based on three elements: international transmission, local switching, and national extension.[13] The FCC predicates all of its cost analyses on these numbers. This approach works for the current means and methods for switched-based voice telecommunications, but such an approach fails when applied to alternative telecommunications approaches. The FCC's proposed model for costing contained these elements—international transmission, local switching, and national extension—to which it applied a specific methodology to come up with certain costs.[14] Rather than using tariffs as the sole arbiter of setting settlement rates, there is also a method for setting those rates on a cost-based basis that reflects the actual costs incurred by the in-country provider. This additional approach shows that there can be an argument made for costs based on forward-looking technology as well as obtaining returns on past investments.

It can be argued that the capital plant and equipment cost is generally the same for any country exclusive of tariffs and other tax-like costs the country must pay on the procurement of the equipment. The country may also have a cost of capital, so when the capital and plant and equipment are equated to an annualized leased rate, the lease rate must reflect the changing costs of capital. For example, in Poland, the respondent sees a 25 percent excise tariff on any imported telecommunications equipment that increases the capital costs base by that amount. In addition, there is a risk premium on capital financing of 2 percent to 2.2 percent that raises the annualized effective lease rates. Table 3.5

Table 3.5
Switching costs in Poland

Effective Life (Years)	Tariff Rate	Interest Rate	Market Premium	Monthly Fee
5	25%	8.00%	1.50%	$0.0263
5	25	10.00	1.50	0.0275
5	25	12.00	1.50	0.0288
5	25	14.00	1.50	0.0301
10	25	8.00	1.50	0.0162
10	25	10.00	1.50	0.0176
10	25	12.00	1.50	0.0190
10	25	14.00	1.50	0.0206
15	25	8.00	1.50	0.0131
15	25	10.00	1.50	0.0146
15	25	12.00	1.50	0.0162
15	25	14.00	1.50	0.0179

Table 3.6
Costs of international Internet telephony operations

Cost Element	Unit Cost	Number of Units	Total Costs
Capital plant	$0.00026	3	$0.00078
Transport	0.00052	2	0.00104
Operations costs	0.00600	3	0.01800
Operations overhead	0.00030	3	0.00090
Sales costs	0.00000	1	0.00000
Total			0.02072

presents a typical example using Poland as a case. If we assume an effective life, a tariff or excise tax rate, an interest rate, and a risk market premium, then for every dollar, the costs of switching per month are as shown in the table.

To complete the cost calculations for international Internet telephony services, further operations derive interesting results, as shown in Table 3.6.[15] In this table, it should be noted that the costs are dramatically lower than AT&T costs. However, they do not include sales costs, a significant factor, nor do they include any R&D, product development, marketing, legal, or other similar costs. These elements may easily, along with profit, raise the rate to a number comparable to AT&T.

Principle of Cost-Based Pricing
The principle of cost-based pricing states that consumers should pay for each link separately, and they should pay only for those links for which they are customers of that link provider. The payment that customers make should reflect a price that is based on the costs of that link.[16] The basis for the principle is the same as for the Baumol Willig theorem: maximizing consumer welfare. The argument is based on the theory of Ramsey pricing. The classic approach taken by Baumol and Willig is as follows:

maximize$\{P1, \ldots, Pm\}[CS + PS]$; subject to $PS = F$,

where CS is the consumer welfare and PS is the production surplus or the profit of the monopolist provider.[17] If, however, the monopolist is eliminated and one maximizes on the basis of consumer welfare alone, and if one assumes a fully displaceable service, and if one further assumes the changes in technology that eliminate scale in toto, then the resultant position is the principle of cost-based pricing: Each separate provider sells its service on the basis of its own costs; the interconnection is free and reflects no costs to the consumer.

The FCC raised concerns about individual settlement agreements and the possibility of various large international carriers' taking undue advantage of arbitrage opportunities within their own field of operations.[18] Smaller nondominant carriers have no recourse to this procedure and no remedy under international law if the settlement agreements are allowed to be set on a company-by-company basis.

International Policy on Internet Settlements

Data are generally free from settlements. This is the accepted result of the WTO negotiations and has been opined on by various entities. The FCC states its position:

There are other technological developments that accentuate the market distortions caused by above-cost settlement rates. For example, the routing of bilateral traffic through third countries has become increasingly prevalent as a means to arbitrage settlement rate differences. Such re-routing can be helpful in undercutting the settlement rate system, but it can also lead to inefficient traffic routing patterns that are not aligned with underlying economic network costs. Use of the Internet also has emerged as an alternative to higher priced IMTS. Though Internet traffic and switched voice traffic are carried over virtually identical facilities, the price for Internet service is far cheaper because switched traffic is subject to international settlement rates, while Internet traffic is exchanged outside of the traditional accounting rate system.[19]

The Organization for Economic Co-operation and Development (OECD), part of the European Common Union (ECU), has this to say about the introduction of Internet-type telephony and its advantages in its ability to have zero settlements:

Services that by-pass the international telecommunications charging system . . . include international simple resale, which is already being offered in some countries. Other services, such as telephony using packet-switched networks, including the Internet, would also be included in this group of services.

An overview of the different charging and settlement rates for a number of technologies is shown in the table. The services where there is no settlement are

Applications, Architectures, and Industry Structures

to a large extent used mostly by large business customers, but they are becoming increasingly available to the smaller customers given developments in technology, and regulation.

Collection charges and settlement for different services

Service	Technology	Collection Charge Type	Settlement
Telephone	Switched line	Subscribe line, trunk line Time/flat/time, distance	Accounting rate system
Packet	Packet	Time, volume, volume	Settlement by traffic volume
×400	Store-and-forward	Volume	No settlement
Leased line	Leased line	Flat	Half split (no settlement)
Frame relay	Frame relay, asynchronous transfer mode	Flat	Half split (no settlement)
Internet	Packet/ others	PSTN, integrated services digital network, leased lines, flat	No settlement

In general, the pricing structure for telecommunication services other than telephony does not depend on time and distance, and does not normally incur a settlement between the operators. Telephone collection charges have also shown a trend toward being less time and distance related reflecting the digitalization of networks. There is, therefore, precedence for using systems other than accounting rates. Despite different charging frameworks many of these other services based on technologies other than the PSTN are profitable.[20]

The OECD table depicts the WTO agreements as reflected in the Uruguay Round of GATT talks. Internet is free from settlements and is the only one free on a full-circuit basis. The OECD report goes on to state that based on this logic, Internet telephony should be free from settlements.[21] Thus under the WTO and the terms of the WTO agreements on services, especially in telecommunications, data are free from both transit fees and settlement fees. Because TCP/IP is defined as a form of data, it is free from such fees. If a country that is a signatory to the Uruguay Rounds decides to violate those terms, then it subjects itself to the severest penalties under the WTO.

Globally Disaggregated Telcos

Internet and telecommunications technology and industry now make it possible to affect all elements of a business in a virtual form. By obtaining all functions necessary to deliver a service by purchasing them from third parties, each of which has other similar customers, each can thus deliver its element of the functionality in a minimal marginal cost manner. The disaggregation theory then concludes with the result that in many technologically intense services businesses, a virtual company can exist where all the functions can be purchased from third parties, or capital equipment may be purchased in a fully interconnected fashion so as to achieve near equality between average and marginal costs from the very start of the business. The disaggregated IP telephony company is the embodiment of the virtual business.

An example shows the elements of any telephone company and how they may be disaggregated:

Switch. The ability to switch traffic as well as provide for the interface between the customer's lines and the backbone network. It is not merely the physical switch but includes all software needed for the deployment of the services to be provided.

License. The license to operate. This may not be just one license but may be a collection, or it may be the position to operate without a license in certain circumstances.

Services. Advanced services, such as call forwarding, automatic number identification, voice mail, and other similar services that are generally software based but require access to a switch and a network.

Operating support systems. The billing, customer care, provisioning, and network management services, separately or integrated.

Sales. The sales channel.

Transport. Local and backbone transport; may include any necessary interfacing with protocols to provide that transport.

This segmentation into disaggregated elements is not unique; moreover, each of the elements may be further divided. In today's "telecommunications" market, there are separate vendors for each of these services. One can create a "telephone company in a box" approach by adding and aggregating vendors in all areas. The corollary, however, is that to be a telephone company, one needs all of these elements, albeit disaggregated into separate elements and provided by various vendors. An IP telecommunications carrier cannot be a telecommunications services provider and not have all of these elements provided in some fashion.

The theory of disaggregation states that technology and industry have developed in such a fashion that it is possible to affect all elements of a business in a virtual form by obtaining all functions necessary to deliver a service. These functions are purchased from third parties, each of which itself has other similar customers and thus can deliver its element of the functionality in a minimal marginal cost manner. The disaggregation theory then concludes with the result that in many technologically intense services businesses, a virtual company can exist where all the functions can be purchased from third parties or capital equipment may be purchased in a fully interconnected fashion so as to achieve near equality between average and marginal costs from the very commencement of the business. The disaggregated company (Figure 3.13) is the embodiment of the virtual business.[22]

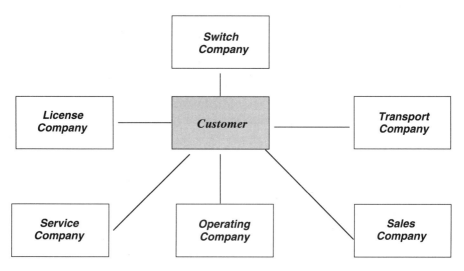

Figure 3.13
The disaggregated telco (Source: Zephyr Telecommunications)

The existence of the disaggregated business is a challenge to the antitrust laws, especially the implementation of the 1996 Telecommunications Act. This implies that as a disaggregated company, any new entrant can achieve the same or better efficiencies of operation of its business as any incumbent, and from the start. This then suggests that competition is based solely on the actions of the monopolistic incumbent and that these actions relate to only one area: interconnection and unbundling.[23]

Disaggregation falls into three dimensions:[24]

Technical disaggregation—the ability to overlay applications and platforms across a disparate backbone of transport facilities and create a whole. An example is the client-server architectures and the local area networks in common use. This type of disaggregation is a result of the many technological advantages that have occurred in telecommunications as a direct result of the 1984 MFJ agreement.[25] Another example is the ability to use a distributed system, such as PCS (personal communications services) and have the actual "switching" occur at the end users' handsets rather than at the old-fashioned hierarchical central office. By distributing the technology and the intelligence, we marginalize the capital deployment requirement and thus achieve technical disaggregation. One example is the concept of providing airtime: the ability of a competitor to unbundle not only the local loop, namely copper wire, but also the frequency spectrum, namely airtime from an existing carrier.[26]

Operational disaggregation—the breaking apart or reassembling in any fashion the operational or business elements to effect the successful provision of service. We can separate billing, transport, sales, service, and network control into different pots and create a virtual corporate entity. We no longer have to do all; we only have to do the part we do well. An example is the outsourcing business, whereby a company, such as a Bell Operating Company, would use an outsourced customer service center to provide this function, or a bank that outsources its entire telecommunications network.

Relational distribution—who does what to whom in such entities as electronic marketing and distribution channels in a telecommunications cybernetwork. This is the most recent example of building a cybernetwork via relationships. Unfortunately, many of the examples are of failure: Prodigy with IBM, CBS and Sears, or MCI and News Corp. on the Internet side.

This disaggregator entity is a key differentiation in the market. The disaggregator is one that may use the existing license holder's access facilities as one of several means to provide service to a fixed customer base. The disaggregator is a different entity altogether and, more important, the most likely evolutionary entity to change as full competition is presented in the wireless market.

By acting as a disaggregator, the international Internet telephony network operator can affect this competitive position. The disaggregator works on the principle that the provision of wireless services is based on the integration of the service elements. This integration may be performed as an aggregation or a disaggregation approach. The aggregation is the way most of the carrier entities now work, having control over all of the elements of "production." The disaggregator may have control of certain strategic elements but will "outsource" others.

Hubbing, shown in Figure 3.14, uses a hub or transit switch to connect the locations. The location of the transit switch is such that the overall costs of the network are minimized. The circuits from the country to the transit switch are generally sized on total traffic emanating from a country. At the network hubs, the IVNs in the listed cities are connected via a backbone Intranet using 1.5 Mbps, 512 Kbps, or 128 Kbps links. This is the airline analogy and generally is the least-cost approach.

Subhubbing is an alternative that uses subhubs that may or may not be termination points on the network (Figure 3.15).

Conclusion

There are admittedly limits to our vision of the future. The positive and negative network externalities stemming from the convergence of voice and data networks will ultimately determine the extent to which international Internet telephony services become a substitute for, and not just a complement to, circuit-switched telephony services. The emergence of new applications for differentiated services on Internet protocol networks is to be expected, even if it is impossible to predict exactly

Virtually Global Telcos

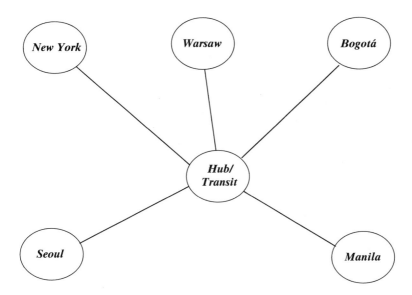

Figure 3.14
Hubbing international IP telephony (Source: McGarty 1999)

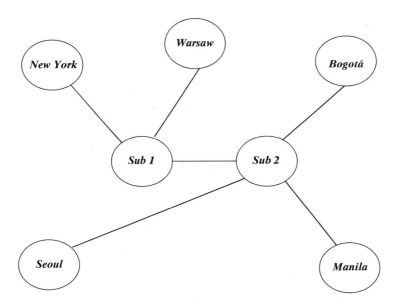

Figure 3.15
Subhubbing international IP telephony (Source: McGarty 1999)

what those novel applications will look like or do for human communication. Network interconnection strategies and policies will also affect the growth of Internet telephony and other advanced Internet services and the extent to which network convergence is realized. Nonetheless, there are several overall conclusions that can be reached at this time. The ability to disaggregate telephony functions and services was identified as a key benefit, beyond the possibly limited cost savings for voice bandwidth, for the emergence of international Internet telephony networks. A global "phone" company can be built a router and a lease at a time. This opens the door to competition in telecommunications much wider than was ever possible in the circuit-switched world of traditional telecommunications systems.

Additional conclusions with regard to architecture, bandwidth versus minutes, regulation, markets, services, and competition are presented below.

Architecture

There are several different architectures available for international Internet telephony services but no clear-cut path to identify which of these will survive. The issues determining survival and dominance are economic, institutional, regulatory, and market acceptance. We have argued that there is a common level of service for voice "telephony" that will dictate a single standard and not a bifurcation of voice quality into high-cost and low-cost voice. We may be wrong in that assumption, and thus there may be other surviving architectures as Internet telephony merges and converges with other Internet multimedia and real-time applications. Perhaps with IP telephony, the customer will come to expect CD-quality voice services, since there is not an intrinsic upper bound on Internet services.

Bandwidth versus Minutes

The architectures will dictate what will be sold: bandwidth or minutes. Also, is the "bandwidth" IP bandwidth or clear channel bandwidth?

Regulation

The FCC has begun to address the settlement and accounting rate issue. Growth in international telecommunications traffic and the pursuant growth in the international economy will be strongly reliant on free and open trade. An element of that trade is telecommunications. The telecommunications market is internal and external. We have argued that the internal portion is generally under the control of the local country, and as best we might, we can influence that in the normal course of trade and tariff discussions. The traffic in international voice, data, and other services, however, is a new development within WTO and thus demands close attention. The trade barriers of telecommunications must be realigned to meet the changes in these markets.

Markets

Different carriers have focused on different market segments. ATT/BT has focused on the multinational company market. Delta Three, Zephyr, and others have focused on the carrier's carrier market. Some have tried to enter the retail market of the end user. Others have focused on calling card customers, who may not know what network their call is crossing. Where are the real markets? The carrier's carrier market is a simple entry point. The retail market is large and high revenue, but expensive as a cost of entry. We see the carrier's carrier market being both the entry point and the growth point at this stage.

Services

The services we have seen are dominantly voice, but we have discussed multimedia, data, fax, and other services. This means that we can envision a wide set of IP-based services. The question with multimedia is again what standards they apply in the standard telephony context, whether there is a set of ITU-compatible IP to SS7 to C7 interfaces, and whether ISDN-like service is portable to IP.

Applications, Architectures, and Industry Structures

Competition

There will be clear competition on many fronts. The barriers to entry to this market are operational and regulatory, and not just economic. The Internet players can provide the degrade quality at low entry costs. We have argued that such quality may be unacceptable; however, with advances in Internet QOS parameters, this may be less of a problem. Over time, international Internet telephony becomes a market dominated by the need for ubiquitous connectivity. Low entry cost means that any player can enter, and therefore the game becomes a marketing and sales game and not one of operations.

However, there will always be the need for interconnection to the global telecommunications network. Despite the advantages of the Internet approach, a switch, or at least a switch-like device, will be required. Thus, there will be a barrier to entry based on technical and operational competence as well as marketing. Having operations in multiple countries is key to long-term success for global firms, even for well-architected international Internet telephony networks.

Notes

1. The view that telecommunications systems are centrally and hierarchically controllable by a single or limited number of players is still alive in the minds of many telecommunications industry executives. A distributed "telephone" network with intelligence at the edge involves a fundamental rethinking of communications architecture, such as the Internet has already done for data communications. It is in this sense that we speak of new worldviews.

2. One can best understand the protocol evolution of the Internet by looking more closely at TCP/IP. To quote Cerf:

IP [the Internet Protocol] provides for the carriage of datagrams from source hosts to destination hosts, possibly passing through one or more routers and networks in the process. A datagram is a finite length packet of bits containing a header and a payload. ... Both hosts and routers in an Internet are involved in processing the IP headers. The hosts must create them ... and the routers must examine them for the purpose of making routing decisions, and modify them as the IP packets make their way from the source to the destination. TCP is a protocol designed ... to provide its clients at higher layers with a reliable, sequenced, flow-controlled end-to-end octet stream.

The rationale for many of the TCP mechanisms can be understood through the following observations:

a) TCP operates above IP and IP provides only best efforts datagram transmission service.

b) End to end recovery . . . leads to sequencing.

c) Flow control requires that both ends uniquely agree. . . .

d) In a concatenation . . . it is possible for a packet to circulate. . . .

e) Termination . . . should be graceful.

f) Every process should be able to engage in multiple conversations

g) . . . the arrival of information should contain no semantic differences.

For an excellent analysis and clear conceptualization of the design of the Internet Protocol and its effects on the architecture and operation of the Internet, see the groundbreaking report by the National Research Council's Computer Science and Telecommunications Board, *Realizing the Information Future: The Internet and Beyond* (Washington, D.C., National Academy Press, 1994).

3. See Neuman, McKnight, and Solomon (1997, 1999) for more information on the historical and technical development of the telecommunications system, as well as the strengths and weaknesses of the 1996 act. For more information on the economic history of the U.S. phone system and its transformation into a competitive marketplace, see Temin (1987).

4. An E1 is the standard measure for telecommunications circuits in much of the world and is equivalent to 2.048 Mbps. *Primary rate interface* means an ISDN interface format at this transmission rate.

5. The capital plant requirements may be determined as follows:

a. Consider a single user who talks 100 minutes per month.

b. Assume that there are 5 days per week, or 22 days per month.

c. Assume that there are 8 hours per day or 176 hours per month or 10,568 minutes per month.

d. Then the average load is 100/10,568, or 1 percent.

e. If we assume a two-to-one peak to average, this increases this amount by about 25 percent.

6. A 1 percent Erlang load generates 100 minutes per month per user.

Following from these assumptions, the calculated IVN numbers and the interconnection facilities may be determined as follows:

a. Assume that an IVN uses 8 Kbps compression.

b. Each port on an IVN can support 100 users at 1 percent Erlang load.

c. This means that a port can handle 100 users ×100 minutes, or 10,000 minutes per port per month.

d. An E1 or 30-port system can handle 300,000 minutes per month.

e. An E1 or 30-port system generates 30 × 8 Kbps or 240,000 bps, or it fills a 256 Kbps channel.

Applications, Architectures, and Industry Structures

f. If a 256 Kbps channel is, for example, $4,000 for U.S. half circuit plus $12,000 for country half circuit, or $16,000 per month, then the per minute rate is $0.0533 per minute for connection.

7. For international Internet telephony operators, the strategy should be to purchase links in bulk, get IRUs for lower costs, and own key facilities.

6. For more information on the negotiations that led to the agreement to form the WTO and its implications for trade in services, including telecommunications services, see Drake and Noam (1997).

7. The following is the FCC's estimate of the size of the settlement process: "The United States paid roughly $5 billion in settlements to the rest of the world in 1995, up from $2.8 billion in 1990. The U.S. out-payment results in part from the fact that U.S. consumers make more telephone calls to foreign countries than foreign consumers make to the United States. In fact, the size of the imbalance between U.S.-outbound and inbound minutes has accelerated in recent years. . . . To the extent that these settlement payments exceed the actual costs foreign carriers incur in terminating U.S.-originated calls, they represent a significant subsidy to foreign carriers. Based on our estimate of the costs of international termination services, we estimate that at least three-quarters of the $5 billion in out-payments is such a subsidy from U.S. consumers, carriers and their shareholders to foreign carriers." Federal Communications Commission, FCC 96-484, Washington, D.C. 20554 In the Matter of International Settlement Rates, IB Docket No. 96-261, Adopted: December 19, 1996, 17.

8. See FCC IB Docket No. 96-261, which describes the process of accounting rates, and see Frieden (1997).

9. Federal Communications Commission, FCC 96-484, Washington, D.C. 20554 In the Matter of International Settlement Rates, IB Docket No. 96-261, Adopted: December 19, 1996, para. 6.

10. This tradition is not compelled by the international legal regime. See Article 9, International Telecommunication Regulation (Melbourne, 1988), and Article 31, Constitution of the International Telecommunication Union (Nice, 1989).

11. See, e.g., Regulation of International Accounting Rates, CC Docket No. 90-337 (Phase II), Second Report and Order and Second Further Notice of Proposed Rulemaking, 7 FCC Rcd 8040, n.3 (1992).

12. Every carrier is required to file a copy of its settlement agreements with the commission. 47 C.F.R. sec. 43.51.

13. See para. 35 of IB Docket No. 96-261, FCC 96-484, December 19, 1996.

14. See para. 37, where the components are defined as:

> **International facility component:** The international facility component consists of international transmission facilities, both cable and satellite, including the link to international switching facilities. This component includes only the half-circuit on the terminating end because originating carriers have traditionally been responsible for the half circuit on the originating end of a call. High-capacity circuits are offered by most telephone administrations to customers on a dedicated basis. The cost element for this component, therefore, is based on foreign carriers' private line rates for dedicated

circuits. Multiple 64 Kbps circuits are derived from the high capacity channels and multiplexed into voice grade circuits based on standard U.S. operating practices. This information, along with average monthly traffic volume per circuit, is used to convert the private line rates to a charge per minute for each country. **International gateway component**: The international gateway component consists of international switching centers and associated transmission and signaling equipment. Foreign carriers do not generally offer a separate tariff rate for the international gateway component, so the study relies on information published by the ITU. The cost of this component varies with the level of digital facilities. **National extension component:** The national extension component consists of national exchanges, national transmission, and the local loop facilities used to distribute international service within a country. Foreign carriers' domestic rates and the distribution of U.S. billed service within a country are used to compute an average charge per minute for cost of this component.

15. The results shown in Table 3.6 were derived from the following calculations: Assume that each trunk associated with switching is approximately $200, a reasonable cost for switching in large numbers. If one then further assumes a usage of 100 minutes per month per use or, equivalently, a 1 percent Erlang load, a trunk can then support 100 subscribers. Thus, the capital per subscriber per month and corresponding per minute amount is as follows:

Per month per subscriber. Assume a 10-year, 8 percent rate, and we have $2.60 per trunk per month, or $0.0260 per subscriber per month.

Per minute per subscriber. On a per minute basis, this is $0.00026 per minute for switching. The general conclusion is that switching is de minimis as a cost element.

Transport costs. The transport costs are the costs for the fiber or other telecommunications facilities. They are generally distance sensitive, but with fiber being more prevalent, this distance sensitivity is no longer a significant factor. Assuming similar capital costs for transport but doubling it to be conservative, it is $0.00052 per minute as with the above argument.

Direct operations costs. These costs include the provisioning of network management, customer services, billing, provisioning, inventory management, and repair and dispatching. These costs are generally personnel driven and thus are produced at local market rates. Frequently these costs dominate the overall cost element of the system. The total cost for these elements is between $4 and $8 per month per subscriber. This is allocated across all of the subscriber's usage—local, long distance, and international. If one assumes that a typical international call represents 10 percent of the total usage, a high number, we have an average of $0.60 per subscriber per month. This is $0.006 per minute.

Overhead operations costs. Generally this represents a 40 percent to 70 percent overhead. We use 50 percent in these calculations based on the most likely costs as an overhead on the operations costs. This then is $0.003 per minute.

Sales and marketing costs. These should relate solely to local in-country operations.

16. The issue here is a quid pro quo issue of parity in providing interconnection in a market that can be commodicized. For example, if two or more LEC or LEC-like carriers enter a market, then there should be no interconnection fee, and each carrier should price its services at the price based on its costs and have no third-party intervenor establish a de facto subsidization. If, however, one carrier provides a service such as aggregation to interconnect more efficiently, then this added non pari passu facility should be compensated at an equal, comparable, and costs-based level, shared among all players. The Baumol-Willig approach can apply here if we eliminate the artifact of ensuring a profit

Applications, Architectures, and Industry Structures

to the monopolist, as Baumol has consistently done. By maximizing consumer welfare at the expense of the suppliers, that is, by creating a competitive market, one arrives at the principle of cost-based pricing.

17. See Brown and Sibley (1986, p. 39).

18. See para. 75, ID-96-261.

19. See Federal Communications Commission, FCC 96-484, Washington, D.C. 20554 In the Matter of International Settlement Rates, IB Docket No. 96-261, Adopted: December 19, 1996, para. 17.

20. Organization for Economic Co-Operation and Development, Paris, 1997, "New Technologies and Their Impact on the Accounting Rate System," p. 35.

21.

> Internet Telephony, the ability to provide voice services based on network technology, is increasingly providing a competitive threat to traditional public switched telecommunication networks. Although the use of this technology for voice is only emerging, there is considerable interest in its potential. This interest is being fuelled by the fact that time-based usage charges are not traditionally used for packet-switched networks. The Internet is providing the underlying infrastructure to begin experiments with providing international voice communications over networks based on packet-switched network technology. Although initially voice communications tended to be computer-to-computer communications, developments are now emphasizing computer-to-telephone communications. The advantage of packet-switched networks also includes, as well, the ability to handle integrated voice, data, and video services which many customers are increasingly requiring for day-to-day business. The fact that there is no international usage charge and only the price of local calls is paid is evidently providing an impetus to Internet telephony. Although arguments have been made that existing Internet capacity will not be able to handle an explosion of voice communication on these networks, it is not evident that the required capacity will not be forthcoming if the demand for services is there.
>
> The development of Internet telephony . . . threatens the viability of the existing accounting rate system. The fact that telecommunication operators, and many governments, seem to continue to support high collection charges (and accounting rates) is in fact accelerating the development of new technologies which help by-pass the existing payments system. Long-term strategy by operators, if they wish to maintain their viability, would argue for lower, more competitive prices, which would serve as well to slow down the development and diffusion of alternate calling procedures.
>
> Governments, given the increasing liberalization of data networks and in PSTN markets, will have difficulty in regulating the entry of many new services, which use packet-switched network technology, including voice communications. First, there is the problem in differentiating one type of digital message from another. Second, there is the difficulty in disrupting communications with anyone in that re-routing of traffic is a simple procedure. Third, there is the policy emphasis that many governments have placed on the diffusion of broadband infrastructures to create the information infrastructures of the future. To have an economic impact, usage prices on these infrastructures need to be low otherwise new services and on-line applications will be slow to develop. Many of these new services will gravitate to packet-switched networks because of price advantages. (OECD, pp. 39–40).

22. See McGarty (1996a, 1996b).

23. See Coll (1986). William McGowan, one of the founders of MCI, recognized this in the IEC business. He used a two-prong approach to effecting his competitive position, first through the FCC and second via the antitrust laws.

24. McGarty (1996a).

25. The first attempt to open the data monopoly of AT&T was by Bob Kahn, the father of the Internet, by obtaining a 300 bps modem from AT&T. AT&T refused to support the Advanced Research Projects Agency and Kahn and his team thus were forced to create a modem apart from AT&T. This led to the proliferation of PC modems and the introduction by Intel of a 56 Kbps dial-up modem that supplants ISDN.

26. The FCC expressly stated that the carrier was not an LEC and thus was not required to unbundle. In addition, in the FCC First Report and Order on Interconnection, August 8, 1996, it stated that a regional Bell operating company's LEC was not a subsidiary even though one of us (McGarty) argued against that based on the theory of agency.

4

Vertical Integration, Industry Structure, and Internet Telephony

William Lehr

The growth of the Internet is helping to propel industry convergence, blurring the boundaries among the telecommunications, broadcast, cable television, and computer industries. Convergence is occurring in applications and services such as multimedia applications, for example, interactive entertainment or business groupware that mix voice, video, and data; in infrastructure such as interconnection among a growing array of heterogeneous network architectures, including circuit- and packet-switched networks, asynchronous transfer mode (ATM), and frame relay; and in business models and industry structures such as the cross-industry mergers and alliances of content and infrastructure providers and across providers of different types of infrastructure facilities. Internet telephony is the application most prominently at the nexus of the convergence of the traditional public switched telephone network (PSTN) and the emerging, next-generation global information infrastructure based on Internet protocol (IP) technology.

There are several reasons for this. First, international, domestic toll, and local telephone revenues are a large source of potential revenue. According to estimates by the Organization for Economic Co-operation and Development (OECD), the public telecommunications service market produced estimated revenues of $519 billion in 1995 in OECD countries.[1] Capturing a share of this stream is a potent lure to firms in the Internet space. Second, expanding the IP protocol suite to support quality-differentiated services across multiple network domains in order to transport delay-sensitive services reliably is necessary to make the

Internet a viable platform for an integrated global information infrastructure. Third, adding telephone services to the Internet will force policymakers, service providers, and customers to rethink traditional models of basic and enhanced telecommunications services and future architectures for industry provisioning.

The Internet industry is undergoing rapid change as a consequence of telecommunications deregulation, growth in the demand for and supply of IP-based services and products, and the need and desire to provide integrated voice, video, and data services on a single network platform. Currently the public Internet runs on infrastructure that is owned by a combination of Internet service providers (ISPs) and traditional telephone companies. In the United States, there are over 4,000 ISPs, ranging in size from small mom-and-pop operations that provide basic Internet access services to large international backbone providers.[2] In the United States, there are more than thirty-two backbone ISPs at the time of this writing (Table 4.1), although most

Table 4.1
National ISPs in the United States

@home Network	Global One
ANS CO + RE Systems, Inc.	Global Village Communications
Apex Global Info Systems (AGIS)	GoodNet
Ascend Communications	IBM Global Network (Advantis)
Ashton Communications	ICon International
AT&T	LDS-iAmerica
BBN Planet	MCI
Cable & Wireless, Inc.	NETCOM
CRL	PSINet
Data Research Associates	Qwest Communications
DIGEX (Digital Express Group)	Sprint
Digital Equipment Corporation	TheOnRamp Group, Inc.
DirectNet Corporation	ThoughtPort
Fibernet	UUNET Technologies, Inc.
Genuity Inc.	VBCnet (GB) Ltd
GetNet	Verio

Source: CIX membership, listed as national network. See http://www.cix.org. As of January 1998, the Web site listed 146 members. Of those, 32 are described as having national (or international) networks.

Table 4.2
Telecommunications carriers in the United States

Carrier Type	Number in 1996
Competitive access providers (CAPs) and competitive local exchange carriers (CLECs)	109
Interexchange carriers (IXCs)	143
Local exchange carriers (LECs)	1,371
Total	1,623

Source: Table 8.17, *Statistics of Communications Common Carriers 1996/1997*, Federal Communications Commission, Washington, D.C., December 1997. These are counts for the number of carriers that pay into the telecommunications relay service fund.

Internet traffic is carried by the largest four or five among them. These ISPs rely on transport services provided by the more than 1,600 traditional facilities-based local and long-distance telephone service providers (Tables 4.2 and 4.3).

This industry structure is largely a consequence of legacy regulation and network design. Historically, telephone service providers were subject to rate regulations and line-of-business restrictions, under the presumption that they were a natural monopoly. Traditional telephone networks were optimized to support a single service: 4 KHz voice telephony. The need to support universal service in a network comprising multi-vintage, long-lived infrastructure deterred anything more than incremental service innovation. Although the quality of service and reliability of telephone service have increased while the real price of service has fallen dramatically, the basic functionality of plain old telephone service (POTS) remains largely unchanged since its introduction. The basic interface remains the dual tone multifrequency keypad (DTMF). Integrated digital services are still not widely available.

Telecommunications deregulation and the development of new wireless and local access technologies such as low-power multipoint distribution service (LDMS), digital subscriber line (DSL), wireless fixed loops, and cable modems enhance prospects for increased local telephone competition and an expansion in the range of services offered by traditional infrastructure providers or new entrants. For example, cable systems operators may add local telephone service over IP networks accessed over cable modems, while local telephone companies may

Applications, Architectures, and Industry Structures

Table 4.3
Major telecommunications carriers in the United States

Company	Carrier Type	Operating Revenues ($billion 1996)
AT&T	IXC	39.3
MCI	IXC	16.4
Worldcom (formerly LDDS)	IXC	4.5
Sprint	IXC and LEC	10.8
GTE	IXC and LEC	12.6
Ameritech	LEC	11.3
Bell Atlantic (merged with Nynex)	LEC	25.2
BellSouth	LEC	14.4
SBC (merged with PacTel)	LEC	18.0
US WEST	LEC	9.8

Source: Table 1.2, *Statistics of Communications Common Carriers 1996/1997,* Federal Communications Commission, Washington, D.C., December 1997.

add video and Internet access services over copper loops using DSL technologies. Long-distance companies and other potential entrants into local services may take advantage of the resale and network unbundling requirements of the Telecommunications Act of 1996 to lease the incumbent local telephone companies' facilities to compete in local services. With the emergence of effective local telephone competition, the path will be cleared for more complete deregulation and the elimination of the regulatory-mandated separation between local and long-distance services or between basic and enhanced services. This will enable even more innovation in services and infrastructure provisioning strategies.

The ability to offer telephone service using IP technology over a managed intranet (to facilitate offering higher-quality service and to support greater network security) or even over the public Internet opens the competitive arena to an even larger subset of potential competitors. For example, both Internet service providers (the firms that provide basic Internet access services, Web hosting, and related services) and next-generation telcos (the firms that principally provide telephone service using IP technologies or Internet infrastructure) may compete for the pool of traditional telecommunications revenue. This further

Table 4.4
Sample of significant communications company restructurings attempted and completed, 1997–1998

Event
Bell Atlantic acquires Nynex. GTE seeks to acquire Bell Atlantic.
British Telecom tries to acquire MCI; GTE bids for MCI; Worldcom finally acquires MCI.
SBC acquires PacTel. SBC seeks to merge with Ameritech.
Microsoft invests $1 billion in TCI.
AT&T seeks to merge with SBC. AT&T acquires Teleport. AT&T acquires TCI. AT&T in strategic international marketing agreement with British Telecom.
Worldcom acquires MFS and UUNET. As part of MCI merger, Worldcom spins off Internet holdings to Cable & Wireless.
Worldcom acquired CompuServe, divests retail business to AOL in return for AOL network and service contract.
TCI starts @home network.
Qwest seeks alliances with Ameritech, US WEST, and other ILECs to offer long-distance telephone services.

expands the space of potential and actual competitors in the converging markets for communications services.

This changed environment has already promoted significant restructuring in the participating industries (Table 4.4). In addition to new entrants at all levels within the value chain, there have been numerous horizontal and vertical mergers, divestitures, and restructurings.

This chapter presents an analytical framework to examine incentives of service providers at various stages in the ISP value chain to integrate vertically. The focus is on residential, dial-up subscribers to simplify the analysis.[3] This chapter addresses the following questions:

• What are the incentives of firms at various stages in the Internet value chain to integrate vertically?

• What does this imply for Internet industry structure today and in the future?

• Is the market for a commodity IP bearer service sustainable?[4]

Because the principal suppliers of facilities to the Internet are traditional local and long-distance telephone providers, the integration or disintegration of the value chain will have profound implications for how telephony services are offered in the future. Internet telephony is at the center of this evolution.

A Framework for Analyzing Internet Industry Structure

Following Coase (1937), we can investigate firm structure (the boundaries of the firm) by considering the advantages of integrating production stages within a single firm relative to the alternative of using market exchange to transfer intermediate goods. The value chain for Internet services, including Internet telephony, may be decomposed into the four elements that must be present in order to offer end-to-end services:

- Retail-level Internet access provider (IAP)[5]
- Local area transport services (LAT)
- Backbone Internet transport services (ISP)
- Wide-area transport services (WAT)

Figures 4.1 and 4.2 provide two views of how these types of firms or essential activities are organized. The retail-level IAP is the furthest downstream, providing the interface by which the end user residential consumer accesses the Internet. The typical IAP is a local or regional firm offering basic Internet access services and Web hosting services. To deliver its services, it relies on the LAT to deliver traffic from the customer's premises to the IAP's point of presence (POP) and from the IAP's POP to the backbone ISP's network.[6] The typical LAT is a local telephone company. The backbone ISP provides the IAP with connectivity and transport services to the rest of the Internet. The ISP may lease bulk transport capacity from wide-area transport (WAT) providers, typically long-distance telephone companies. These activities may be combined within a single fully integrated firm,[7] may be provided by four independent firms,[8] or may be provided by some combination of partially integrated firms. Considering all possible combinations, thirteen types of firms might exist (Figure 4.3). An industry structure would consist of some combination of these thirteen firm types.

The value chain gives rise to five potential types of market transactions between activities as follows (Tables 4.5 and 4.6):

Vertical Integration, Industry Structure, and Internet Telephony

Internet Industry Value Chain

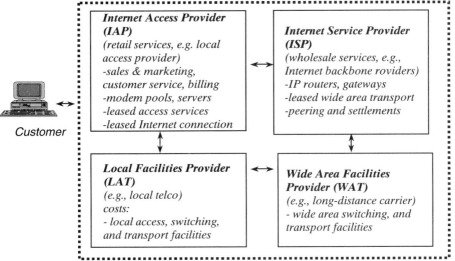

Figure 4.1
A model of Internet industry structure

- Customer to IAP
- IAP to ISP
- ISP to ISP
- IAP to LAT
- ISP to WAT

Each of these transactions involves different types of participants, yet all are related insofar as the customers are the ultimate source of revenue that can be captured by the suppliers at successive stages in the value chain.[9] While the aggregate willingness to pay or final demand of the customers sets an upper bound on the total revenues that can be transferred from customers to suppliers, the aggregate costs of suppliers set a lower bound on the amount of revenue that must be extracted in order to make the service viable. The difference between these two sets the amount of surplus that can be generated in these markets. Each of the transactions could take place in an open market

Internet Services Value Chain

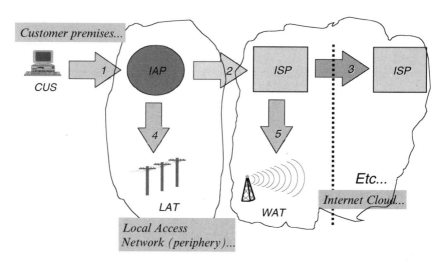

Figure 4.2
The Internet services industry

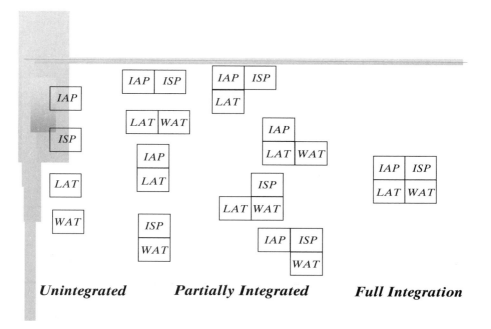

Figure 4.3
Potential firm types

Table 4.5
Internet industry structure: Market interfaces

Interface	Buyer	Seller	Market or Good Purchased	Comment
1	Customer	Internet access provider (IAP)	Internet access and Web hosting service for small businesses and residential customers. Could be transaction or monthly purchase.	Pricing interface between final demand and supplier value chain. This is the source of all revenue that flows into the network. This is a logical interface because it is possible to imagine separate contractual arrangements with each of the providers in the value chain.
2	Internet access provider (IAP)	Internet service provider (ISP)	Bilateral interconnection agreements to provide wide-area Internet transport and universal termination.	Retail-wholesale relationship, where the IAP provides all customer interface functions and the ISP provides wide-area transport and ubiquitous connectivity. Potential for vertical integration.
3	Internet service provider (ISP)	Internet service provider (ISP)	Interexchange points and bilateral interconnection agreements to provide wide-area Internet transport and universal termination.	Wholesale-wholesale relationship between peer ISPs. Potential for horizontal integration to expand scope of service.
4	Internet access provider (IAP)	Local area transport (LAT)	Regular tariffed business line service from LEC for dial-up access and leased lines to ISP POP.	Pricing interface for essential input for IAP to provide service. ISP typically leases local access facilities from regulated monopoly LEC. Potential for vertical integration.
5	Internet service provider (ISP)	Wide area transport (WAT)	Leased lines and virtual private network services purchased in wholesale toll market for WAT.	Pricing interface for essential input for ISP.

Table 4.6
Examples of Internet industry market interface transactions

Interface	Buyer Example	Seller Example	Market or Good Purchased	Comment
1	Residential consumer	TIAC, Barnet	$20 per month unlimited usage for dial-in Internet access. Implicitly, this is end-to-end service for Internet applications.	Customer purchases flat-rate local telephone service and uses 28.8 modem to access IAP over local dial-up call.
2	TIAC, Barnet	MCI	DS-1 or DS-3 interconnection.	Capacity-based pricing for interconnection; may include traffic-sensitive component. This is a hierarchical relationship.
3	MCI	UUNET	DS-1 or DS-3 interconnection.	Revenue-neutral peering relationship.
4	TIAC	Nynex	Regular tariffed business line service from LEC for dial-up access and leased lines to ISP POP.	IAP avoids paying access charges for traffic.
5	MCI, UUNET	MCI, AT&T	Leased lines and VPN services purchased in wholesale toll market for wide-area transport.	Bulk transport services purchased in competitive wholesale market for $0.01–$0.03 per minute.

between independent firms or as an internal transfer within an integrated firm.

If each of the supplier markets is competitive, then consumers will capture all of the surplus, and prices will be no higher at each interface than is required to recover costs. In the more realistic case where firms in one or more of these supplier markets possess market power, we may observe a much more complex array of strategic interactions. Firms may have incentives to exploit their control of bottleneck facilities (e.g., LAT providers) to extract additional surplus. Any sort of entry barrier (e.g., regulatory restrictions, scale economies, sunk costs, customer switching costs) can provide the basis for market power. Generically, firms prefer suppliers in other stages of the value chain to face as stiff competition because this weakens their relative bargaining position.

To understand incentives to integrate vertically in the Internet industry, one must consider the characteristics and cost structure of each of the production activities in the framework. (Tables 4.7 and 4.8 summarize these characteristics).

Internet Access Provider

The Internet access provider (IAP) is the Internet service retailer that provides dial-up access to residential consumers.[10] The IAP provides basic Internet access, e-mail, and Web hosting services that are delivered over facilities leased from the telephone company (the LAT) and from ISPs or WATs (the Internet cloud). The IAP is the downstream retailer or reseller of ISP transport services. There is a wide array of IAPs, ranging from mom-and-pop operations offering service to a small number of subscribers in a specific locale to national IAPs that offer access across the country (such as AOL and Mindspring) and are typically vertically integrated ISPs (or even facilities providers such as AT&T).

Intrinsically, the IAP has the cost structure of a retail firm, with operating expenses that include corporate overhead, sales and marketing, customer service, and telco and ISP service fees for leased transport services. The capital equipment owned by the IAP includes modem banks (to support dial-up access) and the servers (Web hosting, e-mail, file server).

Table 4.7
Internet industry structure: Participant characteristics

	Characteristics
Customer	• Residential subscriber (commercial customers much more complex because they have many more options to self-provision and contract at different stages in value chain). • Buyer of Internet access services and customer premises equipment (CPE). • Inherently local. • Very heterogeneous willingness to pay. Many subscribers. Diverse quality-of-service requirements and tolerance for congestion. • Often risk averse, so prefer flat-rate pricing. Demand is multidimensional, defined over multiple applications (Web, telephony, e-mail, etc.). • No market power. Each small relative to market. Demands are not coordinated. • Demand of individual customer is very bursty and hard to predict, but application demand in aggregate may be relatively easy to predict depending on application.
IAP	• Sell Internet access services to residential subscribers and buy network equipment, local transport services, and ISP services. • Inherently local, although may be active in multiple local markets. • Diverse size ranges from quite small to large. Large are typically vertically integrated with ISP to provide national access and possibility of improved congestion control (e.g., by segregating traffic).
ISP	• Sell Internet backbone/termination services to IAPs and buy network equipment, wide-area transport services, and backbone-termination services from other ISPs. • Inherently regional or national. May be integrated forward into IAP services. • Medium to large size ranging from regional to global backbone providers. In most cases, single interconnection between ISPs is sufficient to connect source and destination. • Offer transport and universal termination services to enable IAP to sell end-to-end access to final consumer.
LAT	• Sell local-area access, termination, and transport services to ISPs. • Inherently local. • Large regional Bell operating companies (RBOCs), currently seeking to expand into inter–local access and transportation service.
WAT	• Sell wide-area transport services to ISPs. • Inherently regional, national, or global. • Large, national IXCs; currently seeking to expand into local access service.

Table 4.8
Internet industry structure: Costs

	Costs
Customer	• Zero incremental cost for usage under current regime beyond opportunity cost of user's time. Significant adjustment costs to change interface (learn, purchase new CPE). Potential for large congestion costs in aggregate. • Largest usage-sensitive cost is opportunity cost of consumer's time (and negative impact of congestion). Fixed cost small; sunk cost may be significant (first-mover advantage).
IAP	• Retailer cost structure. Operating expenses include corporate overhead, sales and marketing, customer service, and telco and ISP service fees for transport. Capital equipment includes modem banks and servers. • Most costs variable with customer count, including capital costs that scale with modems. Modem costs vary with usage, but retail-level costs are not usage sensitive.
ISP	• Wholesaler cost structure. Operating expenses include corporate overhead, network operations (maintenance), and telco service fees for leased lines. Capital equipment includes routers, gateways, and backbone transport facilities. Network operations and maintenance. • Capital costs vary with capacity but not usage. Large share of costs is sunk or fixed. Potential for significant variable costs if usage-sensitive termination fees charged for settlements. • Gateways and shared transport (e.g., international undersea cable plant when ISP-ISP interface), which need to be recovered.
LAT	• Cost structure of RBOC. Operating expenses include corporate overhead, retail-level costs, and network operations. Capital costs include local distribution plant and switches; former dominate. • Large fixed and sunk costs. A significant share of costs is customer specific. Large-scale economies and expectation that no more than a few facilities-based carriers in any locale.
WAT	• Cost structure of IXC. Operating expenses include corporate overhead, retail-level costs, network operations, and local access charges. Capital costs include POPs, switches, and long-haul transport facilities. • Large fixed and sunk costs; however, much less capital intensive than RBOC. Large-scale economies. Retail-level costs more significant because of increased competition (includes customer churn). Inherently national.

Because entry costs to become a local IAP are low, this is the least capital intensive of the activities considered. There are only limited opportunities to realize capital scale economies (modems and servers reflect constant returns to scale). For this reason, it is not surprising that we observe significant entry and exit by IAPs.

Internet Service Provider

The Internet service provider (ISP) is the Internet service wholesaler. It offers IP connectivity to the Internet cloud for the IAP and provides backbone transport (this includes routing and basic transport). The ISP is the upstream supplier of Internet services to the IAP. Most of the ISPs are integrated forward into IAP services. These may be regional or national service providers such as UUNET.

The ISP has the cost structure of a wholesale facilities provider. Operating expenses include corporate overhead, network operations (maintenance, network planning), and telco (and perhaps other ISP) service fees for transport.[11] Capital equipment includes the Internet routers, gateways, and some backbone transport facilities.

The ISP is more capital intensive than the IAP but less so than the facilities-based providers (LAT and WAT). Setting up and operating a national IP network (even on leased WAT facilities) and managing the interconnection arrangements to IAPs and other ISPs present significant entry barriers.

Local Area Transport

Local area transport (LAT) is the local access facilities provider. It is the upstream supplier of the underlying physical infrastructure to support IAP access. For dial-up access, this is usually the telephone local exchange carrier (LEC).[12] The existing physical access infrastructure supports other types of service besides Internet access (telephone calling, cable television).

The LAT has the cost structure of a wholesale facilities provider such as an LEC. Operating expenses include corporate overhead, network operations, and retail-level costs (e.g., for telephone service). Capital costs include local distribution plant and local switching, as well as the billing and signaling network infrastructure.

The LAT is the most capital intensive activity in the value chain. Today, LAT services are provided by monopoly LECs, whose core business is providing local telephone access and calling services in a contiguous geographic area. As a consequence, the LECs remain heavily regulated with respect to interconnection policies, prices, and market participation. Regulatory policy is seeking to promote competition in local services, and if successful, deregulation. In the future, cable TV companies and wireless providers may provide competitive local access alternatives.

Wide-Area Transport

Wide-area transport (WAT) is the wide-area transport provider—the upstream supplier of the underlying physical infrastructure to support the ISP. These are typically long-distance carriers. WATs are the wide-area analogs to the LAT firms.

The WAT has the cost structure of a wholesale facilities provider such as a telephone interexchange carrier (IXC). Operating expenses include corporate overhead, network operations, and retail-level costs (e.g., for telephone service). Capital costs include long-distance switching and transport plant, as well as the billing and signaling network infrastructure.

The WAT is also quite capital intensive, but significantly less so than for a LAT. Because WAT markets are much larger geographically[13] and less capital intensive, effective competition already exists in U.S. long-distance telephone markets. Consequently, long-distance carriers are subject to significantly less regulatory oversight.

Review of the Economic Theory of Vertical Integration

Although much of the discussion will proceed as if the choice between vertical integration and market-based transactions is dichotomous, in reality, there is a continuum of organizational forms.[14] They range from arm's-length, anonymous, "take-it-or-leave-it" market transactions (as in competitive markets), to term commitments, to complex bilateral contracts, to full vertical integration (i.e., consolidated ownership). The more likely it is that the buyer and seller interact in a nonanonymous fashion, the more likely their interactions will be constrained by implicit or explicit contracts that will reflect vertical integration.[15]

There are a number of motivations for vertically integrating:[16]

• *Scale and scope economies.* Average costs are reduced through vertical integration because of the existence of fixed shared costs.[17]

• *Transaction costs.* Internal transfers may be less expensive than market-based transactions (e.g., because of metering or contracting costs).

• *Coordination and control.* There are co-specialized assets in the multiple stages that are more valuable if used together in a coordinated fashion.[18]

• *Product differentiation or price discrimination.* Downstream integration to facilitate price discrimination may be necessary for cost recovery (e.g., the market for an undifferentiated upstream IP bearer service may be unsustainable).[19]

• *Innovation and strategic positioning.* A firm may need to integrate vertically if new product and upstream (downstream) firms do not exist.[20] Or it may vertically integrate to develop complementary skills to enhance its strategic position.[21]

• *Market power.* Integration to protect or extend (leverage) market power is a common motivation that is hypothesized for vertical integration. This may also include a desire to protect quasi-rents associated with sunk investments (e.g., guarantee cost recovery of facilities investment).

The first five motivations are all efficiency enhancing (that is, cost reducing), and public policy should encourage vertical integration that can be justified on these grounds. The last motivation is likely to be opposed by public policy.[22] Historically, U.S. antitrust policy proscribed a number of vertical relationships as inherently anticompetitive. Subsequent economic theory has raised serious doubts about per se restrictions against vertical integration by identifying efficiency-enhancing motivations that are not anticompetitive and by calling into question the effectiveness of vertical integration as a strategy to extend market power. For example, if the downstream (or upstream) market is already competitive, then vertical integration to extend market power may not make sense.[23] Potential rationales for vertical integration to extend market power include the desire to avoid regulation[24] or to protect market power in a core market.[25]

In the following discussion, we examine the costs and benefits of each of the suppliers in the value chain to integrate vertically with adjacent stages.

Vertical Integration in the Internet

One may use the industry taxonomy set out already to explore opportunities to integrate vertically and horizontally. The natural question to ask is what types of firms exist today and what types of firms may exist in the future.

The industry taxonomy partitions the Internet service function into retail (IAP) and wholesale (ISP) services that use the capacity of local- (LAT) and wide-area (WAT) facilities providers. With these four types of activities, there are thirteen possible types of firms, and it is possible that multiple types will coexist simultaneously (see Figure 4.3).[26] In the future, we expect to have an even larger number of possible firm configurations. The following overall conclusions and predictions emerge from this analysis (Table 4.9):

Incentives to integrate vertically in the Internet are strong. Incentives to integrate vertically are strong at all stages within the value chain, and so we should expect to see the emergence of fully integrated facilities-based service providers.[27]

The viability of a wholesale IP bearer service market is enhanced. The availability of wholesale IP bearer services from these and other facilities-based providers will permit the continued existence of nonfacilities-based Internet service providers, implying that the industry will consist of a variety of types of firms.[28]

Downstream integration is more likely than upstream. Incentives to integrate vertically are asymmetric and are stronger for upstream firms to integrate downstream (ISP into IAP, LAT into IAP, WAT into ISP, LAT into WAT) than the reverse.

ISPs will integrate into IAP services. Stand-alone ISPs are unlikely because ISPs have a strong incentive to integrate into IAP services, and national IAPs have a strong incentive to maintain backbone facilities.

Applications, Architectures, and Industry Structures

Table 4.9
Vertical integration and industry structure

Type of Firm	Today?	Future?
IAP	Yes. Low entry costs. Small (e.g., TIAC).	Yes. Small in future. Large are national.
ISP	No. If ISP, then also IAP.	No (maybe if sufficient market of standalone IAPs; could avoid retail-level costs).
LAT	Yes. Regulation and economic entry barriers (e.g., RBOCs—Bell Atlantic).	No. Incentives to integrate forward.
WAT	Yes. Regulation and low entry costs because of active reseller market (e.g., AT&T).	No. Incentives to integrate forward.
IAP-ISP	Yes (e.g., UUNET, AOL).	Yes. Taking advantage of wholesale bearer service market.
LAT-WAT	No (exceptions GTE, International).	Yes, because of Telco Act and technology.
IAP LAT	No. Regulation.	Yes.
ISP WAT	No. If ISP, then also IAP.	Yes. If WAT, then why not ISP?
ISP LAT-WAT	No.	No. If ISP, then why not IAP also?
IAP LAT-WAT	No.	No. If WAT and IAP, then why not ISP also?
IAP-ISP WAT	Yes (e.g., MCI).	Yes.
IAP-ISP LAT	No.	Yes.
IAP-ISP LAT-WAT	No (but GTE, international yes).	Yes.

Facilities-based providers will integrate into Internet services. Stand-alone facilities-based providers (LAT, WAT) are unlikely because they have the incentive to offer Internet services to complement existing offerings (e.g., telephone service) and to respond to competition from resellers (Internet telephony offered by nonfacilities-based providers in competition with traditional PSTN offerings).

These conclusions are based on an assessment of key underlying trends and rely on several important assumptions:

One-stop shopping. Consumers will demand and service providers will seek to offer one-stop shopping services that bundle multiple communication services into a single bill. One-stop shopping services will appeal especially to risk-averse (reputation-sensitive) and convenience-minded (less cost-sensitive) consumers who will value the simplicity of consolidating multiple electronic bills. This will provide a strong market demand driver for vertical integration.

Scale and scope economies. There are significant retail-level scale and scope economies that encourage suppliers to offer one-stop shopping services. This is the cost-side driver for vertical integration. In addition, there are scale and scope economies associated with expanding nationally or even internationally, which will also encourage vertical integration.

Open interface standards. The Internet is distinguished in part by its reliance on and promotion of open interface standards that allow heterogeneous network environments to be flexibly interconnected. This means that it is not essential to be vertically integrated to provide service, especially with respect to the network-related cost economies. Without such standards, vertical integration would be even more important, and the viability of nonfacilities-based providers or partial facilities-based providers would be suspect. The prevalence of such standards increases the relative importance of non-network cost economies (retail-level costs, overhead costs).

Procompetitive regulatory policy. Public policy would like to promote competition at all stages in the value chain. To the extent that such policies are successful, they will promote the coexistence of both vertically integrated and nonintegrated types of firms. The viability of these programs is most suspect with respect to the promotion of competition for local access facilities.[29] If competition is not successful here, then it is likely that local access will continue to be regulated as a bottleneck facility, with the potential for continued restrictions on access pricing, interconnection policies, and participation in adjacent markets. If facilities-based local access competition is not sustainable, then regulatory policy will be required to sustain nonfully integrated firms (e.g., equal access, common carriage). However, I have assumed that local competition will be viable.

Availability of bandwidth. The viability of an active reseller market for non-integrated carriers presumes the existence of a competitive wholesale market for facilities-based transport. This presumes that there will be excess capacity.[30] For WAT services, this already exists and will continue to exist because of the relatively low entry costs and excess capacity in wide area transport.[31] For LAT services, access pricing is regulated and will continue to be regulated until there is effective competition. Because of the costs of installing local outside plant, when competition comes, there is likely to be excess capacity.

The following sections provide the reasoning behind each of these five conclusions and predictions.

Incentives to Integrate Vertically in the Internet Are Strong

There are strong incentives to integrate vertically (and horizontally) for each of the participants in the service provider value chain. Consideration of each of the motivations indicates that there are efficiency incentives to integrate vertically.

Scale and Scope Economies

Scale and scope economies exist whenever there are large fixed or shared costs. Fixed costs do not vary with the volume of traffic actually handled (or number of customers served). Therefore, increasing the volume of traffic (or expanding the subscriber base) will decrease average total costs (scale economies). Shared costs are those that cannot be uniquely assigned to a single product or customer. Therefore, expanding the number of customers served or products offered can result in reduced average total costs (scope economies). For all of the participants in the value chain, there are significant fixed and shared costs, giving rise to scale and scope economies that will encourage vertical integration. This can be best understood by reviewing the cost characteristics of each of the major cost categories.

Network Capital and Operations Costs

• There are significant increasing returns to scale associated with capacity expansion costs. Because of the costs of installing outside plant, it is typical to install excess capacity to provide room for future growth.

• Because of the need to size the network to accommodate peak demand and because peak network demands are not perfectly correlated across domains, there is generically excess capacity in the network (although local bottlenecks may exist at different places and times in the Internet).

• Network operations expenses (planning, maintenance, management) are driven more by the network capacity than by the actual traffic handled. Also, network operations expenses may reflect increasing returns to scale (it does not cost twice as much to manage a network twice the size).[32]

• Off-peak traffic shares peak capacity, so the assignment of costs is somewhat arbitrary and depends on classification of peak.

• End-to-end services share backbone capacity, especially in the Internet, where route may vary with each packet.

• Large shared and fixed costs mean there are large-scale and scope economies. These are likely to be largest for LAT providers because these are more capital intensive than WAT. Similarly, network-related scale and scope economies are likely to be larger for ISPs than for IAPs.

• There are likely to be some scale and scope economies from integrating local and long-distance access network facilities. For example, these may come because some of the facilities used to support WAT services will be shared by local services (e.g., tandem switches, signaling networks, intermachine trunks).

Retail-Level Costs

• Advertising costs show significant scale economies, and brand advertising yields scope economies. Brand advertising of a specific firm's name is likely to be especially important when reputation effects are important, as they may well be until consumers are more experienced and knowledgeable about Internet service options.

• Customer service costs yield moderate scale economies because of the need to be sized for peak usage.

• Bad debt yields moderate scale economies (because of diversification).

• Product innovation and management costs are fixed.

• Sales costs (customer acquisition costs), including original contact and setting up or modifying the customer account, include a number of nonrecurring charges that do not vary with the number of services sold to the customer. This is the retail cost side of providing one-stop shopping. These costs become more important as competition heats up and customer churn increases (reducing the amount of time over which nonrecurring customer costs can be recovered).

• Billing costs include a significant nontraffic-sensitive component that does not vary when the customer is sold multiple services.

• It is unclear whether there are significant scale and scope economies.

• Retail-level scale and scope economies are perhaps not as large as network-level scale and scope economies in absolute terms, but they are likely to become more important strategically as nonfacilities-based providers become more important and as network-related costs become a smaller share of total costs.[33]

Corporate Overhead

• Corporate-overhead-associated general support services and head-quarters operations are largely fixed and shared across multiple services.

• These will provide scale and scope economies from vertical integration.

Closely related is the demand-side driver of network externalities (it is more valuable to be connected to a larger network). In the absence of market power considerations, networks would choose to interconnect to expand the value of their networks.[34] The Internet promotes ubiquitous interconnection, which means that smaller networks can share in the benefits of universal termination supported by larger networks.[35] Because these interconnection policies and settlements arrangements are in flux, smaller networks may be at a disadvantage to larger networks that may seek to exploit the advantages that network externalities yield to larger incumbents.

Therefore, an analysis of the cost structure indicates that there are significant scale and scope economies that can be exploited through vertical integration.

Transaction Costs

One of the justifications for not employing usage-sensitive pricing in the Internet today is the costs of metering traffic. This includes both creating the appropriate infrastructure (modifying existing routers and servers) and the administrative overhead to meter traffic.

Coordination and Control

The LAN and WAT facilities may be regarded as co-specialized assets in the sense that demand forecasting and management, capacity planning, and network management may be easier for end-to-end services if the underlying facilities are controlled end to end.

The importance of this motivation for integrated ownership of facilities is less important today than it was before the development of equal access capabilities in the telephone network and the development of open interface standards. The reliance of the Internet on open interface standards makes this rationale for integrating network facilities end to end less important than it was before divestiture of the Bell system.

An important driver for end-to-end integration, however, may be associated with the need to provide integrated quality-of-service (QOS) differentiated services. This may provide a powerful incentive for an IAP to integrate into ISP services in order to ensure reliability and customer security, and to support QOS guarantees for Internet services. An IAP that does not have end-to-end control over Internet services may be constrained in the sorts of services it can offer. This motivation for integration is logically separable from the motivation to integrate facilities end to end or for an Internet service provider to own its own facilities.

Product Differentiation or Price Discrimination

The need to recover the sunk and fixed costs of constructing network facilities will provide a powerful inducement for facilities-based providers to integrate forward to permit product differentiation and price discrimination to offer value-added services.

Because there is likely to be excess capacity and because short-run incremental costs are significantly less than long-run average costs (which include fixed and shared costs), it will be difficult for facilities-based providers to avoid aggressive "Bertrand-like" price competition. (This argument is explained at greater length in Srinagesh and Gong, 1996.)

In order to price-discriminate, facilities-based providers will have a strong incentive to offer bundled services (one-stop shopping and services that bundle transport with value-added features such as enhanced billing and new features). Creative bundling will facilitate a wider range of targeted discount programs that can be used to target customer groups more narrowly. Moreover, one-stop shopping bundles offer opportunities to offer forward discounts (rebates to customers who stay with you or volume discounts over multiple services) that reduce customers' incentives to switch to a competing carrier.

While this will provide an extremely powerful motivation for facilities-based providers to integrate downstream into services, it will not preclude the existence of nonfacilities-based service providers.

Innovation and Strategic Positioning
In technologically advanced markets, the need to integrate vertically to fill a new opportunity (no current supplier upstream, no distribution channel downstream) is often an important motivation. Similarly, vertical integration may be needed to develop complementary skills.

It seems less likely to be important for integration of local- and wide-area facilities providers, because these services already exist and the skills associated with each are not substantially different. However, this may provide a motivation for IAP-ISP integration or for facilities integration into IAP or ISP services. In both cases, integration may result in an expansion of firm-specific skills. Moreover, IAP-ISP integration may be required to offer quality-differentiated services.

Market Power
Vertical integration is often pursued or considered as a strategy to protect, exploit, or extend market power. Because this is harmful to

competition, antitrust policy scrutinizes the effects of vertical mergers for their effect on competition. Although this is an important motivation, discussion of its impact is beyond the scope of this chapter.

The Viability of a Wholesale IP Bearer Service Market Is Enhanced

The existence of nonfacilities-based providers requires a wholesale market for an IP bearer service. I am assuming that there will be an IP bearer service as suggested in the open data network (ODN) model described in the National Research Council (1994) report, *Realizing the Information Future*. According to this model, multiple technologies will be able to support an enhanced version of IP services flexibly and interoperably across a wide array of applications at higher protocol levels.

Facilities-based providers will have a powerful incentive to integrate forward into product services in order to differentiate their products and price discriminate (Srinagesh and Gong, 1996). Kavassalis, Lee, and Bailey (1997) argue that such differentiation will be possible even at the facilities level because of differences in the ability of applications to support the full spectrum of applications. They argue that the bearer service market will not be a commodity market and hence will support multiple types of organizational structures. The analysis presented here complements their work and reaches a substantially similar conclusion.

Moreover, even if Kavassalis, Lee, and Bailey (1997) are incorrect in arguing that bearer services will be differentiated, it is likely that a wholesale bearer service market will exist. Such a market already exists in long-distance telephone services. The following factors will contribute to the existence of such a market:

Excess capacity. There are fundamental cost and demand drivers that will result in excess capacity. This will include capacity that was installed for future growth (e.g., dark fiber) as well as capacity on different vintage networks.[36] Moreover, competition will imply churn and excess capacity inventory to accommodate uncertainty in market shares.

Free-rider problem of disciplining competition. Unless facilities provisioning is a natural monopoly, there will be multiple facilities providers from which potential nonfacilities-based resellers can lease capacity. Even if

Applications, Architectures, and Industry Structures

reseller competition harms facilities-based providers as a whole, it will be difficult for them to collude on an anticompetitive strategy to resist competition. (It will always be privately profitable to defect from the high "bearer service" price strategy to capture reseller business at the margin.)[37]

Open interface standards and architecture of the Internet. Because IP can run on many technologies and can be used flexibly to interconnect heterogeneous networks, it will be relatively easy for competing facilities based on competing transport technologies (e.g., ethernet, frame-relay, ATM) to support competing versions of an IP bearer service.

It is likely that bearer services will be available under a variety of terms and conditions. These will range from relatively short-term contracts (approaching spot markets for WAT) to longer-term capacity commitment contracts. These latter sorts of contracts may approach full vertical integration as the reseller assumes a greater proportion of the capital risks and residual control rights associated with the underlying capacity.

Downstream Integration Is More Likely Than Upstream

The incentives to integrate vertically are strongest for the facilities-based providers. Moreover, the economic barriers to entry are greater for upstream integration.[38] Therefore, it is more likely that upstream firms will integrate downstream (ISP into IAP, LAT into IAP, WAT into ISP, and LAT into WAT) rather than the reverse.

ISPs Will Integrate into IAP Services

National IAPs are likely to have important advantages in a number of markets, and it seems unlikely that a national ISP would not seek to exploit this opportunity by offering retail-level services. Therefore, it is expected that most ISPs will also offer IAP services. A stand-alone ISP seems unlikely in the future because it would compete as a wholesaler and would be at a disadvantage relative to a facilities-based reseller.

There will continue to be a competitive fringe of stand-alone IAPs because entry costs are quite low as long as there is a viable resale market for IP bearer services offered by IAP-ISP facilities and nonfacilities-based carriers. These IAPs will be pure resellers (reselling bulk services purchased from other IAP-ISPs) or facilities-based resellers that lease the capacity from LATs. These service providers will continue to survive because of their strategic advantage in providing retail-level services to niche customer groups, but they are not expected to earn excess profits. Examples of niche opportunities are vanity credit cards and mom-and-pop operations. A potentially rich source of such firms are firms that have local access capacity installed for another reason that can be expanded to support IAP at a low incremental cost. This may include shared tenant services networks in apartment buildings or malls that could be extended to offer IAP services to the surrounding community or even, perhaps, private intranets.

Facilities-Based Providers Will Integrate into Internet Services

Local telecoms infrastructure entry into Internet access provisions or long-distance network operators' entry into Internet service provisions would involve a relatively small incremental cost, especially because these providers are already providing retail-level services to consumers. Adding Internet-level services would provide them another opportunity to offer one-stop shopping and to respond to competition from Internet telephony. In the near term, entry by an LAT into IAP may be limited by regulatory considerations.[39]

LAT entry into WAT faces significantly lower economic entry barriers than does the reverse because LAT entry is more capital intensive.

Implications for Internet Telephony

The analysis predicts the emergence of an industry structure in which vertically integrated, facilities-based carriers compete with nonfacilities-based value-added resellers. This is a model that is similar to the type of industry structure that exists already in the long-distance telephone industry in the United States. In the case of long-distance telephone services, the increased competition has led to significant price reductions.

Internet telephony intensifies this competition, and its impact is already apparent in international and toll telephone services where IP-based carriers are offering lower-priced per minute calling plans.[40] IP carriers that do not pay inter–local accepts transport area access charges or international settlements fees or otherwise contribute to subsidizing universal service have a cost advantage that allows them to arbitrage existing telephone pricing. This highlights discrepancies in the current regulatory regime, increasing pressure to eliminate implicit subsidies and move pricing more in line with economic costs. Moreover, Internet telephony is helping to drive out other noncost-based pricing discrepancies such as overly distance-sensitive pricing. Internet telephony reinforces the trend toward flat per minute "postalized" rate plans.[41]

Competition also propels innovation. Although we have seen some innovation in telephone services, this has occurred within the narrow confines of enhanced telephony services. In an Internet world, we should see an explosion of service innovation options and even more aggressive competition. The principal upshot of this change should be that telephony will become just one of many applications running on the Internet, generating revenues to recover the fixed costs of the shared infrastructure. In this world, the range of services and types of value-added resellers that may participate will be both larger and more diverse than in the long-distance telephone industry today.

Notes

This chapter builds on earlier work with Dave Clark prepared on behalf of the Massachusetts Institute of Technology's Internet Telephony Consortium (MIT ITC) that was presented my paper, "Vertical Integration and Internet Industry Structure: An Application of the Pricing Taxonomy," presented at the ITC meeting in Cambridge, Massachusetts, November 1997, and "Vertical Integration in the Internet," paper presented at EURO CPR'98 Conference, Venice, March 1998.

1. See *Communications Outlook 1997* (Paris: OECD, 1997), p. 33.

2. See "Internet Service Providers Directory," *Boardwatch* (1997). In spite of consistent predictions of industry consolidation, the number and size of ISPs continues to expand.

3. Large, commercial customers are more complex because they are more heterogeneous and because they face a larger array of outside options. Examining the behavior of large, commercial customers requires considering their needs for intranet services and their

Vertical Integration, Industry Structure, and Internet Telephony

decisions to self-provision, which mean that one must examine interactions between equipment vendors and service providers. Because all of the challenges and opportunities present in residential (or small business) Internet service markets are present in commercial markets as well, focusing on the former provides a good starting point.

4. This refers to the model for an IP bearer service market outlined in Clark (1995) and the National Research Council (1996) report.

5. The notations IAP and ISP used here are new; they were developed within the context of the work of the Internet and Telecoms Convergence Consortium. Typically, in the trade press, all of the service providers that offer Internet access services are referred to as Internet service providers (ISPs). I introduce the IAP/ISP distinction to separate the provision of local access services (at the periphery of the Internet) from Internet backbone services (within the Internet cloud). In many cases, the same firm provides both types of services.

6. In the United States, in most cases, the end user customer pays for a flat-rate local access telephone line that provides connectivity between the customer's premises and the IAP's POP. The IAP purchases regular business lines from the local telephone company (the LAT) to complete the call from the telco switch to the IAP's POP. The IAP leases a private line from the local telco to connect from the IAP's POP to the backbone ISP's POP.

7. For example, in many countries, the PTT provides both long-distance and local telephone services and Internet access.

8. For example, in the United States, there are local IAPs that rely on local telephone carriers to deliver traffic to their POP and from their POP to the ISP that provides them with Internet backbone services. The ISP may lease its transport facilities from interexchange carriers.

9. We ignore the possibility of separate contracting arrangements between the end user and other stages in the value chain (e.g., separate service contracting for IAP and ISP services) on the grounds that such relationships seem unlikely for residential consumers. Large, commercial customers are more likely to consider this a viable option because they consider private networks and the use of the PSTN as substitutes. The largest corporations are likely to have complex pricing agreements with players at all levels in the value chain.

10. We will focus on the model of providing service to residential consumers to ease the discussion. Service to commercial customers is inherently more complex and heterogeneous because they have a larger array of needs and a wider selection of outside options for meeting those needs.

11. Typically backbone providers peer with other backbone providers using "bill and keep," wherein each agrees to terminate each other's traffic at no cost. Larger ISPs may decline to peer with lower-level regional ISPs and require them to pay capacity or usage-sensitive transport fees.

12. Although in the future it may include other types of local access providers such as community TV providers (cable) using cable modems, or wireless providers (e.g., PCS, mobile cellular, spread spectrum).

Applications, Architectures, and Industry Structures

13. That is, local access markets are very local. A local access plant that does not pass a home does not offer a viable substitute, whereas in long-distance services, switches in San Francisco and San Jose can offer competing long-distance services.

14. There is an extensive economics literature on vertical integration, including the following: Grossman and Hart (1986), Krattenmaker and Salop (1986), Perry (1989), Katz (1989), Riordan and Salop (1995), and Williamson (1987).

15. An expectation of repeated future interactions can give rise to implicit contracts.

16. Horizontal integration increases market share. The principal motivations for horizontal integration are to scale and scope economies and extend or protect market power (monopoly—over buyers; monopsony—over suppliers).

17. This may include reductions in the costs of managing risk (i.e., insurance) as when an upstream supplier sells into diverse downstream markets subject to uncorrelated demand shocks. This reduces diversifiable risk in the form of demand uncertainty (analogous to investing in a market portfolio rather than a single stock).

18. Co-specialized assets are assets that are more valuable when used together in a coordinated way. The classic example is a coal mine and the rail facilities that serve that coal mine. Independent ownership of these assets can result in excessive bargaining costs as each player tries to "hold up" the other.

19. Srinagesh and Gong (1996) argue that a competitive market for an undifferentiated bearer service may be unsustainable because of the existence of substantial sunk costs, the likelihood of excess capacity, and aggressive "Bertrand-like" price competition that would prohibit cost recovery. According to Srinagesh and Gong, to resolve this dilemma upstream, suppliers of bearer services will need to integrate forward to differentiate themselves, or they will use long-term contracts to shift the risk of cost recovery toward downstream customers. Kavassalis, Lee, and Bailey (1997) disagree with this assessment, arguing that the bearer service market need not be a commodity because service providers will be able to differentiate their bearer services successfully.

20. For example, an Internet telephony software company may have to integrate backward to produce board-level product if no supplier can be found to provide it. Or on upstream supplier may need to integrate forward to develop new distribution channels for new products.

21. A firm may vertically integrate to acquire additional skills and expertise, especially in technologically complex environments.

22. Public review of mergers by the U.S. Department of Justice focus on the likely effect of the merger on competition. For horizontal mergers, the focus is on postmerger market concentration. The analysis of vertical mergers is inherently more complex.

23. If the target market is already competitive, then prices should not exceed economic costs. Moreover, the firm with market power should be able to extract its monopoly rents without forward (backward) integration by pricing its goods at monopoly levels. Vertical integration to establish market power over a previously competitive market is often difficult unless it is possible for the entering firm to force the exit of competitors and erect entry barriers that will prevent reentry.

24. For example, an upstream provider of a bottleneck facility (e.g., local access services in telephone) may seek to integrate downstream to avoid price regulations intended to constrain monopoly power over the bottleneck facility.

25. For example, if the upstream supplier has substantial sunk investments in sunk capacity, it may seek to integrate forward to deter competition that could destroy the quasi-rents associated with this sunk capacity.

26. For example, today we have stand-alone IAPs (e.g., TIAC), IAPs that are vertically integrated with ISPs but do not own wide-area transport facilities (e.g., UUNET), and IAPs that are vertically integrated with facilities-based ISPs (e.g., MCI).

27. That is, IAP-ISP-LAT-WAT firms.

28. That is, IAP and IAP-ISP firms that do not own facilities but act as either pure or facilities-based resellers of underlying transport services.

29. That is, are local access facilities a natural monopoly?

30. The existence of excess capacity to support a facilities resale market does not preclude congestion problems. I am presuming that usage pricing or admission control procedures will be adopted to address congestion problems such as wasteful use of the Internet. What is necessary is that at any point in time there will be a carrier willing to lease local or long-distance transport services to retail-only resellers.

31. In the near term, this is not true for international service along certain routes; however, international capacity should be expanded rapidly.

32. It is likely that the returns to scale for network management first decrease significantly. That is, very small networks are easy to manage, but quickly become more difficult as they grow larger. An extreme example, is that a firm has no problem with a single computer but a big problem with a network of two computers. Then returns to scale increase over some range, and then eventually decrease again (it is possible for a network to be too large).

33. Technological advances have been reducing network costs in absolute terms and have facilitated the development of more scalable and modular technologies that reduce the effects of increasing returns to scale.

34. A large network may choose to deny interconnection or offer interconnection at higher prices or of inferior quality to a smaller network in order to lessen the competitive threat posed by the smaller network. Because of the importance of network externalities, manipulation of interconnection policies to exploit, protect, or enhance the market power of a dominant incumbent will remain an important concern for procompetitive regulatory authorities.

35. Currently, large backbone carriers exchange traffic using bill-and-keep arrangements. These presume that the costs of termination are minimal or that traffic is balanced. This raises the interesting question of who should be allowed to peer with whom, which is ultimately a question of what smaller networks should pay for universal termination services. Currently, a number of large backbone carriers refuse to peer with smaller networks and charge those networks capacity and usage-sensitive interconnection fees for transport services.

36. If customers switch to cable modems, the copper plant in the ground will become available for other uses.

37. Facilities-based providers could deter reseller competition by colluding to set the wholesale price for bearer services too high. Such a strategy would violate antitrust law. And although it may be collectively profitable, it would be privately rational for an individual facilities provider to defect and offer wholesale bearer services to resellers.

38. In order of increasing entry barriers, the markets may be ordered by IAP, ISP, WAT, and LAT. Facilities-based entry is more capital intensive, and LAT entry is the most capital intensive. Moreover, the LAT market is relatively small for the capital investment, so is most likely to exhibit natural monopoly characteristics.

39. Were the RBOCs suddenly to become the dominant Internet access providers, squeezing out existing IAPs, regulatory authorities may be moved to impose additional regulatory restraints. Similarly, cable TV providers may be reticent to provide telephone service competition (if Internet telephony takes off) for fear of becoming subject to telephone regulation (e.g., subject to equal access provisions, required to contribute to universal service).

40. For example, in February 1998, Qwest starting offering long-distance calling at $0.075 per minute in contrast to prices available from AT&T and other long-distance companies of around $0.10 per minute. Qwest could price lower in part because it is not required to pay interLATA access charges. See *TelecomAM*, February 11, 1998.

41. Postalized rates have been around for quite some time in telephone services. The current trend for applying these pricing plans to basic residential long-distance services was started by telephone resellers and emerged before the advent of Internet telephony.

5

Local-Loop Technology and Internet Structure

David D. Clark

Although the shape of the future of the impact of the Internet on the deployment of technology for advanced residential Internet network access is certainly not clear, certain considerations provide a basis for conjecture. The high cost of new wireline facilities, the emerging ability to provide higher-quality Internet service over the existing wireline facilities of the incumbent local exchange carrier (LEC) and cable providers, the rapidly changing nature of the Internet and its service requirements, and the open nature of the Internet's interfaces tend to inhibit vertical integration of the Internet and the higher-level services provided over it.

One possible outcome, considering these factors, is a future in which there is only a limited degree of competition in the provision of residential Internet service. It would be a future in which the degree of actual consumer choice changes rapidly due to the changing nature of the Internet and the investment decisions of the facilities operators. Research and innovation in alternative modes of residential Internet access might improve the future options for competition.

The industry structure surrounding the local loop, as the network infrastructure and equipment for local telecommunications network are commonly referred to, is changing quickly. The continuing process of deregulation combines with the advent of new service offerings such as the Internet to provide a powerful push for evolution. In attempting to examine this market, the factors that are easier to assess are those that surround the more mature telephone and television services. Attention is naturally directed there because of the level of current and past investment and the size and influence of the industry players.

Nonetheless, it is important to look at the possible shape of the industry that might emerge around new services, particularly the Internet, as they relate to the deployment of advanced local-loop facilities. While such a look must be speculative, it can provide a common framework for discussion, and perhaps a common understanding of the range of options within which the future will evolve. It is possible that within a decade, society will be as concerned with the industry structure behind the Internet—the nature of competition, the range of consumer choice, the rate and level of investment in support of innovation—as we are today with the telecommunications industry.

It is difficult to predict the future course of the Internet. It is a creature of the computer industry, and it evolves rapidly, as do all other parts of that industry. It evolves in response to the emergence of new computer-based services, with the services and the Internet driving each other. The rapid rate of innovation interacts with the need for new investment to sustain the advances, and this interaction creates a future that is difficult to predict.[1] But there are specific factors that seem to constrain the future, especially when looking at the local loop.

The key issues facing the potential provider of advanced access to the residence are as follows. To install a new generation of access technology that reaches the residence and small business is expensive. This level of investment is not likely to happen many times in a given location in any technology cycle, especially for wireline services that imply a large up-front investment. The business case justifying any such investment will be built on three major service offerings: telephony, television, and Internet. The first two are relatively well understood, but the rapid evolution of the Internet makes it harder to predict the nature of the higher-level services to be delivered there.

Nevertheless, predicting future Internet-based services is critical, because these determine the importance and utility of advanced access facilities. One must ask whether in the life of any current or new access facility, the Internet will evolve to deliver new services such as television and telephone service, or just continue to provide the "traditional" Web and e-mail. There is thus a tension between the apparent drive for the Internet to evolve and the difficulty of justifying the necessary investment.

This chapter focuses on possible shapes of the industry surrounding the local loop, which provides network access to the residence and small business, looking at the Internet as a shaping factor. The intention is to provide a framework for debate and identify certain constraints on the future, while acknowledging the speculative nature of this sort of discussion.

Baseline: The "Old" Structure

To provide a baseline for discussion, Figure 5.1 presents a simplified and abstracted illustration of the past, showing the three major communication services that reached the home and the technologies that carried them. Telephone was carried over copper pairs, radio over metropolitan broadcast, and television over broadcast or coaxial cable.

There are two important points about this structure. First, there is a direct linkage between the delivery technology and the service, for example, the provider that installed and operated copper pairs knew that the service being provided was telephone. This clarity in defining the line of business allowed the provider to design the system to optimize the known service and made it somewhat straightforward to construct a business plan for investment in infrastructure. Second, and related, the service and the technology were provided by the same

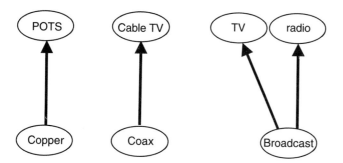

Figure 5.1
Past industry structure of residential access

Applications, Architectures, and Industry Structures

company. The facilities provider and the service provider were vertically integrated.

The Emerging Structure

Divestiture, and the resulting recognition that it was potentially benefi-cial to be in multiple lines of business, caused the simple picture to evolve toward a more complex structure. Figure 5.2 represents a view of what we might expect in the near future; the solid lines represent what is available today and dotted lines represent reasonable possibilities in the not-too-distant future. The services represented are the same with the addition of the Internet. Two new wireless delivery technology modes have been added: satellite and cellular (in contrast to single-tower metropolitan broadcast).

There are several points about this picture. The first is that the strong vertical pairing of Figure 5.1 is replaced by a matrix structure. Many services are coming over several delivery technologies. Second, the Internet is in an interesting intermediate position. It is delivered over lots of technologies, and lots of services are (or can be) delivered over it.

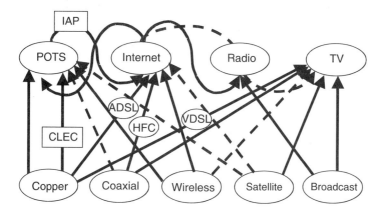

Figure 5.2
Emerging industry structure of residential access

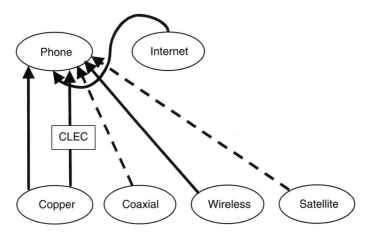

Figure 5.3
Alternatives for access to telephone service

The Telephone Industry as an Example

Figure 5.3 extracts from Figure 5.2 the subset of links that relate to telephone service. The way the copper pair is being used has expanded, in that (at least in the United States) unbundling has been mandated as a way to increase competition. But telephone service is also available using cellular communication, is now becoming available from satellite, has been provided in certain areas over coaxial cable, and is emerging as a service over the Internet. Although some of these modes are not yet technically mature (such as certain forms of Internet-based telephony)[2] and some like telephone over cable are being pushed by only some of the potential providers (for reasons that may have to do with economics and regulation as much as technology), this picture illustrates the complexity of the situation that the consumer, the industrial players, and the regulator must address.

The regulatory situation is certainly more complex than in the past because it is much less clear what (if anything) is to be regulated. In the old structure, the vertically integrated industries were easy to identify. But in this picture, should one look at diversity in facilities, higher-level services, or some other criteria to assess the potential need for regulation? From the perspective of the consumer, the concerns are quality and choice in the high-level services—telephone, television, and so on. The consumer is not directly concerned with the range of technology choices—how many fibers, coaxid lines, and copper pairs reach the house. This suggests that regulators should look at the higher-level services to determine if consumer needs are being met by the competitive marketplace. However, the regulatory history, at least in the United States, applies a different regime to different providers based on the facilities they own. When a cable company and a telephone company propose to offer Internet service, they are subjected to different constraints because they are covered by different parts of the law.[3]

The Unique Nature of the Internet

In Figure 5.2, the Internet occupies a unique position. It can be provided over almost the full range of current and emerging local access technologies, and it can provide (or will be able to do so in the future) all of the enumerated services. It thus has the potential to be a universal means of facilitating the delivery of high-level services to the consumer. Figure 5.4 extracts from Figure 5.2 the relationships relevant to the Internet.

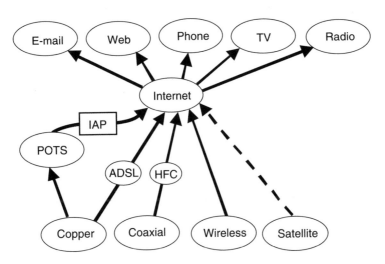

Figure 5.4
Potential industry structure surrounding the Internet

This way of looking at the Internet is not new. A report from the Computer Science and Telecommunications Board (1994) illustrated the Internet as an hourglass, providing a single common means (by way of its standardized interfaces) to make a wide variety of technologies available to a wide variety of services. Tennenhouse, Lampson, Gillett, and Klein (1996) proposed the concept of a virtual infrastructure, where a range of technologies supports a range of services via a single intermediate layer that they refer to as the brokerage. As Figure 5.4 makes clear, this role as a cross-connect between technology and service is a significant one for the Internet in the context of the local loop.

Services over the Internet

Looking first at the upper half of Figure 5.4, how will higher-level services over the Internet evolve, and what will be the implications? More specifically, what will inhibit or enhance the introduction and offering of each sort of service over the Internet? Second, are there forces that would favor or inhibit the integration of the higher-level service with the provision of the basic Internet service itself?

This second question of who provides the higher-level services and applications over the Internet is critical in predicting the future of the Internet and the industries that drive and shape it. The services that are illustrated in Figure 5.2 do not include the "old" services that we traditionally associate with the Internet—e-mail, the World Wide Web, file transfer, and so on. For completeness, some of these are added to Figure 5.4. To an experienced user of the Internet, these services are what the Internet is "for" today. I did not include them in Figure 5.2 because they are not services that are today provided by a "service provider." They do not represent services that somebody sells and consumers purchase. They come into existence through the combined efforts of all the producers and consumers of content and information exchange. People may make money by selling a particular file, but no service provider makes money by selling the file transfer service.

The new services I illustrate have more direct analogs in the preexisting world of consumer communication—telephone, radio and music delivery, and television. The cable television industry, if not the broadcast industry, sells access to television as a subscription service, which it presents as a bundle with options, all of which it packages and selects for marketing.

An important speculation about the Internet is whether this more integrated model will emerge for some higher-level Internet services, in which these services are bundled with the lower-level delivery service for the Internet itself. Past experience would suggest that the answer is no. As noted, current high-level services are not sold by Internet service providers as bundled products. Computer-to-computer Internet telephony is emerging as a collection of stand-alone software packages and network-based products being sold by independent third parties, not as a service being provided by Internet service providers (or anyone else). Other high-level services that are now evolving seem to have a similar structure.[4]

Internet Radio and Music

Internet radio, which is emerging as a significant offering on the Internet, provides a chance to observe the development of an industry in its early stages. There are content packagers, such as Broadcast.com,[5] that are assembling a large amount of material and provisioning their own wide-area infrastructure to deliver it better. At the same time, individual performers, radio stations, and other "small" sources of audio material are making their content available in piecemeal fashion. Whether the large or the small providers of audio content succeed in the market, the Internet service providers do not seem to be a significant provider of any of this service. Their only role is to upgrade the Internet to carry this sort of content better and perhaps thus justify a higher fee for their Internet service.

Internet Television

This application of the Internet does not exist at the time of this writing, but it is informative to speculate on the different forms it might take. A simple option is that television over the Internet works exactly the same way television does today. Very high bandwidth access links are installed, and fifty to one hundred or more channels are broadcast over these links. An alternative model might be that the consumer subscribes to a number of sources of content, and these are downloaded in advance on to a local disk at the site of the consumer, where they can be watched at will. Some sorts of content, like the full-time news and weather channels, which provide highly repetitive material, might achieve a tremendous reduction in required bandwidth to deliver their material by downloading the various pieces just once in the background, and then letting the viewer watch them later. This model of video distribution would contribute to much greater diversity of programming, because channels with only limited content (insufficient to fill a cable slot full time) could still develop a market.

This model of Internet television cannot instantly come into existence because it requires simultaneous evolution of the local loop, the consumer equipment (the successor to the set-top box), and the mode of content formulation and organization by the producer. This interaction illustrates the point that the Internet and the applications that run over it co-evolve, which makes predicting the future (and especially its timing) very difficult. But depending on which model emerges, the communications technology that supports the Internet, for example, satellites, might be subject to very different requirements—high-speed download of real-time video or "trickle charging" the consumer's equipment with prerequested content, for example.

Technology Base

Turning from the upper part of Figure 5.4, which concerns higher-level services, to the lower part, which concerns the delivery technology, there are again two questions to ask. First, to what extent are all of these technology options the same from the perspective of the user? Second, how rich will the competition be in providing them?

There is a wide range of delivery modes for Internet illustrated in Figure 5.4, and they differ in a number of respects. Some, like asymmetric digital subscriber lines (ADSL) and IP over cable, are capable of rather high-speed delivery, perhaps several megabits per second (at least downstream toward the consumer). Internet over dial-up modem, in contrast, is limited to no more than 56 Kbs today, and is not likely to get faster. Some forms of wireless service will be even slower. Different delivery modes vary not just in speed. For example, Internet over dial-up modem is connected only when the consumer makes a phone call for the purpose. Internet over cable and ADSL (high-speed Internet over copper) are services designed to be available at all times.

Do these differences matter? The answer is that it depends on the higher-level service being used by the consumer. For e-mail, there is little compelling difference between a 56 Kbs modem and a faster link. For cruising the Web, the increased speed seems to be valuable, and for Internet television, when and if that becomes significant, the 56 Kbs modem will not be enough. Some forms of Internet telephony, in which calls are placed to the recipient directly over the Internet, are difficult to bring to market if the recipient is not connected to the Internet at all times. If the user must dial up in advance to receive a call, this prevents receiving a call without prearrangement. This limited service is hardly a replacement for traditional telephone service. On the other hand, using an always-on Internet service, such as is provided by Internet over cable, it is possible to receive an unanticipated call, the way the telephone system works today. So the features the Internet customer will demand will depend on the higher-level services that are currently popular, and if a majority of the users do not have a suitable Internet service, certain high-level services will stall in the market.

Competition in Providing Internet Access Service

Just as we are concerned today with competition in the provision of telephone service, it is important to inquire now as to what degree of competition might finally emerge in the provision of Internet service. There is no certain answer today, of course, but we can see the relationship between decisions now being made and the eventual outcome.

One fact that seems quite certain is that installing a whole new wireline facility is very expensive. It is not likely that there will be many new wires (or fibers) installed to the residence in any technology cycle. At the same time, there is anecdotal evidence that the higher-speed Internet options such as Internet over cable (or, more specifically, cable modems over hybrid fiber-coaxid or HFC) are proving sufficiently popular that they may come to represent a distinct variant of Internet access for which the slower options like dial-up do not provide a direct substitute. Today in the United States, there is typically one provider offering copper pairs for ADSL (the incumbent LEC) and one provider of cable in any given area. (The situation in other countries will vary, as different patterns of deployment and cross-ownership apply in different parts of the world.) These are the only two high-speed wireline infrastructure options currently in the picture. So one extreme for future Internet service is that high-speed Internet service is provided by a duopoly, consisting of the current LEC and the current cable provider. Unless there is some business or regulatory pressure to move away from this outcome, it is a likely one.

There are other outcomes that are not so extreme. The LEC might sell an "ADSL" service and permit the consumer to select from a number of competing Internet services over that ADSL link. Or the LEC might be forced to unbundle the copper loop for ADSL service, by analogy with the current approach to service competition for telephone service.[6]

Although it is not possible to predict with certainty how these options might evolve, one can look at the current approach of the cable industry for a first hint. Currently cable providers that choose to sell Internet service over their cable do so by offering the consumer a bundled Internet service option, which they provide and sell as part of their overall service product. There has been no tendency to give the consumer a choice of Internet service providers over their cable infrastructure. Were the LECs to follow this model, a duopoly in high-speed Internet service would be the outcome.

If high-bandwidth applications of the Internet become popular, so that the dial-up service becomes a second-tier service for customers interested in low price rather than service quality, the current very competitive market for consumer Internet access over modem will become squeezed into one low-value corner of the market, with the high end concentrated in the facilities-based providers, of which there might only be two. This sequence of events would signal a major transformation of the consumer Internet service industry.

The technical innovation most likely to alter this picture would be the emergence of some wireless service with enough bandwidth to compete with the performance of the wireline solutions. But this sort of service raises serious technical challenges, including the availability of sufficient suitable wireless spectrum, the difficulty of achieving the requisite bandwidth to the user, the need to provide the always-on form of the service, and so on. It may be that if the duopoly as the final outcome is not considered an adequate range of choices for the consumer, some intervention in the market may be required.

Hybrid Technology

One interesting issue that is now emerging is that it may be possible to construct a superior Internet service by using more than one sort of residential access technology at a time. For example, one variant of Internet access is provided today using satellite or cable in one direction and telephone links in the other. In the future, we may see more novel hybrids, for example, involving low- and high-orbit satellites. Since, traditionally, one industrial player has installed one sort of technology, these hybrid options will force some sort of relationship between multiple players to provide the overall service that the consumer purchases.

A Next-Generation Local-Loop Technology?

There is continued speculation that some form of advanced access technology might be widely installed to the residence—for example, fiber to the curb or fiber to the home—although there does not seem to be any widespread planning or investment in these next-generation technologies. Nevertheless, a number of observations can be offered concerning this situation. One is that the expense is such that the typical consumer will not see a high level of competition in this offering. Possibly there would be at most one version of a next-generation wireline service for most consumers. Second, any such investment would almost certainly be motivated by the desire to get into as many high-level businesses as possible—telephone, television, Internet, and so on. So were this deployment to happen, it would represent a rather complicated business situation. On the one hand, it might serve to increase the competition in all of these higher-level services. On the other hand, it might represent a noncompetitive presence in the access market that might drive the less capable technologies from the market and leave the consumer with insufficient choice in the basic access service. That outcome might lead to regulation of the new access facilities, specifically enforced unbundling of the new facilities so that competitive providers of telephone, television, and Internet are ensured access. Certainly, anticipation of this regulatory outcome would have a chilling effect on the business plans of potential investors.

Since more than 40 percent of U.S. homes have personal computers, it is a plausible guess (but still just a guess) that at the right price, there would be similar demand for high-bandwidth advanced network access, even if all it did was improve the utility of the personal computer by enabling a better version of Internet service. In fact, if a whole neighborhood is wired at once, the cost to each household might be the same magnitude as the purchase of a personal computer. However, individual consumers cannot make independent decisions to have advanced wireline facilities installed. To keep the cost of installation at a reasonable level, it is necessary to wire (or rewire) a whole neighborhood at the same time. Thus, collective rather than individual decision making is necessary.

Given the risks to the private investor and the inability of the individual consumer to act independently, the future picture might be one in which the access technology is a recognized monopoly or a nonprofit or government-sponsored facility, but there is open competition for all the services that run on top of it, including telephone, television, and the Internet. Currently, a number of local municipal governments are experimenting with the installation of advanced access facilities, such as fiber to the home.[7] Although the approaches vary widely in design, including both the services offered and the model of financing, many require the consumer to pay a significant up-front cost. By asking the consumer to bear some of this cost, the financial risk to the installer is reduced. At the same time, the nonprofit or governmental player makes possible the necessary collective action so that whole neighborhoods or communities can be upgraded at once.

Regions of different demographics, regulatory history, and physical conditions offer different opportunities for competition and can support different technical options. The northeastern part of the United States, which mostly has a dense tree cover, has fewer options for wireless deployment than parts of the West, since the water in the tree leaves is opaque to many of the frequencies used for broadband wireless access. Multifamily dwellings can have a lower cost to wire than the dwellings on the fringes of the suburbs, and thus might better sustain competition in access options. Any speculations about the future, whether business plans or options for regulation, must take into account that different conditions may prevail at different times and places. We are not likely to see either a uniform monopoly or successful universal competition in advanced services. And specific providers may find themselves in different states of competition in different parts of their operating range. These realities will raise new issues for regulators and policy planners.

Conclusion

Wholesale installation of wireline access technology to the residence is expensive, and we therefore cannot expect a rush of competitors to enter this market. At the time of this writing, in the U.S. market there are two incumbents: the local telecommunications and the cable provider. Both are moving to enter new service markets, in particular the Internet market. A number of factors will shape the future of the local loop. In the short run, there do not seem to be any serious plans to install additional wires (or fibers) to the home.

One possible outcome is that there are two providers of high-bandwidth Internet service: the incumbent local telecommunications and cable provider. While there will be other forms of Internet access (wireless, satellite, and so on), these may be sufficiently different in features such as bandwidth and continuous availability that they do not directly substitute for the high-bandwidth wireline solutions. The result is a duopoly in the provision of residential Internet access.

If this outcome is considered undesirable, one way to mitigate it (other than regulatory intervention) would be to encourage research in alternative delivery technologies, including high-bandwidth wireless and hybrid models that use more than one technology to build a single, high-performance Internet service. However, exactly which forms of Internet service are substitutable will depend on which higher-level applications become popular, and that popularity can and will change over time. It is thus plausible to anticipate that the competitive breadth of the residential access to the Internet may change with the pace of the evolution of higher-level services, which can happen much faster then the pace of infrastructure investment.

The implication of the Internet for consumer access to higher-level services is that there may be increased competition in the provision of these services, including those such as telephone and television that are limited in competitive breadth today. This derives from the open character of the Internet design that militates against vertical integration of the Internet service provider and the higher-level service provider.

Notes

An earlier version of this chapter appeared as David D. Clark, "Implications of Local Loop Technology for Future Industry Structure" in *Competition, Regulation, and Convergence: Current Trends in Telecommunications Policy Research*, ed. Sharon Eisner Gillett and Ingo Vogelsang (Mahwah, N.J.: Erlbaum, 1999), pp. 283–296.

1. For a general discussion of the uncertain but inevitable evolution of the nation's communications infrastructure, see the report by the Computer Science and Telecommunications Board (1996).

2. Clark (1998) provides an analysis of different sorts of Internet telephony and the factors that limit the deployment of each.

3. A recent working paper from the FCC Office of Plans and Policy (Esbin, 1998) offers a good discussion of the history and current status of regulation in this context and uses the phrase *parallel universes* to describe the possible outcome of the straightforward application of today's regulation.

4. The question of whether the Internet will lead to layered or integrated industry structure is discussed in a number of papers. Tennenhouse, Lampson, Gillett, and Klein (1996) argue that a horizontally layered system with decoupled layers will evolve naturally given the properties of digital technology, unless convergence activities create a temporary monopoly condition. Gong and Srinagesh (1997) argue that the open structure, a natural consequence of the open interfaces, may lead to reduced investment in facilities. Kavassalis, Lee, and Bailey (1998) discuss the factors that lead to different market structures and conclude that a layer such as the Internet can be sustained as an open interface to some extent because Internet service, in contrast to raw capacity (e.g., fiber), is not a commodity but a differentiable product that will permit providers to set prices based on their value to the customers.

5. See http://www.audionet.com/about/ for information on this company and its offering.

6. The recent filing by NTIA (1998) to the Federal Communications Commission advances both these options as desirable outcomes and supports regulatory unbundling of digital subscriber line facilities. This suggests they believe regulation is necessary, even at this early stage of the emerging market for advanced services, to mitigate the power of the facilities owner.

7. Examples include Ashland, Oregon (http://www.projecta.com/afn/), Palo Alto, California (http://www.city.palo-alto.ca.us/palo/city/utilities/fth/index.html), and Glasgow, Kentucky (http://www.glasgow-ky.com/). The term *community networking* covers a range of activities, from municipal wiring to library-based access and community Web pages. Useful sites that relate to community networking include a Web site maintained by David Pearah at the Internet Telephony Consortium at MIT (http://itel.mit.edu/communitynetworks/links.html), the site of the Center for Civic Networking (http://civic.net/lgnet/telecom.html), the Community Networking page of Big Sky Telegraph (http://macsky.bigsky.dillon.mt.us/community.html), a resource page from the Association of Bay Area Governments (http://www.abag.ca.gov/bayarea/telco/other.html), the Directory of Public Access Networks maintained by the Council on Library and Information Resources (http://www.clir.org/pand/pand.html), and an online guide maintained by Paul Baker at GMU (http://ralph.gmu.edu/~pbaker/index.html).

II

Networks and Media

6

Internet Telephony and the Datacentric Network

Philip Mutooni and David Tennenhouse

The increasing proliferation of data communication in the past few decades is unveiling a new paradigm in communications. While telecommunication's technology has largely been associated with telephony and the public switched telephone network (PSTN) for the better part of this century, we are in the process of a rapid shift from a voicecentric to a datacentric communication network. In general terms, the demand for voice services has been increasing at 5 to 10 percent per year, while that of data services has been expanding at 75 to 300 percent annually. Granted that these two rates are applied to different base values, it is not surprising that aggregate data traffic has surpassed aggregate voice traffic.

This chapter examines the rapidity with which aggregate voice traffic is being eclipsed by aggregate data traffic and provides an understanding of how the rate of the transition may affect the final outcome. We model trends in backbone capacity growth and define three key milestones in this network evolution.

Capacity Peak Traffic and Average Compound Annual Growth

In this section, we develop a model that is used to characterize the circuit-to-packet shift. Its goal is to analyze the transition from voice-dominated to packet-data-dominated network traffic. There are two important assumptions used in the formulation of the model. These pertain to the relation between traffic and capacity and the nature of the growth rates used. Throughout this chapter, the term *capacity* is used with reference to installed capacity. This term is also used interchangeably with peak traffic. In our investigation, we have found that installed capacity and peak traffic are closely matched. Furthermore, to simplify the model, we have assumed that the capacity is growing at a relatively constant compounded annual rate. Although past growth is not indicative of future growth, this is a reasonable assumption provided that the interval under projection is of limited duration. We therefore maintain that if the transition interval is sufficiently small, errors due to this assumption are not consequential to our conclusions. We explore the sensitivity of our calculations to the precise growth rates and find that the basic premise of rapid crossover holds over a wide range of growth values.

Model Formulation

Consider a backbone network supporting voice services based on traditional circuit switching, growing in their capacity demand at a constant annual rate, rv, and a suite of data services based on packet switching, growing at a different constant rate, rd. The capacity required to support either category of service is given by the function

$$C(\ ) = C_o(1 + r_x),\tag{6.1}$$

where C_o is a base capacity, r_x is a voice or data growth rate, and 1 is a time duration. For some reference point in time, to the base capacities in voice and data, C_{ov} and C_{od} are related:

$$C_{ov} = C_{od}.\tag{6.2}$$

A plot of these relative capacities is shown in Figure 6.1. Figure 6.2 shows the equivalent base 10 logarithm plot, and includes the curve representing the aggregate capacity: the sum of the voice and data capacity requirements.

We define the following quantities as the results we wish to obtain from the model:

• t_l, the lead user point—the point at which packet data traffic requires 10 percent of the total capacity

• t_c, the crossover point—the point where both types of service require the same capacity

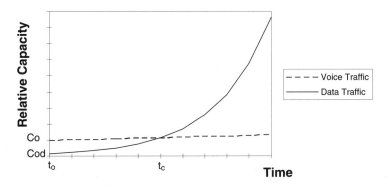

Figure 6.1
Time series plot of the relative growth of voice and data capacities. *Note*: The general function used to plot these graphs was $k(1 \pm x)^+$. A different value of x was used in both the voice and data cases with x(voice) < x(data)

- t_e, the eclipse point—the point at which packet data traffic consumes 90 percent of the overall backbone capacity

- $t_c - t_l$—the time interval from the lead user point to the crossover point

- $t_e - t_c$—the time interval from the crossover point to the eclipse point

The quantities t_l and t_e are arbitrarily chosen at 10 percent from the crossover point. However, they serve as convenient reference points that aid in understanding the rate of transit through the crossover point.

Through this parameterization of the capacity values, r_v and r_d can be calculated. The value of r_x, the average annual rate of growth of data or voice, is calculated by fitting known or derived capacity quantities $\{C_{t1}, C_{t2}, \ldots, C_{tn}\}$ to the curve defined by the equation 6.1.

Microsoft Excel's GROWTH and LOGEST functions are convenient tools for performing compounded growth curve-fitting calculations. These have been used in the MCI, AT&T, and aggregate industry model calibrations.

Calibrating the Traffic Transition Model

In order to apply this model, we perform a calibration through which we ascertain the growth rates of data, r_d, and voice traffic, r_v, and

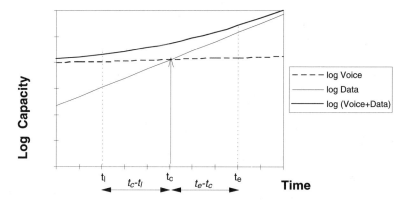

Figure 6.2
Log(capacity)-time series plot of the relative growth of voice and data capacities

determine the proportionality constant of the capacities at a specific time. This calibration is done in four steps:

1. Obtain the overall capacity at known points in time.

2. Decompose this capacity into voice and data components.

3. From the results of step 2, obtain the growth rates for voice capacity (r_v), data capacity (r_d), and total capacity (r_{total}).

4. Determine t_l, t_c, and t_e.

This procedure is then applied to two data sets: one for a selected MCI point of presence (POP) and one for a selected AT&T POP. Later, we use both the data sets and Federal Communications Commission (FCC) market share information to obtain the industry-wide model results.

Analyzing Growth at a Selected MCI POP
We consider IXC carrier capacity as a metric of both voice and data capacity growth. Table 6.1 shows the growth of aggregate capacity deployed at a specific MCI POP for the period between 1991 and 1996. We decompose this into voice and data components in Table 6.2. The plot of Figure 6.3 shows the relative growth trends.

Internet Telephony and the Datacentric Network

Table 6.1
Growth of capacity at a selected MCI POP

Year	Total Number of DS1s[a]	Equivalent Capacity (Mbps)[b]
1991	900	1,386
1994	3,696	5,691.84
1996	11,424	17,592.96
1997 (est.)	18,424	28,372.96
1998 (est.)	25,424	39,152.96

[a] DS1 is Digital Service Level 1.
[b] We assume that one DS1 has a capacity of 1.54 Mbps.

Table 6.2
Breakdown of the capacity in Table 6.1 into voice and data components

Year	Voice Capacity (Mbps)	Data Capacity (Mbps)
1991	1,247.00	139.00
1994	4,553.47	1,138.37
1996	12,315.07	5,277.89

Table 6.3
Results of the MCI data analysis

Quantity	r_{total}	r_v	r_d	α (1996)
Value	0.66	0.58	1.07	2.33

Equation 6.1 now can be used to obtain r_v, r_d, and r_{total}, and equation 6.2 can be used to obtain α.[1] Table 6.3 summarizes the results obtained for MCI's case for r_{total}, r_v, r_d, and α. Based on these rates, we can project MCI's capacity deployment for voice, data, and total capacity.

Having obtained the r_x growth rates, we can apply the traffic transition model to obtain the relevant MCI quantities plotted in Figure 6.4 and summarized in Table 6.4.

Analyzing Growth at a Selected AT&T POP
The interview data points summarized in Table 6.5 provide insight into the growth of aggregate capacity deployed at a selected AT&T POP

Networks and Media

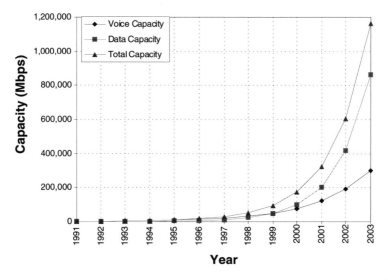

Figure 6.3
MCI capacity growth into interpolated values for voice and data

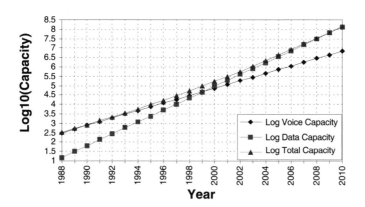

Figure 6.4
MCI's estimated capacity

Internet Telephony and the Datacentric Network

Table 6.4
Summary of the quantities of interest for MCI's case

t_l	t_c	t_e	$t_e - t_l$	$t_e - t_c$	α (1996)	r_v	r_d	r_{total}
1991	January 1999	2007	8 years	8 years	2.33	0.58	1.07	0.66

Table 6.5
Capacity growth data points for a selected AT&T POP, 1991–1999

1. Aggregate capacity in 1996: 10.2 Gbps (six routes operating at 1.7 Gbps each)
2a. Voice/data traffic mix in 1996: 60 percent/40 percent
2b. Voice/data traffic mix in 1988–1989: 90 percent/10 percent
3a. Year-over-year voice traffic compounded growth during 1988–1993: 4 percent–8 percent
3b. Annual data growth during 1988–1993: 2 percent–3 percent of previous year's aggregate capacity
4a. Voice/data mix of all new capacity installed during 1994–1996: 50 percent/50 percent
4b. Voice/data mix of all new capacity installed during 1997–1999: 20 percent/80 percent
5. Year-over-year data traffic compounded growth during 1994–1997: 12 percent–15 percent
6. Newly installed capacity in 1997 is more than the aggregate capacity in 1991.[a]

[a]Frank Ianna, AT&T's executive vice president of networks and computing services, made this statement in a meeting with Wall Street analysts on March 3, 1997. See http://www.att.com/speeches/.

for the period between 1991 and 1996. The voice and data capacity components of this total are deduced as shown in Table 6.6.

Although these data points do not directly address the quantities of interest, the five-step process described in Table 6.6 is used to deduce the AT&T POP's capacity growth from 1988 to 1997. A summary of the results of the spreadsheet analysis of this procedure is shown in Table 6.7.

We then use equation 6.1 to obtain r_v, r_d, and r_{total} and equation 6.2 to obtain α. Based on these rates, we can project AT&T's capacity deployment for voice, data, and total capacity. We therefore apply the traffic transition model to obtain the desired, t_l, t_c, and t_e quantities. The results of applying the traffic transition model to obtain the relevant quantities for AT&T are plotted in Figure 6.5 and summarized in Table 6.8.

Networks and Media

Table 6.6
Procedural steps used to obtain the rates and capacity values for AT&T, 1988–1997

Step	Procedure
1	Refer to data points 1 and 2a. Calculate the values of $C_{v(1996)}$ and $C_{d(1996)}$.
2	Use the result of step 1 and data points 5 and 4a to reconstruct C_v and C_d for 1994–1996.[a]
3	Work from values of $C_{v(1994)}$ and $C_{d(1994)}$ and data point 4a to obtain $C_{v(1993)}$ and $C_{d(1993)}$.[b]
4	Apply data points 3a and 3b to the result of step 2 to obtain C_v and C_d for 1988–1993.[c]
5	Use the result of step 1 and data points 6 and 4b to obtain C_v and C_d for 1997.

[a] The voice capacity quantities for 1994–1996 are obtained by working backward from the 1996 values. The data capacity quantities for this period are then obtained using data point 5.
[b] Here the 1993 values are obtained iteratively from the 1994 quantities subject to the data point 4a constraint. A convenient tool for this sort of analysis is the Goal Seek function in Microsoft Excel, which is generally used for scenario modeling and what-if analysis.
[c] Verify that the results of this step are consistent with data point 2b (voice/data ratio in 1988 is close to 90 percent/10 percent).

Table 6.7
Summary of the results of five-step spreadsheet analysis procedure to obtain AT&T capacity values and growth rates

Year n	1988	1989	1990	1991	1992	1993	1994	1995
Voice capacity (Gbps)	2.10	2.25	2.44	2.64	2.85	3.08	5.12	5.5
Data capacity (Gbps)	0.23	0.35	0.48	0.63	0.82	1.05	3.09	3.5
Total capacity, $T(n)$ (Gbps)	2.33	2.60	2.92	3.27	3.67	4.13	8.21	9.1
$T(n) - T(n-1)$			0.32	0.35	0.40	0.46	4.08	0.9
% new voice							0.5	0
% new data							0.5	0
Voice fraction	0.90	0.87	0.84	0.81	0.78	0.75	0.62	0.6
Data fraction	0.10	0.13	0.16	0.19	0.22	0.25	0.38	0.3
Checks	90/10							

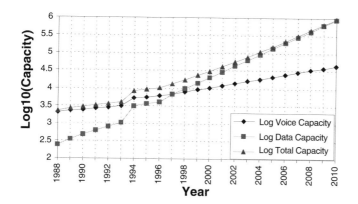

Figure 6.5
AT&T's estimated capacity

Table 6.8
Summary of the quantities of interest for AT&T's case

t_l	t_c	t_e	$t_c - t_l$	$t_e - t_c$	(1996)	r_v	r_d	r_{total}
1988	April 1997	2006	9 years	9 years	1.5	0.16	0.46	0.23

Aggregate Industry Model
Before applying the model and using the results of AT&T and MCI to obtain industry-wide growth, it is necessary to understand how the market share for both of these IXCs has varied over this period. To do this, we use FCC data describing long-distance market share for both AT&T and MCI between 1991 and 1996.

Over this period, these two carriers had a combined total voice market share ranging from 88.5 percent to less than 80 percent in 1996. Given their combined dominance of the market, it is possible to obtain reasonably accurate industry-wide growth rate estimates based on the MCI and AT&T data sets. Aggregate capacities are obtained by fitting a curve through the sum of the derived AT&T quantities of Table 6.7 and the yearly interpolated MCI quantities calculated from Table 6.2. Equation 6.1 is used to obtain r_v, r_d, and r_{total}, and equation 6.2 is used to calculate α.[2] Table 6.9 summarizes the quantities of interest for the industry-wide model, plotted in Figure 6.6.

Table 6.9
Summary of industry-wide model results

t_l	t_c	t_e	$t_c - t_l$	$t_e - t_c$	r_v	r_d	α (1996)
1988	November 1998	2007	10 years	9 years	0.38	0.69	1.97

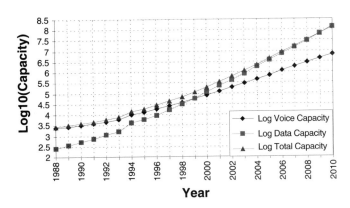

Figure 6.6
Industry-wide estimated capacity

Sensitivity Analysis

This section investigates how the key quantities we have obtained vary with changes in r_v and r_d. A key outcome of this sensitivity analysis is that the crossover transition is relatively independent of the precise growth rates (Table 6.10).

A key determinant of postindustry structure is the transition interval $t_e - t_{NOW}$, namely, $t_e - t_{1997}$. Table 6.10 summarizes the results of a sensitivity analysis performed to assess how this interval is affected by changes in the growth rates. Based on this information, we conclude that the transition period occurs relatively quickly over a wide range of growth rates.

Table 6.10
Sensitivity analysis results on transition period

r_v (%)	r_d (%)	$t_c - t_{NOW}$ (years)	$t_c - t_l$ (years)	$t_e - t_c$ (years)
10	40	1	10	9
10	100	−4	5	4
20	50	1	10	10
20	90	−3	6	4
30	60	2	11	9
30	80	−1	8	4
38	69	1	10	9
40	80	0	9	5
60	90	3	12	9

Alternate Voice Growth Rate Assumption

It is important to note that the value of r_v from Table 6.9 is much higher than the commonly accepted industry average of 5 to 10 percent. Given that these carriers are serving the same market, this high growth raises several questions about their market's characteristics. Such a high growth rate seems to indicate that there may be an oversupply of voice capacity at both facilities. If there were a high surplus of voice capacity, this would imply that a price war is imminent. Alternatively, this buildup of excess capacity can be used to stimulate and absorb the growth of data transmission.

Estimates of the traffic transition model's voice growth rate parameter (r_v) can be derived from alternative industry sources. Assuming this new r_v, we now investigate how the circuit-to-packet transition differs from the section calibrating the traffic transition model. This alternative derivation involves the following steps:

1. Derive r_v based on published IXC and regional Bell operating company (RBOC) telephone traffic volumes.

2. Project the voice capacity $C_{v(t)}$ based on this r_v.

3. Determine the parameters of interest.

To derive the industry-wide growth rate of voice traffic, data from the RBOCs and IXCs are used. Table 6.11 summarizes the data obtained.

Table 6.11
Annual rates of network traffic volume increase for RBOCs and IXCs

Company	1991	1992	1993	1994	1995	1996	Traffic Metric
ATT			162,945	171,907	184,800	195,888	Billed minutes
MCI	36,567	42,735	49,452	58,233	70,095		Overall network traffic
USWest	35,144	37,413	40,594	43,768	47,801		Interstate access minutes
PacTel	43,872	46,800	49,674	53,486	59,193		Carrier access minutes
SBC		41,235	44,203	48,430	53,681	58,668	access minutes

Source: The data were obtained from the 1991–1996 annual reports of each of these service providers.

A weighted average calculation is performed to obtain a voice traffic growth rate, r_v, of 8.8 percent. Using this alternative voice growth rate, two cases are modeled: an idle voice capacity scenario and an accelerated data growth scenario.

Idle Voice Capacity Scenario
In this scenario, it is assumed that voice capacity is growing at 8.8 percent and that the "excess" voice capacity reported by AT&T and MCI remains unused. It is also assumed that data capacity is growing at 69 percent. Based on these assumptions, estimates for the annual values of total capacity were obtained as: $C_{total(t)} = C_{total(t)} - (C_{v(t)} - C_{v(t)})$. Using the resulting total capacities, equation 6.1 gave an estimate for r_{total} of 0.27. Finally, the traffic transition model was applied using these alternative r_v and r_{total} rates and the 1996 aggregate capacities, as base capacities, to obtain the parameters of interest. The results of this scenario are summarized in Table 6.12.

Accelerated Data Growth Scenario
In this scenario, it was assumed that voice capacity is growing at 8.8 percent and total capacity is growing at 45 percent. The "excess" voice capacity was apportioned to data capacity, yielding an accelerated data growth. Based on this optimistic data assumption, estimates for the

Table 6.12
Summary of results for the idle voice scenario

t_l	t_c	t_e	$t_c - t_l$	$t_e - t_c$	r_v	r_d	r_{total}
1988	September 1997	2008	9 years	11 years	0.088	0.69	0.27

Table 6.13
Summary of results for the accelerated data-growth scenario

t_l	t_c	t_e	$t_c - t_l$	$t_e - t_c$	r_v	r_d	r_{total}
1988	February 1997	2001	9 years	4 years	0.088	0.988	0.45

annual values of data capacity were obtained as $C_{data(t)} = C_{total(t)} - C_{v(t)}$. Using the resulting data capacities, equation 6.1 gave an estimate for r_d of 0.98. Again, the traffic transition model was applied using these alternative r_v and r_d rates and the 1996 aggregate capacities as base capacities to obtain the parameters of interest. The results of this scenario are summarized in Table 6.13.

In both cases the transition occurs; the only question is when it happens. The accelerated data growth scenario appears to be favored by industry consultants, but in the end, the conclusion is the same: the growth of the Internet overwhelms voice networks. We turn our attention to this question.

Applying the Traffic Transition Model to Estimate Internet Growth

Since the introduction of Internet competition, it has been difficult to determine aggregate Internet backbone traffic levels. Here, we combine 1993 NSFnet data that put average monthly Internet traffic at 7.8 E+13 bytes per year with the growth rates determined earlier to extrapolate an Internet traffic estimate, $C_{d(1997)}$. The growth of the capacity is projected using the 69 percent r_d rate determined from the aggregate industry model and the 98 percent r_d rate calculated for the accelerated data growth assumption. Applying these rates as annual compounded growth rates to the 1993 traffic quantities gives estimates of $C_{d(1997)}$ of 6.4 E+14 bytes per year and 12 E+14 bytes per year, respectively.

Implications

A key result of the model is a characterization of the interval between the lead user and eclipse points. This interval defines the rate at which the crossover point transpires. In this section, we highlight and address some questions that arise from our results.

Industry Structure: Who Will Supply the Switching?

From our earlier analysis, we observe that the entire interval $t_e - t_c$ is likely to be less than ten years in length. Closer examination of this interval shows that in the space of a decade or less, the communications network will migrate from a predominantly voice-service-oriented network to a predominantly data-service-oriented network. Moreover, the process accelerates, so progress toward a scenario where voice traffic is less than 10 percent of total traffic occurs faster once the crossover point is reached.

This rapid change in the network environment influences the market competitiveness of telco players—switch vendors or service providers—directly correlating their competitive position after the crossover to how well they adapt to the rapid change in the network. Therefore, the ability of such a telecommunication market player to compete in the post-crossover industry structure will arguably be constrained by a window of opportunity described by $\pi = t_e - t_{NOW}$. The smaller π becomes, the more constraining the window.

Following this reasoning, there exists a critical value below which it becomes inconsequential for the player to act. The question then becomes what this critical valve of π is. In fact, it may already be too late for badly positioned market players to act. The key point here is that the faster π shrinks, the less significant that technical or strategic choices become in influencing the final outcome. Therefore, the ability for a market player to compete is constrained by the rate of this transition, as much as or more than by any other factors.

We now briefly discuss two of these potentially constrained players: the RBOCs and time division multiplexing switch vendors. We further consider whether the emergence of Internet telephony services exacerbates or mitigates the challenges these industry players are confronting.

Case 1: The RBOCs versus ISPs

Two key roles of the RBOC were defined at divestiture: (1) providing the last mile and central office serving the customer's premise and (2) providing regional switching and interoffice transmission within a local access and transport area (LATA). This discussion focuses on the second function.

As other types of service providers, namely, Internet service providers (ISPs), have gradually established themselves as the premier provider of packet-switching services within the LATAs, a turf war has developed between them and the RBOCs. While the RBOCs provide access and connectivity between the end customer and the ISP, the ISP serves as an alternative provider of onward traffic switching and transmission (Figure 6.7).

It is likely that at time t_c, the bulk of the packet-switching "assets" will be in the hands of the ISPs and that, beyond t_c, ISPs would switch more traffic than RBOCs. Further, the RBOCs are unlikely to ramp up switch installation fast enough to forestall market share erosion by ISPs and will quickly find their switch base eclipsed by that of the ISPs. Finally, once the ISPs are switching 80 to 90 percent of all traffic (t_c), it will be difficult for the RBOCs to displace them from this role. The effect will be to hollow out the RBOCs before they can place orders and take delivery of the necessary equipment.

Case 2: Traditional Circuit Switch Vendors

We have identified traditional switch vendors as a second market player whose focus, based on the combination of market segment served and business model used, may lead to sudden demise. The business model used here is based on a stream of regular payments from the customer, as contracts usually spanning a period of several years.

Generally the sale of the switch system is bundled as a total solution that includes installation, network management, switch maintenance, and system integration. These latter services and products serve as a key revenue stream for the vendor and are usually contracted for a period of several years. We observe that beyond t_c, as data begin to become the predominant component of traffic, new sales drop off quickly, as does the upgrade and maintenance revenue stream. Moreover, the large

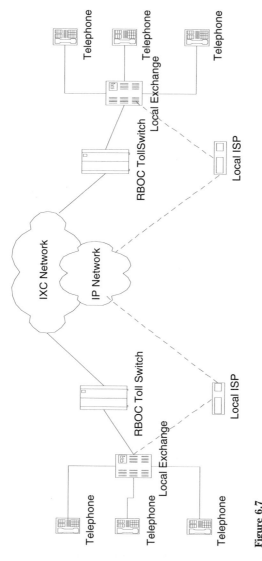

Figure 6.7
Topological representation of network connectivity

labor force that currently captures this downstream revenue becomes very costly to maintain or even dismantle.

Industry Structure: Consequences

As we have seen from the model, voice traffic becomes a minority contributor to overall backbone traffic beyond the crossover point. We now consider some economic and policy consequences of this transition.

Mutooni (1997, appendix A) has developed a separate revenue transition model, based on a similar methodology to the traffic transition model, that provides further insight into economic issues. In particular, it finds that there exists a lag between the capacity crossover and the revenue crossover. During this lag, data traffic exceeds voice traffic, yet voice revenues are significantly higher than data revenues, possibly reducing the likelihood that the RBOCs and traditional switch vendors will act in a decisive and timely manner. Alternatively, their revenue stream may provide a financial cushion to enable them to make a successful transition to the new marketplace.

In addressing industry structure consequences, we first consider how significant the voice market will be after the crossover point. The economic definition of a market, as a congregation and interaction of buyers and sellers of a good or service, would suggest that a voice market would exist as long as there was demand for voice services. A more difficult notion is ascertaining the relevance of this market relative to the data market. From the traffic transition model, we can deduce that the fraction of resources (capacity) used to effect voice communication becomes negligible as we move onward from the crossover point, t_c. Consequently, the marginal cost of providing capacity to carry voice in the overall communication network also becomes negligible.

Based on this argument, we begin an exploration of three important issues that affect telecommunication policy and business strategy: Internet voice substitution effects, market economics, and universal service.

Internet Voice Substitution Effects: The Input of Internet Telephony
The role of substitute technologies, such as Internet telephony, in the post-crossover world, is interesting. The plot of Figure 6.6 suggests that

the fraction of voice traffic in the network is rapidly diminished, becoming a small part of the overall traffic in a relatively short time. Therefore, contrary to contemporary thinking, packet voice technologies in and of themselves cannot power the growth of IP or data traffic. Nonetheless, their success may be significant and very sudden, driven by the arbitrage opportunity they present.

As we move away from t_e, it will become increasingly expensive to maintain a resource-intensive worldwide circuit-switched voice network, whose traffic requirements represent a small fraction of overall capacity, a factor that will become suddenly apparent to service providers and their customers. As t_e approaches, these players will decisively migrate to technologies such as Internet telephony, so that they may dismantle their circuit-switched networks and rid themselves of the costs these networks represent. Because of migration to one packet-based network, technologies such as Internet voice will be immensely successful. However, we suggest it is the potential for infrastructure sharing, and not bandwidth savings as commonly believed, that will drive the growth of these technologies.

Market Economics: The Voice Data Bundle

We now consider the dynamics of the post-eclipse industry structure. We note that AT&T, MCI, and Sprint have dominated the long-distance transmission market. At the same time, the ISP market is dominated by UUNET, MCI, BBN, and PSI. An economic argument may be made that both markets are oligopolies and that these firms can exercise their market power by adopting a bundling strategy.

Beyond t_e, since the incremental cost of transporting voice over a packet infrastructure is close to zero and a customer's demand for data service is more easily stimulated, bundling is a feasible strategy for the service provider. Indeed, the bundling of voice and data goods is practiced today. What is important is that this bundle may evolve to suit a datacentric market.

Whereas today a long-distance carrier may offer five free hours of Internet access per month if a customer signs up for its telephone service, after t_e, a customer is likely to get a bundle that includes close-to-free long-distance telephone service by signing up for a suite of data services.

Universal Service

Universal service has been a key goal of telecommunication policy in the United States since the first decades of the twentieth century. To understand the role of universal service in the post-crossover era of the twenty-first century, we consider one of the primary ways through which it has been implemented to date: subsidization.

One area in which the universal service policy has been applied is the local access subsidy that long-distance carriers pay local telephone companies (RBOCs) to access their subscriber loop. A consideration in setting up such a subsidization policy is the demand for the service. An argument could be made that because local residential service is priced to support saturated demand, then growth in long-distance residential service could subsidize local service. Similarly, in a datacentric market, voice traffic imposes minimal demands on the overall network and could leverage data traffic growth through subsidization.

We can make two observations. First, there is a potential new role for data as a subsidization mechanism for voice. Because of the high-growth nature of the data network, it is capable of being an effective subsidization mechanism, supplementing and even substituting the existing mechanisms. Second, we may witness the evolution of the universal (telephone) service concept to a universal (data) service concept, ensuring equitable data access and services.

Conclusion

This chapter analyzed the implications of the circuit-to-packet transition. The overall transition was characterized using three key milestones: the lead-user point (t_l), the crossover point (t_c), and the eclipse point (t_e). The most significant result was the time interval between now and the eclipse points, $t_e - t_{NOW}$. The implications of this model are to suggest that the telecommunications industry will experience sudden and severe dissuption as data traffic eclipses traditional circuit-switched voice traffic.

Using data from MCI and AT&T, the model was used to analyze the growth of these IXCs and to calibrate industry-wide growth. The model's industry-wide results suggest that the times for t_l, t_c, and t_e are 1988, 1998, and 2007. A sensitivity analysis was then done on the model to gain an understanding of how the three points are affected by growth rate changes. Most important, this sensitivity analysis showed that the $t_e - t_{NOW}$ interval period was not as sensitive to precise growth rates as expected a priori and that its occurrence is sudden across a range of values. By 2007 the traditional telecommunications industry literally will be history, destroyed by the creative forces unleashed by new technologies (McKnight, Vaales, and Katz, 2001).

We have also considered the telecommunication's business and policy implications of the suddenness of the crossover event. We found that the ability of market players to compete in the post-crossover industry structure may largely be determined by the rate of the transition rather than by technical, economic, or other external factors. Two cases were discussed to highlight this implication: RBOC versus ISPs and traditional circuit-switched vendors. We found that the RBOCs will quickly have their switch base eclipsed by that of the ISPs, which would be switching more than 50 percent of the traffic at t_c and 80 to 90 percent of all traffic by t_e. Consequently, in a decade, the RBOCs will be displaced from their switching role by ISPs. In considering the impact the shift will have on the makeup of tomorrow's switching industry structure, we observed that beyond t_e, traditional switch vendors like Lucent and Alcatel may see revenues from new sales, equipment upgrades, and maintenance contracts drop off quickly.

The consequences of the resulting industry structure were then discussed for three cases. The substitution effect of packet voice technologies for circuit-switched voice was the first outcome of traffic migration to a predominantly data dominated network. Here, it was found that although the success of packet voice technologies will be significant and sudden, they will be driven by the potential for infrastructure sharing and not bandwidth savings, as commonly thought.

The consequences for the voice-data bundle were also briefly discussed, arguing that the composition of the bundle is likely to change to reflect overall traffic composition and that because the incremental cost of transporting voice over a packet infrastructure will be close to zero after t_e, the bundle will evolve to suit a datacentric market, conceivably incorporating close to free voice service. Finally, the consequences for universal service were addressed. We suggested that data traffic could be used as a potential subsidization mechanism and that the universal service concept may evolve to a universal data policy as data traffic dominates the network.

Notes

1. The LOGEST and GROWTH functions in Microsoft Excel were used to interpolate the data and obtain projections, respectively.

2. The LOGEST and GROWTH functions in Microsoft Excel were used to interpolate the data and obtain projections, respectively. Data points 3b and 5 use difference metrics for describing the data growth, leading to a discontinuity in C_d growth between 1993 and 1994. This may have also coincided with the replacement of older 565 Mbps equipment by the 1.7 Gbps FT series. Accordingly, in deriving r_d we have fitted a compounded growth curve to the C_d values over the entire period in accordance with the model's constant compounded growth rate assumption.

7

After the Web: Diffusion of Internet Media

Lee W. McKnight and Marc S. Shuster

The rapid pace of innovation of the Internet renders many business practices obsolete. Internet products and services exhibit a fundamentally different life cycle from industrial era products and services. The Internet, acting as a communications medium and a marketplace, facilitates adoption by diffusing information about the product and, in some cases, the product itself. The consumer has direct access to information about the offering and a high degree of choice in deciding which product to adopt or not to adopt. In many cases, the offering may be redesigned by the end users, altering the original conception of the product. Managers must cope with the rapid rate of change and develop strategies that are sustainable and adaptable to these dynamic forces of Internet-based innovation processes.

And yet the Internet is a fundamentally unpredictable, decentralized network of networks. Users on the network's periphery drive adoption patterns. Successful adoption and diffusion of next generation–networked innovations are shown to be of critical importance for future business strategies as Web growth has begun to slow. Firms positioning themselves to take advantage of Internet innovations as either users or suppliers must prepare for what will come after the Web.

This chapter reviews Internet diffusion patterns and identifies factors critical for successful market growth of the next wave of Internet innovations. It also considers the challenges to enabling voice communications and other advanced services on the Net. The chapter first briefly reviews the historical development and technical architecture of the

Internet and projects future expansion of network applications. Data on the number of Internet hosts, World Wide Web servers, the multicasting backbone, USENET, and Internet telephony were fit to an S-shaped logistic curve. The results of the models predict the applications' growth rate, halfway points of growth, and saturation limits. According to the model, the number of Internet hosts was expected to saturate at about 39 million hosts by the early part of this century, while according to the model, the number of Web servers will saturate at about 40 percent of responding Internet hosts. These forecasts are built on a number of assumptions, which are also explained in this chapter.

The adoption rate of Internet telephony was estimated by analogy to adoption patterns of more established applications. The factors necessary for successful deployment of Internet telephony include network architecture and user interface development. Internet telephony, and multicast applications that require reserved network resources, were concluded to be in very early stages of diffusion. By 1999, only a small fraction of the users who had tried Internet telephony applications were willing to adopt and use the technology. This might indicate that further augmentations to Internet services are necessary to improve the usability of real-time applications, such as Internet telephony.

User behavior is the most crucial factor in technology adoption. The consumer's willingness to try new technologies determines the future of communications networks (Noam, 1987). The design of modern networks typically allows user needs to be accommodated by configuring end-node equipment instead of the network itself.[1] With end users gaining greater control of network usage, analysis of network traffic trends is becoming an important tool, as McKnight and Leida note in chapter 8. Enhanced data services are unregulated, providing the opportunity for unlimited entry and innovation (Mehta, 1998). But the distinction between voice and data blurs as voice transmissions are digitized. Mutooni (1997) concludes that by the year 2007 at the latest, packet-based data traffic will dwarf voice traffic. However, analyses of traffic trends alone are likely to be inadequate in predicting the future use of networks and the demand of applications. The most important issue for analyzing future Internet diffusion patterns is clearly defining the uses of network applications and understanding what they will become.[2]

Network Convergence

Traditionally, communications services were tightly coupled to their transportation medium (Werbach, 1997). Radio, television, and telephone service have all been bound to a dedicated network. The Internet, however, has demonstrated that a diverse set of content and applications may be provided across heterogeneous networks. The Internet protocol (IP) allows a spanning layer between the network substrate and applications (Kavassalis, Lee, and Bailey, 1997). The capabilities of the Internet can be extended without modifying the underlying structure of the network. By disassembling content into computable units, a universal, interoperable, and ubiquitous network of interconnected devices theoretically can be obtained.[3] The challenge to realizing the ideal of convergence will be interconnecting a diverse set of networks and devices and overcoming the limitations of cost and capacity.

The concept of convergence dates back to the early days of the telephone network.[4] Historically, AT&T fought vigorously against the interconnection of independent phone companies and the attachment of third-party devices. Paradoxically, the creation of a truly universal network through the interconnection of foreign networks and devices increases the value of the network to its users while eroding the power of the incumbent network service provider. Interconnected networks serve as both complements and competitors. The merger of the Internet and telephony will provide new features and benefits to users and competition for established players.

Internet Applications

Application architectures can be described as either peer-to-peer or client-server. Peer-to-peer applications involve two or more users interacting directly through end-node terminals or computers. In client-server applications, the user interacts with a server to store information or retrieve previously recorded information (Mueller, 1996). The single best-effort quality of service afforded by the Internet has been essential for expansion of the Internet as a low-cost communication medium, and yet it can create problems for almost all applications. For example, to ensure the integrity of a conversation, voice traffic must be delivered reliably, with a minimum delay. On the other hand, voice applications can tolerate some packet loss due to the redundancy of the human language. Data packets can tolerate longer and variable delays but typically only minimal loss (Apostolidis, Merakos, and Wao, 1993).

The real-time protocol (RTP), reservation setup protocol (RSVP), integrated services protocol (infserv), and differentiated services protocol (diffserv) were designed by the Internet Engineering Task Force to alleviate some of the difficulties of implementing real-time applications on IP networks.[5] RTP works by attaching packet-timing information and a sequence number to user data protocol (UDP) packets. This ensures that packets reach their destination on time and in the proper order, which is essential for IP telephony. RSVP allows bandwidth to be allocated along different levels of quality of service (QOS). An RSVP session involves two processes: admission control, which determines whether the router has sufficient resources to accommodate the requested QOS, and policy control, which determines whether the user has permission to make the reservation (Branden et al., 1997).[6] The integrated services protocol (infserv) and differentiat Services protocols (diffserv) are still under development at the time of this writing, but hold promise for supporting a variety of Internet applications with different service quality characteristics.

Real-time peer-to-peer voice applications, such as telephony, are sensitive to delay and require QOS guarantees if the network is not overprovisioned. Table 7.1 summarizes characteristics of various network applications. QOS ensures that little delay occurs in transmission between peers. Delay has much less of an effect on the usability of information in a client-server environment. E-mail requires only a deferred level of QOS. That is, application messages can be temporarily stored at intermediate points in the network without noticeably affecting the performance of the application. Thus, applications in which data can be stored and forwarded at a later time, such as fax, are amenable to networks with limited immediacy of QOS transport. On the other hand, transmission errors have a greater effect on data applications than voice or video applications. A voice message can still be understood with some amount of noise. However, a small change in a sequence of computer code will cause the information in data applications to be unusable. Client-server applications that involve user interaction such as Web

After the Web: Diffusion of Internet Media

Table 7.1
Application QOS characteristics

Application	Architecture	QOS Requirements	Content
Telephony	Peer-to-peer	Immediate	Voice
E-mail, news, messaging	Client-server	Deferred	Data
Web browsing	Client-server	Delay tolerant	Data
Fax	Peer-to-peer	Delay tolerant	Data
Fax over IP	Client-server	Deferred	Data
Voice mail	Client-server	Deferred, delay tolerant	Voice
Video/audio broadcast	Multicast	Immediate	Data

browsing are delay tolerant. Delay does not affect the usability of information but may cause frustration if users must wait to receive a response from the server.

Inefficiencies arise when applications are implemented on unsuitable network systems. The switched connections of the public switched telephone network (PSTN) maintain a high degree of synchronism and symmetry (Rockström and Zdebel, 1998). Such connections are unnecessary and expensive for many data-based applications. The Internet, however, provides an efficient mechanism for asynchronous data transmission and replication, but is unreliable for video broadcast and real-time voice applications (Table 7.2). An ideal network would provide an adaptive and flexible model to accommodate the distinct technical characteristics of each application. An IP network, such as the Internet, that exploits asymmetries, provides suitable capacity, and is augmented with the means to reserve resources may approach such an ideal model.

Adoption of Technology

Modeling Adoption Behavior

Everett Rogers, in his classic book, *The Diffusion of Innovations* (1995), presented the mathematics of diffusion and adoption behaviors. The

Table 7.2
Delay and error properties of network applications

	High Delay Tolerance	Low Delay Tolerance
High error tolerance	Client-server voice/video example: Voice mail	Peer-to-peer voice/video transmission example: Telephony, broadcast
Low error tolerance	Data replication example: Backup	Data retrieval example: WWW browsing

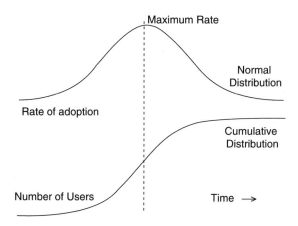

Figure 7.1
Diffusion and adoption curves

processes involved in the diffusion and adoption of technology can be characterized by the two curves in Figure 7.1. The normal gaussian distribution curve illustrates the rate of adoption at time t. The S-shaped logistic curve illustrates the cumulative growth in number of users of the technology by time t. Adoption behavior can be divided into three stages: growth, maturity, and saturation. During the growth stage, the rate of diffusion and number of users grow as communication increases knowledge about and acceptance of the innovation. The earliest period of the growth stage may be approximated by the exponential curve, $N(t) = ae^{bt}$, where N quantifies the users at time t. The rate of diffusion reaches a maximum at the halfway point indicated by the vertical line in Figure

7.1. The maturity stage is at the maximum point of the curve. The curve begins to level off during the saturation stage as all potential users have adopted the technology. The saturation stage often coincides with the growth stage of a competing technology. An additional stage of decline may occur as users substitute one technology for another. In some cases, a new diffusion wave for the technology may follow as additional uses are identified, current users replace or upgrade their existing equipment, and the technology itself is improved.

The rate of adoption can be described by the differential equation,

$$\frac{dN}{dt} \propto N(M - N), \tag{7.1}$$

where M is the saturation point of the diffusion process. Thus, diffusion is proportional to the amount of the innovation adopted and the amount remaining to be adopted.[7] The variable, N, can be expressed as either the percentage of the total market or the absolute number of users adopting the technology. The saturation level, M, can be expressed as the total percentage of the market or the absolute number of users whom the technology will reach. When an innovation acts as a simple substitute, substitutions have been observed to replace older technologies almost completely if substitution progresses a few percentage points (Fisher and Pry, 1971). In this case, M may be approximated as 100 percent. If M is not known beforehand, an M may be calculated that results in the best statistical fit of the model with existing data points (Griliches, 1957).[8]

The diffusion model describes the transfer of knowledge and experience from early adopters to the rest of the population. The innovation adoption decision process typically consists of four steps: knowledge, persuasion, decision and implementation, and confirmation (Rogers, 1995). Individuals obtain knowledge of the innovation and evaluate it in terms of perceived characteristics. The validity and reliability of the information are assessed, and then the decision to adopt or reject the innovation is made. This decision is reassessed and confirmed based on the actions of other individuals. The adoption rate increases as uncertainty decreases, with a larger community sharing information concerning the innovation. Members of the community learn from the experiences of others and imitate the behavior of the innovators. There may be a significant time lag between the point at which one learns and tries a technological innovation and actually adopts the technology by making some commitment and including the innovation as part of routine usage.

Adoption of Network Applications

As a communications medium, the Internet naturally facilitates rapid diffusion of novel network applications through the transmission of information about applications and the applications' software itself. The most important attributes of innovations, according to Rogers (1995), are relative advantage, compatibility, complexity, trialability, and observability (Table 7.3):

Relative advantage—the degree to which an innovation is perceived as superior to its predecessor. Users migrate to applications that provide benefits over existing applications. Figure 7.2 illustrates the percentage of traffic originating from three popular applications on the NSFnet backbone. Note that on April 30, 1995, NSFnet was transitioned to a new architecture in which traffic is exchanged at four network access points; therefore, comparable traffic data do not exist after this date. Traffic from World Wide Web browsers surpassed both ftp and gopher traffic. The advantages provided by the Web resulted in users substituting the Web for gopher and ftp. IP telephony applications must present some

Table 7.3
Summary of innovation attributes of the Web and IP telephony

Innovation Attribute	Web	IP Telephony Software
Relative advantage	Multimedia, hypertext information format	Cost savings Call management features
Compatibility	Compatible with ftp, gopher	Can interconnect with PSTN through gateways
Complexity	Easy-to-use graphical interface	Varies by implementation
Trialability	Free client software requiring no commitment	Many implementations are free to download Some applications require service commitments
Observability	Highly observable URLs	Limited

After the Web: Diffusion of Internet Media

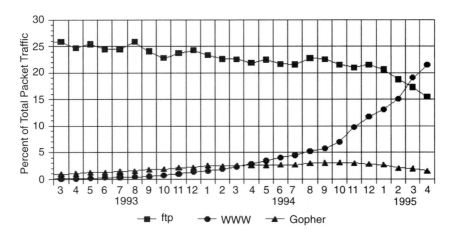

Figure 7.2
Traffic on the NSFnet backbone (Sources: Merit NIC, James Pitkow, GVU)

benefit over traditional forms of telephony. Cost savings have attracted early adopters of these applications. Although cost savings do exist, quality may be lower due to latency and other factors. Lower quality tends to be a result of network characteristics, not the application layer. However, the perception of overall poor quality may hamper future adoption even as bandwidth availability improves or new priority routing protocols are adopted.

Compatibility—the degree to which an innovation is perceived as consistent with the existing values, experience, and the needs of potential adopters. Interfaces that are compatible with familiar applications will increase the rate of adoption. Web browsers provided a similar interface and compatibility with ftp and gopher browsers. Users could continue to access ftp and gopher services as well as Web services. Computer-based telephony applications appear to be incompatible with methods of interacting with existing technology. Connecting with another party may require different directory lookup procedures, such as locating an IP address, and similar system platforms or software. Improved gateway services may help achieve more compatible telephony applications.

Complexity—the degree to which an innovation is perceived as relatively difficult to understand and use. It impedes the adoption of innovations.

For example, the Web achieved widespread acceptance due to the easy-to-use interface of browsers. For users unfamiliar with computers, telephony applications have a more complex interface and are more difficult to set up than standard telephone equipment. However, with the emergence of gateways and, perhaps in the future, more advanced, easy-to-use computer telephony interfaces, this impediment to the adoption of advanced Internet services such as IP telephony may be less significant.

Trialability—the degree to which an innovation may be experimented with on a limited basis. Many successful network applications have been very trialable. Web and gopher clients could be downloaded for free and experimented with without any commitment. Most telephony applications do not require any commitment by the user and do not present any difficulties in discontinuing use. Users can simply install the software without modifying their primary telephone system. Some Internet telephony applications permit users to try Internet-based services without switching their primary telephony service provider.[9] Adoption of Internet telephony gateways of special-purpose hardware by business users or service providers presents different dynamics for adoption than consumer services.

Observability—the degree to which the results of an innovation are visible to others. Innovations that have observable benefits are adopted more quickly. Rogers (1995) notes that software-based innovations are less observable than hardware-based innovations. Some software innovations such as the World Wide Web had certain aspects that were highly observable, such as widely advertised URLs. New telephony applications may use existing addresses such as telephone numbers or host names that will not differentiate them. However, the peer-to-peer nature of telephony applications may cause early adopters to encourage others to try the applications.

Diffusion of the Internet

Several factors affect the growth of the Internet. Communications systems are characterized by both positive and negative externalities. Positive externalities arise when growth in the user population increases the value of the network for individual users. New adopters derive more

After the Web: Diffusion of Internet Media

value from the network than early adopters because of the greater availability of information and the number of users with which to communicate. However, as the size of the network's knowledge base grows, information may become more difficult to locate and organize. Negative externalities arise when the performance or usability of the network degrades due to increased usage and traffic. Heightened costs, congestion, and growth in complexity often occur in expanding networks. Each additional user produces a network with different qualities. New applications also change the nature of the network. For example, the demand for Web access created the need for direct connection to the Internet instead of simple access methods such as mail gateways.

Internet Hosts

Figure 7.3 illustrates the growth of hosts on the Internet from 1969 to 1998.[10] From 1969 to 1998, Internet host expansion exhibits an exponential growth pattern, but growth rates during different periods are inconsistent due to different host count methods. The solid line in Figure 7.3 illustrates the exponential regression curve for the data. The host count describes only the number of visible machines connected to the Internet and does not provide information on usage. There exists no accurate calculation of Internet users. Multiple users accessing the network through the same machine obscure the actual size of the Internet community. For example, many individuals may read-mail through a single machine acting as a mail server or access the Internet

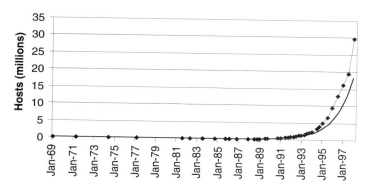

Figure 7.3
Growth of Internet hosts (Source: Network Wizards)

Networks and Media

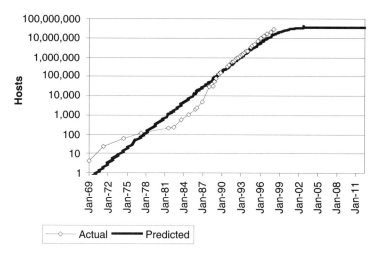

Figure 7.4
Predicted growth of Internet hosts

using public terminals. Internet hosts that act as public file servers may have an unlimited number of potential users. The ratio of users to machines has been decreasing as network services are being accessed with personal computers instead of time-shared mainframes. Despite the fact that hosts may be private terminals or public servers, the Internet host count currently provides the most reliable measure of the size of the Internet.

Figure 7.4 projects the growth of Internet hosts by fitting data to the equation. The upper limit of hosts, 39 million, was calculated by finding the best statistical fit. The logarithmic scale more clearly distinguishes several waves of Internet host growth in which host counts do not fit the predicted curve. The host count observations begin to converge on the predicted curve around 1989, with the commercialization of the Internet or the implementation of the domain name system. Although the growth of Internet hosts is predicted to saturate in the early part of this century, this does not imply that expansion of the Internet will discontinue. The stabilization of the number of hosts may be coincidental with the increased growth of private networks, often called intranets—virtual private networks, or networks of communities of interest. Many hosts within these private networks are hidden from the surveying devices described earlier. Organizations that create intranets isolate internal users from the rest of the Internet behind firewalls, proxy servers, and gateways. These organizations provide internal content on private servers and decide what content and services from the external network they will allow users to access. The rise of an intranet-dominated Internet may be a response to the need for improved security, filtering of content, or differentiated levels of service. Another trend that might also cause a slowdown in the growth of the number of hosts is the use of the Internet as a transport mechanism. Users can access a gateway device that uses the Internet for transport through terminals that are not Internet hosts, such as plain old telephone service (POTS) equipment. There may, of course, be a new wave of adoption of Internet hosts if, for example, Internet security improves and new applications attract new users. The question, as we note in the title of this chapter, is what will come after the Web—and that we do not profess to know.

The Web

In 1989, the World Wide Web was conceived as a distributed hypertext system to manage information about a lab's accelerators and experiments. The first multimedia browsers were introduced in 1992 and 1993. No accurate count of Web users exists. The number of Web servers or sites is displayed in Figure 7.5.

The Web has experienced tremendous growth, but the data indicate that this growth is beginning to slow. To predict an upper limit on Web growth more accurately, Web servers were plotted as a percentage of the total number of responding Internet hosts (Figure 7.6).[11] All public Web servers are responding Internet hosts. Other types of responding hosts include other forms of servers and networked machines that are always on and are outside a firewall.

The number of Web servers should not exceed the number of responding hosts. An upper limit of 40 percent of responding hosts functioning as Web servers was obtained. This is equivalent to approximately 8.6 million Web servers by mid-2000. The halfway point of Web growth occurred in December 1996. These results are consistent with the fact that many organizations have already created a presence on the Web. A new wave of growth may occur if individuals were to set up private Web servers as personal computers gain the ability to be continuously connected to the network. Such a capability would enable the transition from Web content hosted on a single server to content hosted on local

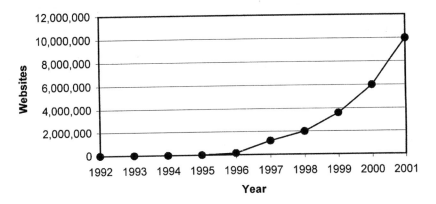

Figure 7.5
Growth of web sites (Sources: W3 Consortium; Matt Gray, MIT)

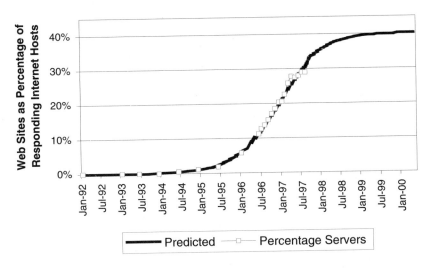

Figure 7.6
Predicted web site growth as a percentage of responding Internet hosts

After the Web: Diffusion of Internet Media

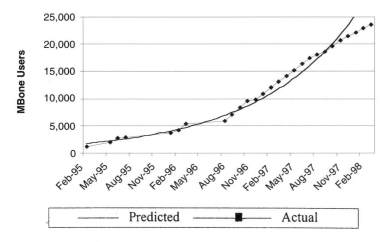

Figure 7.7
Mbone growth (Source: Kevin Almeroth, UCSB)

personal computers. However, this would not necessarily increase the total information base of the Web.

Multicast Applications
The IP multicast backbone (Mbone) is an early Internet-based real-time video and voice application. The first multicast session was established between BBN and Stanford University in 1988. The Mbone distributes information in a one-to-many fashion rather than a one-to-one fashion, as is the case with peer-to-peer IP telephony.[12] Figure 7.7 describes the usage of the Mbone from 1995 to 1998 in terms of the cumulative number of distinct IP addresses identified. The Mbone has experienced rapid exponential expansion, but this growth is beginning to slow based on the intersecting of the data with the fitted exponential curve.

The histogram in Figure 7.8 describes the number of days between a user's first and last Mbone connection. Each unique IP address appearing in the *mlisten* log files was considered to be an Mbone user. The first bar in the figure represents the number of users having zero days between connections. Therefore, about 10 percent of the total number of users participated in the Mbone only once. About 54 percent of the users used the Mbone again within fifty days or fewer. These results suggest that most users tried the application a few times and then

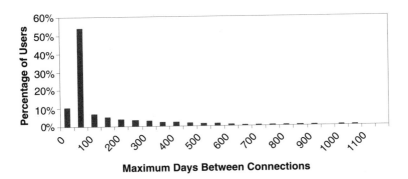

Figure 7.8
Histogram of maximum days between Mbone connections

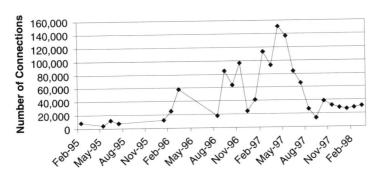

Figure 7.9
Number of Mbone connections made each month

discontinued use. The remaining 36 percent of the total user population made use of the Mbone within a fifty-day or more period of time. Of the users observed in Figure 7.7, only a small percentage decided to adopt the technology. Most users experimented with the Mbone over several days and then discontinued use.

The number of connections made by Mbone receivers per month is displayed in Figure 7.9. Instead of increasing in a regular manner, connections fluctuated and exhibited several peaks in usage. These peaks coincide with the presentation of events on the Mbone such as Internet Engineering Task Force (IETF) meetings or space shuttle or Mars exploration audio and video provided by NASA. The number of new users joining the Mbone, in Figure 7.10, fluctuates in a similar manner, and

After the Web: Diffusion of Internet Media

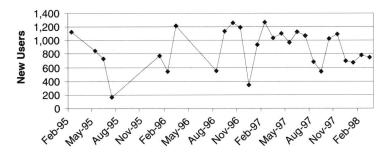

Figure 7.10
New Mbone users by month

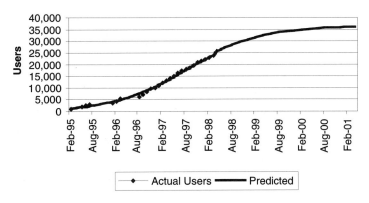

Figure 7.11
Predicted Mbone growth

peaks also coincide with the availability of certain content. This suggests to date that new users join the Mbone to participate in special sessions and find little reason to participate in subsequent sessions. Thus, the number of Mbone adopters is very small compared to the number of users observed.

The number of Mbone users is expected to reach only 36,500 (Figure 7.11). The small size of the Mbone user community can be attributed to the adoption patterns described and competition from newer multicast and telephony applications. The Mbone may also experience a decline in usage as users migrate to these newer applications. In sum, the MBONE may end up as a historical footnote, superseded by more robust multicast applications.

IP Telephony Applications

Clark (1999) identifies three general classes of IP telephony applications. Although these applications are often referred to as Internet telephony applications, they may be implemented on any IP-based network, not just the public Internet. Class 1 connects POTS equipment, with the Internet serving only as a conduit. Class 3 uses computers attached to the Internet for voice communications and other advanced applications. This class does not involve any interaction with the PSTN or equipment, with the possible exception of a telephone line and modem for dial-up access. Class 2, a hybrid of classes 1 and 3, allows communication between computer-based telephony systems and POTS equipment. Thus, a computer telephony application resides on one end node, and a PSTN phone resides on the other end node. Some applications provide both class 2 and 3 capabilities. The number of IP telephony software users over a three-year period is displayed in Figure 7.12.

In this section, IP telephony software refers to class 2 and 3 applications. The data were approximated from software sales of Vocaltec's Internet phone product that has an estimated 90 percent market share. IP telephony like the Mbone appears to be in an early exponential growth phase based on the close fit of the data in Figure 7.12. Projections for IP telephony are likely to be very unreliable based on the limited availability of data. A model for the growth of IP telephony was developed by analogy to other applications discussed. An upper limit

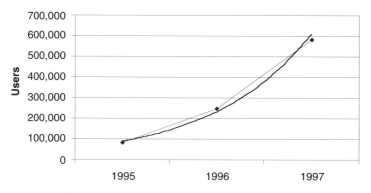

Figure 7.12
Growth of IP telephony users (Source: Scott Wharton, Vocaltec)

After the Web: Diffusion of Internet Media

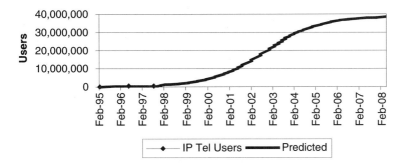

Figure 7.13
Predicted growth of IP telephony

was chosen as identical to the upper limit of Internet hosts. The saturation of telephony clients was approximated as not exceeding the total number of Internet hosts. A growth constant was then derived that best fit observed data points. IP telephony adoption was predicted to reach its halfway point in January 2002 and had a t value of 5.5 years. The growth of telephony software users displayed in Figure 7.13 is not as dramatic as some other predictions. For example, International Data Corporation predicted there would be 16 million IP telephony users by 2000, whereas this model suggests that telephony applications are still in an early stage of growth. The more conservative results of this model may reflect the exclusion of class 1 applications in which the Internet is used solely for transport and accounting only for active users of the software.

According to Vocaltec, 3 million individuals have tried telephony software, but only 500,000 are active users and make frequent calls. As is the case of the Mbone, there are many users in the knowledge or trial stage of the adoption process who are not yet willing to adopt the technology.

Internet Applications After the Web

The forecasts of the growth of Internet hosts, Web servers, and Mbone and IP telephony users are based on a simple model of the diffusion and adoption of innovations, based on the work of Rogers and others. We

Table 7.4
Growth rates of network applications

Technology	Growth Constant	Halfway Point	t in Years
Internet hosts	0.00162	October 1998	7.2
Web servers	0.00501	December 1996	2.4
MBone users	0.00344	August 1997	3.5
IP telephony software users	0.00218	January 2004	5.5

do not purport to have captured the full complexity of user behavior, competitive dynamics, regulation, macroeconomic conditions, or future innovations for Internet telephony or these other convergent product and service markets. We do, however, hope that our models can bring a measure of reality to the hyperbolic rhetoric surrounding the growth of the Internet, the emergence of the global Internet economy, and the convergence of the Internet and telecommunications industries.

The growth rates for the Internet itself, based on host counts, were slower than for most applications (Table 7.4). The expansion of the Internet was delayed until the arrival of easy-to-use software, such as Mosaic, and the commercialization of Internet backbone. For many years the Internet was restricted to academia and scientific research networks. The Web experienced the most rapid growth of the applications studied, with a takeover time of 2.4 years. (The takeover time is the time required for adoption to proceed from 10 percent to 90 percent of the saturation point.) Information placed on the Web was immediately accessible to all Internet users. The value of the Web to users was related to available content and the suitability and organization of information. The longer takeover time for IP telephony and network news can be attributed to the application's limited value during early stages of development.

The Mbone was determined to have a takeover value of 3.5 years. Although Mbone growth occurred quickly, the Mbone was attractive to only a limited number of users. This growth rate reflects diffusion through a much smaller user community than other applications. Several reasons explain the Mbone's failure to attract more users. Unlike the Web, limited content was available to Mbone users. Mbone sessions also tended to suffer from poor transmission quality. Handley (1997) found that 80 percent of sites observed reported intervals with packet loss rates greater than 20 percent, which is regarded as the threshold above which audio without redundancy becomes unintelligible. If problems related to poor transmission continue on the public Internet, the growth of IP telephony applications may slow as future users may be less tolerant of inferior performance than early adopters. Alternatively, IP-based, overprovisioned private networks may be used to overcome this problem.

Technological Substitutions

The adoption of technology can be understood in part as the replacement of old technologies by newer, more efficient ones. E-mail acts as a substitute for postal mail, content available through the Web serves as a substitute for paper-based magazines and journals, and IP packet-routed telephony can substitute for conventional switched telephone services. The overall trend of media convergence is driven by the underlying substitution of general-purpose programmable systems for special-purpose devices (Griliches, 1957). Substitution itself is catalyzed by the need to improve efficiency. Digitization permits more efficient delivery of information, increasing its availability in time and place (Bane, Bradley, and Collis, 1997).

Based on the takeover times listed in Table 7.5, the Internet and network applications, on average, experienced much greater adoption rates than traditional technological substitutions, which typically required from nine to fifty-eight years to reach the halfway point (Fisher and Pry, 1971). Advances in computing performance, rapid diffusion of information, standardization, and positive feedback can explain the unusual rates of adoption for network applications. Positive feedback occurs as advances in networks and computing produce conditions that fuel further expansion (Werbach, 1997). As higher-capacity networks become available, demand for bandwidth-intensive applications also grows. Positive feedback occurs as users increase the value of this and attract additional users. Users of the Internet have produced most of its content and developed many of its applications.

Table 7.5
Technological substitution rates

Substitution	Halfway Point	t in Years
Synthetic/natural rubber	1956	58
Synthetic/natural fibers	1969	58
Water-based/oil-based paint	1967	43
Plastic/hardwood floors	1966	25
Plastics/metal in cars	1981	16
Organic/inorganic insecticides	1946	19
Synthetic/natural tire fibers	1948	17.5
Detergent/natural soap	1951	8.75

Source: Fisher and Pry, 1971.

Standardization and the Effect of Gateway Devices

The interconnection of incompatible systems has the effect of nullifying competition between contending variants. For example, the interconnection of alternating and direct current electric power distribution networks through the rotary converter neutralized the rivalry between these competing systems (David and Bunn, 1988). Interconnection of the IP network and the PSTN through gateways allows elements of both systems to coexist. Gateways achieve compatibility and integrate different modes even if undesired or unintended by the designers of the original network. The early Bell telephone system could technically be interconnected with independent companies but interconnection was usually refused in order to control the telephone business and induce operating companies into becoming Bell licensees (Mueller, 1996). In modern telecommunications systems, the presence of voice transmissions over IP networks and interconnections of the PSTN with IP network are difficult to detect. The PSTN system does not derive any advantage over IP-based systems from having a larger user base because traffic originating from IP networks cannot easily be eliminated or treated differently. From the user's perspective, an Internet-based telephone connection could appear identical to a PSTN-based telephone connection.

Gateway devices impose costs in the form of speed, accuracy, capacity, and availability to achieve compatibility. Additionally, the limited deployment of gateways provides IP telephony applications access to a small number of PSTN exchanges. Gateways will become bottlenecks as they are more widely deployed and their usage increases. When gateway inefficiencies become more apparent, incentives to interconnect IP networks and the PSTN transparently will arise. Telephony applications will evolve such that the distinctions between application classes will be eliminated. The earliest adopters of IP telephony applications, Internet users and hobbyists, were restricted to communicating with other Internet users (class 3 applications). Later adopters, including corporations and intranet users, could communicate with PSTN telephone users (class 2 applications). Subsequent adopters of class 1 applications used the Internet as a transport mechanism only and made calls through PSTN equipment by service arrangements with certain long-distance carriers. New generations of telephony systems will transparently incorporate elements of all applications. Thus, computers will seamlessly provide voice and data services, and telephone calls will be routed over the most efficient network.

Conclusion

The forecasting and modeling of innovation diffusion in this chapter have relied on a narrow definition of each application. The IP telephony model included only software products, and Internet hosts were modeled instead of all Internet users, as it is not precisely understood who qualifies as an Internet user. However, the Internet's emphasis on end-node processing and user participation is resulting in dynamic applications. The design and implementation of applications are rapidly evolving according to user requirements and the constraints of technology. Telephony applications will quickly change as network capabilities are upgraded and user needs are realized.

Therefore, we emphasize the limitations of our own work and urge readers to revisit our assumptions as the Internet and its applications continue to change. New concepts based on and defined in terms of old technologies tend to hinder the development of new technologies (Rockström and Zdebel, 1998). Most telephony systems are still based on the assumption of technology as a scarce and expensive resource. The Internet has the potential of transforming communications services as antiquated notions of technology are discarded. IP telephony application not only can reproduce existing telephony features, but can also incorporate multicast and information retrieval features to form new types of applications, similar to but more capable and easier to use than the Mbone. The differences in the capabilities of Internet enhanced telephony and conventional telephony imply that the path of innovation diffusion may not strictly adhere to the linear model of simple technological substitution. New applications will emerge that are not incremental improvements over current communication systems.

As network services change and diversify, they have become increasingly difficult to classify. The nature of modern networks renders the distinctions in types of content, transport, and applications irrelevant. The Internet transports and processes bits without regard to distance or intended use. The breakdown of the barriers between services is beginning to reveal the irrelevance of regulatory and policy models that distinguish different modes of communication. Along with the convergence of technologies, it is necessary for regulatory frameworks to also converge (McKnight, 1997). Inappropriate regulations will hinder innovation. For example, an attempt to regulate or impose fees on Internet telephony service providers may simply accelerate the growth of PC-based telephony applications (see chapter 2).

Adoption of Internet services is very rapid, but Web growth is slowing. Businesses therefore need to begin planning, at Internet speed, for future opportunities and threats from the next wave of Internet innovations. Real-time applications, such as Internet telephony, Internet radio, and Internet television, will most likely drive this wave of growth. Although the market acceptance of Internet telephony to date has been limited, this network innovation is on the verge of rapid growth due to user demand for more interactive applications, cost savings, and increased flexibility compared to traditional services. The Internet is transforming business processes worldwide. Firms positioning themselves to take advantage of Internet innovations as either users or suppliers must prepare for what will come after the Web.

After the Web: Diffusion of Internet Media

Notes

This chapter is based on Marc Shuster's thesis, "Diffusion of Network Innovation: Implications for Adoption of Internet Services" (MIT, 1998). Support from the MIT Internet and Telecoms Convergence Consortium (ITC) is gratefully acknowledged. Feedback on this research provided by ITC research staff members Bill Lehr, Sharon Eisner Gillett, and Petros Kavassalis was very helpful in honing the arguments made here. Kevin Almeroth's willingness to share his insights about the Mbone data analyzed in this chapter was greatly appreciated and very helpful. Additional assistance of ITC members in conference calls and following presentations at the ITC November 1997 and June 1998 meetings is gratefully acknowledged, as is feedback from MIT electrical engineering and computer science faculty during 1998 Masterworks presentations, as well as from attendees of the International Telecommunications Society 1998 Conference, held in Stockholm, Sweden. Any errors of fact or omission are the responsibility of the authors. The views expressed are those of the authors and are not necessarily shared by Tufts University, MIT, or the ITC.

1. For example, the World Wide Web emerged as a result of the demand for easy-to-use information retrieval software and the widespread adoption of browser software by Internet users.

2. This use of data networks for voice applications may have a significant impact on the revenue of traditional carriers, unless they also prepare to offer new services. Estimates of the revenues to be lost and gained from Internet telephony and Internet multimedia services are beyond the scope of this chapter.

3. The union of computers and communication systems has enabled this unbundling of network elements. In theory, the computation performed by one computer can be emulated by any other computer. British mathematician Alan Turing proved that any mathematical operation that could be performed on one machine could be accomplished on a single universal machine.

4. Theodore Vail, president of AT&T, envisioned the Bell System in 1910 as based on "a common policy, common purpose, and common action; comprehensive, universal, interdependent, intercommunicating like the highway system of the country" (Neuman, McKnight, and Solomon, 1997).

5. See the IETF Web page on applications (http://www.ietf.org/html.charters/wg-dir.html#Applications Area) for more information on Internet protocols and standards.

6. Before applications may take advantage of these protocols, deployment problems must be addressed and pricing models must be developed to produce incentives so as not to overburden the network.

7. The solution to this differential equation is

$$N(t) = \frac{M}{1 + e^{-(a't + b)}},$$ (7.2)

where a describes the rate of adoption and b is the constant of integration. The halfway point of the process is identified by the relation,

$$t_{1/2} = -\frac{b}{a}.$$ (7.3)

The halfway point is also the point of inflection of equation 7.2,

$$\frac{d^2N}{dt^2}(t_{1/2}) = 0. \tag{7.4}$$

A useful relation to compare the diffusion of different technologies is •t, the time, in years, required for diffusion to proceed from 10 percent to 90 percent of M, or the takeover time.

$$\Delta t = \frac{1}{83.06 \cdot a}. \tag{7.5}$$

Equation 7.2 can produce a form in which the parameters a and b can be calculated with linear regression methods,

$$\ln\left(\frac{N(t)}{M - N(t)}\right) = at + b. \tag{7.6}$$

8. The mathematical equations of adoption processes make assumptions that do not necessarily reflect actual adoption behavior. Specifically, the adoption curve is symmetric about the halfway point, an asymptote exists that diffusion cannot proceed beyond, and adoption begins in the infinite past and goes to completion in the infinite future. The model is intended only to be a descriptive tool and provides no insight into driving forces or causality, if not accompanied by further analysis.

9. Trialability is more important to early adopters, who have less assurance of the viability of the applications. Late adoptions are assured of the application's success through observation of previous adopters.

10. The data were obtained from several sources and may not be consistent throughout the entire time series because of different host count methods. From 1969 to about 1988, all Internet hosts were registered in host tables with the Network Information Center. In 1988, the domain name system (DNS) was implemented and deployed, and host counts were performed by querying the DNS system (Lotter, 1992). Beginning in January 1998, the survey mechanism was modified to account for organizations' restricting access to domain data. The new survey counts hosts by querying the domain systems to discover IP addresses assigned names.

11. Responding Internet hosts were estimated by Network Wizards by querying a statistical sampling of the Internet (Network Wizards: http://ftp.nw.com).

12. Information about hosts participating in the Mbone was collected using the *mlisten* tool that continuously monitors multicast addresses used to advertise Mbone sessions. The data may not reflect the actual size of the Mbone user community. More than one user may use a computer with an assigned IP address, and problems in the collection method may also distort the results. Unreliable transmissions that cause packet loss may result in group members' appearing to leave a session but not actually doing so. In addition, abnormal Mbone behavior may occur as a result of software bugs and performance experiments. Unique IP addresses were counted from the *mlisten* tool log files.

III

Economics and Costs

8

Internet Telephony Service Providers

Lee W. McKnight and Brett Leida

Telecommunications transport, plus customer service and sales and marketing costs, represent a large proportion of an Internet service provider's (ISP) total costs in extending its product offerings to include managed Internet telephony services. The chapter suggests that pricing and management models supporting Internet voice services might be employed for other Internet differentiated services as well, possibly realizing some economies of scope for the provider. Because of convergence, an integrated regulatory framework will be required to formulate policies for multimedia services. We conclude that governments should develop appropriate policies without introducing economic and technical distortions into the market for Internet telephony and other advanced Internet services, even as the "creative destruction" of traditional industries and services unfolds.

There are a wide variety of mechanisms by which customers may use Internet telephony services. We take the term *Internet telephony service provider* to mean an intermediary organization such as an ISP (which might also be a telephone company) that aggregates and terminates Internet voice traffic. Many other kinds of entities are engaged in providing Internet voice services, whether to fixed or mobile devices, but are not explicitly modeled in this chapter. This chapter does present a cost model of ISPs and Internet telephony and assesses its business and policy implications.

The term *Internet telephony* has been broadly applied to a family of applications that typically includes (real-time) voice communication, at least partially over a network using Internet protocols. This is in contrast to traditional telephony (or plain old telephone service—POTS) that occurs solely over a circuit-switched telephone network. However, distinctions between Internet telephony and traditional telephony become less clear when one considers telephony services that bridge packet-switched and circuit-switched networks. Clark, in Chapter 2, classifies various types of telephony services that can be realized using these once disparate networks. The type of Internet telephony analyzed in this model is what Clark calls class 3 Internet telephony—computer-to-computer Internet telephony in which two computers communicate over the Internet via a modem connection or a direct network connection.[1] Moderate use of computer-to-computer Internet telephony can have a significant impact on the costs of an ISP. Pricing and policy issues arising from Internet telephony services are also briefly addressed in this chapter. We conclude that both new pricing strategies and supportive policy frameworks are needed for Internet telephony services to recover costs and to integrate the Internet and telecommunications industries.

Cost Model of Internet Service Providers

A cost model of ISPs developed by the MIT Internet and Telecoms Convergence Consortium (ITC) and the MIT Research Program on Communications Policy (RPCP) quantifies the impact on an ISP's cost structure that would result from an increased use of Internet telephony.[2] Two scenarios are modeled: a baseline scenario representing current ISPs in which the principal use of the network is for Web browsing and there is essentially no Internet telephony, and an Internet telephony scenario in which the ISP sees a substantial increase in use of computer-to-computer Internet telephony by its subscribers.[3] The model is not intended to provide a realistic view of any individual business, but rather presents results for a generic ISP of specified characteristics. The model is presented here as an example of the type of analytic tool that may be helpful to business and to governments as both continue to reflect on where Internet telephony will fit in the long run and what is needed for it to work in a rapidly evolving Internet and telecommunications industry.

The model is used to identify the costs of end-to-end Internet service for various types of users (e.g., dial-in, leased-line). These costs are broken down into five categories:

Capital equipment—the hardware and software of the network

Transport—the leased lines of the network and interconnection costs

Customer service—staff and facilities for supporting the customers

Operations—billing, equipment and facilities maintenance, and operations personnel

Other expenses—sales, marketing, general and administrative

Key Model Assumptions

The ISP cost model presented here has more than three hundred input parameters. Here we present the key assumptions.[4]

ISPs come in all shapes and sizes. Firms with international, facilities-based networks are called ISPs, as are firms with a few modem racks and a leased line. Therefore, a model that captures the costs for both types of firms must be carefully designed.

Figure 8.1 shows a hypothetical market where there are two principal types of ISPs: backbone ISPs (1 and 2 in the figure) and access ISPs (A–F). Each access ISP has a backbone ISP that connects it to other access ISPs. The backbone ISPs interconnect at network access points (NAPs). The ISP entity represented in the cost model is a single-backbone ISP and its associated access ISPs. Hence, the model results do not necessarily correspond to the costs of any particular ISP given the current (U.S.) market structure of separate backbone and access ISPs. Nevertheless, the model results do represent the total costs of providing end-to-end Internet service, which is the intended goal of the model.

The network of the modeled ISP is shown in Figure 8.2. The backbone links are connected at nodes called tier 2 POPs (point of presence), and the access nodes, tier 1 POPs, are connected in a star network to a tier 2 POP.[5] It is further assumed that identifying costs for the following types of subscribers captures sufficiently the costs of an ISP:

Economics and Costs

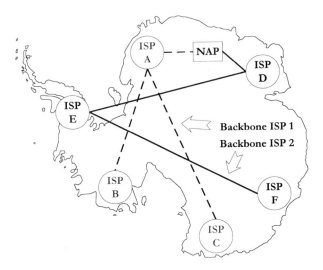

Figure 8.1
Hypothetical ISP network architecture. *Note*: The model represents an access and back
bone ISP with leased transport

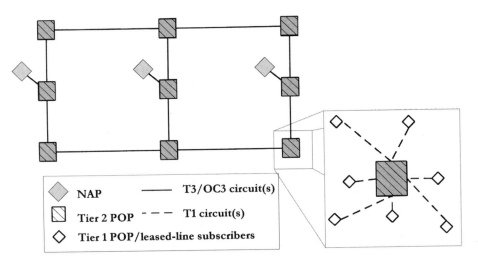

Figure 8.2
ISP topology

residential dial-in subscriber, business dial-in subscriber, ISDN (128 Kb dial-in) subscriber, 56 Kb (leased-line) subscriber, and T1 (leased-line) subscriber.[6] Statistics from 1996–1997 for the pricing of ISP services and the number of subscribers for the various services in the United States were used to determine revenue for the modeled ISP.[7]

It is assumed that Internet telephony is used 33 percent of the time in the IT scenario. The result is that per user bandwidth increases by a factor of 1.66 in the IT scenario.[8] Further, it is assumed that dial-in subscribers will increase their holding time and call arrival rates by 20 percent in the IT scenario.[9]

Principal Cost Categories

The ISP's costs are separated into five principal categories: capital equipment, transport, customer service, operations, and other expenses (which include sales and marketing and general and administrative).

Each cost element (e.g., router, billing or marketing costs) is determined based on assumptions about how large the costs would be for the given number of subscribers. Once the total cost of an element is known, its cost is allocated to each type of subscriber based on the relative amount of use by each type of subscriber. Carrying out similar calculations for each cost component permits the model to determine the cost per subscriber for each type of subscriber.

Capital Equipment
Capital equipment includes that which is found in the tier 1 and tier 2 POPs. Figures 8.3 and 8.4 show how the ISP capital equipment is interconnected at a (tier 1 and tier 2) POP.[10] Capital investments are converted from a one-time, fixed cost to a leveled annual cost by using a cost of capital rate.[11]

Each piece of capital equipment is sized based on assumptions of users' access patterns and bandwidth requirements. Once the total cost of a piece of equipment is known, its cost is allocated to the various types of subscribers based on the relative amount of use by each type of subscriber. For example, analog modems are sized based on how often the residential and business dial-in subscribers call and how long they stay connected. Once the required number of modems is known (and,

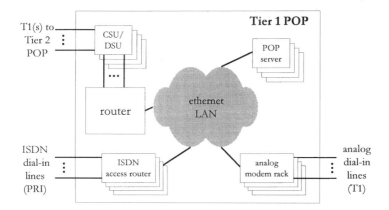

Figure 8.3
Tier 1 POP

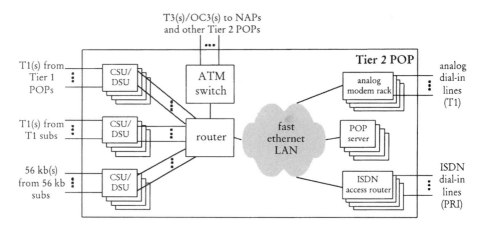

Figure 8.4
Tier 2 POP

hence, the cost), the cost is split between the residential and business dial-in subscribers based on how much traffic each type of subscriber generates. For this particular piece of capital equipment, no modem costs are allocated to the ISDN, 56 Kb, and T1 subscribers since they do not use this type of equipment. Similar calculations are carried out for each piece of capital equipment.

Transport

The transport costs of the ISP comprise costs due to leased lines to connect the tier 1 and tier 2 POPs (T1s, T3s, and OC-3s) and costs due to incoming analog and integrated services digital network (ISDN) phone lines (T1 and PRI) to connect the dial-in subscribers. In addition, monthly costs for the ISP to interconnect at an NAP are included in transport costs.

The costs for the leased lines are based on published tariffs by telecommunications providers such as AT&T. Many providers offer substantial discounts for a customer, such as an ISP, that leases circuits in bulk. If the customer commits to a certain number of dollars per month, it will receive a discount according to the range in which its commitment falls. Such bulk discounts are taken into account in the model and are based on published figures by the carriers.

As with the capital equipment costs, transport costs are allocated to the various types of subscribers (e.g., ISDN primary rate interface costs are allocated entirely to the ISDN subscribers), whereas the backbone costs are allocated to each type of subscriber according to the relative amount of bandwidth required for each type of subscriber.

Customer Service

Customer service is furnished by representatives who provide technical support over the telephone to the subscribers. It is assumed that all dial-in subscribers (analog and ISDN) will be making calls to customer service. Additionally, technical representatives of subscribers with leased lines will also call customer service, but it is assumed that these subscribers will have their own internal end user support, so that the end users are not calling the ISP's customer service.

For the model, the perspective is taken that customer service is outsourced by the ISP. Hence, instead of determining how large a staff is needed, one determines how many call minutes there are and what the cost per minute is that is charged to the ISP.

Operations

Operations correspond to the routine tasks necessary to keep the ISP functioning. Operations costs fall into three principal sections: network operations and maintenance, facilities, and billing.

Network operations and maintenance costs are those for maintaining the hardware and software of the network, as well as the personnel needed to carry out these responsibilities. The costs for maintenance are based on a percentage of the total costs for the capital equipment, and the personnel costs are based on the number of people needed to maintain the given number of POPs.

Facilities costs are those associated with maintaining a physical space for each POP—for example, building rent, electricity, and heat. The costs are based on an expenditure in dollars per month for each type of POP.

The costs of billing for Internet service include those of rendering a monthly bill. There is a fixed fee for generating each bill, and each subscriber receives one bill per month.

Other Expenses

The remaining costs seen by an ISP—sales/marketing and general/administrative—are included in an "other expenses" category. Although these costs are not the focus of this study, they are nonetheless part of an ISP's costs and are included to provide a perspective relative to the other cost categories.

Sales and marketing costs—costs used to attract and retain subscribers—are based on a percentage of revenue. The value for the percentage is based on figures taken from annual reports of ISPs and other telecommunications service providers.

General and administrative (G&A) expenses consist primarily of salaries and occupancy costs for administrative, executive, legal, accounting, and finance personnel. Similar to sales and marketing costs, G&A costs are based on a percentage of total costs. The value for this percentage is also derived from annual reports of ISPs.

Internet Telephony Service Providers

Table 8.1
Revenue and cost comparison

	Magnitude	Residential	Business	ISDN	56 Kb	T1
Revenue	$26.7 million	69.9%	0.3%	1.3%	2.7%	25.8%
Cost	30.7 million	69.3	0.3	1.0	2.2	27.2

Source: Leida, 1998.

Table 8.2
Baseline scenario cost summary

Category	Cost	Distribution
Capital equipment	$3,349,000	11%
Transport	7,242,000	24
Customer service	7,927,000	26
Operations	3,445,000	11
Sales, marketing, G&A	8,725,000	28
Total monthly cost	30,688,000	

Source: Leida, 1998.

Cost Model Analysis and Interpretation

Baseline Scenario Results

The baseline scenario represents an ISP whose users are primarily browsing the Web in the 1997 time period. Table 8.1 shows the cost results for the baseline scenario. The initial conclusion—that the cost is slightly greater than the revenue—is not necessarily surprising since many ISPs have had difficulty operating profitably.

The cost and revenue distribution across the subscriber base indicates that no type of subscriber is being substantially subsidized.[12] This indicates that the market for providing Internet access services is relatively efficient and competitive.

Table 8.2 shows the results across the various cost categories. Capital equipment and operations costs each represent approximately half the

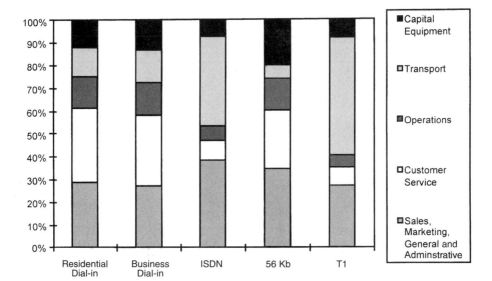

Figure 8.5
Subscriber cost distribution for baseline scenario

costs of the other three categories. In general, however, no particular cost category dominates the ISP's costs. Taken from another perspective, all cost categories play an important role in determining an ISP's costs.

Figure 8.5 shows the cost distribution for each type of subscriber. Note that this distribution varies substantially among subscriber type. For example, transport represents only a small portion of cost for dial-in subscribers but a large portion of cost for T1 subscribers. Similarly, customer service is a larger share of dial-in subscribers' cost than T1 subscribers' cost.

The baseline scenario analysis yields the following conclusions:

• No particular cost category dominates the ISP's costs.[13]

• There is a substantial variation in cost distribution among the different types of subscribers.

• The ISP's total cost distribution will vary with the subscriber mix and the individual cost distribution.[14]

• Nontechnical components represent a substantial portion of each subscriber type's costs.

• ISPs are losing money.

Baseline Scenario

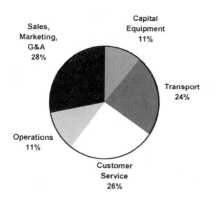

Internet Telephony Scenario

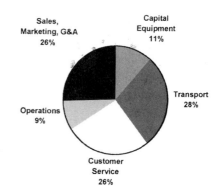

$ 30.7 Million	Cost	$ 43.5 Million
$ 26.7 Million	Revenue	$ 31.8 Million

Figure 8.6
Comparative cost results (Source: Leida 1998)

Internet Telephony Scenario Results

Comparing the Internet telephony scenario to the baseline scenario, costs in all categories increase in the Internet telephony scenario; however, some categories are affected more than others. The bottom line for an ISP is that revenues will increase slightly, while costs will increase substantially with only a moderate use of Internet telephony. Hence, ISPs need to consider how to minimize the cost impact of Internet telephony or how to recover additional revenue if they hope to operate at profitable levels (or both). The first thing to do is to consider differentiating voice service and charging per minute for that, as traditional telecommunications firms do. This is what most Internet telephony service providers do, even as the telecommunications industry faces increasing pressure to adopt simpler, Internet-style flat-rate or tiered-pricing structures.

The comparative results for the baseline and Internet telephony scenarios are shown in Figure 8.6. At 28 percent of total costs, transport costs become the largest cost category in the Internet telephony scenario. The implication for ISPs, based on this result, is that an ISP that

Table 8.3
Subscriber cost increase

	Residential	Business	ISDN	56 Kb	T1
Capital equipment	45%	45%	80%	66%	63%
Transport	75%	75%	85%	64%	64%
Customer service	44%	44%	44%	43%	44%
Operations	7%	7%	30%	26%	25%
Other expenses	7%	7%	7%	78%	78%
Total	33%	34%	48%	59%	64%
Cost	$30	$32	$126	$745	$2,375

Source: Leida, 1998.

operates its network most efficiently will have a competitive advantage over other ISPs if the Internet telephony scenario takes place. Such efficiencies could come from scale economies, facilities-based networks, or network optimization techniques. However, if one believes that the market for transport is already efficient and that transport is essentially a commodity, then there would be fewer opportunities for competitive advantage resulting from owning a network. Even so, network optimization techniques would prove advantageous whether the ISP owns or leases its network.

Subscriber costs are affected in different ways. Table 8.3 shows the percentage increase in each cost category for each subscriber type. For example, transport costs increased by 75 percent for the analog dial-in subscribers. In general, transport costs are substantially affected for each subscriber type. Costs in the "other expenses" category increase for the leased-line subscribers due to an increase in sales and marketing costs. This is based on the assumption that leased-line subscribers would purchase enough capacity to maintain their circuit at the same level for both scenarios. Hence, additional revenue is received from the leased-line subscribers in the Internet telephony scenario. Because sales and marketing costs are based on a percentage of revenue, these costs also increase.

Drawing conclusions based on comparing the change in costs between the different types of subscribers is not valid because the revenue is also changing, but only for the leased-line subscribers. One method of com-

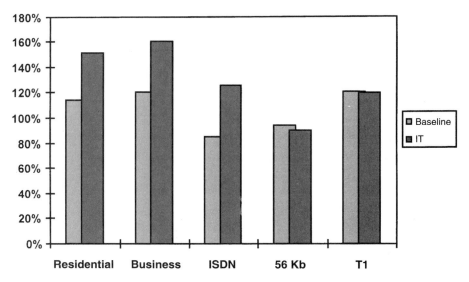

Figure 8.7
Cost/revenue ratio for baseline and IT scenarios (Source: Leida 1998)

paring the impact on the different types of subscribers is to consider a cost-revenue ratio for both scenarios, which is presented in Figure 8.7. It shows that the dial-in subscribers become particularly unprofitable, but the leased-line subscribers remain at about the same level of profitability as in the baseline scenario.

Table 8.4 shows a breakdown of the ten highest-cost elements for residential dial-in subscribers. In the IT scenario, the cost elements for the dial-in subscribers maintain a similar distribution as for the baseline scenario. Two transport cost elements (analog dial-in T1 and T1 transport) increased, but only moderately. Nontechnical costs, such as customer service, sales and marketing, and G&A, together represent 59 percent of the per user costs. Hence, as in the baseline scenario, nontechnical costs still play an important factor even in the face of Internet telephony.

As in the baseline scenario, (backbone) transport costs remain the major cost element for the T1 subscribers in the Internet telephony scenario (Table 8.5). Hence, ISPs targeting T1 subscribers can gain substantial cost savings by having the most efficient network. This is in contrast to ISPs that target analog dial-in subscribers, for example, and

Table 8.4
High cost components for residential dial-in subscribers (IT scenario)

Item	Cost	Percentage (IT)	Percentage (Baseline)
Customer service	$10.80	36%	33%
Sales and marketing	4.00	13	18
Analog modems	3.51	12	11
General and administrative	3.01	10	11
Analog dial-in T1	2.68	9	8
T1 transport	2.07	7	4
Billing	1.25	4	5
POP personnel	0.92	3	4
S/w and h/w maintenance	0.78	3	2
T3/OC-3 transport	0.42	1	4
Total of top ten items	29.43	97	

Source: Leida, 1998.

Table 8.5
High-cost components for T1 subscribers (IT scenario)

Item	Cost	Percentage (IT)	Percentage (Baseline)
T3/OC-3 transport	$1,103	46%	46%
Sales and marketing	398	17	17
General and administrative	300	13	10
Customer service	173	7	8
NAP interconnection cost	116	5	5
Cisco 7513 serial port card	78	3	3
T1 CSU/DSU	61	3	3
POP personnel	44	2	3
S/w and h/w maintenance	37	2	2
Cisco 7513 router chassis	33	1	1
Total of top ten items	2,343	99	

Source: Leida, 1998.

Internet Telephony Service Providers

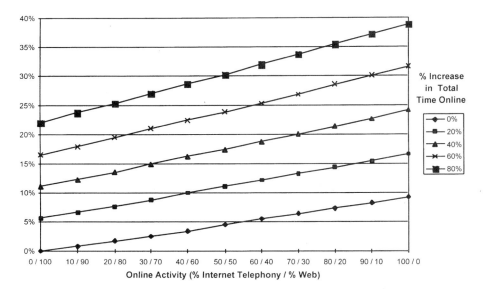

Figure 8.8
Internet telephony and usage level impact on dial-in subscriber's costs

would receive only marginal benefit by optimizing their network. For them, substantial cost savings can also be gained by targeting customer service and sales and marketing areas.

Sensitivity analysis of key parameters can provide further insight into the impact of Internet telephony on users' costs. For dial-in subscribers, modem costs are principally affected by usage patterns. In the Internet telephony scenario, it was assumed that call arrival rates and holding times each increased by 20 percent over the baseline scenario. Additionally, it was assumed that Internet telephony is used 33 percent of the time that a user is online. These two parameters could be varied independently according to various scenarios. Figure 8.8 shows how a dial-in user's total cost would change under these types of scenarios.[15]

The end result is that dial-in users can affect their costs more by increasing total time online than by spending the same amount of time online while solely using Internet telephony. Similar analysis for customer service costs of dial-in subscribers shows that a doubling of customer service requests over the baseline scenario increases total subscriber costs by approximately 35 percent. Hence, any activity that prompts a user to spend more time online and to make more customer service requests will have a substantial impact on an ISP's costs. For T1 subscribers, total costs are sensitive to changes in the usage patterns, which would seem intuitively correct because transport costs represent a large portion of T1 subscribers' costs.[16]

The Internet telephony scenario analysis yields the following conclusions:

• In the IT scenario, the increase in the ISP's costs is double the revenue increase. Hence, ISPs will lose even more money if they do not attempt to recover additional costs.

• Transport costs become the largest cost category in the IT scenario.

• Nontechnical costs still remain a large portion of per user costs, especially for dial-in subscribers.

• Dial-in subscribers' costs are sensitive to access patterns and customer service costs. T1 subscribers' costs are sensitive to bandwidth usage patterns.

Internet Telephony Pricing

ISPs face potential increased cost pressure due to Internet telephony. To a lesser extent, they also face cost pressure due to access charge reform. For ISPs to remain in business, they will need to recover these increased costs. Standards such as the resource reservation protocol (RSVP) and the differentiated services (diffserv) protocol developed by the Internet Engineering Task Force (IETF) could be used as a mechanism for implementation of usage-sensitive pricing to recover those costs.[17] However, whether and where RSVP is useful has not yet been determined. It is clear that RSVP by itself is not capable of resolving the host of network architecture and quality of service (QOS) constraints on Internet pricing models. For example, how RSVP traffic could cross multiple networks has not been resolved.

Diffserv, currently gaining more adherents, is more likely to be used in the backbone networks than in edge networks and thus may not resolve this conundrum by itself. When developing pricing schemes, service providers will have to look beyond the Internet telephony service and consider how to price differentiated and integrated Internet services generally. We argue elsewhere that an integrated regulatory framework will be required to permit the provision of such integrated services.[18]

Alternatives for pricing include flat rate or the introduction of usage-sensitive pricing. McKnight and Bailey present a variety of proposed approaches to Internet pricing, including approaches at the infrastructure level for network interconnection.[19] Experimentation with a variety of pricing models that permit service guarantees for multiple qualities of service, including guarantees for both real-time multimedia and multicast conferencing, is now required.[20]

Employment of yield management techniques, which may enable use of innovative service definitions in the face of highly variable demand to maximize revenue, should also be considered.[21] Yield management, which originated in the airline industry and is discussed further in Leida (1998), uses a combination of service definition, pricing, and admission control. The fundamental principle of yield management is that different classes of service, whether Internet access or Internet telephony, are defined, and only the high-priority classes are served during peak periods of demand. During low periods of demand, discount classes are intended to attract an increased level of demand. The consequence of such techniques is that the system's capacity is fuller on average and revenues are higher.

Additionally, one must consider the state of technology when considering cost-recovery alternatives. Usage-sensitive pricing will not be an option until protocols that monitor the use of Internet telephony are deployed widely.

Internet Telephony Policy

There are a variety of policy issues raised by Internet telephony, none of them addressed by the Telecommunications Act of 1996, which is a recipe for gridlock of a decade of litigation around the issues of the redefinition of market structures.[22] There appears to be a self-correcting quality to the degree to which policy frameworks can become misaligned with technical and economic conditions, but the time lag and social welfare loss may be substantial. Here, we focus particularly on a quantitative estimate of the costs for Internet telephony service providers. In addition, we touch briefly on the regulatory discussions surrounding Internet telephony within the European Union.

The regulatory treatment of the Internet and Internet telephony service providers has attracted substantial attention but little insight as yet. (Broader discussion of a model for a new, convergent regulatory framework, with no distinctions between wireline and wireless, narrowband and broadband, broadcast and switched service, and content and conduit, may be found in Neuman et al., 1997.)

Access Charge Reform

Telephony traditionally has been one of the most regulated industry segments in the United States. Under Federal Communications Commission (FCC) rules (specifically, the Computer II Inquiry), ISPs, being classified as "enhanced service providers," are exempt from regulations imposed on "carriers," such as long-distance telephone companies.[23] These carriers must pay per minute access charges on the order of $0.06 per minute to the local phone companies, which terminate each end of a long-distance call.[24] A trade association of telephone companies—America's Carriers Telecommunications Association (ACTA)—filed a petition with the FCC asking it to regulate Internet telephony.[25] ACTA argued that ISPs providing Internet telephony services should pay access charges to the local telephone companies, as do other long-distance service providers.

In May 1997, the FCC unveiled a reformed access charge system.[26] While not ruling explicitly on the ACTA petition, the FCC chose not to require ISPs to pay per minute access charges.[27] Instead, it imposed increased phone charges on business users, ISPs included, and residential users with a second phone line in the form of an increased subscriber line charge (SLC) and a new presubscribed interexchange carrier charge (PICC).

Under the new rules, ISPs saw an increase in cost of their analog dial-in lines. The SLC went from a cap of $5.60 per line, per month to $9.00 on January 1, 1998 (although few local exchange carriers will be able to charge as high as the cap); the average has been calculated to be $7.61,[28] and the PICC went from $0.53 to $2.75 per line, per month. Using the average charges, the impact on ISPs (or any multiline business) was a $4.23 per month increase for each analog line.[29] Plugging these updated

Table 8.6
Analog dial-in subscriber costs for four scenarios

	Baseline	Baseline with Access Reform	IT	IT with Access Reform
Capital equipment	$2.70	$2.70	$3.90	$3.90
Transport	2.98	3.44	5.21	5.86
Customer service	7.50	7.50	10.80	10.80
Operations	3.07	3.07	3.27	3.27
Other expenses	6.52	6.57	7.01	7.06
Total	22.77	23.27	30.19	30.89

Source: Leida, 1998.

costs into the ISP cost model yields an increase for the analog dial-in subscribers' cost for both the baseline and IT scenarios. Table 8.6 shows the initial results for the two scenarios compared to the results for the two scenarios with the access reform.

An alternative method of access reform could have been to implement per minute access charges for ISPs as proposed in the ACTA petition. The effect of such reform is shown in Figure 8.9. This analysis is based on the residential dial-in subscriber of the baseline scenario who spends 1,233 minutes per month online (approximately 41 minutes per day). The dial-in subscriber monthly cost is displayed as the per minute access charge is varied. The result is that access charges quickly become the dominating cost element for a dial-in subscriber. ISPs would surely have to pass this cost increase on to end users, which would have the effect of greatly impeding the continued growth in dial-in Internet services.

Although no cost increase is advantageous to ISPs, the recent FCC actions should be considered much less threatening than the potential impact of Internet telephony or of per minute access charges. A principal conclusion based on these cost results is that ISPs need to prevent widespread use of Internet telephony or change the current pricing structure of Internet access services in order to recover the increased costs.

European Internet Telephony Policymaking

Perhaps the greatest challenge for Internet telephony is how it will be treated by governments. The Internet is indeed growing in importance

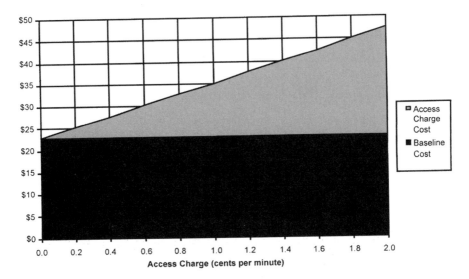

Figure 8.9
Access charge impact on dial-in user cost (Source: Leida 1998)

in the United States and has therefore been focused on at the highest levels of the U.S. government more than in most other nations. But it would be a mistake to ignore regulatory dilemmas and proposed approaches arising elsewhere. In particular, the European Commission's approach to determining policy for Internet telephony merits attention because of the obvious impact that such policies may have in enabling, or inhibiting, the continued growth of a worldwide market for advanced Internet services.

Heterogeneity has been a key characteristic of the Internet from its beginning. The question of how much heterogeneity in Internet policy is tolerable for various classes of service will soon be answered in practice by policymakers and Internet users.

The European Commission has established several criteria that Internet telephony must meet before it will be subject to regulation:[30]

• Such communications are the subject of a commercial offer.

• Such communications are provided for the public.

• Such communications are to and from the public switched network termination points on a fixed telephony network.

• Such communications involve direct transport and switching of speech in real time.

Based on these criteria, Internet telephony is not considered voice telephony because it does not meet the criterion of real-time communication due to the high levels of delay that Internet telephony users experience on the public Internet.[31] Hence, Internet telephony services in Europe are not subject to regulation at this time.

Conclusion

Internet telephony service providers confront a variety of challenges. The costs, the technologies, business and pricing models, as well as the policy environment for Internet telephony are all unsettled and in a state of rapid evolution.

So far, the FCC has taken a relatively hands-off policy approach in the United States, as has the European Union. In spite of misguided efforts in some countries to ban Internet telephony, we believe the real challenge is how to align the costs, technologies, prices, and policies to enable a rich new class of differentiated and integrated Internet services to flourish, subsequently bringing substantial benefits to consumers. Internet telephony is acting as a catalyst, restructuring the telecommunication industry. The rapid growth of new IP-based infrastructures, services, and applications resulting from these trends should benefit consumers and producers worldwide, while hastening the creative destruction of outmoded regulatory regimes, industry structures, and business practices.

Notes

We gratefully acknowledge support for this research from the MIT Internet and Telecoms Convergence Consortium (http://rpcp.mit.edu) and the Edward R. Murrow Center, Fletcher School of Law and Diplomacy, Tufts University. This chapter is a revised version of Lee W. McKnight and Brett Leida, "Internet Telephony: Costs, Pricing, and Policy," *Telecommunications Policy, 22,* pp. 555–569, 1998, which was also published in Jeffrey K. Mackie-Mason and David Waterman, eds., *Telephony, the Internet, and the Media: Selected Papers from the 1997 Telecommunications Policy Research Conference* (Hillside, N.J.: Erlbaum, 1998). The model and analysis was first developed in Brett Leida's S.M. thesis, "A Cost Model of Internet Service Providers: Implications for Internet Telephony and Yield Management" (1998, MIT).

We thank ITC staff members and companies for providing invaluable feedback by conference calls and ITC meetings. We also credit Networked Multimedia Information Services (NMIS) for partial support, NSF grant NCR-9307548, and the students of the MIT Telecommunications Modeling and Policy Analysis Seminar (TPP91) for an initial model, which was presented to the FCC in May 1996. This chapter extends slightly the model in Leida (1998) to explore the impact of FCC policy decisions on costs.

1. Ongoing work within the MIT Internet and Telecoms Convergence Consortium models Internet telephony gateways and call centers. Results of this work are not yet available.

2. More information about the ITC can be found at http:/rpcp.mit.edu/.

3. The issue of gateway traffic is not modeled here. Other ITC work is analyzing gateway issues.

4. For a more detailed description of each model parameter, see Leida (1998).

5. Further discussion about ISP architecture is found in Leida (1998).

6. The sole distinction between residential and business dial-in subscribers is varying access patterns. Residential subscribers are assumed to request access primarily in the evening and business subscribers during the day. See Leida (1998) for more details on access patterns.

7. Sources include: FIND/SVP (1996); Forrester Research Inc. Telecom Strategies Group (1996); Morgan Stanley (Technology/New Media) (1996); and *Boardwatch Magazine Directory* (1997).

8. $1.66 = 300\% \cdot 33\% + 100\% \cdot 67\%$.

9. Because the leased-line subscribers' users are "always on" the network, the concept of dialing in does not apply to them.

10. The following ISP capital equipment is considered in the model: analog modems, content housing server, 56 Kb CSU/DSU, Cisco 7513 serial port card, Fore 4 port DS3 card; ISDN access router, LAN-10Mbps ethernet, T1 CSU/DSU, Cisco 7513 ATM card, Fore 4 port OC-3 card; POP server, LAN-100Mbps ethernet, Cisco 2500 router, Cisco 7513 router chassis, and a Fore ASX-200BX ATM switch chassis.

11. See Leida (1998) for details.

12. This is in contrast to the public switched telephone network, for example, where, based on government desires, business subscribers subsidize residential subscribers.

13. However, this is true only for the mix of subscribers used in the baseline scenario. Other mixes of subscribers would yield different results.

14. Hence, if the subscriber mix changed, the ISP's cost distribution would be weighted by the number of each type of subscriber. For example, if the ISP had only T1 subscribers, its cost would be distributed just as the T1 subscribers' cost is distributed.

15. The cost increase is relative to that of the baseline scenario. Because all other costs are held constant (such as customer service, sales, and marketing), the cost increase shown

in this figure will not be the same as for the Internet telephony scenario where other costs were assumed to increase.

16. See Leida (1998) for further sensitivity analysis.

17. IETF rfc2205 (http://reference.nrcs.usda.gov/ietf/rfc2300/rfc2205.txt).

18. Neuman, McKnight, and Solomon (1997). See also McKnight, Vaaler, and Katz (2000).

19. McKnight and Bailey (1997). See also Bailey and McKnight (1997).

20. The announcement by America Online (AOL) in January 1998 that it was raising the price for its service to $21.95 per month from $19.95 per month suggests that at least one major ISP recognized that the revenue-cost equation must be brought into balance, as we argue here.

21. Paschalidis, Kavassalis, and Tsitsiklis (1997). Ideally, a company using yield management wants to maximize its profit, not just its revenue. However, in most cases where yield management is currently used, the marginal cost of providing service is very small in relation to fixed costs; hence, maximizing revenue is essentially the same as maximizing profit.

22. Neuman, McKnight, and Solomon (1997).

23. In its "Computer II Inquiry" (Federal Communications Commission, 1980), the FCC established the definition of (basic and) enhanced service providers and chose not to regulate them for reasons of public interest. Based on this definition, ISPs have always been classified as enhanced service providers (see Werbach, 1997).

24. Werbach (1997).

25. America's Carriers Telecommunication Association (1996) Students of the MIT Telecommunication Modeling and Policy Analysis Seminar 1996.

26. See Federal Communications Commission (1997a, 1997b).

27. More generally, the FCC is trying to move away from the per-minute charges that were developed in the 1980s when telephone service was generally a monopoly to a system of flat-rate charges that will be more compatible with a competitive market.

28. Federal Communications Commission (1997c).

29. ($7.61 − $5.60) + ($2.75 − $0.53) = $4.23.

30. European Commission Directorate-General for Competition (1997).

31. Short (1997).

9

Local Internet Access Networks: Economics and Policy

Daniel Fryxell, Marvin Sirbu, and Kanchana Wanichkorn

It has taken nearly thirty years for the historically analog telephone network to be transformed into today's end-to-end digital circuit-switched network. Today we are on the verge of a second revolution in telephone technology that will be every bit as radical as the conversion from analog to digital: from circuit-switched to packet-switched technology for the carriage of voice as well as data traffic. The development of technology for carrying voice traffic over Internet protocol (IP) networks has already resulted in the widespread introduction of packet-switched technology in the long-distance network at significantly reduced tariffs (Okubo et al., 1997; Thom, 1996). Avoided access charges account for part of these savings, along with the use of advanced compression techniques to reduce the bit rate of a call to as little as 8 Kbps from the standard pulse code modulation (PCM) rate of 64 Kbps. Numerous firms sell gateway products for conversion between circuit switching and voice-over-Internet protocol (Internet telephony). Several firms have introduced IP-based PBX products as well. As with the conversion from analog to digital, the last part of the network to switch from circuit to packet technology will be the subscriber loop and the residential customer.

The shift from circuit-switched to packet-switched networks is based on several converging trends. The most important is the emergence of data as the dominant form of traffic on the nation's telecommunications networks. Various commentators have set the crossover date between 1998 and 2002. Virtually all agree, however, that with voice traffic growing at only 6 to 8 percent per year while data traffic grows at 30 to 40 percent, it will take only a few years after the crossover for voice to represent but a small proportion of total telecommunications traffic. Thus, in addition to any cost or functionality benefits that may be available by carrying voice over IP networks, carriers will find it irresistible to combine voice and data on a single network in order to simplify network planning and administration.

We present an economic analysis of an IP-based local access network, providing both voice and data services. We compare the cost of this integrated packet network to the cost of a traditional public-switched telephone network (PSTN) with a second phone line used to call an ISP and describe the architecture of the proposed network, the cost model, and its results. We also discuss a number of technical and policy issues regarding the deployment of this integrated packet network.

Proposed Network

The proposed architecture envisions the concept of end-to-end IP technology with asymmetric digital subscriber loop (ADSL) in the local loop to provide complete integration of voice and Internet access (Figure 9.1). ADSL is a digital technology for the local loop that uses the existing copper infrastructure to deliver broadband data rates affordably to customer premises. This technology is attractive to incumbent local exchange carriers (LECs) since it makes use of their ubiquitous copper wire plant. ADSL delivers downstream (from the central office to the customer premises) payloads of up to 6 Mbps and upstream payloads of up to 640 Kbps on 24-gauge loops of up to 12,000 feet. For distances up to 18,000 feet, the data rates decrease to 1.5 Mbps downstream and 160 Kbps upstream. This technology provides sufficient bandwidth for multiple simultaneous Internet telephony conversations.

At the customer premises, an ADSL line terminates at a remote ADSL transceiver unit (ATU-R), which is part of the residential gateway (RG) (Holliday, 1997). The RG is the demarcation point between the customer premises equipment (CPE) and the subscriber loop network. During the initial transition to a totally IP network, RGs may contain an Internet telephony gateway function that converts between analog voice signals and Internet telephony packets. In this scenario, RGs are

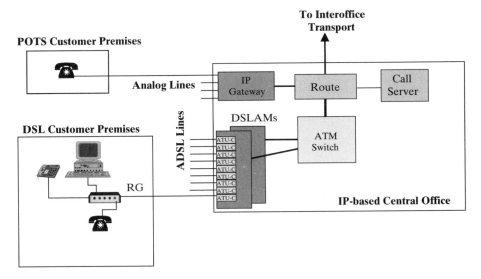

Figure 9.1
IP-based network. *Note*: POTS = plain old telephone service; DSL = digital subscriber line; IP = Internet protocol; DSLAM = digital subscriber line access multiplex; ATM = asynchronous transfer mode

equipped with RJ11 ports for analog telephone handsets and an RJ-45 port to connect ethernet-based equipment, such as a PC. In the future, the RG may be the gateway for a home area network (HAN)—a local area network (LAN) optimized for the home. In the future, handsets may send packets over the HAN as opposed to analog voice. Several technologies have been suggested for this HAN network (Freed, 1998). The Home Phoneline Networking Alliance (HomePNA) is developing ethernet technology that can run over today's in-home wiring with all its multiple taps and splices (Niccolai, 1998). The home RF (radiofrequency) alliance is developing standards for a wireless solution (SWAP: simple wireless access protocol) to the home networking problem (Ohr and Boyd-Merritt, 1998). Other groups are working on IEEE 1364 ("Firewire")–based standards for high-speed home networking that could support video as well as voice and data services. All of these home networks provide enough bandwidth for Internet telephony traffic.

Today's telephone switch consists of three main components: line cards, which terminate subscriber loops and interoffice trunks; the

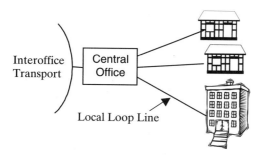

Figure 9.2
Central office area

switch fabric, which connects traffic between lines or to trunks; and the common control computer, which provides call setup and custom calling, and supports advanced intelligent network services.

The IP-based central office (CO) presented in Figure 9.2 provides the same functionality in a radically different way. At the CO, ADSL lines terminate in central office transceiver units (ATU-Cs) that are housed by digital subscriber line access multiplexers (DSLAMs), which statistically concentrate the typically bursty individual streams into high-bandwidth links. A router, which is connected to the DSLAMs via an asynchronous transfer mode (ATM)) switch, provides the logical switching function.

Currently, the most popular architecture for ADSL access networks is based on an ATM layer running over the DSL physical layer. In this model, communication channels between RGs and the router are ATM virtual circuits managed centrally at the CO. The ATM switch provides the ATM user network interface and aggregates traffic coming from different DSLAMs. Running over ATM, the IP layer provides a common communications protocol for the entire network (from CPE to interoffice transport).

Server programs running on one or more stand-alone processors provide common control functions. This element provides the necessary signaling and call control functions. Finally, an IP gateway, which converts analog voice to IP packets and vice versa, provides connection to analog voice lines. This device gives customers with less demanding communication needs the alternative to choose analog voice lines. The functionality required for the gateway can be performed by a class 5 telephone switch with an IP interface on the trunk side. Competitive subscriber loop networks provided by cable or wireless carriers could be similarly configured to provide integrated IP service.

Cost Model

Our cost model for the IP-based broadband architecture compares the cost of the proposed architecture with the cost of a traditional network solution for voice and Internet access using the PSTN. In the PSTN-based architecture, Internet access is provided by dial-in connections that make use of voice-grade modems for data transfer. Currently, the majority of Internet subscribers connect their modems using the same lines they use for voice service. However, in this chapter we assume that Internet subscribers purchase an additional phone line for the modem. We make this assumption in order to have some parallelism with the IP/ADSL architecture, where voice lines are not blocked by Internet access.

Voice and Internet access services do not necessarily have the same quality in both architectures. The speed of Internet access and the "always-on" availability, for instance, differ considerably between the two cases.

Only costs that are directly associated with the network infrastructure—the capital carrying costs and maintenance expenses—are included in the model. Expenses for operations and support, as well as marketing and other costs of running a company, are not included.

Throughout the cost model we assume a forward-looking perspective. This means that we determine the costs for a network built today with current technology. The fact that there are sunk costs in legacy LEC networks is not considered in the cost model.

General Layout

In this chapter we analyze architectures for a network of a LEC within a local access and transport area (LATA) that provides voice and Internet access service. The total area covered by the network is divided into elementary areas served by a local CO. Customer premises are connected to COs by local-loop lines, and COs are connected to each other

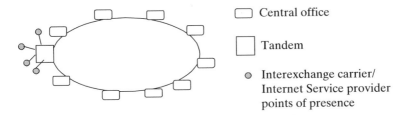

Figure 9.3
Interoffice transport

by interoffice transport facilities. COs are the interconnection point for lines in the same elementary area and the gateway to the interoffice facilities, which provide connection to locations outside the area served by the CO (Figure 9.3).

All COs are assumed connected to a single synchronous optical network (SONET) fiber ring for interoffice transport within a LATA. This configuration is not necessarily the optimal solution for any particular LATA. However, the one-ring architecture assumption provides a simple model to estimate the requirements of the interoffice transport infrastructure.

Interoffice transport facilities also include a tandem office that routes indirect channels between COs and is the gateway to the points of presence (POPs) of interexchange carriers (IXCs) and Internet service providers (ISPs). The connections between the tandem and the IXC or ISP POPs are modeled as point-to-point fiber links. Although the SONET architecture allows the provisioning of direct channels between any pair of COs, routing some connections via the tandem allows a more efficient allocation of bandwidth.

We assume that inter-LATA voice traffic and Internet access traffic are delivered to generic IXC/ISP POPs that accept both voice and Internet access traffic. In current voice networks, there are many small ISPs connected to COs instead of large ISPs connected to tandems. However, the configuration with ISPs at the tandem is more appropriate for the IP/ADSL architecture, where there is no distinction between voice and data. For comparison, we assume the same configuration for the PSTN-based architecture. By assuming that customers connect directly to a few backbone POPs, this PSTN-based architecture internalizes the costs of

Table 9.1
Average number of lines per location

	Household	Small Business Location
Number of voice lines per location	1	3
Number of dial-in lines per location (PSTN-based architecture)	1	1

the dedicated lines that small ISPs currently use to connect to Internet backbones.

Characterization of the Locations Served by the Network

The architectures we analyze are suitable for providing Internet access to households and small businesses. Medium and large corporations have access to higher capacity and more expensive networking solutions. We adopt the simplified assumption that all the customers are either residential or small businesses. In the PSTN-based architecture, the number of voice lines determines the number of loop lines for voice, and the number of dial-in lines determines the number of loop lines to an ISP for Internet access (Table 9.1). This means that two loop lines are needed per household and four loop lines per small business location. In the IP-based architecture, voice and Internet access traffic are carried over a single ADSL line; thus, only one loop is needed per household or small business location.

Traffic

We assume 50,000 voice lines per CO, of which 65 percent are residential lines and 35 percent are small business lines. The LATA has thirty equivalent COs, with a total of 1.5 million voice lines. The total number of locations with Internet access is determined by multiplying the number of locations by the Internet penetration parameter.[1]

Voice Traffic
Busy hour call attempts (BHCA) per line, call completion ratio (calls completed over calls attempted), intra-CO fraction, and tandem-routed

Table 9.2
Voice traffic

Voice Traffic	Residential	Business
Busy-hour call attempts (BHCA)	1.3	3
Call completion ratio (calls completed/calls attempted)	70%	70%
Call holding time (minutes)	3	3
Fraction of intra-CO calls	35%	35%
Fraction of intraLATA calls	50%	37%
Fraction of interLATA calls	15%	28%
Tandem routed fraction of intraLATA	10%	
Tandem routed fraction of interLATA	20%	
Data rate of an IP voice channel (Kbps)	64	

inter-LATA fractions (Table 9.2) are assumed, as suggested by Hatfield (1997). The tandem routed intra-LATA fraction is assumed as an average of the values for local and intra-LATA, as suggested by Hatfield (1997). The fractions of intra-LATA and inter-LATA traffic were estimated based on the values of dial equipment minutes (DEMs) and call completion reported by the Federal Communications Commission (FCC) for the state of Pennsylvania and Hatfield's values (Hatfield, 1997) for the business and residential DEMs ratios for local, intra-LATA, and inter-LATA traffic.

Call holding time (assumed constant) was determined as the value that made the busy-hour CSS3 (BHCCS) derived from the BHCA and the call completion fraction the same as the BHCCS derived from the DEMs, assuming a busy-hour traffic concentration factor of one-tenth of total DEMs divided by 270 business days.

Voice traffic in the IP/ADSL architecture is assumed at 64 Kbps per voice channel (ITU-T Recommendation G.711). Internet telephony standards include codecs such as G.723.1 operating at bit rates as low as 5 to 6 Kbps, but we chose to err on the side of higher bit rate voice.

Internet Access Traffic

For the dial-in architecture, Internet access traffic is expressed in common channel signaling (CCS) because the network is circuit switching. However, for the more flexible packet-based IP/ADSL architecture, this traffic is expressed as a data rate (Table 9.3).

Table 9.3
Internet access traffic

Internet Access Traffic	Residential	Business
Busy-hour activity rate	7.4%	20%
Average downlink data rate in the IP-based architecture (Kbps)	10	
Uplink data rate as a fraction of downlink data rate	10%	

Traffic assumptions for the dial-in architecture are based on a study that monitored ISP lines serving mainly residential subscribers (Morgan, 1998). ISP lines have a peak traffic around 27 CCS. This value goes down to about 20 CCS during the typical busy hours of voice networks. According to Leida (1998), ISPs size their modem access servers to have about ten residential users per modem. Based on these values, we can estimate the busy-hour probability that a given residential customer is connected to his or her ISP as

$$10\% \cdot \frac{27CCS}{36CCS} = 7.5\%,$$

with an expected usage during the peak hour of 2.7 CCS and a probability of

$$10\% \cdot \frac{20CCS}{36CCS} = 5.56\%$$

during the network busy hour (or 2 CCS per subscriber).

For the PSTN-based architecture studied here, probabilities are likely to be higher than these values because Internet subscribers have an extra line for the modem. In order to reflect this factor, we increased the activity rates by 30 percent. The activity rate for small business is assumed twice that of residential subscribers, with the business peak occurring at the voice busy hour.

We assume that the activity rates derived for dial-in connections stay the same for the ADSL architecture. The average bandwidth usage when active is assumed twice the average bandwidth for modem users, as suggested by Leida (1998). The uplink bandwidth is assumed 10 percent of the downlink bandwidth.

Table 9.4
Local-loop Lines

	Investment
Fixed cost per location passed	$413
Incremental cost per line	$205

Local Loop

We assume that local loops are all copper from the customer premises to the CO. Since ATU-Cs must be located where the copper ends, this is a necessary assumption to have all the DSLAMs located in the CO. The inclusion of digital loop carriers (DLC), which concentrate copper pairs at a remote terminal with a fiber feeder from the CO, would introduce extra complexity into the model. In that case, since copper lines would not reach the CO, DSLAMs would have to be moved from the CO to the remote terminals. Our assumption is consistent with the fact that ADSL technology is first being deployed in areas where loops are short and DLC systems have not been deployed.

Estimates for local loop investment are derived using the Hatfield model for an area (Washington, D.C.) where little use of DLC is required (Table 9.4). Thus our loop cost estimates are consistent with the assumption that all the copper lines terminate at the CO.

Loop costs include loop cable, installation, and infrastructure (conduits, poles, cable protection, and so on). Since the last two components account for a large part of the loop cost and are not very sensitive to the number of lines per location, the marginal cost of adding extra lines is considerably lower than the cost of providing the first line. Cost per location passed and incremental cost per line were estimated as the coefficients of a linear regression on the loop cost per location calculated by modifying the Hatfield model versus the number of lines per location (Table 9.4).

Central Office

IP-Based Central Office

The IP-based CO configuration is as discussed earlier. The cost model includes the elements shown in Figure 9.1 plus a main distribution frame

Local Internet Access Networks

Table 9.5
IP-based central office

Main distribution frame	
Cost per line	$17.5
DSLAM	
Cost per line	$400
Installation multiplier	1.1
Administrative fill	98%
ATU-Cs per DSLAM	200
IP gateway	
Cost per line	$100
Installation multiplier	1.1
Administrative fill	98%
ATM switch	
Common equipment	$28,000
OC-3 port	$2,000
DS-3 port	$1,000
Installation multiplier	1.1
Router	
Common equipment	$60,000
OC-3 port	$10,000
Installation multiplier	1.1
Transmission equipment	
OC-48 ADM, installed	$50,000

(MDF) and add drop multiplexers (ADMs) (Table 9.5). The MDF, the end point for the copper lines of the local loop, provides electrical protection and is the interface between the loop lines and the in-office equipment. The MDF investment is computed based on a cost per line, for which we use the value suggested in Hatfield (1997).

The values for cost and capacity of DSLAMs were derived from equipment currently available in the market. Prices of ADSL equipment still show a large variation and rapid price reductions, which are typical for new technologies in the initial phase of deployment.

IP gateways with the level of concentration required for a CO are just now emerging. Commercial products currently targeting the corporate market can terminate only a small number of voice lines. The assumption for the cost of this element, which is only a rough estimate, is based on prices of existing products, taking into consideration economies of scale.

The ATM switch and the router are sized based on the number and type of connections such that their forwarding capacities are not a bottleneck. Links between DSLAMs and the ATM switch are at the DS-3 rate, and all the links to the router are at the OC-3 rate. ATM switch and router costs were derived from current list prices with a 30 percent discount.[3]

The call server in the IP-based architecture performs functions comparable to the common control of a circuit switch in the PSTN. For this reason, the server cost was assumed as the cost of common control for an equivalent PSTN switch. This value was estimated as 70 percent of the switch common equipment (common control plus switch fabric), which was determined as total cost of the switch (computed as in Hatfield, 1997) less the cost of line and trunk cards.[4]

ADMs connect the SONET ring, which supports OC-48 circuits,[5] to the transmission equipment inside the CO. For each OC-48 circuit to which the CO is connected, there is one ADM that extracts or inserts OC-1 channels from or into the OC-48 circuit. ADMs are connected to the router by OC-3 links.[6] OC-1 channels in OC-48 circuits can be individually allocated to establish transport links between pairs of COs, COs and the tandem switch, or COs and IXC/ISP POPs.[7] Direct channels, either between pairs of COs or COs and POPs, are established only if there is enough traffic to justify it. Otherwise traffic follows an indirect path via the tandem router. Nondirect traffic shares the channels that are allocated for transport between the tandem router and COs or POPs.

PSTN-Based Central Office

The basic configuration of the PSTN network used in this chapter is derived from the Hatfield model (Hatfield, 1997).

The MDF and the ADM perform basically the same function as in the IP-based architecture. In this architecture, the basic transport channels, which are extracted (inserted) from (into) the OC-488 interoffice circuits by ADMs are DS-3s (Table 9.6). A narrowband circuit switch is at the core of this architecture. This PSTN switch establishes intraoffice connections between pairs of loop lines and interoffice connections between loop lines and interoffice trunks. The investment in switching

Table 9.6
PSTN-based central office

Main distribution frame	
Cost per line	$17.5
Transmission equipment	
DCS, per DS-3, installed	$30,000
OC-3/DS-1 TM, installed	$26,000
OC-48 ADM, installed	$50,000
Maximum transmission fill	80%
Switch	
A_{switch}	−14.9
B_{switch}	242.7
Line administrative fill	98%
Cost per trunk port	$100
Maximum trunk occupancy (CCS)	27.5
Switch installation multiplier	1.1

equipment is determined by adding the investment in line cards, common equipment (including switch fabric and common control), and trunk ports using costs found in Hatfield (1997).

Grooming equipment for the CO includes digital cross-connect systems (DCSs) and terminal multiplexers (TMs). These elements are sized according to the interoffice traffic, which is computed based on the assumptions for traffic generation and routing. DCSs cross-connect DS-1 trunks between the switch and TMs. TMs, which provide an interface to the switch at the DS-1 level, multiplex DS-1 circuits into the DS-3 channels used in interoffice transport.

Interoffice Cable

The total length of an interoffice ring is determined by summing the lengths of the ring that cross each CO area. In order to estimate the dimensions of each CO area, we assume that these areas are square and there is a uniform line density throughout the LATA of 5,000 lines per square mile. The distance that the ring crosses within each CO area is the side of the square multiplied by a factor of 1.5, which accounts for the fact that the route of the cable is not a straight line. The tandem

Table 9.7
Interoffice transport

Network Infrastructure	Cost
24-fiber interoffice cable (per foot)	$3.5
24-fiber increment (per foot)	1.2
Interoffice cable infrastructure (per foot)	1.1

office is assumed connected to five different IXC/ISP POPs by links that are half a mile long.

The number of fiber strands per cable is a multiple of twenty-four. Each circuit in the ring requires two strands, and each point-to-point circuit, such as the ones between the tandem and the IXC/ISP POPs, requires four strands. We assumed no use of dense wavelength division multiplexing (DWDM).

The costs of fiber cable and cable infrastructure (protection, poles, conduits, and installation) shown in Table 9.7 are the aggregate values of all the subelements into which they can be decomposed (for a more detailed description, see Fryxell, 1998).

Tandem Office

At the core of the tandem office is a router (or a switch for the PSTN-based architecture) that provides the logical switching functionality to handle nondirect intra-LATA and inter-LATA traffic. The tandem office has ADMs that extract or insert basic OC-1 transport channels from or into the SONET ring. These channels include direct channels between COs and IXC/ISP POPs and channels between COs and the tandem router (or switch). Direct channels are physically cross-connected from the ADMs to the links connecting the tandem to the IXC/ISP POPs. Channels between COs and the tandem router (or switch) carry intra-LATA and inter-LATA traffic that, for a more efficient allocation of channels, is indirectly routed via the tandem router (or switch).

The cable links between the tandem and the IXC/ISP POPs use OC-3 circuits. It is not cost-effective to multiplex OC-3 circuits into a higher-capacity OC-48 circuit because these links are very short. Savings in fiber would be outweighed by the extra cost in ADMs. Since these links carry

Table 9.8
IP-based tandem office

Router	
Common equipment	$60,000
OC-3 port	$10,000
Installation multiplier	1.1
Transmission equipment	
OC-48 ADM, installed	$50,000

Table 9.9
PSTN-based tandem office

Switch	
Cost per trunk	$100
Minimum common equipment cost (0 trunks)	$500,000
Maximum common equipment cost (100,000 trunks)	$1,000,000
Switch installation multiplier	1.1
Maximum transmission fill	80%
Transmission equipment	
OC-3/DS-1 TM, installed	$26,000
OC-48 ADM, installed	$50,000
Maximum transmission fill	80%

both direct and tandem-routed traffic, some of the OC-3 circuits come directly from the ADMs, while the rest come from the tandem router (or switch).

IP-Based Tandem Office
In the IP approach, the architecture for the tandem office consists of a router and ADMs. All the links to the router are at the OC-3 level (Table 9.8).

PSTN-Based Tandem Office
In the PSTN-based architecture, the tandem office consists of a circuit switch, ADMs, and TMs (Table 9.9). TMs provide interfaces between the switch and the ADMs, and the switch and the links to IXC/ISP POPs.

Table 9.10
Customer premises equipment

Equipment	Cost
IP-based architecture	$500
PSTN-based architecture	100

The tandem switch investment was determined as in Hatfield (1997). This investment is the sum of two components: an investment in trunk ports based on a fixed cost per trunk and an investment in common equipment that scales linearly with the number of trunk ports.

Other Equipment

Customer Premises Equipment

In the IP-based architecture, the residential gateway is the only CPE included in the cost model (Table 9.10). The cost for this element was determined based on prices of small ISDN routers with analog telephone ports. In the PSTN-based approach, CPE for Internet access is a 56 Kbps modem. The cost of this element was derived from typical prices paid in retail stores.

Analog telephone handsets are also necessary for both architectures, but this low-cost element is not included in the cost model.

In-Building Wiring

The cost model for the IP architecture excludes HAN and CPE costs except for the residential gateway. With SWAP or the HomePNA, these costs will be minimal. By contrast, retrofitting a home for LAN service over CAT5 cabling can easily cost more than one thousand dollars (Bill, 1998).

ISP Equipment

Because the network analyzed in this chapter is a local network, equipment located at IXC/ISP POPs should be out of its scope. However, the IP-based and PSTN-based architectures differ substantially regarding the way inter-LATA traffic is delivered to ISP POPs. While in the former case Internet access traffic is already delivered in IP packets over high-

Table 9.11
ISP equipment

Terminal multiplexers	
Investment per DS-1/DS-3 TM	$8,700
Maximum transmission fill	80%
Remote access servers	
Investment per modem	$250
Administrative fill	98%

capacity circuits, in the latter case traffic is delivered as modem signals over voice lines. For a fair comparison, we include the elements that make the conversion from analog signals over voice lines to data packets over high-speed data lines. These elements are remote access servers, which are banks of modems and access routers, and the TMs that provide an interface to these servers at the DS-1 level (Table 9.11).

The investment per modem for remote access servers was derived from list prices with a discount of 30 percent. The investment per DS-3 TM is estimated as one-third of the investment per OC-3 TM.

Capital Carrying Costs and Maintenance Expenses

Capital carrying costs are determined based on equipment service lives. For the LEC part of the network, with the exception of switching equipment, we use the lives adjusted for net salvage value proposed in Hatfield (1997)[8]. Reflecting the current rate of change in the industry, a value of ten years, rather than sixteen, for switching equipment seems more appropriate for a forward-looking perspective. Moreover, this value is consistent with the life of transmission equipment.

The annual maintenance expense for each of the network elements is determined as the initial cost of the element times its respective expense factor (Table 9.12). Expense factors were derived from historic expense ratios for Bell operating companies,[9] as reported on their balance sheets and expense account information.[10] As suggested in Hatfield (1997), expense factors for switching and transmission equipment are forward-looking values derived from a New England Telephone cost study.[11]

Economics and Costs

Table 9.12
Lives and maintenance expenses for network equipment

	Adjusted Projection Life (years)	Expense Factor
Switching	10	2.7%
Digital circuit equipment	10	1.5
Interoffice fiber cable	23	7.2
Interoffice cable infrastructure	24	3.6
local loops	28	3.7
CPE equipment	10	1.5
ISP equipment (modems and TMs)	10	1.5

Table 9.13
Rate of return on investment

Investment	Rate of Return
Network equipment	10%
CPE	15
ISP equipment	20

Service lives for CPE and ISP equipment are assumed to be ten years (the same as for LECs' switching and transmission equipment). In reality, ISPs use much shorter periods—on the order of three or four years—to depreciate their investment in communications equipment. However, we chose this value in order to have only one life for all the transmission equipment in the network.

The rate of return for the LEC part of the network (Table 9.13) was determined by weighting the return on equity and the return on debt by their respective fractions, as given by Hatfield (1997). The rate of return for ISP equipment is the value suggested in Leida (1998).

Results and Sensitivity Analyses

Monthly Cost per Customer Location
Figure 9.4 compares monthly costs per customer location between the PSTN and the IP/ADSL architectures. The total cost of the IP/ADSL

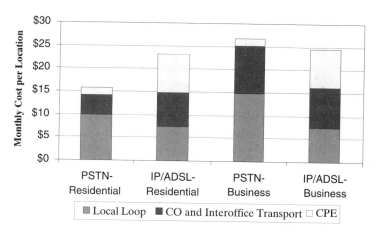

Figure 9.4
Average monthly cost per customer location

architecture is higher than for the PSTN architecture for residential customers but lower for business customers. For both residential and business customers, local loop costs are lower in the IP/ADSL architecture because fewer loops are required. However, for residential customers, these savings are not large enough to offset the higher investment in CPE and CO equipment. On the other hand, for business customers, the savings due to fewer loops outweigh the higher investment in CPE and CO equipment, resulting in a lower total cost for the IP/ADSL architecture.

Figure 9.5 shows the cost breakdown of CO equipment and interoffice transport for the IP-based architecture. It is apparent that DSLAM costs dominate.

Sensitivity Analysis of Residential Gateway and DSLAM Costs
Figure 9.6 presents a two-way sensitivity analysis of the combined effect of variations in residential gateway and DSLAM costs on the monthly cost. The PSTN is preferred when residential gateway and DSLAM costs are high, and IP/ADSL is preferred when the opposite is true. At the default values of $500 for the residential gateway cost and $400 for DSLAM cost, IP/ADSL architecture is preferred for business customers, but PSTN is preferred for residential customers. According to the analysis shown here, we can expect that the IP/ADSL architecture will be

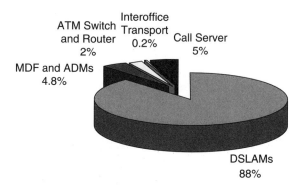

Figure 9.5
IP-based CO and interoffice transport cost breakdown

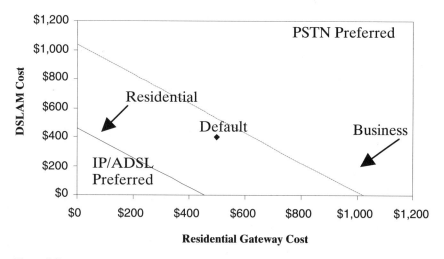

Figure 9.6
Preference regions as a function of residential gateway and DSLAM costs

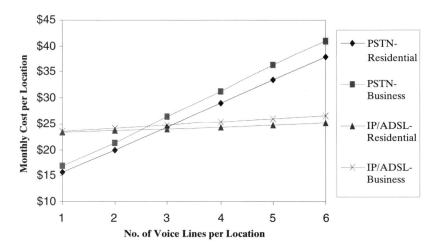

Figure 9.7
Monthly cost as a function of number of voice lines per location

cost-effective for residential customers if residential gateway and DSLAM costs continue to decline.

Sensitivity Analysis of the Number of Voice Lines per Location
Figure 9.7 shows monthly cost per location as a function of the number of voice lines. Breakeven is at 3.0 lines for residential customers and 2.6 lines for business customers. For our default values of 1.0 line per home and 3.0 lines per business location, PSTN is preferred for residential customers, and IP/ADSL is preferred for business customers.

In the PSTN scenario, costs increase proportionally with an increase in the number of voice lines because more loops are required to the customer premises. On the other hand, costs are insensitive in the IP/ADSL case because a single high-speed digital subscriber line can support multiple telephone conversations simultaneously, thereby obviating the need for additional loops to provide additional voice channels.

Sensitivity Analysis of Bandwidth Usage
Figure 9.8 shows cost per location as a function of average bandwidth usage for Internet access. Results are very clear that costs are basically fixed and barely change with bandwidth usage. However, it is important

Economics and Costs

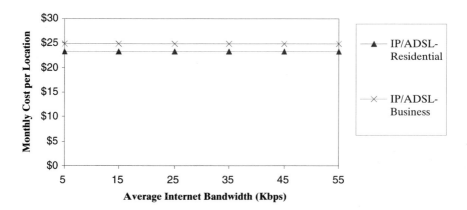

Figure 9.8
Monthly cost per location as a function of internet bandwidth usage

to note that these costs are for the local infrastructure. Internet backbone costs are certainly more sensitive to this parameter. The PSTN architecture is circuit switching, and therefore bandwidth usage in the local exchange area is not a question. Dial-in connections always use the entire circuit independent of the actual data transferred. Costs are similarly insensitive to the bandwidth use per voice channel, as shown in Figure 9.9.

Sensitivity Analysis of Internet Penetration Rate
The results shown are based on the assumption that all homes and business locations in the serving area require both voice and data services. In reality, some may need only a basic voice service. Figure 9.10 illustrates the changes in requirements if not all residential and business customers subscribe to an Internet access service. In the PSTN case, not subscribing to the Internet means dropping the extra dial-in line; in the IP/ADSL case, it means using analog voice lines terminated at the IP gateway (Figure 9.1).

Average costs per location are plotted in Figures 9.11 (residential) and 9.12 (business) against Internet penetration. These costs are the weighted average values between the cost per location with Internet access and the cost per location without Internet access, that is, the average costs per location faced by an LEC at a given value of Internet penetration.

Local Internet Access Networks

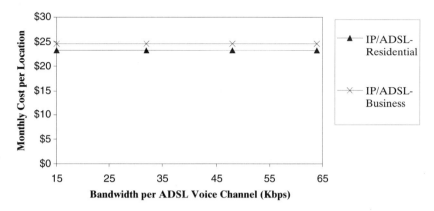

Figure 9.9
Monthly cost per location as a function of BW/voice channel

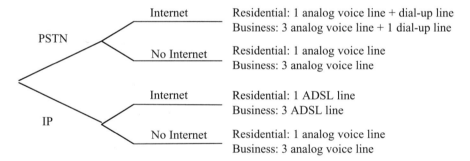

Figure 9.10
Customer characteristics

Economics and Costs

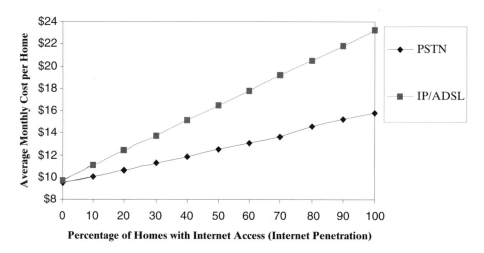

Figure 9.11
Monthly cost per home as a function of Internet penetration

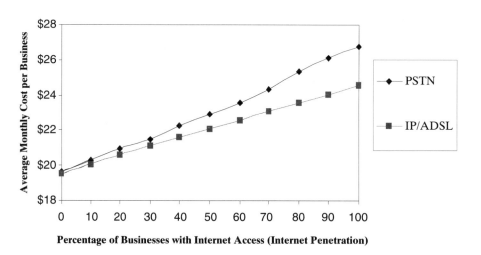

Figure 9.12
Monthly cost per business as a function of Internet penetration

At 0 percent (no home has Internet access), costs of both PSTN and IP/ADSL are approximately the same. Both PSTN and IP/ADSL costs increase almost linearly with an increase in Internet penetration rate. However, IP/ADSL costs increase at a higher rate (steeper slope), resulting in a higher cost at any given value of Internet penetration rate. Costs of PSTN and IP/ADSL for business customers (Figure 9.12) are about the same at 0 percent. However, in contrast to the residential results, PSTN costs increase at a higher rate, making IP/ADSL always preferable for business customers.

Note that the values at 100 percent correspond to the results shown in Figure 9.4. IP/ADSL is not cost-effective for residential customers at our projected equipment costs. Although it requires fewer loops to the homes, savings in loop costs are not high enough to justify the higher investment in CPE and CO equipment. IP/ADSL is cost-effective for business customers because savings in loop costs more than offset higher CPE and CO equipment costs. Results shown in this section confirm that this finding still holds true no matter how high or low the Internet penetration rate is.

Conclusion

Even without the additional revenue that an LEC might be able to earn for provisioning superior Internet service via DSL, in a greenfield setting, an integrated IP/ADSL network is cost-effective for small businesses simply on the basis of lower loop and interoffice transport costs. If the costs of premises gateways and DSLAMs continue to decline, we can expect that an IP/ADSL architecture eventually will be cost-effective for residences as well. Moreover, we have not examined any potential benefit to consumers of an IP/ADSL service in the form of lower interexchange calling costs. Elsewhere, we have shown that these can be substantial (Wanichkorn and Sirbu, 1998).

These results suggest that small businesses, Centrex users, and multiple dwelling units might be the first customers targeted by an LEC seeking to migrate to an integrated packet network. The transition from circuit switching to Internet telephony raises a number of technical and policy issues that will also have to be addressed before the conversion can become widespread.

Technical Issues

While it is possible to put together proof-of-concept systems using currently available technology, widespread diffusion will require resolution of a number of still-unresolved issues.

Internet Quality of Service

Today's public Internet provides only a "best-effort" level of service. At peak hours, packet delay and loss rates, particularly at exchange points between carriers, can be significant. There are two approaches to dealing with the QOS problem. Many of today's Internet telephony service providers carry the traffic over private internets, where loads are managed to ensure minimal packet delays. At the same time, new protocols to provide differentiated service over the public Internet are being discussed within Internet standards' bodies. Agreement on standards, and their deployment among the diverse carriers comprising the Internet, will take several years. Furthermore, the introduction of differentiated services requires differentiated prices. New pricing and billing mechanisms will be needed to accompany the introduction of differentiated QOS (Clark, 1997). Finally, the reliability of today's Internet—as measured by the frequency and severity of service outages—still does not meet the standards of today's PSTN.

Operations Support

As the faltering rollouts of ISDN demonstrated, the development of operational support systems—including network management, ordering, provisioning, and billing—can stall the deployment of a technology that works perfectly at small scale. Because so many elements of the network will change, many new operations systems will be required.

Directory Services

Voice telephone users today are identified using the ITU's E.164 standard for telephone numbers. Internet telephony end points use Internet addresses. In order for callers to be able to identify those using a uniform name space, most Internet telephony phones will be assigned an E.164 number as an alias. This then poses the need for a directory service that maps E.164 numbers into the appropriate Internet address. For Internet telephony users who wish to reach callees on the legacy PSTN, there must be an equivalent service for mapping the callee's E.164 number into the IP address of the most appropriate gateway. Standards for these directory services have yet to be developed. Moreover, as the current controversy over domain names demonstrates, developing a worldwide infrastructure for name space management is no easy task.

Policy Issues

Power and Emergency Service

Today's telephone service is powered from the central office and continues to function when the electric utility fails. However, residential gateways and Internet telephony handsets are likely to draw considerably more power than today's telephones, requiring connection to household power outlets. Thus, during an electric utility outage, the telephone might not operate. Potential solutions to this problem include backup battery power integrated into the residential gateway or substantial reductions in the power consumption of both an Internet telephony handset and gateway that would allow both to be powered from the central office. It is not clear whether home area networks based on the HomePNA standards will support powering through the home wiring. For the case where the HAN is based on wireless technology, such as SWAP, we can assume that the handsets are already battery powered. However, the need to power the DSL remote and the wireless base station remains.

Competition in Vertical Services

In the PSTN, the local telephone central office integrates the line card, switching fabric, and common control processor into a monolithic telephone switch. In the Internet telephony world, switching and common control functions may be physically, and even administratively, separated. Thus, it is perfectly feasible for a subscriber to purchase DSL and ISP service from vendor A, while contracting with vendor B for all of the vertical services traditionally associated with a telephone call—services such as callerID, call forwarding, three-way calling, voice mail, or advanced intelligent network services. This will have important consequences for the profitability of local service vendors. Currently, vertical services, such as custom calling features, are highly profitable, providing a subsidy to basic access (Huber, 1997). Increased competition for the provision of these vertical services should lead to a reduction in their profitability and a corresponding need to raise basic access prices closer to cost.

Competition in the provision of vertical services also raises technical questions. The ITU-T standards framework for Internet telephony, H.323, defines a gatekeeper function as the locus of vertical service provision. However, the standards as currently drafted do not easily accommodate the notion that subscribers might switch between multiple gatekeepers at will or even use multiple gatekeepers simultaneously for different services. The use of multiple gatekeepers for different purposes would also complicate the provisioning of E.164 to IP directory services.

E.164 Number Management

The average residence today has 1.2 telephone lines. However, in an Internet telephony environment, the number of distinct simultaneous voice calls is limited only by the upstream bit rate, which can easily support a half-dozen calls. Under these circumstances, residences may choose to acquire multiple E.164 numbers—one for each person or extension in the home. This could easily lead to even more rapid exhausting of number space in the North American numbering plan. Alternatively, as with ISDN, a single E.164 phone number may be associated with multiple call appearances on different handsets. This conserves numbers at the expense of requiring consumers to learn some new conventions for call management.

Availability of DSL

The future of DSL as a service offering of the LECs faces significant regulatory uncertainty. The FCC has recently issued a Notice of Proposed Rulemaking, which presents the LECs with an uncomfortable choice: They can provision DSL service on an integrated basis, in which case they will be subject to the unbundling requirements that mandate that the service be made available to competitors at regulated TELRIC rates. Or they can provide DSL on an unregulated basis through a separate subsidiary. In that case, the separate subsidiary must acquire copper loops pursuant to the parent's UNE tariffs. This would force the LECs to become serious about UNE provisioning, which would then open the door to competitive local exchange carriers that wish to provide DSL service on a competitive basis using the same UNE loops (FCC, 1997).

Notes

Support for this research was provided in part by a grant from Bellcore. The opinions expressed in this chapter are those of the authors and do not reflect the views of Bellcore or Carnegie Mellon.

1. We use a default of 100 percent, implying that all household and business locations in the serving area purchase Internet access.

2. Hundreds of call seconds. One circuit occupied during one hour is equivalent to thirty-six CCS.

3. For list prices, see http://www.networkcomputing.com/.

4. For this purpose, the cost per line card is assumed to be $60.

5. An OC-48 circuit carries 48 OC-1 channels at 51,840 Mbps each, for an aggregate data rate of 2,488,320 Mbps.

6. An OC-3 circuit carries 3 OC-1 channels.

7. An OC-48 circuit carries 48 DS-3 channels, which is equivalent to 1,344 DS-1s or 32,256 DS-0 voice channels.

8. These values are based on the average projection lives as determined by the three-way meetings (FCC, State Commission, and ILEC) for the regional Bell operating companies and SNET.

9. The numbers were calculated as the average of the values for the states of Pennsylvania, California, and Maryland and the District of Columbia

10. This information may be found on the ARMIS report, which is in the appendix of the Hatfield model.

11. New England Telephone, 1993 New Hampshire Incremental Cost Study, provided in compliance with New Hampshire Public Utility Commission Order Number 20, 082, Docket 89-010/85-185, March 11, 1991.

10

Internet Telephony in the Corporation

Kanchana Wanichkorn and Marvin Sirbu

Internet telephony, or low-bandwidth voice transmission over Internet protocol (IP) networks, offers a number of features of interest to business and consumer users. By having local Internet connections, Internet telephony users can make a long-distance call for the price of a local call. Companies with offices across countries, as well as across continents, can use their corporate networks and Internet telephony to handle their long-distance calls and save on long-distance charges. In addition to the ability to bypass the long-distance carrier, Internet telephony also allows companies to integrate their voice and data network by overlaying the voice network on top of the IP data network. This integration has the power to invoke fundamental shifts in business behavior since an integrated voice-data network can deliver a broad range of applications not possible using traditional separate voice and data networks—for example, desk-to-desk videoconferencing. An integrated network may potentially reduce management and maintenance costs by eliminating the need to maintain two separate networks.

This chapter presents an economic analysis of corporate Internet telephony. A cost model was developed to estimate the impact of installing an IP-PBX on the cost of premises, local, and long-distance calling and to compare it with the cost of traditional Centrex service.[1] The installation of an IP-PBX enables the use of Internet telephony over an existing corporate local area network, thus allowing a complete integration of corporate voice and data networks. The analysis estimates the impact of installing an IP-PBX on the cost of premises, local, and long-distance calling. Results show that an IP-PBX is more expensive than traditional Centrex when only premises telephony costs are considered. This is largely due to the current high costs of gateway equipment to interface an IP-PBX to the public switched telephone network (PSTN), which are projected to decline sharply over time.

The higher short-run costs of an IP-PBX can be offset by savings in toll calls, particularly for medium and large firms. These savings are largely obtained on intracorporate calls, which are assumed to travel entirely as IP between IP-PBXs at each end. Internet telephony interexchange carriers (ITXCs) currently provide low-cost toll services. They realize cost savings through the avoidance of access charges paid by traditional IXCs. Both Centrex and IP-PBX users may make use of an ITXC to lower toll calling costs. However, an IP-PBX user, by delivering calls already in packet form, enables the ITXC to avoid incoming gateway costs. We hypothesize that these savings, because of competitive forces, will eventually be passed on to consumers. Thus, users of an IP-PBX can expect to pay lower toll calling costs than a Centrex user wherever such ITXC services are available.

IP-PBXs are not as reliable or available as conventional alternatives, nor do they provide the full range of features found on the most advanced PBX and Centrex systems. They do present some advantages, however, with low-cost support for interactive voice response and unified messaging.

Corporate Internet Telephony

IP-PBX Architecture

In a traditional PBX (Figure 10.1), telephone handsets are connected by twisted wire pairs to a central PBX box. Inside the box there are:

• Line cards, which convert traffic from the handsets into the internal format needed for switching

• Trunk cards, which interface to the PSTN via analog or digital trunk lines

• A switching fabric for making connections between line cards for premises calls or between line and trunk cards for off-premises calls

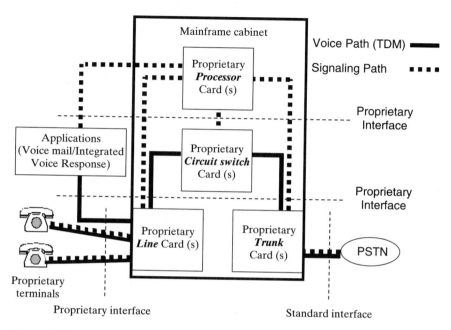

Figure 10.1
Traditional PBX architecture

• A computer control system, which manages call setup and provides advanced features

In order to provide auxiliary services such as voice mail or automated attendant, a computer server, which functions as a voice station, must interface with line cards on the PBX.

An IP-PBX blows apart this conventional model (Figure 10.2). In place of line cards, there are station gateways or terminal adapters to convert standard handsets to IP. Alternatively, the handset itself produces voice over IP (VOIP). Or, in lieu of a traditional handset, one could even use a PC equipped with sound card, headset, and appropriate software. In place of trunk cards, there are trunk gateways. In place of a circuit switching fabric, there is simply an IP network infrastructure. Finally, the processor and call management applications reside on a standard PC running call control software.

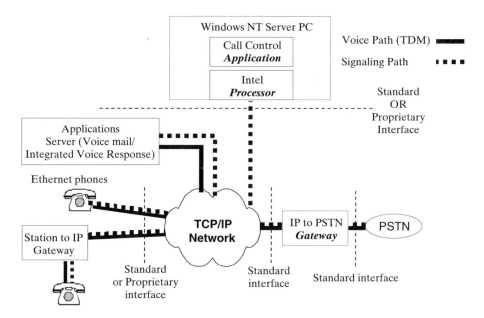

Figure 10.2
IP PBX

Established firms such as Cisco, 3Com, LM Ericsson, and Nokia have all acquired IP PBX startups and are offering products in competition with independents such as Shoreline Teleworks, Alti-Gen, and 8×8.[2]

This new architecture has several important implications. First, the office local area network (LAN), not twisted pair wiring, is the primary network for linking phones on premise. Second, phones linked as a single logical PBX can be distributed anywhere across the global Internet or intranet; the only requirement is that the IP network provide adequate capacity and quality of service for handling voice traffic. Third, call control need not be located adjacent to the handsets or gateways. For example, 8×8 corporation is promoting a hosted IP-PBX model in which an Internet Service Provider (ISP) or other third party runs the call control server in a secure machine room at the ISP in support of phones and terminal adapters at the customer premises.[3] Finally, enhanced services, such as voice mail or integrated voice response (IVR), can be provided with a simple computer server, without the need

Internet Telephony in the Corporation

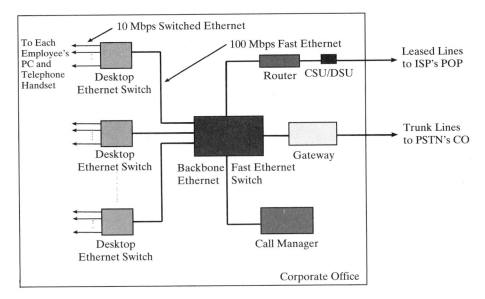

Figure 10.3
LAN network architecture

for special speech digitizing hardware, because the speech has already been digitized by handsets and gateways. In call center applications, an IP-PBX easily supports a PC running a soft phone application, which facilitates integration of calling data (e.g., caller ID) with customer support software.

For the purposes of cost modeling, we assume the firm has an LAN based on switched ethernet (Figure 10.3). Our model assumes a central 100 Mbps, fast ethernet switch as the backbone, connected to an exterior router, and a set of local ethernet switches. The local switches provide at least 10 Mbps to every office outlet. The router connects to a channel service unit/data service unity (CSU/DSU) that has an interface with leased lines to the ISP's point of presence (POP).[4] All of the data network equipment and wiring costs are assumed sunk and therefore not part of the cost of an IP-PBX.

IP-PBX costs include the costs of terminals, trunk gateways, and the call manager. The gateway converts premises IP telephony to traditional analog or digital voice signals and routes them to the PSTN over voice

Economics and Costs

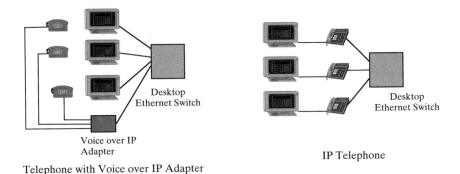

Telephone with Voice over IP Adapter

IP Telephone

Figure 10.4
End user equipment configuration

trunks. The gatekeeper or call manager provides services such as address translation (mapping a phone number with an IP address), admission control, and directory services.

The connection between the desktop ethernet switch and the telephone handset depends on the type of handset to be used. Two configurations are considered in this chapter (Figure 10.4):

Traditional telephone with voice-over IP adapter. Each telephone handset is connected by telephony twisted pair wiring into a port on a VOIP adapter.[5] The adapter then connects to the desktop ethernet switch and is typically located adjacent to it in the wiring closet. Each employee's computer also connects directly to the desktop ethernet switch.

IP telephone. An IP telephone operates externally like a traditional telephone but contains embedded VOIP hardware and an ethernet network interface.[6] Therefore, it can be attached directly to the LAN. Typically the network interface includes an uplink port for connecting to the ethernet switch and a downlink port so that the user's computer can share a single office ethernet outlet via the handset. Companies such as 8×8 and Lucent have reduced all the logic necessary for an IP phone to a single chip with processor, digital signal processors (DSP), network interface, and keyboard and display drivers.

A critical issue for an IP-PBX is emergency power provisioning. A traditional PBX or Centrex powers handsets over the twisted pair wiring. The PBX itself would have an uninterruptible power supply (UPS) to

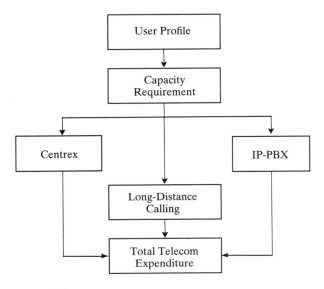

Figure 10.5
Model organization flowchart

enable both the central unit and the telephones it supports to work through a power outage. Providing comparable capability for an IP-PBX is more difficult. All active equipment in the corporate LAN, such as ethernet switches, as well as trunk gateways and the call manager PC, would need to be on a UPS. As for handsets, category 5 cabling, commonly used for ethernet wiring, has pairs designated for providing power from the wiring closet to terminal devices, though this is rarely implemented. Alternatively, a terminal adapter located in the data closet and backed up by a UPS could provide power over traditional twisted pair to a conventional handset. Providing a UPS in every data closet is more costly to acquire and to maintain than the central UPS used for a traditional PBX.

Cost Model Description

Figure 10.5 shows the basic submodules of our cost model.[7]

User Profile
The user profile module contains information about network users and traffic patterns (shown in Table 10.1). The number of users was varied

Table 10.1
Model parameters and default values

Parameter Name	Default Value	Parameter Name	Default Value
User information		*Equipment cost*	
No. of users (small, medium, large location)	20, 100, 200	*Handset*	
No. of users per computer	1	Centrex telephone handset	$150
No. of users per voice line	1	IP telephone handset	$395
Data traffic information		Time to install an IP telephone handset	30 minutes
Average data rate per computer	5 Kbps	*VOIP gateway and call manager cost*	
Percentage active in peak hour	100%	2-port gateway	$2,995
Fraction of internal data traffic	0.5	4-port gateway	$3,995
Voice traffic information		8-port gateway	$4,995
Average call length, minutes	3	24-port gateway	$10,000
Peak combined calls per hour	10	Call manager server and software	$14,995
Peak-to-average number of calls ratio	3	Discount received from vendor	20%
Fraction of internal calls	0.2	Time to install VOIP equipment	8 hours
Inbound-to-outbound calls ratio	1	*Uninterrupted power supply*	
Fraction by type of inbound/outbound calls		48V DC UPS for 48 VOIP handsets	$1,400
Local calls	0.5	110V UPS (one per telecom closet)	$700
Intracorporate calls	0.2	Network computers per telecom closet	48
Toll calls	0.3	*Maintenance, move, and change cost*	

Data rate of an IP voice channel	15 Kbps
Grade of service	1%
PSTN local calling cost	
Centrex rate (low estimate, base, high estimate)	
Installation per line (low estimate, base, high estimate)	$40, $70, $100
Monthly rate per line	$30, $50, $70
Trunk price (low estimate, base, high estimate)	$40, $70, $100
Installation per trunk line	$40, $70, $100
Monthly rate per trunk line	$25, $55, $75
ISP leased line (installation, monthly cost)	
128 Kbps	$2,200, $750
256 Kbps	$2,400, $1,100
512 Kbps	$2,600, $1,600
T1	$4,500, $2,300
2xT1	$9,000, $4,600
Multiplier for premium ISP service	1.2
Centrex case	
Maintenance plan purchased from PSTN (low estimate, base, high estimate)	$2, $3, $5
No. of moves and changes per line per year	0.5
Time spent per move and change	30 minutes
VOIP case	
Maintenance cost (% of equipment cost)	10%
Move and change (time spent per line per month)	30 minutes
Reduction in assistance time after first year	50%
Long-Distance calling cost	
IXC rate	$.07 per minute
Dial-in gateway ITXC rate	$.055 per minute
Remote gateway ITXC rate	$.035 per minute
Fraction of traffic routed via IXC	0.2
Personnel cost ($50,000 per year)	$25 per hour
Cost of capital	10% per year
Economic life of equipment	3 years

from 20 to 200 representing small, medium, and large locations. The default traffic values represent averages for corporate users. Individual firms may exhibit patterns that differ substantially from these averages.

Capacity Requirement Module
The capacity requirement module analyzes traffic pattern and determines the appropriate type of PSTN and ISP connection. The following major steps are performed in this module:

1. Determine the number of internal voice lines and data lines required for the network.

2. Estimate the average required bandwidth for voice and data traffic at the backbone and to and from the ISP.

3. Calculate peak voice traffic intensity, and determine the minimum number of required trunk lines to the PSTN based on Erlang B statistics.[8]

4. Select the appropriate gateway capacity and the corresponding number of trunk lines to the PSTN.

5. Select the appropriate capacity ISP connections.

Module Assumptions

• Low bandwidth Internet telephony—approximately 15 Kbps per voice channel.

• One percent grade of service (probability of call blocking) used to determine the minimum number of trunk lines to the PSTN.

• Gateways come with various numbers of ports. It is assumed that gateways are available with two lines, six lines, and in increments of six lines up to ninety-six lines. Given the minimum number of trunk lines needed to provide the required grade of service, the model will choose the next higher available gateway capacity and adjust the number of trunk lines to the corresponding gateway capacity.[9]

• The available ISP access capacities are 128 Kbps, 256 Kbps, 512 Kbps, T1, and 2xT1.

Centrex Module
The Centrex module calculates the cost of using Centrex service. Start-up cost, monthly charge for local calls, and maintenance costs are estimated.

Module Assumptions and Default Values

• Since different local exchange carriers use different Centrex pricing schemes, three estimates of Centrex price are used in the model.[10]

• Start-up cost includes handset cost and Centrex installation. It is assumed that each telephone handset costs $150 and the company does not require new inside telephone wiring.[11]

• Monthly charges include Centrex basic rate, usage charges for local calls, touchtone charges, 911 charges, and tax.

• The model assumes that the corporation buys a maintenance plan that covers inside wiring maintenance from the phone company. Moves, adds, and changes (MAC) are estimated at 0.5 per line per year at a cost of $25 each.

IP-PBX Module

This module calculates the cost of installing an IP-PBX on an existing corporate LAN as well as the associated monthly operating cost. The initial start-up cost is the sum of handset, gateway, and call manager costs, including installation, PSTN trunk line installation cost, and ISP leased-line installation cost. The monthly operating cost includes PSTN trunk line cost, ISP leased-line cost, maintenance, and move and change cost.

Module Assumptions and Default Values

• We assumed the use of ethernet phones as opposed to terminal adapters.[12] Installation and configuration were estimated at 30 minutes per handset.

• Gateway and call manager costs are estimated based on the price of Cisco (formerly Selsius) equipment. Cisco offers gateways supporting two, four, eight, and twenty-four trunk lines—models AT-2, AT-4, AT-8, and DT-24, respectively.[13]

• The gatekeeper or call manager consists of a computer and call management software. The model assumes that a separate server class computer is dedicated for the use of the call manager. It has dual power supplies, dual disks, and memory.

• The model assumes that it takes eight hours to install a trunk gateway and a call manager.

• Since different phone companies charge different trunk prices, three estimates of PSTN trunk prices are used.[14] Monthly rate includes hunt group (which ensures that calls to a busy line are switched automatically to a free line), usage charges for local calls, touchtone charges, 911 charges, and tax.

• ISP leased line and port costs vary with capacity.[15] Installation cost includes the cost of CSU/DSU and ISP leased line setup cost. Monthly cost includes the cost of the telco access line and ISP monthly charge. The model assumes that the corporation pays a 20 percent premium on top of this monthly basic service rate in order to get a higher quality of service for voice telephony. Since both data and voice network share the same ISP leased lines, the model sets the fraction of ISP leased-line cost allocated to the voice network to be proportional to the data rate of voice divided by the total data rate of voice plus external data.

• Annual software and hardware maintenance cost is assumed to be 10 percent of equipment cost. Move and change cost is estimated as the cost of additional person-hours needed for the voice network. During the initial stages of use, there will be adjustments that need to be made and a number of requests for assistance from the users. After a period of time, users will learn to fix the problems themselves. The model assumes that each voice line requires thirty minutes per month for assistance and MAC service during the first year. The time required for assistance and MAC service is assumed to decrease by 50 percent every year.

• Personnel cost is estimated to be $50,000 per year, which includes any benefits that the corporation must pay for this employee. This translates to a cost of approximately $25 per hour.

Long-Distance Calling Module

The long-distance calling module estimates the cost of toll services. Figure 10.6 shows different choices of long-distance call routing for the Centrex and IP-PBX cases, respectively.

In the Centrex case, the corporation has two alternatives: to use a traditional interexchange carrier (IXC) for long-distance service or an Internet telephony interexchange carrier (ITXC), which provides a dial-in remote gateway service.[16] In the IP-PBX case, the corporation has three choices. For the call destination that does not use an IP-PBX, it

Internet Telephony in the Corporation

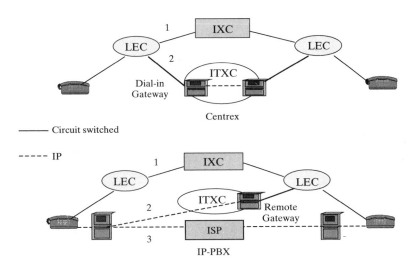

Figure 10.6
Choices of long-distance call routing. *Note:* LEC = local exchange carrier

can route via a traditional IXC or an ITXC that provides a remote gateway service.[17] For the destination that also uses an IP-PBX, it can route the call directly via an ISP.

Module Assumptions and Default Values

• The model assumes that where the infrastructure exists, corporations always choose to route toll calls over an ITXC.

• In the Centrex case, the model assumes that all intracorporate calls and 80 percent of toll calls are routed via an ITXC that provides a dial-in gateway service. The remaining 20 percent are routed via a traditional IXC.

• In the IP-PBX case, all intracorporate long-distance calls are routed via the ISP. The destination office has either an IP-PBX or a gateway to convert the received IP voice packets back to the voice signals. Other toll calls could be routed via either an IXC or an ITXC, which provides a remote gateway service. The model assumes that 20 percent of toll calls are routed via an IXC. The remaining are routed via an ITXC, which provides a remote gateway service.

- The model assumes an IXC rate of 10 cents per minute.[18] ITXC dial-in gateway rate and remote gateway rate are assumed to be 7.5 cents and 5.5 cents per minute, respectively.[19]

Total Telecom Expenditure Module
This module takes all costs from the other modules and categorizes them into initial start-up costs and monthly operating cost. Initial start-up cost is then amortized and added to monthly operating cost to reflect total monthly telecom expenses.

Module Assumptions and Default Values

- Centrex contract length and economic lifetime of Internet telephony equipment is three years.
- Cost of capital is assumed to be 10 percent.[20]

Results

Table 10.2 shows the resulting user calling pattern when the default values are entered in the model, and Table 10.3 shows the estimated monthly cost per line for Centrex service. Table 10.4 shows the impact of corporate size on total traffic and trunking requirement. Gateway capacity is chosen based on the number of trunk lines. Table 10.5 summarizes the calculation of the Internet access capacity needed to support both data and voice uses as a function of firm size.

Table 10.6 shows the resulting monthly cost per user line for the IP-PBX scenario. Start-up cost, monthly recurring cost, and annualized

Table 10.2
User calling patterns

Type of Call	Inbound and Outbound Calls per Line per Month	Minutes per Line per Month
Intraoffice	117	351
Intracorporate	94	282
Local	235	705
Toll	141	423
Total	587	1,761

Table 10.3
Centrex total monthly cost per line

	Low Estimate	Base	High Estimate
Start-up cost per line			
Telephone handset	$150	$150	$150
Centrex line installation	40	70	100
Total start-up cost	190	220	250
Annualized start-up cost per month	6	7	8
Monthly recurring cost per line			
Centrex line monthly charge	30	50	70
Maintenance, move, and change	3	4	6
IXC charge (42 min. at $0.7/min.)	3	3	3
ITXC charge (310 min. at $0.055/min.)	17	17	17
Total monthly recurring cost	53	74	96
Total monthly cost per line	59	81	104

Table 10.4
Trunking analysis

	Large Corporation	Medium Corporation	Small Corporation
Number of users	200	100	20
Average minutes per hour on phone	10	10	10
Peak-to-average traffic ratio	3	3	3
Total minutes per peak hour	6,000	3,000	600
Percentage of traffic to/from PSTN	54%	54%	54%
Total Erlangs to/from PSTN	54.4	27.2	5.4
Required trunk lines for 1% blocking probability	69	38	12
Gateway capacity (no. of trunk lines)	72	42	12

Table 10.5
ISP access analysis

	Large Corporation	Medium Corporation	Small Corporation
Required bandwidth for voice (Kbps)	384	192	38
Required bandwidth for data (Kbps)	500	250	50
Total required bandwidth (Kbps)	884	442	88
Type of leased line	T1	512 Kbps	128 Kbps
Percentage of cost allocated to voice	43%	43%	43%

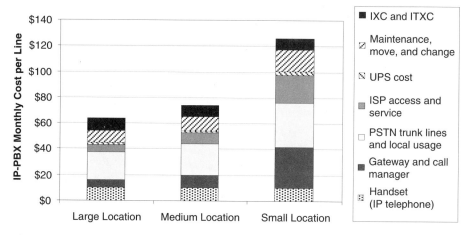

Figure 10.7
IP-PBX total monthly cost breakdown

total monthly cost are summarized by category. Three values of PSTN trunk line cost represent the low, base, and high estimate, respectively. As the table shows, the total monthly cost per line for the large corporation is the lowest. This reflects economies of scale since more users share the call manager, trunk gateways, and ISP service.

Figure 10.7 shows a breakdown of the IP-PBX monthly costs for the base parameter values. PSTN trunk lines and local usage are the largest contributor to total monthly cost. Actual equipment costs—call manager, gateway, and handsets—are dwarfed by usage and maintenance costs.

Table 10.6
IP-PBX total monthly cost per line

	Large Location	Medium Location	Small Location
Start-up cost per line			
Handset (IP telephone handset)[a]	$329	$329	$329
Gateway and call manager	$181	$282	$969
PSTN trunk line installation	$14, $25, $36[b]	$17, $29, $42[b]	$24, $42, $60[b]
ISP leased-line installation	$10	$11	$48
UPS cost	$53	$63	$105
Total start-up cost	$586, $597, $608[b]	$701, $714, $727[b]	$1,475, $1,493, $1,511[b]
Annualized start-up cost per month	$19, $19, $20[b]	$23, $23, $24[b]	$48, $48, $49[b]
Monthly recurring cost per line			
PSTN trunk lines and local usage	$9, $19, $27[b]	$11, $24, $32[b]	$15, $33, $45[b]
ISP access and service	$6	$8	$20
Maintenance, move, and change	$10	$10	$16
IXC charge (42 min. at $0.07/min.)	$3	$3	$3
ITXC charge (169 min. at $0.035/min.)	$6	$6	$6
Total monthly recurring cost	$34, $44, $52[b]	$38, $51, $59[b]	$60, $78, $90[b]
Total monthly cost per line	$53, $63, $72[b]	$61, $74, $83[b]	$108, $126, $139[b]

[a] Both equipment and installation costs are included.
[b] Low estimate, base, and high estimate, respectively.

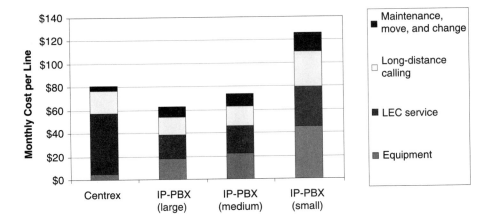

Figure 10.8
Cost comparison between Centrex and IP-PBX

Figure 10.8 compares total monthly cost per line of the base estimates for the Centrex and IP-PBX scenarios. Various cost components of both Centrex and IP-PBX are grouped into four categories. For the Centrex scenario, equipment cost is the cost of the handset, LEC service cost is the cost of Centrex service, and long-distance calling cost is the sum of IXC and ITXC charges. For the IP-PBX scenario, equipment cost is the sum of handset, gateway, and call manager costs; LEC service cost is the cost of PSTN trunk lines and local usage; and long-distance calling cost is the sum of IXC charge, ITXC charge, and fraction of ISP cost allocated to the voice network. The result shows that total monthly cost per line for an IP-PBX is cheaper than Centrex for both large and medium corporations but costlier for the small corporation. As is true for a conventional PBX, an IP-PBX trades higher equipment cost for a reduction in the cost of LEC service. An IP-PBX allows the large and medium corporation to save on long-distance calls—approximately 30 percent and 20 percent, respectively, over Centrex. But the small corporation has to pay about 20 percent more when using an IP-PBX. This is because ISP service is relatively more expensive at low port speeds. Maintenance, move, and change costs for an IP-PBX are much higher than for Centrex for all corporate sizes. This reflects higher personnel costs needed to support an IP PBX voice network. Due to its higher equipment cost per line, maintenance cost in the small corporation is much higher than the others.[21]

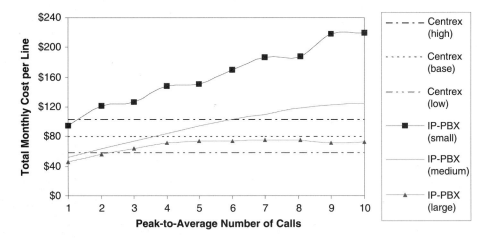

Figure 10.9
Total monthly cost per line as a function of peak-to-average number of calls

Sensitivity Analysis

The flexibility of the cost model allows us to examine the effect of changes in the input values on total costs. The model contains more than fifty input values. This section examines the results from changes in some of the variables that give nonlinear responses.

Variations in Usage

Figure 10.9 shows the effect of changes in the ratio of peak-to-average number of calls on total monthly cost per line. We assume that total monthly call volume remains constant but that more calling is skewed toward the peak hour. In general, this type of calling pattern favors Centrex over any type of PBX because the equipment and trunk costs for the latter must be based on peak demand. Results show that total monthly cost per line for the IP-PBX scenario increases substantially when changing the values of peak-to-average number of calls from one to ten. On the contrary, Centrex cost does not change at all. The jump in the curve of the small corporation indicates a move to a larger-capacity gateway. Since the appropriate capacity is determined from peak traffic, a company with a lower peak-to-average number of calls

Economics and Costs

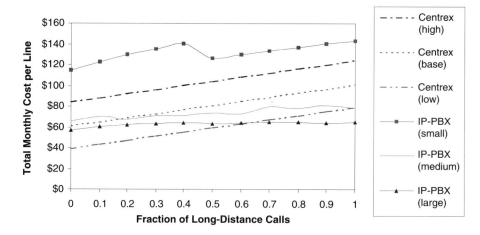

Figure 10.10
Total monthly cost per line as a function of fraction of long-distance calls

ratio generally bears less cost of gateway and trunk lines per minute of use than the one with a higher peak-to-average number of calls ratio. Therefore, an IP-PBX—or any other PBX—is more attractive to the company with a more evenly distributed traffic pattern.

The effect of the fraction of long-distance calls on total monthly cost per line is shown in Figure 10.10. As the fraction of long-distance calls increases, total monthly cost per line for both IP-PBX and Centrex increases. However, they increase at different rates. Total monthly cost per line for Centrex increases at a faster rate because Centrex users are assumed to pay a higher ITXC rate. The rapid decline shown on the graph of IP-PBX for a small corporation when the fraction of long-distance calls increases from 0.4 to 0.5 is due to the fact that lower gateway capacity and fewer trunk lines are required while the same capacity ISP service can be used. The trend of the graph also implies that IP-PBX compares favorably to Centrex for the firm that makes many long-distance calls because the IP-PBX allows for toll cost savings not available to a Centrex user.

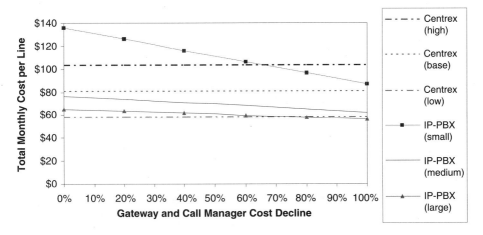

Figure 10.11
Effect of IP equipment cost reductions on relative prices

Variations in Gateway, Call Manager, and ITXC Remote Gateway Costs

IP-PBXs are relatively new technology. Equipment costs for gateways and call managers should decline in the future. A sensitivity analysis was performed to see the combined effects of declines in gateway and call manager costs on total monthly cost per line. The ITXC dial-in rate, IXC rate, and other input variables were held fixed at default values. Figure 10.11 shows that for a large corporation, an IP-PBX is always preferable to Centrex. For a small corporation, an IP-PBX could prove to be preferable to Centrex only in the high Centrex cost scenario and only following substantial equipment cost reductions. In the base and low Centrex cost scenario, no matter how low the cost of gateway and call manager, Centrex is always cheaper than an IP-PBX. For a medium-sized firm, an IP-PBX is always preferable to Centrex in the base and high Centrex cost scenario.

Economic and Policy Implications

Scenarios 1 and 2 in Figure 10.12 show the total costs of premises and long-distance voice service for users of Centrex or an IP-PBX under the assumption that all toll calls, including intracorporate calls, are carried

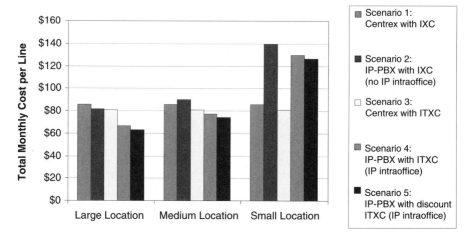

Figure 10.12
Cost comparison among different scenarios

over a traditional IXC. As the figure clearly shows, when toll call costs are identical, Centrex is preferred over an IP-PBX for firms of all sizes. It is only when we introduce the possibility of carrying toll calls using IP that the picture begins to change.

To keep the comparison fair, scenario 3 shows the effect on total voice communications costs for a Centrex user if the firm switches as many toll calls as possible to a dial-in gateway ITXC. This is the only extent to which the traditional Centrex user can benefit from VOIP technology.

In scenario 4, we show the impact on total voice communications costs in the IP-PBX-using firm if it too routes most calls over an ITXC and in addition routes all intracorporate traffic over an IP network rather than via an IXC. These savings are possible because the firm is assumed to have an IP-PBX at all corporate locations, and no conversion to circuit switching is necessary. These savings alone are enough to shift the decision away from Centrex toward an IP-PBX for medium and large firms. Finally, in the fifth scenario we show the effect of assuming that IP-PBX users benefit from a per minute discount when using an ITXC by virtue of saving the ITXC the costs of the dial-in gateway. The additional savings here are modest, showing that the greatest toll savings come from costs avoided on end-to-end VOIP calls within the firm.

Table 10.7
Optimal choices between Centrex and IP-PBX

Local Exchange Carrier Cost	Small corporation	Medium Corporation	Large Corporation
Low	Centrex	Centrex	IP-PBX
Base	Centrex	IP-PBX	IP-PBX
High	Centrex	IP-PBX	IP-PBX

In general, it is more economical for a small corporation to use Centrex and for a large corporation to use an IP-PBX. However, for a medium corporation, the optimal choice depends on the costs of LEC service—the Centrex rate and PSTN trunk line cost. In general, in areas where Centrex rates are high, PSTN trunk line costs are also high, and vice versa. If this assumption holds true, a medium-sized corporation located in an area where LEC service is offered at a low rate is better off using Centrex. Table 10.7 summarizes these findings.

This analysis yields the following conclusions:

• The major saving of IP-PBX over Centrex comes from the saving in intracorporate long-distance calls.

• Even without a discount in the ITXC rate, an IP-PBX costs less than Centrex as long as there are some calls made directly from one IP-PBX to another.

• The incremental cost of allocating more voice traffic to IP is less than the incremental cost of allocating more voice traffic to the PSTN.

• An IP-PBX is not economical for small corporations.

Conclusions

Internet telephony is an alternative to a traditional PBX or Centrex service for corporate telephony. If one compares only the costs for equipment and local service, Centrex is more economically attractive than IP-PBX for firms of all sizes. The dominant IP-PBX cost is the cost of gateway equipment and associated trunks to interface the PBX to the PSTN. The cost of the Internet equipment is high due to low volumes of production. With rapid change of technology and more competition in the market, these costs are projected to fall rapidly, reducing the advantage of Centrex.

However, the choice of a premises communication solution must also take into account the impact of that choice on long-distance communications costs. Moving to an IP-PBX makes possible significant savings in toll charges immediately. When these savings are included in the analysis, we find that medium to large—but not small—firms may find an IP-PBX preferable to Centrex even at today's equipment costs. Analysis shows that the major saving of IP-PBX over Centrex comes from the saving in intracorporate long-distance calls. That is, the use of an IP-PBX at each company location allows intracorporate calls to be easily carried inexpensively over an IP network at considerable savings. Further savings are available if at least some external toll calls can be made through an ITXC, which accepts calls as IP and routes them over an IP network to a dial-out gateway. While an ITXC may offer savings even to the Centrex user over traditional IXC pricing, we assume that the ITXC provides an additional discount for net to phone service, which saves the ITXC the costs of an originating gateway. Continued growth in the number of remote gateway ITXC providers increases the fraction of toll calls for which such savings are available, thus further encouraging the deployment of an IP-PBX. As the number of firms using an IP-PBX increases, remote gateway service providers have more incentive to expand their infrastructure, which feeds back positively on the use of IP-PBX.

When queried as to their reasons for considering an IP-PBX, two issues dominated the responses of corporate telecommunications managers: long distance-cost savings and less expensive implementation of IVR and unified messaging systems. This raises the most compelling, but also most difficult to quantify, reason for firms to consider adoption of Internet telephony: to enable the firm to incorporate more easily advanced IP-based services and applications into its internal operations and its interfaces with the external world.

Notes

An earlier version of this chapter was presented at the Internet and Telecoms Convergence Consortium Meeting, Helsinki, Finland, June 15–16, 1998. Comments, suggestions, and support from consortium members are gratefully acknowledged.

1. Centrex is a business telephone service offered by local exchange carriers from a central office.

2. Meir, E., *et al*, "PBX- The Next Generation," *Business Communications Review*, Jan, 2000, pp. 38–42., Rigney, S., "PBX Meets the LAN," PC Magazine, Nov 24, 1999.

3. For details, see http://www.8×8.com.

4. A CSU/DSU converts between the different encoding schemes used for internal data equipment and for PSTN leased circuits.

5. See, for example, the IP PBX from Shoreline Teleworks at http://www.shoretel.com/product_info/index.htm.

6. An example of an IP telephone handset is Selsius-Phone by Selsius Systems. See details at http://www.selsius.com.

7. The model was constructed using ANALYTICA, a visual software tool that provides an alternative to the spreadsheet. See http://www.lumina.com/software/index.html for more details.

8. With the assumption that calls will arrive in Poisson distribution and given a target grade of service, the Erlang B formula can be used to determine the number of voice lines needed.

9. For example, if the minimum number of trunk lines to PSTN, which is determined by the Erlang B formula, equals 23 lines, the model will choose the appropriate gateway capacity of 24 lines and adjust the number of required trunk lines to 24 lines.

10. For example, for a thirty-six-month contract, US West offers a monthly rate of $36 per line for unlimited service in Denver. Bell Atlantic charges a monthly rate of $27 plus a usage charge of $0.07 per local call in Pittsburgh. Ameritech charges $44 per month for the first seventy-three local calls and $0.08 for each additional local call in Cincinnati. The values are estimated from Centrex prices collected from Ameritech, Bell Atlantic, BellSouth, NYNEX, Pacific Bell, and US West.

11. For example, AT&T MERLIN 34-DLX handset, $150; NORTHERN TELECOM Meridian M-2008 handset: $170.

12. Costs are based on the cost of the Cisco/Selsius etherphone handset.

13. The current price of Cisco AT-2, AT-4, AT-8, and DT-24 is $2,995, $3,995, $5,995, and $12,000, respectively. See http://www.selsius.com for more details.

14. The values are estimated from PBX trunk prices collected from Ameritech, Bell Atlantic, BellSouth, NYNEX, Pacific Bell, and US West. A nationwide average for a local PBX business trunk as of October 15, 1995 is $53.22. See Lande and Waldon (1997, p. 24).

15. ISP leased line cost is estimated based on UUNET dedicated access price for a three-year contract.

16. A dial-in remote gateway accepts an analog voice call and converts it into IP voice packets. The carrier that provides this service then forwards these voice packets through

a wide area network to whichever of its POPs is closest to the call destination. IP voice packets are converted back to an analog voice call and forwarded to the nearest PSTN central office. Examples of ITXCs that provide this kind of service are Qwest and AT&T.

17. An ITXC that provides a remote gateway accepts IP voice packets. It then forwards these IP voice packets through the wide area network to its POP closest to the location of the call destination. IP voice packets are converted back to an analog voice call and forwarded to the nearest PSTN central office. Currently, no carrier provides this service using open standards. Net2Phone provides PC-to-phone Internet telephony using proprietary software on the user's PC.

18. AT&T, MCI, and Sprint offer a long-distance rate of 10 cents per minute to anywhere in the United States.

19. Qwest and AT&T charge 7.5 cents per minute. Since there is no carrier offering a remote gateway service at the time of this research, it is assumed that the cost of providing a remote gateway that converts analog voice signals to IP voice packets is 2 cents per minute. Hence, the ITXC that offers a remote gateway service will charge 2 cents lower than the ITXC that offers a dial-in gateway. The corresponding remote gateway rate is then assumed to be 5.5 cents per minute.

20. The Hatfield model, which calculates costs of local telephony, uses default values for the cost of equity of 12 percent, the cost of debt of 7.7 percent, and the debt ratio of 45 percent. The resulting cost of capital is $55\% \ (12\%) + 45\% \ (7.7\%) = 10\%$.

21. Annual maintenance cost is assumed to be 10 percent of equipment cost.

IV

Markets, Strategies, and Regulation

11

Internet Telephony Markets and Services

Terrence P. McGarty

Real-time international Internet protocol (IP) telephony markets and services have been an early successful application of voice technologies to the Internet. This success has not stemmed solely from the excessive regulatory burdens and astonishingly high prices (relative to costs) for voice telephony in certain markets. This chapter first describes new market mechanisms for exchanging bandwidth of minutes and then addresses the resultant need for new metrics and measures of service quality for Internet and other new real-time telecommunications services, including voice quality and security. Multimedia communications are then discussed as examples of emerging alternative varieties of Internet telephony and other advanced Internet services.

Telecommunications is in a formative stage, but it is poised for rapid growth subject to a well-developed national plan. The main concern in the existing telecommunications industry structure is that the post, telephone, and telegraph (PTTs) and the other quasi-governmental players may actually delimit growth. Also of concern is the development of an infrastructure. There is a battle of concepts between federalism for telecommunications and a full, open, free market. The free market has proved to be the most effective in the United States and the United Kingdom, and the lack of the free market in many countries has clearly delimited telecommunications growth.[1] It has been tried only in a limited way in other countries, and Russia has been one of those. It is argued that the free market approach is much more effective than federalism.

Regulatory changes globally and their impact on world markets will be significant. The General Agreement on Tariffs and Trade and GATS treaties and the World Trade Organization agreements, as well as the recent Federal Communications Commission (FCC) challenges to settlements and accounting rates present a real threat to Russia's position as a world player if it attempts to ignore them and not become a proactive player in that process. Russia must join the WTO to be an effective player, and such joining is consistent with the goals of a free market player.

Longer-term, network interconnection issues and the resultant positive and negative network externalities stemming from the convergence of voice and data networks and the emergence of differentiated services will be critical for the growth of advanced forms of Internet telephony and other advanced Internet services. This chapter concludes that the development of new varieties of real-time Internet telephony, such as real-time multimedia communications involving video, text, data, and voice information, will lead to the emergence of growing markets for telecommunications bandwidth and related goods and services.

Real-Time Telecommunications Markets and Exchanges

There are markets for various commodities in the world today. These markets have various forms of derivatives, namely combinations of puts and calls.[2] The same is true for the development of a worldwide market for telecommunications services. Consider two types of services that exist today: bandwidth and minutes. Bandwidth is in E1s, fractional E1s, or multiple E1s.[3] This is the bandwidth market. The minute market is in minutes of traffic to a particular place. In each case, one can construct a price per unit: a price per E1 between two places or the price per minute between two places. In this regard, there have been several approaches recently to the sale of bandwidth as a market entity.

Approaches to the Sale of Bandwidth

Bandwidth Exchanges
Companies such as Band X, Rate Exchange, and ArbiNet have developed what they perceive is an exchange market for the buying and

selling of bandwidth and minutes. They have tried to establish exchanges where companies buy and sell bandwidth or minutes of traffic for a certain period between certain specific destinations of a certain quality. The companies act as brokers in the process. There is no real-time settlement or guarantee of delivery. In certain ways, it is not even the telecommunications equivalent of e-Bay. None of the entities has real-time interconnection. However, they are trying to get this capability in place; for example, Band X is currently allowing for interconnectivity in a gateway in London.

If one wants to buy and sell minutes and is connected to a switch with the other party also connected, then the process might work. In fact, such a process is the essence of the current resale market. However, bandwidth is not that easy. Even an existing circuit, such as an E1, might have to be rerouted, reestablished, or reconnected, a process that requires 90 to 120 days—hardly a real-time process. In effect, there is no intermediary taking the risk of having the facilities in place, since the locations for termination are the most uncertain elements. For example, one may relocate an E1 termination a dozen times depending on the local interconnection issues.

Real-Time Switch Partitioning

Real-time switch partitioning is a market where companies may meet at a switch and interconnect at the minute of service or bandwidth approach, using the switch in a partitioned fashion. The owner of the switch, such as General Telecom at 60 Hudson Street, allows for the interconnection of many players on the switch and thus permits the real-time brokering and completion of sales.

Today, such switches are at the heart of the resale business. They allow for low capital cost entry and essentially allow bandwidth and minute brokers to interconnect. The dealing is all "off the books" in the sense that the switch operator receives a fee independent of the actual revenue generated by the switch.

This approach is an intermediary to the general market where buyers and seller meet. It is more akin to what we see today in oil markets where closed groups trade oil on the spot market. There is no concept of a day trader in either business model.

IP Dial Tone

IP dial tone is going to become a major issue. Conceptually we believe we know what it is: there is an "outlet" that will automatically connect to the global Internet and give global interconnectivity if any IP-enabled device is connected to it. However, there are many unanswered questions. What is it really? What are its architecture and elements? According to whose worldview is it implemented? There is no good definition of IP dial tone. The reason is that we think it is a work in process.

One thinks one knows what IP dial tone looks like when one sees it. There is a "plug" in my "wall," and if I "plug" anything into "it," "it" allows full IP connectivity across a large IP network and allows me and the others interested in this IP device to use certain applications that may be beneficial to one or both of us. But this is a vague definition. Let us say that GE makes IP devices in my refrigerator. Then let us say that the plug is the electrical outlet and that GE has an agreement with the power utilities to carry IP over the power lines. Let us assume that GE has an agreement with Kraft to place small, electronic, wireless devices in my cheese coverings, and that each time I open the refrigerator and take out a piece of Kraft cheese, it tells the refrigerator, which in turn tells Kraft. Kraft and GE know what I eat and when. Maybe this is good for them, but maybe it is not good for me. Is this IP dial tone? I think it is one embodiment of it.

Now consider Bell Atlantic and its IP dial tone. We replace the RJ 11 jacks with interfaces that use the jack for interconnection of any IP-dial-tone-compatible device—say, my television, computer, or IP telephone. Who controls the content? Is Bell Atlantic in a position to become an @home?

If there is such a thing as IP dial tone, then what is the construct of a market? One at the IP level? One at the bandwidth level? Clearly not one at the minute level.

Transit Switches

The transit switch is a set of telecommunications nodes on the East and the West or North and South that are connected by a fiber link or links, owned, leased, shared, or otherwise, in between. The nodes provide for interconnection by the most advanced telecommunications methods available and thus allow the transit switch operator to become the market maker in telecommunications interconnection. As New York and London make financial markets, places like Bangkok, Seoul, Bombay, Moscow, and Vladivostok can have the potential to make international telecommunications markets brokering telecommunications capacity to all players, East and West.

The approach taken in this chapter is to focus on the provision of services via a transit switch and then to utilize technologies such as TCP/IP and speech compression to establish the first global multimedia network supplying video, voice, and data. The transit switch concept proposed for Russia is one that uses TCP/IP as a means to lower the capital of switching costs, to use existing resources more efficiently, and to leverage the technology to implement a full multimedia network capability. Currently, companies such as Teleglobe have been trying to become transit switch entities.

The transit switch concept can be stated as follows. A country or entity may become a transit switch if it is placed in a location or locations where the tariffs, circuit availability, traffic flow, and interconnectability are such that the provision of telecommunications service can be done at or in a least-cost manner for the region or regions to be served.

Implementation of the Transit Switch Concept. The transit switch construct is a paradigm for telecommunications industry development. It has three elements; the switch infrastructure, the ability to buy transport "long" and sell it "short" in the world telecommunications market, and the need for a global fiber infrastructure building on the plans and developments already in progress.

Security of Telecommunications Networks. If the transit switch is to become a reality, then security is a key and essential guarantee to anyone seeking to use this facility. Security encompasses physical security, access security, and ultimately transaction security. The world technology base may play a significant role in this development process.

Packet Telecommunications. The deployment of standard telecommunications switches is merely an extension of what world carriers are doing. The use of TCP/IP type carriage, that is, extended packet telecommunications, moves the intelligence to the edge of the network. This is a critical move that must be deployed and must be used as a strategic advantage. The network can readily take advantage of its new start and do it in the vein of a TCP/IP world rather than in a hierarchical telecommunications world.

Policy Developments and Global Responses. The main focus on the transit switch concept is that an open market policy will allow for significant external investment and rapid growth. The main problem is the lack of clear laws and legal structures globally and the debatable concepts of contracts, property, and the ability to seek remedies in a structured and reliably consistent legal system.

Market Intermediaries

The last approach is the intermediary services broker. Companies such as ITXC and GXC have taken this approach, assuming the following:

• There are many "naive" and unconnected ISPs that need a clearinghouse or middleman to effect their transactions.

• Currency transactions and settlements can be done by a multiplicity of third parties.

• Third-party billing, network management, and infrastructure provisioning must be established.

• There will be no entry by the more typical telephone carriers into the IP telephony market.

These assumptions are critical to the "broker" approach, but they are highly problematic, given the needs of this market to have telephony and telecommunications expertise. In short, the approach has fundamental instabilities. It rests on having contractual agreements with third parties that frequently are in weak regulatory and operational control. This approach may show "rapid" growth, but such growth is carefully scrutinized as a Potemkin Village of facades and lacking in sustainable substance.

Table 11.1 presents a detailed comparison of the market makers in the IP world.

Table 11.1
Internet telephony markets and services

Type	Offering	Strengths	Weaknesses	Examples
Bandwidth exchanges	The provision of a real-time market for the buying and selling of "contracts" on bandwidth and minutes.	Provides an open forum for the pricing. Open market pricing should "clear the market."	Fails to allow completion of the sale.	Band X, Rate Exchange, ArbiNet
Real-time switch partitioning	The provision of the real-time partitioning of a switch, which is a physical meet point of a "group" of common interest that can interconnect between each other and create a closed market.	Ease of access. Provides a controllable switch and interconnection point. Determines the "trading" rules and players in a defined space.	Closed market, may not provide lowest prices. Open to only a select few. May limit provisioning to single points.	General Telecom
IP dial tone	The provision of IP interconnectivity wherein a bandwidth on demand may be brokered and quality of service may be achieved at a price point.	Provides complete IP interconnectivity end to end. Allows for greatest breadth of service offerings.	Places a single broker in charge. Risk of a single control point.	Bell Atlantic, AT&T&BT
Transit switch	The provision of a single point of access wherein a single carrier through a self-controlled switch partition allows for bandwidth and minute markets.	Allows for complete end-to-end provisioning.	Places a single broker in charge. Risk of single control point.	Teleglobe
Market intermediaries	A single point of contact among local contracting entities to broker interconnection among a common technology platform.	Lowest cost of entry	Poorest level of service and quality. Subject to the most regulatory risk. Uncertain operational integrity with local partners.	ITXC, GXS

The Commodity Concept

Commodities are goods or services that may be bought and sold in relatively standard, undifferentiated bundles. For example, in the oil market, oil is bought and sold on the basis of its barrels, and wheat is sold in grain markets based on its moisture content, as well as a bushel. As with any other market, one can call bandwidth commodity C and the price $P(C)$. Thus one may pay \$50,000 per month for an E1 between New York and Moscow or \$0.1855 per minute between New York and Warsaw.

More complexly, however, one might construct the commodity C as follows: $C = \{\text{Location}_1, \text{Location}_2, \text{Duration}, \text{Capacity}, \text{Start Date}, \text{Volume}, \text{Other}\}$—for example, $C = \{\text{New York, Warsaw, 2 Years, E1, October 15, 1999, 2.5 million min/month, PRI/C7}\}$. That is, one wants to buy an E1 for two years from New York to Warsaw that can carry at least 2.5 million minutes per month and has a C7 PRI interface. Then, one has a price $P(C)$ on that commodity as of today. One can further create derivatives—puts and calls, or rights to buy and sell that commodity or derivatives thereof at some time in the future—as one can do with stocks and agricultural and mineral commodities.

One would further assume that one could see a declining curve for such commodities: $C_1 = \{\text{New York, Warsaw, E1, 1 year, now}\}$ and $C_k = \{\text{New York, Warsaw, E1, } k \text{ years, now}\}$. Thus, one would assume some form of declining costs: $C_1 > C_k$ for all k.

Likewise, one could assume that if such a market existed for bandwidth, calls and puts could be constructed, and the usual approaches for option pricing would most likely apply.

The flow in our model can then be perceived to be from IRUs (Indefeasible Rights of Use), to bandwidth, to IP interfaces, to minutes of use. By using some form of technological transformation, such as IP telephony, one can then look at all four markets. Let C^{IRU} = an IRU commodity unit, C^{BW} = a bandwidth commodity unit, C^{IP} = an IP commodity unit, and C^{MOU} = a voice minute of use commodity unit. Let us assume that one has the following transformations: an IRU is an ST3 or 155 Mbps of bandwidth, or 77 E1s, and an E1 can handle 2.5 minutes of use (MOU) as an IP circuit. There is as yet no clear IP unit, so one shall avoid this at this time. Thus, one would logically have: $C^{IRU} < 77\ C^{BW} < 77\ (2,500,000)\ C^{MOU}$. Failure of this would allow arbitrage in the market.

Now there must be clearinghouses for these commodities. Several exist, all operating on the Internet and in their early stages of development.[4] One would assume that there could be some real-time exchange mechanism for such trades; however, the infrastructure is not yet there.

The essence of an efficient telecommunications commodity market is the ability to "buy long and sell short," or to take advantage of the inherent price arbitrages that will exist. Another advantage of such a market, if it is efficient, will be to value the "value added" to each step in the change from raw bandwidth to MOUs. If one knows the conversion rate from an E1 to an MOU and if the market values this at some multiple of the conversion rate, then this is the value added by the technological conversion. The same is true in, for example, the oats market, where a bushel of oats has a price, but an oat bran muffin is significantly higher on a per pound basis.

Requirements for an Efficient Real-Time Telecommunications Market

There are several simple requirements for a real-time telecommunications market:

• A fungible product unit such as bandwidth or MOUs. These exist.

• A readily accessible means to get access to the product units. This does not exist. There must be a way for someone who holds E1s to be able to give access to another who desires to buy them on a real-time basis. There must be an exchange mechanism. In the commodity markets, there is, however, never an exchange of the actual train car load of commodities; there is only a market on the derivative. In this case, however, there may be a "contract," but there also must be a delivery mechanism. This can be done on a futures basis, but for real-time efforts, there must be a real-time interconnect facility.

• A readily efficient and trustworthy broker of services and prices. So far these have been the Band X and Rate Xchange players. This may not be the case for a long period of time. Generally, the "exchange" is some controlled and independent third party.

Thus, two elements are missing: the exchange mechanism on a real-time basis and the actual exchange broker. There are ways to create contracts to void the deficiency of the mechanism, but there still needs to be a workable broker.

Least-Cost Routing

The success of any IP telephony model that relies on dedicated networks will depend on least-cost routing. This section presents an analysis and methodology to determine and implement least-cost routing for the company in a dynamic fashion so as to ensure a minimal net present value cost to the network portion of the intranet network. The approach builds on my work in the mid-1970s in the deployment of least-cost routing for dynamically variable satellite circuits with a traffic matrix constraint using integer programming techniques.

The cost of a link, L, is defined as P, and P depends on the vendor, the from and to locations, the data rate, and the duration of the contract. Thus, P may be parameterized as follows:

$$P = P(M_i, M_j : D_k, T_m : V_n),$$

where M is the city or location, D the data rate, T the duration of the contract, and V the vendor. The capacity of the link, C, defined by the above, is given in the following:

$$C_{i,j} = D_k / E_k,$$

where E is the efficiency of the Internet voice node (IVN) at that link.

Table 11.2 depicts the prices per link for a specific vendor and for a specific set of locations parameterized on data rates and duration of contracts. Table 11.3 depicts the prices for a specific vendor and for a six-month contract between several locations and at various data rates.

Consider the following illustration. An international IP telephony company selects nodes for operation in New York, Warsaw, Seoul, Manila, and London. The traffic matrix in minutes per month is shown in Table 11.4.

It is possible to do a direct connect mesh network or to select a hub network using a transit switch approach as is done in the airline business. A subhubbing approach is also possible. It all depends on the pricing matrix between countries as to which approach is most cost-effective for a particular firm. Note that pricing may include a

Internet Telephony Markets and Services

Table 11.2
Vendor and location by data Rate and duration: New York to Moscow

Duration	Date Rate			
	128 Kbps	256 Kbps	512 Kpbs	E1
12 months	$14,000	$27,000	$36,000	$39,500
24 months	13,000	25,000	34,000	35,500
36 months	12,000	23,000	32,000	32,500

Source: McGarty, 1999.

Table 11.3
Vendor and duration rate by location and data rate: One-year agreement

Location	Date Rate			
	128 Kbps	256 Kbps	512 Kpbs	E1
London	$4,000	$8,000	$12,000	$12,000
Frankfurt	6,000	12,000	18,000	22,000
Warsaw	9,000	18,000	24,000	36,000
Moscow	14,000	27,000	34,000	39,500

Source: McGarty, 1999.

Table 11.4
Minutes per month between five locations

From/To	New York	Warsaw	Seoul	Moscow	London
New York		500,000	700,000	400,000	400,000
Warsaw	300,000		100,000	100,000	100,000
Seoul	700,000	200,000		100,000	200,000
Moscow	300,000	200,000	100,000		500,000
London	500,000	100,000	100,000	100,000	

Source: McGarty, 1999.

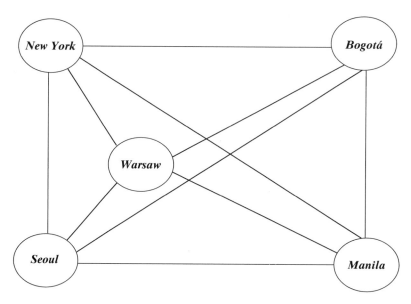

Figure 11.1
International point-to-point IP network (Source: McGarty 1999)

differentiator between transit only and termination only. For the purposes of illustration of the general concept, a point-to-point network connecting the five nodes of (New York, Warsaw, Bogotá, Manila, and Seoul) is shown in Figure 11.1. (The hubbing and sub-hubbing approaches are discussed in Chapter 3.) In this network, the design is to procure the links on a fully interconnected basis, and each link matches the traffic requirement for the network traffic matrix. This is generally the most straightforward but also most inefficient use of network resources.

Bandwidth can be obtained on a long-term basis, built, or purchased on what can be called a spot market. The intelligent use of bandwidth will allow significantly lower costs to all parties, especially emerging nations. The issue of real-time least: cost routing (LCR) is a complex issue that means that costs are available, routing tables can be dynamically changed, and there may be a bidding mechanism for bandwidth that can be sent down ultimately to the end user. This becomes a resource utilization issue as well as an end user and market pricing mechanism. The issue is one of implementing, controlling, informing,

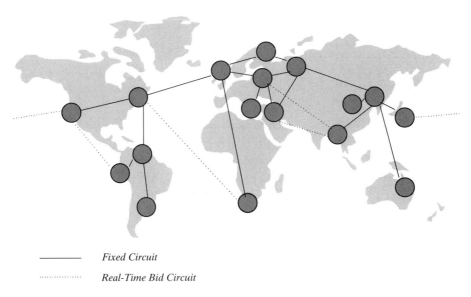

——————— *Fixed Circuit*

················ *Real-Time Bid Circuit*

Figure 11.2
A fixed and real-time bid network (Source: McGarty 1999)

and communicating pricing information and decisions in a fully distributed fashion and using this at the IP layer as well as the TCP layer. Where should this be accomplished? What protocols in terms of bandwidth bidding should be used? And what are optimal schemes? Figure 11.2 illustrates how an internal Internet telephony carrier could extend its "virtual global" network by interconnecting with real-time bandwidth exchanges.

A dynamic LCR functions as follows:

• There exists a market mechanism to price bandwidth on demand—for example, one of the carrier's clearinghouses such as Band X, Rate Xchange, and Arbinet.

• There exists a mechanism to interface with such a carrier in real time.

• There exists a capability in the router to determine the least-cost route and to adjust the router table to provide for that approach.

• The routers can communicate with the central facility and the market-clearing mechanism to permit real-time adaptation and least-cost routing.

IP Telephony Service Qualities

Quality of service (QOS), levels of service, and grades of service may be characterized by various metrics. There is generally no consensus at this time as to what metrics are the most useful for quality differentiation. However, the International Telecommunication Union and the Internet Engineering Task Force are currently working on such standards. There are also many government entities that have the role and responsibility for obtaining and facilitating the dissemination of the information provided by carriers. There may already be entities that have the authority to provide end users with this information. The general position is that there should be no mandated values, that it is generally appropriate to respond to end user concerns, and that government should not mandate certain levels of performance but at most should be an information-gathering and -disseminating entity.

The major problem generally is defining what QOS is and how it may relate to levels of services and grade of service. *Grade of service* means the probability that a call presented to a telephone system is actually carried by that system. *Quality of service* a widely disputed term. In the telephony world, the QOS is generally stipulated by the telco along with mandated values given by the public utility commission (PUC) that detail such elements as time to get dial tone, voice quality (subjectively determined), time to respond to customer calls, and similar measures. In the asynchronous transfer mode (ATM) world, the issues include cell error rations, cell loss rations, and cell delay variability. In fact, there are currently four classes of ATM service, ranging from that of a private line to that of a connectionless data protocol.

Grade of Service

AT&T has defined grade of service as follows. Let R be the rating of a call by a customer in category R, and let M be the system performance measurement. Let M be measured from the system. For example, in a voice call, a customer may measure a call quality, using MOS score, as 4.1, given a packet delay of 20 msec. Figure 11.3 depicts the process of grade of service. The grade of service (GOS) is defined as:

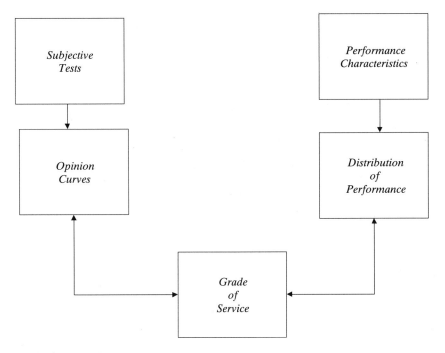

Figure 11.3
The grade of service process

$$GOS = \int P(R/M)p(M)dM.$$

In other words, GOS is the expected R averaged over the anticipated M.

Quality of Service

There is a growing issue regarding QOS on the Internet. For the most part, the Internet was an "as is" facility: users took what they got and liked it. There were and are ways around this issue, but for the most part they are patchworks of improvement. The issues of quality of service, level of service, and grade of service will dominate the evolution of Internet II as well as the evolution of new IP-based networks such as those proposed by Bell Atlantic and the AT&T and British Telecom joint venture. Will the Internet evolve into the network of last resort if QOS, GOS, and level of service are better on private IP-based networks? Is this a threat to the Internet, or will there be a natural tiering of such service grades?

The Internet is more distributed and adaptive but more difficult to control if QOS is to be achieved. In the public switched telephone network (PSTN), traffic congestion is managed such that under overloads, connections may not be made. In the Internet, originating traffic will access the destination end point and receive some level of service even though that service level may not be useful (this is referred to as "best effort"). Thus, certain applications (e.g., voice or video) may be restricted in their use unless service management capabilities are introduced to ensure acceptable performance levels. And although higher-priced high-speed links may be made available, there is no guarantee that the unmanaged core of the network will provide high-speed throughput.

Established and new entrant international carriers and the standard set of telecommunications offerings are migrating over time to IP technology. The IP services to be offered include highly secure, global virtual intranets and associated IP-based applications; multimedia networks with point-to-point and multicast data, video, and audio capabilities; global call centers providing twenty-four-hour, multilanguage customer support; and communications services to support traveling executives and allow virtual meetings to take place with anyone, anywhere, as well as toll-grade voice quality.

Of the elements listed above, security is the most important. Many carriers recognize that this order of priority must be incorporated into any system design. Multimedia communications and customer support are also critical. The last item is a "follow me anywhere" concept.

Telecommunications Voice Quality

Telecommunications networks generally have levels of performance that are tested in the normal acceptance of a circuit. Typical criteria for acceptance are shown in Table 11.5. These acceptances are determined by means of a set of detailed tests. Table 10.6 depicts several of these tests, the objective of the tests that are generally performed, the procedures used, the desired results, and the level of performance sought.

Results on voice quality are shown in Figure 11.4 for a link on a clear channel IP telephony system as measured by both ends. Note that on

Table 11.5
Voice quality factors

Performance Factor	Value
Call blocking rate busy hour	<5%
Call setup time	<12 sec, 95% of the time
Call setup failure rate	<5%
Dropped call rate	<3%
No answer rate	<5%
Echo suppression	>20 dB
MOS speech quality	>3.8

Source: McGarty, 1999.

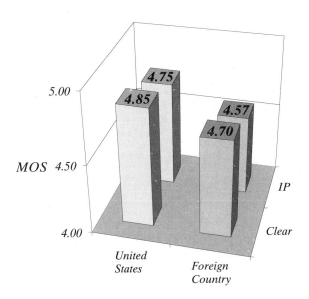

Figure 11.4
Mean objective scores (MOS) for IP telephony (Source: McGarty 1999)

Table 11.6
Voice quality tests and measurement

Test	Objective	Procedure	Level of Performance
Call setup time	To test the time to set up a call measured from the time the last digit is entered until the time that end party ringing is commenced.	This will be an A/B test procedure using the circuit and a standard reference on a time-of-day basis. The standard reference shall be a U.S.-generated AT&T clear channel circuit. The test shall include the measurement of the time between the last digit dialed and the time of the commencement of end number ringing. The test shall include measurements for 50 calls of type A and B.	<25% difference
Link loading	To determine the maximum loading on each circuit to meet the blocking probability requirement.	This will include the loading of the circuit to its maximum handling capability by placing calls onto the circuit and determining the maximum number of simultaneous calls before blocking exceeds the 5% level.	Maximum loading with blocking probability < 5%
Call completion	To determine the fraction of calls terminated without problem.	This test shall consist of the placing of 100 calls in a row and determining the number, a terminated successfully. This shall be done on both ends of the circuit.	>95% call completion
Call blocking	To determine the call blocking probability on the circuit.	Calls shall be made at three levels of loading—50%, 100%, and 125% of maximum peak busy hour capacity—and call completion shall be recorded.	<5% call blocking at load
Voice call quality	To determine the voice quality of the circuit.	This will be an A/B test procedure using the circuit and a standard reference on a time-of-day basis. The standard reference shall be a U.S.-generated AT&T clear channel circuit.	<15% determining difference in average

Test	Purpose	Procedure	Criteria
		The procedure will be to place twenty calls on each end of the circuit in a double-blind fashion. There will be a 50:50 mix of the standard reference and the company circuit. The caller will be asked to determine whether the quality was acceptable. Then the two will be compared for statistical significance of difference using a student t-test.	
Bit error rate	To determine the end-to-end bit error rate (BER) of the circuit.	Use a BER tester on the loop-back circuit.	$BER < 10^{-6}$
Fax quality	To determine if the fax transmissions are acceptable.	Transmit fax ten times.	Readable fax
Modem test	To determine if the modem transmissions are acceptable.	Try data modems up through 56Kbps.	Modem connection via synch
Failure reporting tests	To determine if the failure reporting procedure is followed.	Failures will be generated at each end of the circuit. Calls will be placed to the network operations center and the time to determine and report the trouble will be measured.	Time to report < 15 min. Failure to report rate < 5%
Trouble tickets[a]	To determine if trouble tickets are prepared properly and if the clearing process is commenced.	Trouble tickets shall be prepared and circulated.	Time to issue shall be < 15 min.
Trouble clearing	To determine if the trouble clearing process is working.	This will entail the end-to-end clearing of the created trouble.	Time to clear shall be < 75 min.
Billing	To determine if the billing system integrity is in operation.	Traffic shall be loaded for 48 hours from both ends of the circuit. Bills and customer detail records shall be prepared.	<1% billing errors.
Customer care test	To determine if customer care system integrity is working.	Calls shall be placed at random to customer care.	Time to answer shall be <45 sec.

Source: McCarty, 1999.

[a] Trouble ticket is the term that carriers use for messages sent within their own network and to their partner networks to identify hardware, software, or congestion problems.

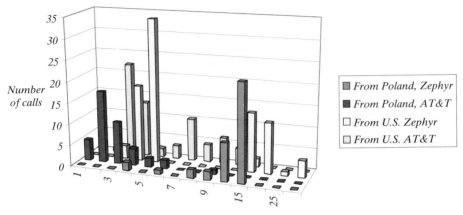

Time (seconds (nb nonlinear scale))

Figure 11.5
Call setup times: IP vs. AT&T (Source: McGarty 1999). *Note:* Zephyrisan IP carrier

this link, one compares IP to the clear channel AT&T links. There is no noticeable difference in voice MOS and QOS. Several carriers have already achieved this QOS, but few IP carriers have even begun to test for this factor.

Mean objective scores for IP telephony clearly match those of the clear channel telephony, whether they originate from the United States or from a foreign country. There is at most a 10 percent difference, which, given the size of the sample, makes its statistically insignificant. Figure 11.5 shows results from call setup time measurements on an IP versus standard call setup procedure. Note the bimodal characteristics.

Figure 11.6 summarizes the results of these call setup tests, which were performed between the United States and Poland. The two networks that were compared were those of Zephyr Telecommunications and the alternative pairing of AT&T and the Polish PTT's networks. While an IP network may have longer call setup times, this was found on further investigation to be largely due to the process of having a non–primary rate interface interface and in establishing a call on a second dial tone basis.

Calls terminating via a C7 interface are shown in Figure 11.7. Note the dramatic difference in call set-up time. There are still some differ-

Internet Telephony Markets and Services

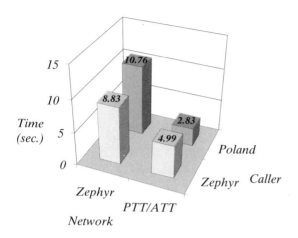

Figure 11.6
Poland-United States call setup times: IP vs. AT&T (Source: McGarty 1999)

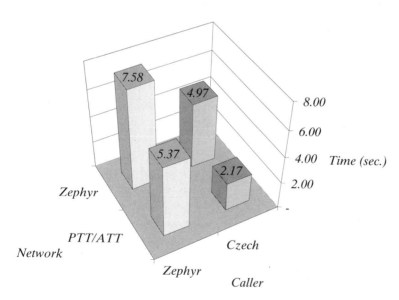

Figure 11.7
Czech Republic-United States call setup times: IP vs. AT&T (Source: McGarty 1999)

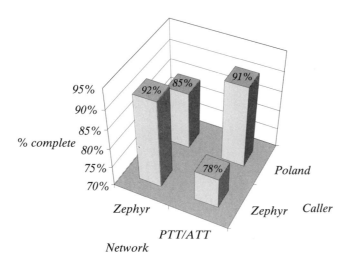

Figure 11.8
Call completion rates: IP vs. AT&T (Source: McGarty 1999)

ences since the interface is a local switch, albeit with C7 and not an international tandem switch with C7.

The last measurement that can be shown is the call completion rates. Figure 11.8 depicts some of these rates. Note that they are comparable but generally reflect the network configuration.

Security

Security is a key element in the deployment of any IP telecommunications service. IP-based networks, by the very fact that they are relying on widely known protocols, are vulnerable to attack from those seeking either financial gain or simply the psychic gains of maliciously or benignly hacking a system. Safeguards against such security threats are of paramount importance for an IP telephony system. Security falls into three categories:

Physical security—the securing of the physical network to compromise, penetration, or misappropriation

End-to-end security—the security associated with end user access (voice, data, or information security)

Logical security—the security to penetration by an adversary who can cause errors or faults or otherwise compromise the system, end user, or information through access to the logical elements of the network

There are many typical security functions that can be considered. These common functions are listed in Table 11.7.

Security begins with the analysis and determination of threats, compromise protocols, and similar security risks and what can architecturally be done to ensure a secure environment. The overall issues of network security are at the levels of physical attacks of resources, transport compromise between resources, logical attack at software in its broadest sense, and end user compromise. One can view the issues in an open and a closed network environment. Table 11.8 presents an overview of these extremes.

The network alternatives and their implications for network security are shown in Figure 11.9. There are two closed networks, the open Internet, and a virtual private network (VPN), which is encapsulated by some form of security from the Internet. The VPN is constructed by and within the Internet. The gateways (GW) are interfaces between the networks, and it is at these points that protocols and techniques must focus on the security issues.

The security elements discussed in this section must use all three dimensions—Internet, closed, and VPN—as a means to specify and evaluate the issues of network security. Security is also at the heart of any defense against information warfare.

Multimedia Communications

Multimedia communication is simply displaced conversation. From the new user perspective it represents a truly transparent medium of talking—of sharing ideas and conversations with others in a simple fashion, blending seamlessly all elements of communications in any typical human conversation. Multimedia communication does not consist merely of the devices and displays; it is not merely advanced CD players with enhanced sound. It is a conversation with others, using all of the available senses, combining meaning and content between individuals displaced in time and space. The key architectural and

Table 11.7
Network security functions

Function	Details
Unauthorized access control	A system should be designed so that there shall be no unauthorized access of any Internet voice node (IVN), router, switch, or backbone element. The IVN should provide for total and complete firewall capabilities to ensure secure access and shall not permit any unauthorized packet flow through any IVN-connected router.
Billing control	The IVN should provide for a complete secure billing collection system with complete and full real-time redundancy. It must also provide alarms for any attempt to penetrate the system in an unauthorized fashion and should provide for a complete and secure keyed access system for company access.
Wiretapping implementation	The system should allow for any and all legally authorized wiretaps to be implemented on the system. The taps must be in a standard format and must be able to be obtained in a secure and compartmentalized format.
Remote instantaneous cutoff	The system must have the capability of remotely and instantaneously being cut off to prevent any unauthorized breach of security.
Packet streaming control	The system must prevent packet streaming. It must prevent the unauthorized use of the routers, whether they are connected via an intranet or Internet, by others for the purpose of sending packets over the network or through the routers. The IVN must have the capability to authorize every packet before transmission.
Network management compartmentalization	The network management system must be fully compartmentalized from the system. Any access to any voice channel must be monitored and must have a key control access capability. No user of the system may access any voice circuit in any fashion without having that access monitored.
Code key control	The system must use a secure code key access technique for any access to, modification of, reconfiguration of, or material change to the system, its configuration, connections, or any other operational function.

Source: McGarty, 1999.

Internet Telephony Markets and Services

Table 11.8
Open and closed network security challenges

Level	Open Network	Closed Network
Physical	Physical breach	Uncontrolled access
Transport	Intercept versus destruction	Intercept versus destruction
Logical	IP/TCP header swaps Delay/intercept/intrusion	Intrusion via compromise
User	Encryption and authentication	Encryption and authentication

Source: McGarty, 1999.

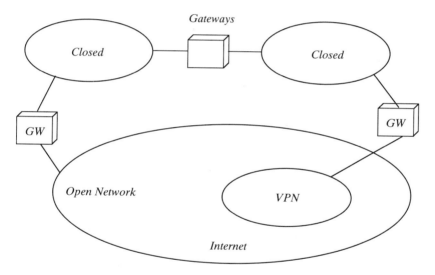

Figure 11.9
Security across networks of networks (Source: McGarty 1999)

technical question is whether the Internet can and will support the types of multimedia communications that are envisioned.

When one introduces the multimedia communications concept, one does so in the context of having multiple users share in the use of the multimedia objects. Thus, multimedia communication requires that multiple human users have sensory interfaces to multiple versions of complex objects stored on multiple storage media. In contrast to data communication in the computer domain, where humans are a secondary afterthought and optimization is made in accordance with the machine-to-machine connection, multimedia communication is a human-to-many-other-human communication process that must fully integrate the end user into the environment. Multimedia communication thus generates a conversational sense, is sustainable over longer periods, and has an extreme fluidity of interaction. The current Internet affords a conversational sense. Expanding that conversational quality to a wider array of multimedia objects is the challenge.

Critical issues in the area of multimedia communication are the data objects, the conversational quality of the interaction, and the overall communication's architecture. It is this concept of conversational quality—of displaced sharing of information and creating transactions of the mind—that makes this definition of multimedia communication more expansive and represents a challenge for integration into the Internet fabric. This concept of displaced conversational quality demands interaction, and such transparent interaction is the inherent capability and functionality of the Internet, especially as it addresses the new user.

The major observation that can be made is that the standard approach to the communications system design, from the physical layer and up, is the wrong way to proceed for multimedia. In a multimedia environment, one must, perforce of user acceptance, design the system from the top layers down.

Conclusions

There are several overall conclusions that can be reached:

Bandwidth versus minutes: The architectures will dictate what will be sold: bandwidth or minutes. Also is the "bandwidth" IP bandwidth or clear channel bandwidth?

Markets: Delta Three, Zephyr, and others have focused on the carrier's carrier market. Some have tried the retail market of the end user. Where are the real markets? Will be an evolving question. The carrier's carrier market is a simple entry point. The retail market is large and high revenue, but expensive as a cost of entry. One sees the carrier's carrier market as being the entry point but also being the growth point at this stage.

Services: Services thus for are dominantly voice, but a wide set of IP-based services—multimedia, data, fax, and other services—can be envisioned. The question with multimedia is what standards apply in the standard telephony context. Is there a set of ITU-compatible IP to SS7 to C7 interfaces? Is ISDN-like service portable to IP?

Competition: There will be clear competition on many fronts. The barriers to entry to this market are operational and regulatory and not just economic. The Internet players can provide the degrade quality at low entry costs, but such quality may be unacceptable. With advances in Internet QOS parameters, this may be less of a problem. Thus, there would be ubiquity, low entry costs, and any player can enter; the game becomes a marketing and sales game and not one of operations. One might counterargue, however, that there will always be the need for interconnection to the global telecommunications network so that despite the simplistic Internet approach, a switch or switchlike device will be required. Thus, there will be a barrier to entry based on technical and operational competence as well as marketing. One might argue further that having operations in foreign countries is the key to success after having achieved the sales and operational levels. This means partners, affiliates, or other experienced players. Competition is the ultimate barrier to entry. It will be seen as these three forces are brought to bear.

Notes

1. McGarty, TPRC 1997. The author delineated the Asian markets and predicted the fall of many of the economies by determining the strength or weakness of the telecommunications infrastructure.

2. An E1 is a 2.024 Mbps line, the standard in much of the world.

3. At the time of this writing, Band X, Rate Xchange, iBasis, ITXC, Arbinet, and Enron are among the leading purveyors of bandwidth.

4. The details of what it will take to achieve true multimedia functionality in the Internet are significant. Such issues as what is needed, what barriers in the current Internet design must be overcome, who will do the changes, and what the risks are would need a lengthy exposition. Suffice it to say that there are no fundamental barriers to introducing multi-media into the Internet environment. In fact, there are small efforts already underway that show how to do this. The Internet Users Society will be one vehicle. More important, it will be the innovativeness and creativity of the end users that will make it a reality.

12

Internet Telephony Carrier Strategies

Husham Sharifi

Internet telephony started in the mid-1990s as a service meant to subvert the traditional scheme of international telephone calls. Its audience, almost exclusively technology enthusiasts, viewed the idea as intriguing but no more than whimsical. Now, it has risen as a seminal part of the Internet revolution, but it is, of course, just one part. Were carriers to realize its utility as a subset of the vast opportunities before them, they could dominate more than ever before.

Characteristics of the Internet Telephony Industry

Supply Chain

To understand an industry, we should understand its supply chain. Figure 12.1 is provided to structure the analysis in this chapter. The access points (levels 2 and 4 in the figure) are where Internet telephony will be deployed, especially since it can be integrated with other applications at these points. The fact is particularly relevant to the strategic recommendations given to the carriers in the conclusion. The innovative, added value that is advocated in that section should occur at levels 2 and 4. The infrastructure that should be leveraged is generally from level 1.

Incumbents in different countries stretch across varying parts of the telecommunications supply chain. Telebras, for example, before privatization, owned everything in Brazil's telecommunications sector. By

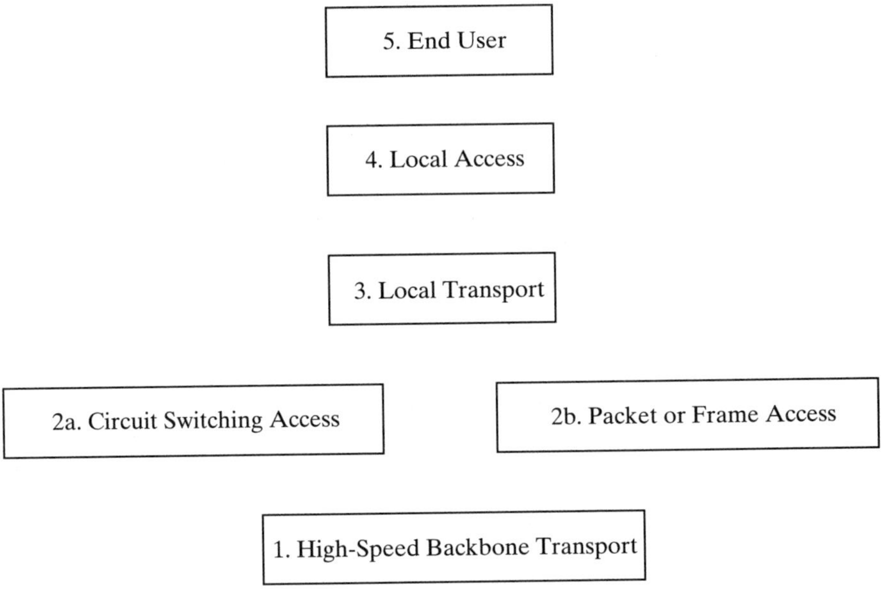

Markets, Strategies, and Regulation

```
┌─────────────────────────────┐
│                             │
│       5. End User           │
│                             │
└─────────────────────────────┘

┌─────────────────────────────┐
│       4. Local Access       │
└─────────────────────────────┘

┌─────────────────────────────┐
│      3. Local Transport     │
└─────────────────────────────┘

┌──────────────────────────┐    ┌──────────────────────────────┐
│ 2a. Circuit Switching    │    │  2b. Packet or Frame Access  │
│     Access               │    │                              │
└──────────────────────────┘    └──────────────────────────────┘

        ┌──────────────────────────────────────┐
        │  1. High-Speed Backbone Transport    │
        └──────────────────────────────────────┘
```

Figure 12.1
The telecommunications market chain

contrast, GTE in the United States has traditionally owned only local transport infrastructure. The responses and positions of traditional carriers are heavily influenced by where they lie on the supply chain.

Generally networks have interconnections at the raw bandwidth or long-haul voice level, depending on their needs. This type of activity occurs at level 1, the high-speed backbone transport level. The form of interconnection here could in theory take on any character. However, given market realities, it occurs almost exclusively between very large networks on a peer-to-peer basis. The major networks of the world, such as NTT, AT&T, and Deutsche Telekom, engage in considerable activity at this level.

The second level comprises the switching equipment and its necessary peripherals, required to translate voice or data for transport by level 1. At level 2 there is typically a fee for connection to the switch. In market lingo, this is a port fee for backbone access. The port is, of course, in the switch, which sits in a hub—a point of presence (POP), network access point (NAP), or a telehouse. For example, Internet service providers (ISPs) pay, directly or indirectly, to connect to the backbone through level 2b. (Notice that ISPs are not intrinsically part of this supply chain, as they should not be. The distinguishing features of traditional carriers come not from their service but from their ownership of infrastructure, divided here into five levels.)

The local loop consists of roughly two sections. These are in fact analogous to the larger network, but they exist within a local context. Just as signals must be transmitted across long distances by the backbone at level 1, signals must be transmitted across local distances by the local cables, usually fiber optic, at level 3. To access the backbone, one must connect to the level above it—level 2. Identically, to access the local cables, one must connect to level 4.

The traditional Bell operating companies (BOCs) in the United States have owned the infrastructure at both levels 3 and 4. Companies such as GTE and MFS, which would build rings around cities, have owned infrastructure at level 3 only. To get to the end user at level 5, they have had to purchase the right for local access from the BOCs. This is what made BOCs in the U.S. monopolies: they owned the central offices through which almost everyone ultimately must pass, and they owned the lines between the central office (level 4) and the residential premises (level 5). (Note, however, that central offices could potentially be bypassed in cases where providers would build cables directly into industrial parks or use specific wireless solutions.)

Competitive local exchange carriers (CLECs) have become slightly more prominent. They usually exist at level 4 exclusively. They often lease transport (level 3), as an unbundled element in the United States, between the central office area, where the CLEC's switch is located, and the residential premises. They also often lease transport (also level 3) between the central office area and the point for backbone access.

In a certain sense, this situation puts CLECs and others constrained to access points at a competitive disadvantage. They rely on potential competitors for transmission of their signals. Looked at in a different way, one can see unique opportunities arising from a business design that concentrates on access points. These are the points where the provision of integrated services occurs. The bundling of e-mail, Web browsing, video streaming, and Internet telephony must be handled at access points. Those who control the hubs (access points) have greater influence on the form and character of network content. Management of content seems to be the market's greatest promise.

The presentation of the market in this light highlights its character as an intrinsic networked economy. Before we dismiss this statement as tautological, we should consider that people often miss its implication. In other words, a certain set of economic principles apply to networked economies.

Networks Effects

A number of attributes related to the networked economy make Internet telephony so potentially potent. These include positive network externalities, economies of scale, economies of scope, public policy subsidies, access charges, local-loop bypass, and the international accounting rate regime. The first three are systemic; the last four are the result of policy.

Positive network externalities exist because the Internet is a network of many, many networks. ISPs, even small providers, can take advantage of the externalities provided by the interconnection of myriad networks. They can compete directly with the networks with which they connect, because they can use those networks to achieve the same geographical reach. Typically they must offer compensation for this privilege. It could be in the form of giving the interconnected network a commensurate additional reach, riding over a network of similar technological sophistication. This would be a peer-to-peer interconnection. For a smaller, less technologically advanced network connecting to a larger network, a form of monetary compensation would be necessary. This would be a hierarchical bilateral interconnection. There are multilateral options for interconnection too, for which a network may have to pay. But the increase in potential market capture eclipses the costs.

The result is that in a world of many customers aggregating their preferences into a demand curve, many suppliers compete for the same market share. Especially as newcomers, suppliers may have only the price of their service to distinguish themselves. This could lead to an environment that approximates Bertrand competition, with the price coming very close to the maginal cost of service.

Contrast this with the public switched telephone network (PSTN), which has exhibited a stronger reliance on *economies of scale*. This has been due to the monopolistic or sometimes oligopolistic history of the industry. Many countries have considered, and still do consider, their telecommunications ability as a matter of national security. Consequently, traditional carriers have been mostly singular, state-owned monoliths. This phenomenon, currently based on an ideological choice, has led to a certain type of capital-intensive economic activity. A traditional carrier, as a single entity, has had the expense of creating a nationwide infrastructure, at both the local and the long-distance levels, along with all the hardware to support it, such as the various massive electronic switching systems switches that have been developed over the years. The only possible way to recover these costs has been to inflate margins and necessarily serve millions of customers.

The Internet industry started with numerous actual suppliers and thousands of potential suppliers. Due to this large number of players and their geographical spread, interconnection standards allowed an ISP to operate successfully without becoming huge—that is, without achieving economies of scale.

Due to the dynamics of convergence—increased interoperability and cross-compatibility—the Internet can also achieve *economies of scope*. Within the Internet context, this means that offering two services jointly is cheaper than the sum of offering each service separately. For example, one company offering e-mail service jointly with Web browsing is more cost-effective than the sum of the costs of two companies—one that offers e-mail exclusively and another that offers Web browsing exclusively.

The economies-of-scope phenomenon potentially cuts across all applications of telecom: information aggregation and search facilities, e-mail, hosting, browsing, directory service, transport, video on demand, audio-conferencing, and videoconferencing. The economic implication is that there are overlapping capital costs, operations costs, and management costs. The latter two are generic to any industry. The former, capital, refers to server hardware, server software, lines to and of the backbone, routers, gateways, switches, and miscellaneous application-level programs. They could run as one service or they could run as two, or twenty, just as easily.

Public subsidies make up another factor that has afforded the Internet a special economic position. (Notably, though, subsidies have also been significant for the PSTN.) Having started in the United States, the predecessors of the Internet were benefiting from public subsidies during their developmental period. There have been, of course, costs associated with the research and development of ARPANET and NSFNET. But like the costs of virtually every other government project, these can be treated as economic sunk costs. They never need to be recovered and therefore do not influence future decisions. Users of the research and development, and the results that have built on them, suffer no loss of alternative opportunity. These users include everyone in the world who uses the Internet.

Interexchange carriers (IXCs), which are domestic long-distance providers in the United States, must pay an average of 6 cents per minute to local exchange carriers (LECs) for access to the local loop. This *access charge* creates a situation in which data providers, or more pertinently voice over Internet protocol (VOIP) providers, in the United States are exempt from the per minute local access charge. They can arbitrage at least by several cents per minute. There is therefore no advantage to bypassing local operators, which charge a flat rate for local service.

In Europe, the prevailing usage-based pricing for the local loop encourages *local-loop bypass*. In order to arbitrage, start-ups running VOIP will search for ways to avoid the incumbents' local networks. This is not a benefit related to IP telephony as a technology per se, but it presents itself as a concomitant phenomenon within the same marketplace.

Finally, Internet telephony *bypasses the international accounting rate system*. A service provider with an Internet telephony gateway in a foreign territory needs to pay only a national interconnect payment (Kelly, Sharifi, and Petrazzinni, 1997), such as that in a hierarchical bilateral agreement. Depending on the service provider's interconnection scheme, they may never even lease a line that leaves the country. Although Internet interconnection is the single most prohibitive cost for a provider, it eats up less of the profit margin, given an adequate customer load, than payments to the international accounting rate system. This distinction holds especially true for operators in developed countries. Their payments per minute to developing countries are often much higher than payments in the reverse direction.

One should note, as accounting rate expert Tim Kelly of the ITU points out, that between 1992 and 1997, settlement rates dropped by an average of 9 percent per year. In comparison, commercial tariffs dropped by only 3 percent per year. Obviously this suggests that the difference between MC and tariffs has become less dependent on the rates of settlement.

Demand Drivers

While price, and a consequent arbitrage opportunity, is what had initially sparked commercial interest in Internet telephony, the future will exhibit a different form of demand. Specifically, the phenomena driving demand will be reliable and customizable quality of service (QOS), interoperability, appropriate application of regulation, and value-added on top of IP telephony service.

Quality of Service

Without a reservation scheme or any way to establish secure, end-to-end traffic flows, IP manages congestion by queuing and directing packets. It queues packets when a router's potential throughput is less than the rate of packet arrival. A router directs packets by both final destination and according to network congestion. Hence, improving routers in size and capacity should improve the quality and the delay of IP telephony. At least, this is a realistic short-term alternative to protocols like real-time protocol and resource reSerVation protocol.

Studies have been done on how to translate this into reality (Partridge et al., 1998). But QOS is a matter of management. To satisfy QOS requirements, one should consider delay, bandwidth, probability of lost packets, costs, and jitter. An algorithm that decides the order in which to consider these attributes would be useful. It would be implemented at the packet scheduler on the output port of routers.

Figure 12.2 offers a possible segmentation of policies. The spectrum in the figure should be viewed as a continuum; the four categories are offered only as heuristics. Category 1 has no lower bound to quality but does have an upper bound. The quality could be bad to the point of uselessness but could never be better than a certain level. Category 2 has no bounds above or below. This is better than category 1 in that quality could

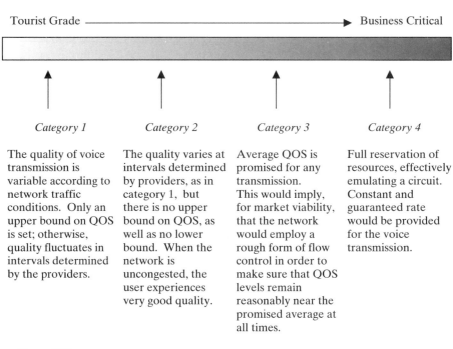

Tourist Grade ⟶ Business Critical

Category 1	Category 2	Category 3	Category 4
The quality of voice transmission is variable according to network traffic conditions. Only an upper bound on QOS is set; otherwise, quality fluctuates in intervals determined by the providers.	The quality varies at intervals determined by providers, as in category 1, but there is no upper bound on QOS, as well as no lower bound. When the network is uncongested, the user experiences very good quality.	Average QOS is promised for any transmission. This would imply, for market viability, that the network would employ a rough form of flow control in order to make sure that QOS levels remain reasonably near the promised average at all times.	Full reservation of resources, effectively emulating a circuit. Constant and guaranteed rate would be provided for the voice transmission.

Figure 12.2
Differentiated service for voice

be great during off-peak periods. Category 3 promises an average level of quality, and category 4 promises a distinct level of quality.

Notice that this spectrum is based on the mechanics of the reservation process. Within even the best reservation mechanic (full circuit emulation), a very low-quality service could be established and guaranteed. It would nonetheless be controlled, which would be the salient consideration for network management and the consequent experience felt by users. In fact categories 1, 3, and 4 could have five predefined levels, fewer, or many more. That character depends on the service provider's configuration.

Interoperability

The industry trend that has clearly prevailed over the past several decades has been a movement from intelligence being centered at the core of the network to intelligence being distributed at the network's nodes. The familiar intelligent-network/dumb-network dichotomy describes this movement. As a result of it and concomitant rhetoric about convergence, however, many commentators have taken this evolution to imply that there will be a singular network of the future. It would, the argument goes, just transmit data, an activity that is so simple that it would not require more than one generic network.

One example is multicast, a network design that would, for example, be used for Internet telephony conference calls. In fact, for otherwise compatible networks, we have no rules to communicate between different multicast protocols. Each autonomous system (AS)—essentially any one network that is under a single administration—can use a different multicast protocol. For interoperability, we need an interdomain protocol. It would be used to multicast datagrams among different ASs, which would be a necessary but not a sufficient condition for higher-level policy decisions regarding interconnection.

To support differentiated QOS, there must exist interoperable schemes for operations and billing between networks. Resource reservation at a particular level for one provider may represent a different cost from resource reservation at the same level for another provider. Conducting a form of settlement payments, as a means of compensation to close cost gaps on a bilateral basis between providers is extremely difficult. First, a large ISP could have many other ISPs, both small and large, connecting to it. Trying to forge an acceptable contractual agreement with each one would be burdensome. And if each agreement were different, it would result in enormous costs to process settlement schedules. Each schedule would have to be calculated in its own way.

Second, ISP No. 1 may be satisfied with the network performance for reservations of ISP No. 2 and may thus choose to forge a settlement scheme. But perhaps ISP No. 2 has an agreement to exchange reservations with ISP No. 3. Suppose ISP No. 1 considers ISP No. 3's reservation network performance to be decidedly mediocre. This complicates their decision to enter into any agreement. The complications increase exponentially with thousands of ISPs.

Both of these considerations could lead to balkanized interconnected networks, which would obliterate many of the advantages of integrated services, positive network externalities, economies of scope, and more.

A broad, standardized framework should be offered as a baseline for guidance in this activity, and it should occur at an industry-wide level.

Regulation

Regulation could prove a major stumbling block in the demand for Internet telephony. Likewise, an absence of regulation in pivotal areas could allow oligopolists and monopsonists to structure the market in a way that kills several market sectors, one of them possibly being Internet telephony.

Regulation can take many forms. For example, it can be done through technological means. Blocking user data protocol (UDP) packets represents such a short-term solution. ISPs can simply drop UDP packets with certain port numbers over 1024, a range that is open to individual control.

The potentially deleterious effects of thoughtless absence of regulation depends on certain large players, especially after the tidal wave of mergers succeeding the 1996 Telecommunications Act in the United States and the World Trade Organization agreement in Geneva. (The latter applies to sixty-nine countries that together constitute 95 percent of the global market in basic telecom services.) Large companies, and alliances of large companies, are well positioned to exert enormous market pressure, as both sellers and buyers, to create oligopolistic or nearly monopsonistic environments (or both). If these large players are left entirely to their own devices, they could easily stifle not only the deployment and uptake of IP telephony but of Internet technology in general.

Value-Added Service

Internet telephony presumably will exhibit two trends. First, its quality will approach the quality of PSTN service or, alternatively, the two will move toward a common, third model. Second, the prices of these two services will move closer and closer to each other, to the extent that customers will no longer choose one or the other exclusively on the basis of price. The result of both of these trends will be that in order to drive demand for Internet telephony, service providers will have to add value.

They will have to offer package solutions, in which, for example, video display is integrated with audio delivery. Web browsing could be aptly juxtaposed with Internet telephony, especially in on-line stores and other situations where interactivity enhances a transaction. E-mail could be used to trigger telephone calls. File transfers could be performed during a phone call, at the utterance of a word. The potential list is long, and much of the integration will necessarily occur at the application level, with software companies constantly providing new solutions. Whatever solutions there might be, IP telephony service providers must deploy them in creative and evolved ways in order to induce customer uptake and stem customer churn.

A more immediate form of integration can be achieved with call centers, a market that grew enormously during the 1990s thanks to advances in telecommunication technology that allow, for instance, caller line identification or call forwarding. Call centers cover a diverse range of applications, including customer support, telephone mail order, telephone sex, and telemarketing. For companies offering these services, the ability to centralize the functions—allowing the company to channel calls coming from all around the country or indeed, the world to a single site—is critical to achieving economies of scale.

For call centers, Internet telephony offers the chance to reduce telephone charges, particularly for international calls. More important, it enables call centers to tie together a voice side of a business to a growing Internet side. For instance, a caller who has browsed a company's Web site and has chosen a product to buy but needs more information could have the option to speak, via Internet telephony, with a call center representative. The representative would be able to trace the choices made by the caller and to assist in closing the sale. This would offer a segue into more sophisticated forms of integration, the possibilities of which are bounded only by the imagination of entrepreneurs.

Bandwidth Commoditization

In the past, infrastructure could be used for purposes of competitive advantage. This is no longer true. Excess capacity has in part encouraged the traditional carriers to promote Internet growth. A thriving Internet has been expected to soak up some of their excess bandwidth without challenging their core business. They also have been continually deploying more capacity in order to remain viable for future demand. Overprovisioning is supported by traditional carriers' business design.

The PSTN is currently configured to meet the demand of the busiest periods. In the United States, for example, the greatest number of standard telephone calls tends to be made on Mother's Day. (Incidentally, the second greatest number of telephone calls tends to be made on Father's Day, but in this case they are predominantly made as collect calls.) U.S. traditional carriers provision for the capacity they need to handle Mother's Day traffic, thus leaving large amounts of bandwidth unused during most of the rest of the year. In fact, under normal circumstances, all long-distance voice calls could be carried on 5 to 10 percent of current circuits, although even these figures would shrink where fiber is deployed (Kelly et al., 1997).

In 1995, AT&T reported to its stockholders that it had added more transatlantic telecommunications circuits between 1992 and 1993 than it had in all of its history before 1992. The new TAT-12/TAT-13 system doubled capacity, with capabilities of carrying up to 5 Gbps. Similarly AT&T, MCI, Sprint, SBC, communications and six Asian carriers in March 1997 signed an agreement to build the first undersea fiber-optic cable to link the United States and China. Its capacity is expected to be 10 Gbps (Lande and Blake, 1997). These oceanic cables have not only increased in capacity; they have significantly decreased in cost. Table 12.1 shows various cost measures. For example, over a forty-year time span, per minute costs plummeted from about $2.44 to about $0.01.

With such overcapacity priced at a negligible cost, traditional carriers are hard-pressed to use congestion as a justification for inflating prices. The entrance of new and structurally different telephony providers, such as those that provide telephony over the Internet, will prompt customers to question why they pay so much for long-distance calls.

Traditional carriers thus have an incentive to sell discretely their down-time capacity, which will eventually succumb to commoditization anyway, while they pursue the more intelligent strategy of offering value-added services, a market segment that will not only grow but will create new market realities (in other words, opportunities to make money) in its wake.

Table 12.1
Oceanic cables and their costs

System	Year	Technology	Cost (millions)	Annual Investment Cost per Usable Circuit[a]	Investment Cost per Minute[b]
TAT-1	1956	Coax. cable	$49.6	$213,996	$2.443
TAT-2	1959	Coax. cable	42.7	167,308	1.910
TAT-3	1963	Coax. cable	50.6	111,027	1.267
TAT-4	1965	Coax. cable	50.4	140,238	1.601
TAT-5	1970	Coax. cable	70.4	18,773	0.214
TAT-6	1976	Coax. cable	197.0	10,638	0.121
TAT-7	1983	Coax. cable	180.0	8,139	0.093
TAT-8	1988	Fiber optic	360.0	10,285	0.117
TAT-9	1992	Fiber optic	406.0	6,628	0.076
TAT-10	1992	Fiber optic	300.0	2,857	0.033
TAT-11	1993	Fiber optic	280.0	2,667	0.030
TAT-12	1996	Fiber optic	378.0	1,080	0.012
TAT-13	1996	Fiber optic	378.0	1,080	0.012

Source: Lande and Blake, FCC, 1999.
[a]The annual investment cost per usable circuit is the annual payment rate for the life of the asset that produces a present value equal to the initial investment cost. This calculation assumes a twenty-five-year cable life and a discount rate equal to the average cost of capital for the firm. For purposes of comparison, the discount rate is based on 40 percent debt at an indebted cost of debt of 9 percent and 60 percent equity at a 14 percent rate of return, with the latter increased to reflect a 33 percent income tax rate. These assumptions translate to a discount rate of 16.9333 percent.
[b]The investment cost per minute assumes that average activated circuits are used eight hours per day for 365 days each year and that 50 percent of circuits are idle (not activated). These assumptions are consistent with the current utilization rates in the industry, but they probably overstate the utilization rates for early cable systems.

Strategic Designs of Traditional Carriers

In 1950 international telephone service presented only 20 percent of international revenues for carriers. About fifty years later, traditional carriers rely on international telephone service for 95 percent of their international revenues, and yet this bulk of service is the very sector under threat from IP telephony. In the light of the tremendous uncertainty traditional carriers face, what should their strategic posture be?

Four possible options for strategic response are presented: joining in the fight directly, seeking protection and inertia through regulation, modifying the pricing structure, and changing the rules of the interconnection game. They are followed by five strategic imperatives (rather than just options): evolving the concept of lock-in, leveraging the installed base, working the channel, pursuing more fruitful growth opportunities, and perceiving the customer in a new light.

Join in the Fray

A traditional carrier can choose to acquire a share of the revenue stream from Internet telephony in a passive way. It can, for example, profit from local call revenues, leased-line revenues, and revenues from the provision of second lines to residential consumers for dedicated tasks such as data telephony and regular telephony (Kelley et al., 1997) A study by the Office for Economic Cooperation and Development (OECD) (1996) shows that these revenues alone would outweigh the loss of revenue from their existing customer base to IP telephony service. Of course, traditional carriers might benefit more from competing directly. If they cannot beat the competition, they could join it. Then, with their marketing muscle, deep pockets, and patience, they could overwhelm it in the long term.

The techniques they could use would not come just from changing prices. A mentality that exclusively sees IP telephony as an instrument for arbitrage assumes that the market landscape will not change. With the constant innovation, convergence, and differentiation of the industry, new market realities are emerging every day. Traditional carriers are in fact in a highly advantageous position to benefit from these opportunities. They must compete directly, though, and they must do so in a creative way.

Protect through Regulation

A traditional carrier could take an insular reaction to Internet telephony, trying to block it or protect itself by encouraging governments to regulate ISPs. Pakistan offers a clear-cut example; regulation there has been applied against telephony over the Internet (Kelly et al., 1997).

The government requires ISPs to write a clause in their contracts forbidding customers from using Internet telephony.

Similar efforts exist elsewhere. In the United States, many traditional carriers have pushed to have ISPs pay local access charges, classify ISPs as telecom service providers, and even ban IP telephony. Some carriers simply tell customers that they will charge them an access fee directly for IP calls that run between telephones on both ends (as opposed to a computer on one end, for example). The general response of the Federal Communications Commission (FCC) has been to determine that data, as opposed to voice, traffic is not subject to local access charges. Additionally, ISPs are not considered telecom providers; they are instead categorized as enhanced service providers (ESPs), a category that places them under fewer restrictions by the U.S. Telecommunications Act of 1996.

Modify Pricing Structure

Traditional carriers could respond to Internet telephony by modifying their pricing structure. Part of the challenge they face is from competitors that exploit the arbitrage opportunities created by existing pricing structures. One reaction is to drop their prices on standard telephone service but push the service through special marketing channels. AT&T, for example, offers a calling card for 9 cents a minute for telephone calls anywhere in the United States. The long-distance threat is particularly pointed for international calls. Voice over IP (VOLI) bypasses the international accounting rate system and consequently offers great savings. (U.S. IXCs, pay an average of 44 cents per minute to traditional carriers of other countries.) In response, traditional carriers could devise ways to reduce their international rates, which could imply withdrawing from accounting rates and moving toward a system analogous to that in the world of Internet interconnection. But eating into profit margins is not a viable long-term strategy.

In order to minimize the impact of decreasing margins and competition at the fringe, traditional carriers can consider two approaches to pricing exclusively or in tandem: (1) move from flat-rate local calls to usage-based local calls, and (2) avoid anonymous packetized long-distance service, which cannot be charged, and implement monitored and managed packetized service, which would introduce a wider variety of billing possibilities. Movement from a capacity-based pricing structure to a usage-based pricing structure would thus be feasible. Usage-based pricing has indeed been determined to be closer to optimality for integrated services, which comprise IP telephony (Bailey, McKnight, and Sharifi, 1998).

Change the Rules of the Game

Traditional carriers are positioned as leaders of the market. An obvious strategy is thus to engage in a form of market leadership. One particularly potent form is constituted by interconnection.

In contrast to the accounting rate regime that governs the PSTN, Internet interconnection merely has a de facto system. An ISP that initiates a connection does not pay anything to the ISP that ultimately receives the connection request. Indeed, the link might pass through several intermediate ISPs, and different bits of the message could even travel by different routes. (The latter is not likely, however, given existing traffic behavior on the Internet.) This model (if it can be called such) obviously differs from the PSTN model. ISPs wanting to connect to the Internet backbone in the United States, typically where most networks of the world want to connect, must pay the full circuit costs of the leased line to do so, even though traffic flow is bidirectional.

Contrast this with metaphorical "half-circuit costs" paid by an interconnecting network in the PSTN. Since traditional carriers in developed economies pay out much more than they receive in settlement monies, they generally feel burdened by the PSTN accounting rate system. The payments for the most part go to traditional carriers of developing economies, which are obviously supportive of the regime.

The roles of the beneficiaries and subsidizers of the Internet system are exactly reversed. Traditional carriers of developed economies receive money flows from traditional carriers of less developed economies. The resulting rhetorical support for this regime is predictable, but, more important, traditional carriers in developed economies are also poised to define the future of Internet telephony. They could simply withdraw from the PSTN accounting rate regime and establish a new regime based on market conditions and their own market power, thereby altering the structure of the industry. There are other options too, but the point is that certain players have the power to take unilateral action, even at the expense of the world, and thoroughly change the rules of the game.

Abandon Lock-in; Embrace Lock-in

Carriers should think about lock-in in new ways, and they should abandon their old forms of lock-in. Lock-in is ultimately a question of switching costs. The old forms of lock-in are based on switching costs from infrastructure. The new forms are based on switching costs from the value of information. Instead of offering money or the like, carriers should consider bundling tactics in order to overcome switching costs. For example, a user who subscribes to IP telephony could be offered 200 free minutes of ISP service, but the user would not have the option of buying the IP telephony service separately. Further, the difference in price between the ISP service alone and the bundle would need to be less than the added utility an IP telephony service would have for the customer. If the carrier could accurately forecast this utility, it could use the strategy quite effectively. Such a tactic would solve the information good dilemma, where a user is unsure of a service's utility until after using it.

Carriers should realize that switching costs for infrastructure-based service such as theirs will soon equal transaction costs. Transaction costs may remain high or become low, but either way, the convergence of switching costs and transaction costs by definition will squeeze margins significantly. Further, the difference between technology lock-in and vendor lock-in is important. Internet telephony could certainly become ubiquitous, which would create an environment of technology lock-in (where no one would want to use anything else). But eventually suppliers would proliferate, making vendor lock-in based on infrastructure highly unlikely. With these issues in mind, executive management of carriers should strive for vendor lock-in (by various means that are not directly dependent on infrastructure) and try to make their money in the aftermarket with service, upgrades, and innovations.

Throughout the dynamic, carriers should not make vague promises to consumers. Consumers will sense the deliberate nonchalance and will fight its underlying lock-in tactic. Consider that there are two execution modes for lock-in: eliminating opportunities for alternative supply and relying on loyalty. Firms accustomed to infrastructure-based lock-in have employed only the former; now they must learn how to employ the latter. As Shapiro and Varian suggested in *Information Rules* (1999), carriers could make sure that consumers have access to their calling patterns so that they can get a broader idea of their own needs for service. This would certainly enable consumers to shop for competition. But it would also allow them to demand more customized service (for which they presumably would be willing to pay more) from their carrier.

The crucial aspect of lock-in for carriers is not to compete for customers based on price. Consumers would use the opportunity to churn constantly, and carriers would be left to stem the tide with no more than pricing schemes, which can be complicated and unfortunately transparent in the telecommunications world. The best way for carriers to achieve lock-in is to search for ways of adding value to their offerings. Internet telephony, especially when packaged with other innovations, could do exactly that, but it cannot do it alone, and it especially cannot do it as a substitute to POTS (plain old telephone service). Carriers should use their current strengths, like a large installed customer base, to leverage innovations.

Sell Access for New Products to the Installed Base

There are a number of ways to do this, and they are bounded only by managerial creativity. One tactic that has already been employed is geographical expansion, which in the case of carriers takes the form of horizontal mergers and acquisitions. Given that interconnection already provides global positive network externalities, the added value to consumers for this is not much. Carriers should consider how to leverage their installed base to sell innovative service. For example, they should measure usage and not mere ownership. The number of telecommunications users in an installed base is not nearly as ripe for exploitation as the character of usage of both individuals and segmented groups. The latter tactic should be the focus of measurement in order to introduce different forms of price discrimination, target innovations to people who want them, and bundle value-added information packages in the most lucrative way possible.

Work the Channel

Consider the Complementors

Carriers must consider the important industry complementors to their service. Cisco, of course, is one, as are Juniper, Lucent, Sycamore, and other networking companies. Carriers should consider where they could best compete in a world of different standards, and then try to encourage their own optimal standards among these complementors in the industry channel. Integrating partly into these areas of the channel is a way to start forcing standards to their favor, especially if they have the business savvy or sheer power to combine that move with a set of alliances in the same area. Despite the channel conflict, Oracle successfully does it. The carriers can too.

Internet Plays

One clever Internet play is the movement into the application service provider (ASP) space. Doing so allows carriers to encourage networks of compatibility between different applications, one of which will certainly be Internet telephony. It allows them even to leverage the ASP infrastructure for purposes of running Internet telephony in integrated packages with other applications. Carriers can then force standards to be adopted for the application programming interfaces and other interfaces built in by companies that license their software to ASPs.

Achieving greater positive network externalities through horizontal mergers is fine, especially in order to service the business-to-business sector of the market. But these movements automatically raise concern among the antitrust set. Carriers should consider that vertical mergers (or mere integration, like the ASP move) allow them to play in the ever-shifting dynamics of distribution caused by the Internet. Taking advantage of new distribution dynamics is more difficult than simply expanding one's network, but it also has a greater potential payback.

Multiplayer Strategies

There are potentially creative ways to offset the actions of certain industry participants against each other. Certainly some of the industry players have interests that partially align with the interest of carriers. As just one example, carriers could give IP telephony for free to CLECs in order to move them in concert against incumbent local exchange carriers. In other words, by having IP telephony being supplied for free from upstream partners, CLECs would be even more aggressive in their attempts to reach the end customer downstream. The increased potential margins (lower cost [zero] with at least the same revenue) may even encourage them to invest in infrastructure that allows partial bypass. Many other positive dynamics could play out for the carrier. In general, the tactic could also lead to a constellation of allies that in the future would affect the channel in other ways. To ensure that its interests are preserved, the carrier would need to maintain its position of leadership among this section of its channel.

Understand Limits to Growth and Better Paths

Economies of scale have limits in industries that are dependent on infrastructure. In other words, a carrier like AT&T eventually found that it experienced diminishing returns after growing past a certain size. By contrast, information-based industries seem to have no natural limit for benefiting from economies of scale. Microsoft can produce 50 million copies of its Excel program just as easily as it can produce 50 copies. Its fixed costs are high, but its variable costs are fixed and low. They neither diminish nor increase with further production (copying).

Carriers should move into the information industry and leave behind their limits to growth. They have the great benefit of being able to leverage their own infrastructure into such an area. Here network externalities are more important than before as driving forces in the economy. The network economy is one where network externalities can combine with economies of scale to produce potent competitive advantage. Carriers are well positioned to leverage one into the other.

Shapiro and Varian (1999) distinguish between revolution strategies and evolution strategies in network economies. Carriers have been insisting on evolution tactics, where they try to achieve backward compatibility and create one interface after another to tie new technologies into old. This may work as a short-term strategy, but the pressure of thousands of new competitors with innovative value to offer makes it futile in the long run. Carriers must prepare and eventually unleash on the market a variety of revolution strategies, all based on added value that has synergy (overlap of resources with a simultaneous diversification of risk) with their existing services. It must be something new and useful, however. Luckily for them, it need not come from in-house innovation. They can gain it through acquisition too.

Realize Your Allies Can Include Your Customers

Local markets in the United States are thirsty for fast Internet service. They would love to see simple, fully scoped, and seamlessly integrated communications devices operated by one button on a computer screen. Consumers often blame a number of different parties, local phone companies included, for not letting this happen. Further, consumers could potentially accept such advancement from almost anywhere in the market.

Carriers should realize that their customers are not just points of revenue. They are allies in the struggle to bring the Internet telephony concept fully to market. They have a surprising number of business interests aligned with the business interests of carriers, which would be wise to tap these interests before on-line consumer collectives like Accompany.com and Mercata.com force the issue on them.

Conclusion

Carriers realize that they own a wonderful resource in the networked economy: the network. But they seem insistent on continuing to use this as a bottleneck. A wiser approach would be to treat it like the commodity that it is becoming and use their current privileged position to open up to competitors in ways that help them achieve synergies. The need to move away from the infrastructure and price-based lock-in model and toward the added value- and innovation-based lock-in model should be high in the minds of carriers' executives. They must treat their channel in new ways, treat their customers in new ways, treat their complementors in new ways, and ultimately treat their product in bold and unprecedented ways. The principles they apply will be proven economic tenets, but the mix and the form of application must conform to the inexorable, competitive, and novel press of the networked economy.

13

Internet Telephony Regulation

Jonathan Weinberg

The communications world is changing, and packet-switched networks are taking over. Traditionally, telephone networks have relied on a circuit-switched architecture; when one user makes a call to another, a circuit within the network is opened and dedicated to that call for as long as the call lasts.[1] In the 1960s, scientists began developing packet-switching techniques for communicating information. In packet switching, the information (a telephone conversation, video clip, computer program, newspaper article, or something else) is sliced up into small packets, each carrying its own copy of the destination address. The packets travel individually to their destination, not necessarily over the same route, and are reassembled in proper sequence when they arrive. Packet switching is the way the Internet works.[2]

The traditional communications world relies on distinct infrastructures for each communications service. Voice travels over a nationwide wired, intelligent, circuit-switched network, with a single 64 Kbps voice channel set aside for each call. Video moves over a separate system of terrestrial broadcast stations, supplemented by coaxial cable or hybrid fiber/coaxial networks carrying video programming from a cable head-end to all homes in a given area. Data are piggybacked onto the voice network via an awkward kluge, under which the information is converted from digital to analog form and back again.

Digitization and packet switching have the potential to change that traditional design. One can convert the information transmitted by any communications service—voice, video, text, or data—into digital form.

Packet switching, with or without the use of Internet protocol (IP), enables the transmission of that digitized information across different networks without regard to the underlying network technology.[3] This means that the digitized information corresponding to any service can be transmitted over any physical infrastructure: copper wires, fiber, hybrid fiber-coaxial, microwave, direct broadcast satellites, or carrier pigeon.[4] Proprietors of copper (or hybrid fiber/coaxial or wireless) infrastructure can offer services not previously associated with those physical facilities, and new services can be delivered, via the Internet, over any physical facilities supporting high-speed data transmission.[5]

Both local exchange carriers and cable operators are now entering the market to provide high-speed data services. Consumers with Internet access can engage in real-time voice transmission via IP. Cable operators are exploring the provision of voice telephony, via IP, over cable facilities.[6] New services, including video, can be offered over various facilities; all that is necessary is bandwidth. And increasingly firms are designing nationwide, packet-switched, backbone networks to carry that traffic.[7] These networks are not designed to support a particular service; they carry whatever information is necessary for the service the consumer wants.

These developments, however, give rise to a regulatory dilemma. American communications law has developed along service-specific lines. It has developed complex and distinct regulatory structures covering telephony (wired and wireless), broadcasting, cable television, and satellites. It has so far left IP transmission largely unregulated. As those technologies become no longer separate, we need to figure out what to do with the old regulatory structures.

In this chapter, I focus on one aspect of that problem: To what extent should (or can) we impose legacy telephone regulation on IP networks? As a broad-brush matter, it seems plain that it would be a very bad idea either to impose such regulation or not to impose it. Imposing legacy regulation on IP networks seems like a bad idea because that regulation was not designed for those networks. It was developed to fit a circuit-switched world, served mostly by monopoly telephone service providers, and it is characterized by extensive cross-subsidies and a general disregard for innovation and competitive markets. Not imposing regulation, though, seems untenable as well: IP and conventional networks are merging. To maintain extensive regulation of the circuit-switched world and minimal regulation of the IP world will simply invite arbitrage and will undercut the legitimate policy goals of the old system.

This problem is made more difficult by the snarl of cross-subsidies that comprise much of modern telephone regulation. Telephone pricing today is characterized by a variety of subsidies: some federal, some state; some explicit, some implicit.[8] On the federal level, the government administers explicit subsidies through "universal service" contributions and disbursements. It implements implicit subsidies through the interstate access charge system[9] and geographic averaging of interstate long-distance rates.[10] States typically administer implicit subsidies via geographic averaging of local telephone rates, business-to-residential subsidies, and the pricing of vertical features, intrastate access, and intrastate toll. The most important of these is geographic rate averaging: high-density urban areas, where costs are lower, underwrite the provision of service to low-density, high-cost rural areas.[11]

The Federal Communications Commission (FCC) thus must face these questions: To what extent should the Internet, and IP networks generally, be brought into the web of subsidies that characterize much of modern telephone regulation? What are the consequences if they are not?

In this chapter, I focus my attention on explicit federal universal service subsidies and, to a lesser extent, the interstate access charge system. After providing some background, I suggest that the distinction between "telecommunications" and "information service," embedded in current law, cannot coherently be applied to IP-based services. Rather than attempting to single out "telecommunications" providers for universal service contribution obligations, it may make sense to impose those obligations on the owners of the physical transmission facilities used for the services. I suggest that in the long run, providers of interstate IP-based services should pay any congestion costs they impose on the local exchange. Such a step may be appropriate, however, in the presence of meaningful competition in the local market, and only on a showing that the failure to require such payments is distorting ISPs' market incentives.

Background

Internet Architecture

The Internet is an interconnected network of networks, communicating using packet-switching technology. A key part of that technology is the IP, which provides the intelligence to transmit packets successfully even if source and destination are on different physical networks. IP converts multiple physical networks, which may run on completely different hardware, into a single logical network. Any computer on any of the underlying networks can thus communicate with any other.[12]

On a more prosaic level, the Internet is a set of computers, packet routers, and the physical communications paths (such as copper wire, or fiber-optic cable, or terrestrial wireless, or satellite transmission, or coaxial cable) connecting them. A packet router is a data communications device whose job it is to tell packets where to go; each time a packet hits a router, the router examines that packet's address information and determines where to send it next.[13] Typically each router is connected to at least two others.[14] For the most part, the Internet's physical transmission paths are copper or fiber lines leased from telephone companies (or fiber-optic cable from other providers).[15] All telephone lines are not the same, though. At one extreme is an ordinary analog voice line, which can be used for data by means of a modem transmitting information at (say) a rate of 28.8 kilobytes per second (Kbps). As one seeks increasing speed, one might lease data lines from the telephone company rated at T1 (1.544 megabytes per second, or Mbps) or T3 (45 Mbps), or an OC3 fiber-optic line (155 Mbps) or an OC12 (622 Mbps). Each of these comes with a progressively higher price tag.[16]

When I am at home in Ann Arbor and send an e-mail message to a *Yale Journal on Regulation* editor who has an account on the Yale University system, the packets constituting that message move something like this. Each packet begins at my home computer and travels over my home telephone line to a server belonging to Msen, my internet service provider (ISP). Msen is in the business of supplying Internet access to residences and businesses. It has modem banks in twenty-four Michigan cities, and provisions its network using telephone lines leased from companies in the state.

Msen has made the business choice to provide service only in Michigan, though. Its network does not extend beyond the state. In order for my packets to leave Michigan, therefore, Msen must pass them to a backbone provider.[17] A backbone provider is a firm that owns high-speed routers physically located in a number of cities across the United States and has leased (or constructed) high-speed data lines to connect those routers.[18] It thus controls a high-speed interstate data pathway. To get my packets to Yale University, Msen will most likely pass them via a Detroit interconnection point to a national backbone provider known as UUNET. (UUNET is currently a unit of MCI Worldcom.)[19] UUNET may route the packets to New York and hand them off to AT&T.[20] CERFnet would then convey the packets to the Yale University network in New Haven; that network would reassemble the packets into my e-mail message and deliver them to the recipient.

Who pays for all this? ISPs and Internet backbone providers interconnect by means of "transit" or "peering" arrangements.[21] Msen pays UUNET for transit. That is, it pays UUNET to accept traffic coming from Msen's network and deliver that traffic to either a destination on UUNET's own network or a third network for ultimate delivery.[22] UUNET and CERFnet, by contrast, have a peering arrangement; each has agreed to deliver traffic to the other, so that the customers of one network can exchange traffic with the customers of the other, and neither network pays the other for that service.[23] As a general matter, the major national backbones peer with one another. Networks that enter into peering arrangements are usually (although not always) more or less the same size, so that roughly equivalent numbers of packets flow in each direction.[24]

My monthly subscription payment to Msen covers my share of its costs for interconnection to UUNET and other backbone providers. It also covers my share of Msen's costs to transport packets within its own network—that is, capital expenditures for routers, servers, modems, and associated equipment and monthly payments for leased lines to connect those pieces of equipment.[25]

Telephone Regulation

All of these relationships developed within the context of a much older, completely unrelated telephone regulatory system. Federal regulation of telecommunications began with the Mann-Elkins Act of 1910, which subjected telephone and telegraph service to the jurisdiction of the Interstate Commerce Commission (whose main job was railroad regulation).[26] Twenty-four years later, Title II of the Communications Act moved the job of telecommunications regulation to the new FCC.[27] For both the substantive standards applicable to telephone and telegraph service providers and the procedural mechanisms used to enforce those standards, Title II looked to then-existing railroad law.[28]

Title II, as enacted in 1934, regulated the conduct of communications "common carriers," defined to include any person (other than a broadcaster) "engaged as a common carrier for hire in interstate or foreign communication by wire or radio."[29] Its keystones were requirements that carriers' rates be embodied in published tariffs[30] and be just, reasonable, and nondiscriminatory.[31] Carriers were required to interconnect with other carriers[32] and to obtain agency permission before building or acquiring new lines.[33] The agency had the power to prescribe just and reasonable charges,[34] suspend and investigate tariffs,[35] and award damages.[36] The FCC administered these provisions with the goals (among others) of safeguarding against anticompetitive behavior, minimizing the potential for improper cross-subsidization, and protecting the quality and efficiency of telephone service.[37] Over time, Congress added new requirements relating to such disparate issues as carriers' disclosure of private customer information,[38] obscene or harassing telephone calls,[39] the use of telecommunications services by the hearing impaired,[40] pay-per-call services,[41] and facilitation of police eavesdropping.[42]

The Federal-State Divide

The Communications Act did not abrogate exclusive control to the FCC. Rather, it divided authority between the national government and the states. It assigned the FCC authority over interstate communication, but left to the states regulation of intrastate communications.[43] Even before the passage of the 1934 act, it became clear that this dividing line between federal and state jurisdictions was problematic.[44] A long-distance call, after all, passes over the network of the local telephone company serving the caller, *and* that of the long-distance company, *and* that of the local telephony company serving the called party. What does such a call do to the act's jurisdictional boundaries? In a 1930 case, *Smith v. Illinois Bell Telephone Co.*, the Supreme Court provided an answer. To the extent that local plant is used for interstate calling, the Court stated, it is beyond the reach of the state regulator. Its costs relate to "property used in the interstate service" and must be included in the interstate rate base, under federal control.[45] The cost of local telephone company plant must thus be allocated between the intrastate and interstate jurisdictions.[46]

In the wake of *Smith v. Illinois Bell*, AT&T increased its per-minute long-distance rates to reflect that portion of local plant costs assigned to the interstate jurisdiction and returned the corresponding revenues to the local companies (which, for the most part, were its subsidiaries, so the reimbursement was just a division of revenues within the AT&T corporate family).[47] After the beginning of long-distance competition,[48] the new long-distance carriers came to make similar payments.[49] Under FCC rules promulgated in 1983, AT&T and its competitors each made competitively neutral access payments to the (now independent) local carriers for the right to originate and terminate traffic on their networks.[50]

As the FCC recognized, though, this impact of *Smith v. Illinois Bell* was economically questionable. Local plant costs are for the most part non-traffic sensitive. That is, the cost of installing and maintaining a wire from an Ameritech central office to my house is the same whether I use that line five minutes each day or eighteen hours. Yet under the access charge system, those costs were recovered through a per minute (traffic-sensitive) charge on long-distance usage. Heavy long-distance users ended up paying more than the costs they imposed on the network; light users paid less. This created arbitrage incentives and raised the possibility that heavy users might turn to solutions in which they bypassed the local telephone networks entirely in initiating long-distance traffic, avoiding access charges and shifting those costs onto an ever-shrinking rate base.

Accordingly, the FCC began moving away from the old structure. It ordered in 1983 that a portion of the local plant costs in the interstate jurisdiction should be recovered through flat, monthly per line charges assessed on all local telephone subscribers. This, the agency reasoned, would be more nearly economically efficient: non-traffic-sensitive costs would be recovered through non-traffic-sensitive fees, so that prices would be based on the true cost characteristics of telephone company plant. At the same time, the FCC established the Universal Service Fund, to be supported by the long-distance carriers, to subsidize rates in high-cost areas.[51] The agency contemplated that over time, it would increase the monthly per line charges paid by local telephone subscribers until those charges covered all local plant costs in the interstate jurisdiction, with the exception of the costs reimbursed by the Universal Service Fund.[52] This goal proved unrealistic, as the FCC faced complaints that allowing the flat charges to rise might cause low-income customers to disconnect their telephone service.[53] Instead, local costs assigned to the interstate jurisdiction ended up being recovered partly through subscriber line charges and partly through interstate carriers' access payments.[54]

Computer II

In the meantime, the FCC was forced to revamp the regulatory structure in an entirely different respect, to confront "the growing . . . interdependence of communications and data processing technologies."[55] In the early days of telecommunications, customers buying telephone or telegraph service got an integrated communications offering managed from top to bottom by the service provider. That changed: "In providing a communications service, carriers [increasingly] no longer control the use to which the transmission medium is put."[56] Instead, carriers came to offer transparent communications channels that subscribers could use as they chose, for the transmission of voice, data, fax, or other information.[57] Users were able to combine the communications paths provided by telephone companies with computing power and thus create new services, such as voice mail or database access, that they could sell to others. The FCC recognized, in a landmark 1980 proceeding known as *Computer II*, that it would be undesirable to subject these new services to the tariffing and other requirements that were the concomitants of traditional telephone regulation. Imposing those regulatory burdens would discourage innovation and distort the new marketplace, as vendors sought to structure their services so as to avoid coming under the regulatory umbrella. And because the markets for the new services were competitive, regulations primarily intended to restrain market power were unnecessary.[58]

Accordingly, the FCC announced that it would distinguish between basic and enhanced services.[59] It limited basic transmission services to the offering of "pure transmission capability over a communications path that is virtually transparent in terms of its interaction with customer supplied information."[60] By contrast, "any offering over the telecommunications network which is more than a basic transmission service" was an enhanced service.[61] Enhanced services included services "offered over common carrier transmission facilities" that "employ computer processing applications that act on the format, content, code, protocol or similar aspects of the subscriber's transmitted information; provide the subscriber additional, different, or restructured information; or involve subscriber interaction with stored information."[62] Thus, for example, any service featuring "voice or data storage and retrieval applications, such as a 'mail box' service," was enhanced.[63]

Enhanced service providers, the FCC continued, should not be subject to regulation under Title II of the Communications Act.[64] Notwithstanding that any enhanced service by definition had a communications component, the FCC found that no regulatory scheme could "rationally distinguish and classify enhanced services as either communications or data processing"[65] and that any attempt to impose regulation on enhanced services would lead to arbitrage, inconsistency, or inappropriate regulation.[66] (There was one major caveat: Ma Bell and her descendants, when they sought to offer enhanced services, were subject to a set of rules designed to ensure that they did not leverage their monopoly power.)[67] That approach was wildly successful in spurring innovation and competition in the enhanced-services marketplace. Government was able to maintain its control of the underlying transport, sold primarily by regulated monopolies, while eschewing any control over the newfangled, competitive "enhancements."

When the FCC revamped access payments in 1983, it initially took the position that both basic and enhanced service providers should pay access charges. Both were "users of access service" in that they "obtained local exchange service or facilities which are used . . . for the purpose of completing interstate calls."[68] On reconsideration, though, the agency abandoned that view. Enhanced service providers, it stated, would experience severe rate shocks if they were to pay the same access charges as long-distance carriers.[69] Accordingly, it exempted enhanced service providers from any access charge obligations. Rather, those charges fell solely on firms offering basic, interexchange services on a common carrier basis.[70]

The 1996 Telecommunications Act

In 1996, Congress passed the Telecommunications Act. This enactment, which significantly rewrote U.S. telecommunications law, did not refer to basic and enhanced services at all. Instead, it characterized communications services as "telecommunications" or "information service."[71] Congress defined *telecommunications*, though, in a manner strongly reminiscent of the basic services category, as "the transmission, between or among points specified by the user, of information of the user's choosing, without change in the form or content of the information as sent and received."[72] It defined *information services* in a manner reminiscent of enhanced services, to include "the offering of a capability for generating, acquiring, storing, transforming, processing, retrieving, utilizing and making available information via telecommunications."[73] The FCC concluded that Congress in the 1996 act intended telecommunications and information service to parallel basic and enhanced services.[74]

At the heart of the 1996 act are provisions intended to enable, for the first time, competition in the provision of local telecommunications service. Local telecommunications competition is problematic because the incumbents already own the key facilities—most important, the lines running from telephone company central offices into every home and business. Accordingly, section 251 of the 1996 act requires incumbent local exchange carriers to make those lines, and other facilities, available to competitors at cost and to allow competitors to place their own equipment in the incumbent's central offices.

Robust competition, though, calls for reform of the subsidy system. Under the pre-1996 status quo, local service was subsidized explicitly, through the Universal Service Fund, and implicitly, through subsidies built into long-distance carriers' access payments. The 1996 act directed the FCC to move toward a system under which implicit subsidies would be eliminated. All federal subsidy support would be distributed through "specific, predictable and sufficient" explicit mechanisms.[75] The FCC accordingly announced that it would seek to reduce access charges so that they covered *only* the traffic-sensitive costs of interconnection with the local network (and thus were cost justified).[76] All other local plant costs in the interstate jurisdiction, it continued, should be covered through either flat, per line charges or explicit, portable subsidies provided by a larger, revamped Universal Service Fund. This fund, by the terms of the 1996 act, would be supported by equitable and nondiscriminatory "contributions" (as the statute put it) from interstate telecommunications carriers.[77]

As the FCC has implemented the 1996 act, the Universal Service Fund has several components. The largest component is the "high-cost" fund. This mechanism subsidizes telephone companies in rural and other high-cost areas where the costs of the local loop—that "last mile" of the telephone network running to the individual home or business—are so high that many users would drop off the network rather than shoulder the full costs themselves.[78] In the second quarter of 1999, interstate telecommunications carriers paid about 2.4 percent of their interstate and international end user revenues for that purpose.[79] The Universal Service Fund also supports the Lifeline and Link Up programs, targeted toward low-income consumers,[80] and a program designed to connect schools, libraries, and rural health care providers to the Internet.[81]

The FCC's reorganization of the Universal Service Fund following the 1996 act greatly increased the scope of explicit federal telephone subsidies, but it did not increase total support. In imposing a charge paid by long-distance carriers to a centrally managed fund and disbursed to local exchange carriers, rather than setting the rate-making boundary between federal and state jurisdictions so that long-distance carriers paid local carriers inflated fees, it simply made explicit what had previously been implicit. For the most part, the same entities (interstate telecommunications carriers) still paid the monies in question, and the same entities (local exchange carriers) still received them. Because the 1996 act was able to carry over existing subsidy patterns in this manner, Congress gave no serious thought to funding universal service from some other source—say, out of general tax revenues.

Universal service support mechanisms, under the 1996 act, may support only "telecommunications [that is, basic] services."[82] The act directs the FCC periodically to reevaluate the definition of supported telecommunications services in the light of "advances in telecommunications and information technologies and services," relying on "the extent to which such telecommunications services are essential to education, public health, or public safety; have . . . been subscribed to by a substantial majority of residential customers; [and] are being deployed in public telecommunications networks by telecommunications carriers."[83] The services supported by the Universal Service Fund today, as defined by the FCC, are no more than single-party voice-grade access to the PSTN, with touchtone signaling and access to emergency services, operator services, and directory assistance.[84]

The Internet and Universal Service Mechanisms

The FCC's April 1998 *Report to Congress on Universal Service* sought to characterize IP-based service offerings as "telecommunications" or "information service" in order to assess their regulatory obligations.[85] That distinction however, cannot coherently be applied to IP-based services. This section explains why, and then suggests and evaluates an alternative approach.

Report to Congress on Universal Service

After the passage of the 1996 act, the FCC consistently characterized IP-based services as information services rather than telecommunications.[86] This meant that the providers of such services were required neither to pay a percentage of their end user revenues as a contribution to the Universal Service Fund nor to comply with any other Title II obligations.[87] The agency was forced to reexamine that judgment, though, in 1998. Opponents, including Senators Ted Stevens (R, Alaska) and Conrad Burns (R, Montana), were urging that all IP-based services should be deemed to involve "telecommunications."[88] Those senators expressed concern that as telephone traffic shifted from conventional to IP networks, a failure to impose universal service charges on IP-based services would endanger universal service.[89] They crafted an appropriations rider directing the agency to undertake a detailed review of its definitions of the terms *information service, telecommunications,* and *telecommunications service* (among others) in the Telecommunications Act of 1996; the application of those definitions to "mixed or hybrid services" (referring in part to Internet access services and IP telephony); and "the impact of such application on universal service definitions and support."[90]

The FCC duly wrote a report responsive to the appropriations rider.[91] It reaffirmed its conclusion that Internet access services were information services (and that the providers of such services therefore were under no obligation to make direct payments to the Universal Service Fund).[92] By contrast, the commission classed the provision of pure transmission capacity to Internet access and backbone providers as telecommunications.[93]

The agency ran into some difficulty, though, when it sought to characterize IP telephony services—that is, services enabling real-time voice transmission using Internet protocols. The FCC first addressed computer-to-computer IP telephony, in which individuals use software and hardware at their premises to place calls between two computers connected to the public Internet.

In that context, the FCC stated, it need not decide whether there was "telecommunications" taking place; Title II requirements (including universal service payment obligations) would not apply in any event.[94] Title II obligations, the agency explained, apply only to the "provi[sion]" or "offering" of telecommunications.[95] When a user, with an ordinary Internet connection through her ISP, uses Internet telephony software to enable real-time voice communication between her computer and that of a fellow enthusiast, the ISP may not even know that the subscriber's packets are carrying voice communications. The ISP is not, in any meaningful sense, "provid[ing]" the voice telephony to that subscriber, and cannot be made subject to Title II on that basis.[96]

The agency was unable to be so definite, though, with respect to phone-to-phone IP telephony services. Those are services in which a customer places a call, using an ordinary telephone and the PSTN, to a gateway device that packetizes the voice signal and transmits it via IP to a second gateway, which reverses the processing and sends the signal back over the public switched network to be received by an ordinary telephone at the terminating end.[97] The FCC was unable to reach a conclusion as to the proper classification of such services, stating only that "the record currently before us suggests that certain forms of 'phone-to-phone' IP telephony lack the characteristics that would render them 'information services' within the meaning of the statute, and instead bear the characteristics of 'telecommunications services.' "[98] It deferred any "definitive pronouncements" on phone-to-phone IP telephony to an unspecified later proceeding.

The *Report to Congress on Universal Service* stressed the FCC's position that the growth of IP-based services would buttress universal service, not undercut it. Notwithstanding that Internet access providers are not required to make universal service payments, they are major users of telecommunications and thus make "substantial indirect contributions to universal service" in the prices they pay to purchase telecommunications.[99] The agency did express concern that exemption of IP telephony providers from universal service contribution requirements might create an incentive to shift traffic to IP networks, increasing the burden on the remaining contribution base and undermining universal service; it found no evidence, however, of "an immediate threat to the sufficiency of universal service support" at this time.[100]

The Breakdown of the Telecommunications/Information Service Distinction

It should not be surprising that the FCC had trouble with the characterization and regulatory obligations of IP telephony providers. On the one hand, the agency was surely correct that Title II obligations should not leap into existence simply because a consumer transmits voice rather than, say, graphics, over an IP connection. It would be highly problematic to treat packets differently just because they carried voice rather than some other sort of information. More important, as the commission noted, in the simplest computer-to-computer case, the customer is buying only Internet access rather than an IP telephony service as such. In other IP telephony services, by contrast, the customer receives enhanced functionality, which goes beyond the plain-vanilla transmission that constitutes "telecommunications."

On the other hand, it is also problematic if the provider of a service that looks and feels to the user just like conventional telephony is subject to regulation far different from that imposed on conventional telephony providers. In particular, it would be odd and unhelpful if huge regulatory distinctions should turn on the question whether a vendor transports an intermediate leg of its telephone calls by IP or some other packet-oriented technology. Conventional telecommunications carriers increasingly are using asynchronous transfer mode (ATM), a different packet-oriented communications technology, in their networks, and it is completely accepted that the use of ATM to transmit a telephone call does not render the carrier an information service provider.

To accommodate both of these concerns, one must devise a way of distinguishing those forms of IP telephony that should be subject to regulation from those that should not, but that turns out to be troublesome. The FCC in the *Report to Congress on Universal Service* suggested the possibility of subjecting to Title II regulation IP telephony services in which the provider "1) . . . holds itself out as providing voice telephony or facsimile transmission service; 2) . . . does not require the customer to use CPE [customer premises equipment] different from that CPE necessary to place an ordinary touch-tone call (or facsimile transmission) over the public switched telephone network; 3) . . . allows the customer to call telephone numbers assigned in accordance with the North American Numbering Plan, and associated international agreements; and 4) . . . transmits customer information without net change in form or content."[101] The effect of these requirements would be to regulate an IP telephony service as telecommunications if the customer's signal travels in unpacketized form over the public switched network to a gateway (as in conventional phone-to-phone service), but not if it is packetized in the customer premises equipment (as in computer-to-computer service).

It is doubtful that would work very well. Consider a telephone handset that packetizes the customer's voice signal and sends the packets via IP to an Internet telephony service provider, but that nonetheless looks and acts, from the user's perspective, like a conventional telephone. If a service should rely on such equipment, it is not obvious what policy goals would be served by treating that service differently from phone-to-phone IP telephony as defined.[102] Indeed, consider business telephone users served by switchboard or Centrex systems. Should the policymaker apply one regulatory paradigm if calls from the business's telephones are directed to an IP gateway on the public switched network, but another if the switchboard serving the business itself serves as such a gateway? Why?[103]

The difficulty extends beyond the particular definition suggested in the *Report to Congress on Universal Service*. What if the phone-to-phone IP telephony provider adds just a dab of functionality—say, it not only enables two people to talk, but automatically records the conversation and makes it available via streaming audio on a Web site? Or—so as to enable anybody to be a talk show host—it allows the originator to conduct a conference call with three or four people, while allowing any member of the public to dial in and listen?[104] Looking to the 1996 act definitions, it seems plain that the recording, storage, and rebroadcast of the conversation in the first example involve enhanced functionality and constitute an "information service"; the more difficult question is whether we have one service or two. That is, does the example involve a single information service or a plain-vanilla telephony service (telecommunications) combined with a separate transcription service (information service)? Similarly, the service in the second example does not appear to qualify as "telecommunications," which the 1996 act defines as "the transmission, between points specified by the user, of information of the user's choosing, without change in the form or content of the information as sent and received," because the transmission does not seem to be "among points specified by the user."[105] Yet should we therefore characterize the overall service as an "information service," or can one again find a regulated telecommunications service by dividing the offering into two?

The anomaly here is that it is easy to build functionality into IP-based services, yet under the "telecommunications"–"information service" dichotomy, an IP-based service will be deemed "telecommunications," and thus subject to regulation and universal service obligations, only if it offers sufficiently crabbed functionality. If the same service gets a software upgrade and offers a little more functionality, it becomes an information service and escapes regulation—unless the new functionality is deemed a separate service, but we do not have any rules for deciding when that should be so.[106] It is hard to see why any of this makes sense.

IP telephony presents yet another puzzle. Under the FCC's current definitions, both phone-to-computer and computer-to-phone IP telephony appear to be information services. In each case, the gateway is providing protocol conversion and processing (translating from unprocessed voice to a series of IP packets, or vice versa); under established rules, that enhanced functionality pulls the service out of the realm of simple telecommunications.[107] Yet put those two services together, and what do you have? Any protocol conversion taking place at one point in the call is undone at another; established law suggests that the concatenated services *are* mere "telecommunications."[108] It is hard to know what to do with that, since the firms providing the two services may not, in a distributed environment, even be aware of one another.[109] The bottom line is that the telecommunications–information service boundary does not seem to divide up the world of IP-based services in any especially useful way.

Nor are these problems limited to IP telephony. Consider a rather more important finding of the *Report to Congress on Universal Service*: that Internet access is an information service. That conclusion seems vulnerable outside of the dial-up context. One of the defining characteristics of IP is that an IP network itself displays no intelligence; it only passes information transparently from one edge to another. In a phrase, the network provides only "commodity connectivity."[110] All of the intelligence and enhanced functionality—the storage and manipulation of user information—take place at the edges of the networks (that is, either before or after the information is transmitted from origin to destination).[111] Simple IP transmission thus seems like a classic example of "transmission, between or among points specified by the user, of information of the user's choice, without change in the form or content", that is, telecommunications. Indeed, the FCC has said essentially that about other packet-based services.[112]

The *Report to Congress on Universal Service* bottoms its finding that Internet access is an information service largely on the fact that ISPs run mail servers, host Web pages, offer Usenet news feeds, operate caches, and engage in other computer-mediated activities that go beyond simple transmission of packets.[113] But not all customers require these services. Where the customer is a corporate intranet, it will maintain its own mail and Web servers. The Internet access provider likely will provide nothing except pure transmission and routing of packets within its internal network and connection to the larger Internet. In such a case, it seems hard to avoid the conclusion that the ISP is offering telecommunications: it is providing transport, and nothing else.

This suggests some really silly accounting problems. Imagine that an ISP leases a fat digital transmission link to a network access point. The carrier leasing that line to the ISP is liable for universal service payments to the extent the ISP uses that connection to serve dial-up customers, because the ISP is providing those customers with an information service, and thus is itself a telecommunications "end user" for universal service purposes.[114] At the same time, if the analysis in the preceding paragraph is correct, the carrier need *not* pay into the Universal Service Fund to the extent the ISP uses the same connection to serve corporate customers, for the ISP is providing telecommunications to those customers and thus is not an "end user." If nothing else, that is administratively unworkable.

The notion that pure Internet connectivity is "telecommunications" within the meaning of the 1996 act, though, is troubling on a more fundamental level. It expands the scope of services subject to Universal Service Fund exactions without any policy-oriented understanding of why that should be necessary or desirable. Put another way, it extends old rules to the Net without adequate consideration of whether that is a good thing.[115]

Why the Telecommunications/Information Service Distinction Doesn't Work

To understand why the telecommunications–information service distinction does not work in the IP context, it is useful to look back to *Computer II*. The *Computer II* categories, like their 1996 act cognates, focused on service offerings. That is, the things being categorized were services rather than (say) equipment or capabilities.[116] That is a natural way to divide up the world from a conventional telephony perspective; folks from the world of computer-to-computer communications, though, tend to use a different set of categories.

The computing world, in thinking about the communications process, tends to rely on the open systems interconnection (OSI) model, which organizes that process into layers.[117] The physical layer is concerned with the physical infrastructure over which the information travels; immediately above that is the data link layer, concerned with the procedures for transmitting data using a particular technology, and the network layer, concerned with the transfer of data between computers and routing.[118] The transport layer defines the rules for information exchange and manages the reliable end-to-end delivery of information.[119] The session, presentation, and applications layers focus on user applications; in particular, the applications layer contains the functionality for specific services.[120]

The service offerings contemplated by *Computer II* cut across the layers of the OSI model. For example, the paradigmatic example of basic service (or "telecommunications") is plain old telephone service (POTS), designed to enable ordinary voice communication. POTS constitutes a vertically integrated intertwining of components from various layers. It relies on a copper twisted-pair infrastructure (the physical layer) organized into a circuit-switched architecture, with 64 Kbps channels set aside for each voice signal (data link, network, and transport layers).[121] Applications such as flash hook signaling rely on elements ranging from the bottom (physical) to the top (applications) layers.[122]

The *Computer II* model in fact contemplated that enhanced services would be constructed in a layered manner, but it relied on an entirely different set of layers. Its fundamental assumption was that POTS services were the foundation on which enhanced services were built. One created an enhanced service by taking POTS service (or a similar but higher-bandwidth service provided by the telephone company), using that service to transmit data, and adding data processing (and thus enhanced functionality). The underlying POTS transport was subject to regulation; the enhanced service, which was "enhanced" in the most literal sense, was not. That made perfect sense in the world of *Computer II*, back in 1980, and for years to come. It was perfectly natural for government to seek to regulate the underlying transport (which was, after all, offered for the most part by regulated monopolies), while eschewing any control over the "enhancements." The 1996 act, as the FCC has interpreted it, carried forward the same model.[123]

That key assumption does not work in the IP world. IP maintains a sharp separation between the various layers of the OSI model. Different components of the network are responsible for the physical infrastructure, the transport of the underlying bits (using the IP), and the applications (or services) that ride on top. One can write applications without having to worry at all about the lower layers; one's service will work over any physical infrastructure and any transport protocol with IP on it. That means, though, that the foundational assumption of *Computer II*—that an enhanced service is a basic service "plus"—no longer works.

In the IP world, there are no vertically integrated service offerings such as POTS that can be seen as the foundation of more elaborate offerings. An IP-based service offering that transmits information transparently does not play the same role in the IP world as POTS does in the conventional telephony world, because it does not provide transport for other, more elaborate IP-based service offerings. Rather, the only foundation of any IP-based service offering is the underlying IP transport.

As applied to the IP world, the distinction between basic and enhanced does not serve the goal of allowing government to regulate underlying transport while leaving the enhancements to the marketplace. Instead, it creates only the anomalous distinction that a service is subject to regulation if it offers little functionality, but free from regulation if it offers somewhat more.[124] It creates the anomalous result that two services, each deemed information services when viewed in isolation, may combine in a distributed environment to form an end-to-end offering magically deemed telecommunications.[125] If regulators wish to carry forward into the IP world *Computer II*'s goal of attaching regulatory obligations to underlying transport, they need to aim those obligations more precisely.

Universal Service Redux

In rethinking universal service support in the modern telecommunications world, how should we draw the line between regulated and unregulated services? One approach might be to revise the universal service payment obligation so as to associate it not with service provision but with the physical facilities along which the information moves.[126] *Computer II*, after all, sought to impose regulatory obligations on the underlying transport, and it is the physical layer that is associated with underlying transport in the most fundamental sense. A payment obligation tied to the ownership of qualifying facilities could apply without regard to whether the information moving via those facilities was in digital or analog form, or was packet or circuit switched.

Such an approach would have a variety of advantages. We could avoid the problems associated with determining which providers were providing "telecommunications," making them subject to the assessment, and which were providing "information services," leaving them exempt. Facilities ownership would trigger the obligation without regard to the nature of the traffic moving over those facilities. Such a rule might be able to do what the *Computer II* distinction itself can no longer do. It might effectuate *Computer II*'s goal of imposing regulatory obligations on underlying transport without burdening the service components higher up the protocol stack. It would thus vindicate *Computer II*'s still-valid judgment that in order not to retard innovation, we should not impose regulatory costs on the new, still unfolding functionalities made possible by the marriage of silicon and data transmission.[127]

Such an approach would be aesthetically appealing. To the extent that the high-cost fund is designed to support the availability of physical infrastructure universally throughout the nation,[128] it makes a nice symmetry to impose the associated costs on physical infrastructure. More consequentially, the approach would be technology neutral. Based on the assumption that a bit is a bit is a bit, no matter how it is transmitted, it would address the concerns of those who fear that a shift of telephone traffic away from circuit-switched voice to packet-switched data will undermine the entire subsidy structure. This seems important. In the ultimate analysis, it is hard to justify a regulatory scheme that assigns different consequences to provision of the same transport using different technologies. Such a scheme leads providers to make technology choices on the basis of regulatory arbitrage, not on the basis of which technology is most efficient, powerful, or inexpensive in the particular context.

Under a facilities-based approach, the facilities owners (telephone companies and others) from which ISPs and backbone providers lease data lines, as well as any ISPs and backbone providers owning their own transmission facilities, would make payments to the Universal Service Fund. One would expect facilities owners to pass on costs to ISPs and backbone providers leasing capacity from them; backbone providers to pass on costs to ISPs paying them for transit; and ISPs to pass on costs to their subscribers.[129] All this would likely increase the share of universal service obligations ultimately paid by consumers of Internet-based services. That without more, though, should not be a dispositive objection. Conventional and IP networks are merging, so that it will no longer work simply to seek to insulate IP networks from regulation.[130] Rather, the goal should be to find ways to recast existing regulation (where it should not simply be jettisoned for circuit-switched and packet-switched networks alike) to be technology neutral and IP friendly—to make sense in an increasingly packet-switched world.[131]

The approach I have detailed is not, in fact, the best one to choose. The simplest and best way to fund universal service would be to take the money from general tax revenues. That would eliminate any arbitrage or distortions caused by taxing one class of communications activity and not another. For the reasons set out earlier, though, Congress did not consider that approach;[132] as a political matter, it is now infeasible. Alternatively, we could reduce the scale of the problem by sharply reducing universal service subsidies to the minimum necessary to keep rural subscribers on the network.[133] That approach too, though, seems politically infeasible. If we are to fund extensive subsidies through assessments on communications providers, we need a method of doing so that is consistent with the nature of IP offerings. A facilities-based approach would satisfy that criterion; our current approach does not.

The FCC would have to overcome considerable practical difficulties, though, before it could adopt a facilities-based approach. How would the agency determine the amount of the fee paid by facilities owners? The agency currently sets universal service assessments as a percentage of the revenues a firm receives from end users for telecommunications.[134] If the agency tied the fact of the payment obligation to physical facilities ownership, then it could sensibly tie the amount of the assessment to revenues only by looking to that limited set of revenues corresponding to physical transmission. Yet typically a telecommunications (or information service) provider provides its customers with a combination of physical infrastructure, transport, and associated features and services, not just physical facilities. The revenues it receives are for the combination. Where a provider itself owns transmission facilities (rather than purchasing raw transmission from a third party) and provides its customers with an integrated service, it is not clear how one can isolate that portion of its revenues that correspond to raw transmission alone.[135]

Tying universal service obligations to a metric other than revenues could be at least as precarious. One possibility might be to make the fee proportional to the raw bandwidth of a firm's transmission facilities. Increasingly, though, carriers are creating bandwidth through improved multiplexing techniques rather than laying new fiber.[136] It would be undesirable if a firm's implementation of such techniques led to a massive jump in its universal service obligations; that might discourage desirable experimentation and capacity expansion. Nor would it always be clear, in the case of innovative technologies, how much bandwidth to associate with a given facility. Indeed, for some technologies (say, unlicensed wireless spread spectrum), the notion of the bandwidth associated with a facility seems essentially meaningless.[137]

It might be possible to impose a fee based on a firm's asset investment in physical facilities or on other such proxies. Alternatively, these difficulties might push us back to a solution based on actual or imputed revenues. Conceivably, a second-best solution might limit the universal service assessment to owners of transmission facilities, require those entities to make payments based on actual revenues in cases in which they provide leased lines or the equivalent, and require them to make payments based on the imputed value of the raw transmission they provide to themselves when they offer other services. Ultimately this issue appears to be essentially one of tax policy: how to devise an appropriate base for raising universal service funds that will not distort infrastructure development.[138]

In the end, an attempt to vindicate *Computer II* principles in the context of universal service obligations may be misdirected. The universal service obligation, after all, is today essentially a tax supporting a particular government program.[139] Under current rules, a firm may receive universal service support for serving customers in high-cost areas, if it provides access to the PSTN sufficient to support analog voice transmission, with touchtone signaling and access to emergency services, operator services, and directory assistance.[140] This reflects the conventional understanding of universal service. Voice access to the PSTN is seen as essential to public safety and participation in society and democracy, and every network subscriber benefits when that network is expanded.[141]

For historical and political reasons, we have chosen to fund this program not out of general tax revenues but through exactions from a class of communications service providers. In defining that class, it may be that our lodestar should not be *Computer II* but rather these more general principles: Any definition (1) should be adequately broad, (2) should not discourage development and deployment of new technology, and (3) should not introduce obvious distortions, which is to say that it should treat substitutable services similarly.

It would not make sense, thus, to limit the universe of universal service contributors to providers of supported services. Such a rule would tax the provision of conventional analog voice telephony connections while leaving untouched other data pathways that consumers could use to secure similar functionality. Indeed, there is no obvious reason to limit the universe of contributors to actors regulated under Title II. Under the current regulatory structure, only telecommunications carriers need contribute to the Universal Service Fund. Providers of cable service need not make payments to the fund, because cable service is not defined as "telecommunications"; it is governed by Title VI rather than Title II of the Communications Act.[142] Yet if the FCC is not to impose distortions, statutory pigeonholes should not overcome considerations of functionality and market substitutability. Under a technology-neutral approach, all services functionally similar to those subject to a Universal Service Fund obligation (or the facilities used to provide them) should be in play.

The Internet and Access Charges

The Universal Service Fund is not the only—or even the most important—federal subsidy mechanism. Telephone pricing today is characterized by a tangle of implicit as well as explicit cross-subsidies,[143] and the implicit subsidies are larger than the explicit.[144] The most important such subsidy mechanism, on the federal level, is interstate access pricing.[145] In part, those charges are designed to compensate the local telephone companies for the costs the call imposes on their networks. Historically, however, they have also included a substantial implicit subsidy component.[146] As a result, access charges today are an opaque blend of forward-looking economic cost, historic costs, and subsidies intended to depress local rates.[147] The FCC is seeking to remove the subsidy element from access charges and to drive those charges down to a level more nearly approximating forward-looking cost.[148]

Where should the Internet, and IP networks generally, fit within the access charge structure? As in the universal service context, I suggest that access charge obligations need not turn on the telecommunications–information service distinction in the long run at all. While universal service payments are pure subsidy, access charges include a cost recovery element. There is no compelling reason that, in the long run, information service providers should not pay charges tied to the costs they impose on the local exchange. Rather, the goal should be to move access charges toward cost for telecommunications and information service providers alike.

The Status Quo

Currently, information service providers do not pay access charges.[149] That exemption should continue for now. As the FCC has explained, it would make little sense to require ISPs to pay interstate access charges as currently constituted: "The existing access charge system includes non-cost-based rates and inefficient rate structures. [There is] no reason to extend this regime to an additional class of users. . . . The mere fact that providers of information services use incumbent [local exchange carrier] networks to receive calls from their customers does not mean that such providers should be subject to an interstate regulatory system designed for circuit-switched interexchange voice telephony."[150]

I have already suggested that attempts simply to insulate IP networks from regulation are doomed to fail. But that is not to say that one should blindly extend old rules to IP networks, no matter how inefficient or ill advised that regulation is. The FCC is currently seeking to remove implicit universal service subsidies from interstate access charges.[151] Against that backdrop, it would not be sensible to extend those subsidies to a new class of users, imposing distortions and inefficiencies on IP networks.

Beyond the Status Quo

The current exemption is not the end of the story. Access charges, after all, recover costs as well as generate subsidies. In the absence of access charges or some comparable payment, there is no mechanism to cause

ISPs to pay any congestion costs they impose on the local exchange. Any traffic-sensitive costs they impose, rather than being reflected in their own rates, are assigned to the local jurisdiction and spread among all local ratepayers.[152]

The extent to which ISPs impose costs on the local exchange is hotly debated.[153] The FCC's Local Competition Order, though, estimated a cost of $.002 to $.004 per minute as a default proxy for the traffic-sensitive component of local switching.[154] This figure, small as it is, suggests the potential for a mismatch between prices and economic costs where ISPs receive huge numbers of calls over the public switched network, since typically such a call is free to both caller (paying flat residential rates) and ISP (under standard local business rates, paying a flat fee for incoming calls). The matter is not simple; local switching costs appear to be essentially congestion costs,[155] and the interested parties fiercely dispute the degree to which Internet access in fact generates congestion on the local network.[156] The associated costs may well be zero except during peak periods.[157] But it seems plausible that Internet access may impose some costs on the local exchange not reflected in the rates that ISPs pay.[158]

The legitimacy of any mismatch between prices and economic costs in this area is usually debated in federalism terms. ISPs urge that the local lines they buy fall within the intrastate jurisdiction, so that it is up to state regulatory commissions to decide whether there is an impermissible disparity between prices and costs. They continue that in receiving large numbers of incoming calls while making few outgoing calls, ISPs are no differently suited from a variety of other local businesses (pizza parlors, say) and should not be singled out for different treatment.[159]

That argument seems unsatisfactory, though, on a variety of levels. To the extent that the bulk of the inefficiencies and subsidies that characterize conventional telephony are built into the intrastate pricing structure, we should be wary of too quick a finding that any IP-based service is properly regulated as part of that structure. Moreover, the federalism argument seems wrong: ISPs provide what is in predominant part an interstate information service.[160] Customers use ISP facilities to exchange traffic with e-mail correspondents, Usenet news participants, Web sites, FTP servers, and other persons or devices without regard to jurisdictional boundaries.[161] Indeed, the entire point of Internet access is to enable communication with persons and sites ranged across the globe.[162]

Dial-up Internet access, to be sure, is an information service under the definitions discussed earlier in this chapter, not a telecommunications service like long-distance POTS. It is by no means clear, though, why that should be relevant to a charge designed to recover actual costs imposed on the local exchange. When the FCC established the access charge system in 1983, it initially contemplated that both basic and enhanced service providers would pay access charges.[163] Even in reversing that initial judgment, it had no doubt that enhanced service providers "employ exchange service for jurisdictionally interstate communications."[164] Because the Internet traffic passing over the local phone lines connecting end users and ISPs is predominantly jurisdictionally interstate, federal policy should govern how the costs associated with that traffic are allocated.[165]

It has been suggested that the fact that ISPs need not pay all of the costs they incur may lead to concrete distortions. Specifically, the most efficient way to move bits from end users to ISPs may well be over digital, packet-switched links that bypass the PSTN entirely (or that use customers' local loops but leave the network before hitting a telephone switch). Yet ISPs' freedom from access charges could motivate them to stay on the circuit-switched network even when that is the less efficient solution. If ISPs were required to pay the economic costs of their connections to the circuit-switched network, the argument runs, then CLECs would have incentives to offer, and ISPs to buy, more efficient packet-switched connections. Incumbent LECs might well then roll out their own comparable services in response.[166]

On the other hand, the scenario just sketched out is vulnerable to a variety of objections. First, it appears that end user demand for digital subscriber line and other packet-switched services, and competition from ISPs affiliated with incumbent local exchange carriers and cable operators, are driving ISPs to seek packet-switched connections in any event. It is by no means clear that ISPs' low rates for connection to the local exchange are significantly affecting ISPs' and consumers' choices in this regard.

Second, the reasoning set out above assumes the existence of local competition. That is, it assumes that some firm is in fact offering packet-switched access in competition with the incumbent local exchange carrier. In the absence of local competition, reforming the rates paid by ISPs accomplishes nothing except that ISPs pay higher prices and incumbent local exchange carriers keep the money, because the monopoly providers have little incentive to develop ways to move the Internet traffic off the circuit-switched network.

Nor would it work simply to postpone the imposition of any new charges on ISPs until after local competition emerges. There is a chicken-and-egg problem. One of the most important factors affecting the willingness of local exchange carriers (competitive or incumbent) to roll out packet-switched connectivity for ISPs is ISPs' willingness to buy that connectivity—yet current regulation diminishes ISPs' incentive to do so. One answer, thus, might be for the FCC to announce now that ISPs will be required to pay a federally tariffed charge for connectivity to the circuit-switched network, reflecting actual economic costs, upon the emergence of local competition in the relevant market. This would encourage competitive local exchange carriers to roll out packet-switched services directed at ISPs, knowing that the imposition of the federally tariffed charge on circuit-switched connectivity would level the playing field and make those services more attractive. The FCC's actual moves, though, have been in the opposite direction. The agency has stressed that "the FCC has no intention of assessing per-minute charges on Internet traffic or changing the way consumers obtain and pay for access to the Internet."[167]

Finally, tying the new charge to the existence of competition might be difficult in other ways. How could the agency determine the actual economic costs imposed by ISP circuit-switched connections on the local network? To the extent that it required local competition as a prerequisite for any regulatory change, how would it measure competition? The FCC's experience with the 1996 act's famously problematic directive that the Bell operating companies may provide in-region long-distance services only after they open up their local markets to competition offers no grounds for optimism that this process would be any easier.[168]

Conclusion

The distinction between regulated "telecommunications" and unregulated "information services" is at the center of the 1996 Telecommunications Act. That distinction, though, is rooted in the conventional telephone network; it does not work in the IP world. We need to develop new ways of reconciling old telephone regulation with new IP networks. For example, regulators should consider associating universal service payment obligations not with the provision of "telecommunications," but with the ownership of transmission facilities. Such a rule might effectuate the underlying goals of the telecommunications–information service distinction, as current law cannot. The exemption of information service providers from access charges should continue for now. In the long term, however, it may make sense for information service providers to pay charges tied to the costs they impose on the local exchange. Ultimately, we will have to reshape the rules governing both old and new technology if we are to find a structure that works.

Notes

During the 1997–98 academic year, I served as legal scholar in residence at the Federal Communications Commission and was among the drafters of the FCC's April 1998 Report to Congress on Universal Service, which I discuss in text. As should be apparent from this chapter, though, the views I express here are not necessarily those of the commission or its staff. For the ideas contained in this chapter, I owe a deep and continuing debt to current and former FCC staffers, including Dale Hatfield, Elliot Maxwell, Mike Nelson, Stagg Newman, Robert Pepper, Stan Trost, and Kevin Werbach. I owe particular thanks to Jessica Litman, Neil Netanel, and Stagg Newman for their comments on an earlier draft, and to David Clark, Shane Greenstein, and Danny Weitzner for their insights. None of them can be held responsible for what I say here, but anything that is useful in this chapter probably comes from one of them. The outright errors and unsupported leaps of logic are all mine.

1. This is oversimplified. Time division multiplexing techniques allow multiple calls to share a given circuit. See Harry Newton, *Newton's Telecom Dictionary* 728–729 (14th ed. 1998). Even using multiplexing techniques, though, it remains the case that each call has a fixed share of network resources allocated to it for the duration of the call.

2. See id. at 527.

3. See RFC 791 (Internet Protocol), http://ds.internic.net/rfc/rfc791.txt.

4. See RFC 1149 (Carrier Pigeon Internet Protocol), http://ds.internic.net/rfc/rfc1149.txt. Carrier pigeons are appropriate only for applications tolerating extremely high latency.

5. Thus, a telephone company recently announced plans to offer eighty channels of cable programming over copper pair using RADSL. See Small Telco Eyes Cable over DSL, *Multichannel News*, Aug. 29, 1998. US WEST is seeking cable franchises for video services it plans to offer over a fiber-copper network using VDSL. See US West Wins Phoenix

Franchise, *Multichannel News*, Sept. 3, 1998. And various players are offering video over the Internet. See Richard Tedesco, Who'll Control the Video Streams? *Broadcasting*, Mar. 8, 1999, at 20.

6. See, e.g., John Markoff, In AT&T-TCI Deal, Cost and Logistical Problems, *New York Times*, July 2, 1998, at D1.

7. These networks may rely on native IP, like Qwest's, or on asynchronous transfer mode (a high-speed packet-like transmission technology), like Sprint's planned ION network. See Jacob Ward, Sprint's Brave New Network, *Industry Standard*, June 5, 1998, http://the-standard.net/articles/display/0,1449,544,00.html.

8. "Implicit subsidy," in this context, means that "a single company is expected to obtain revenues from sources at levels above 'cost' (i.e., above competitive price levels), and to price other services allegedly below cost." Federal-State Joint Board on Universal Service, Report and Order, 12 FCC Rcd 8776, 8784 n. 15 (1997) (Universal Service Order), appeal pending sub nom., Texas Office of Public Utility Counsel v. FCC, No. 97-60421 (5th Cir.).

9. See 47 C.F.R. Part 69.

10. See 47 U.S.C. § 254(g).

11. See Universal Service Order, 12 FCC Rcd at 8784.

12. See RFC 1180 (TCP/IP Tutorial), http://www.rfc-editor.org/rfc/rfc1180.txt, at paras. 2.5–2.7, 5–5.12.

13. See Jack Rickard, Internet Architecture, in *Boardwatch Magazine Directory of Internet Service Providers* 11 (Winter 1998).

14. See id.

15. See id. at 11–12.

16. See id. at 12; Harry Newton, *Newton's Telecom Directory* 508, 695, 696 (14th ed. 1998).

17. See Application of Worldcom, Inc. and MCI Communications for Transfer of Control, 13 FCC Rcd 18025, 18104–18107 (1998) (hereafter, Worldcom-MCI Order).

18. Id. at 18106–18107.

19. See *Boardwatch Magazine Directory of Internet Service Providers* 259 (Winter 1998).

20. See id. at 221.

21. See Worldcom-MCI Order at 18105–18106; OECD Working Party on Telecommunication and Information Services Policies, Internet Traffic Exchange: Developments and Policy 14–15 (1998), available at http://www.oecd.org//dsti/sti/it/cm/prod/TRAFFIC.htm.

22. See Worldcom-MCI Order at 18106.

23. See id. at 18105–18106; Kenneth Cukier, "Peering and Fearing: ISP Interconnection and Regulatory Issues," available at http://ksg222.harvard.edu/iip/iicompol/Papers/Cukier.html.

24. See Cukier, supra note; OECD Working Party on Telecommunication and Information Services Policies, supra note, at 14–17. See generally Padmanabhan Srinagesh, Internet Cost Structures and Interconnection Agreements (March 1995), available at http://www.press.umich.edu/jep/works/SrinCostSt.html.

25. Finally, it covers costs relating to operations, customer acquisition, and customer service. See Lee W. McKnight and Brett Leida, Internet Telephony: Costs, Pricing and Policy, 22 *Telecomm. Pol'y* 555, 557–559; Srinagesh, supra note 24.

26. Earlier statutes—the Pacific Railroad Act of 1862 and the Post Roads Act of 1866— had provided for some governmental authority over telegraph lines built with government subsidies or along public lands. See Kenneth A. Cox and William J. Byrnes, The Common Carrier Provisions—A Product of Evolutionary Development, in *A Legislative History of the Communications Act of 1934*, at 25, 27 (Max Paglin ed. 1989).

27. 47 U.S.C. §§ 201–276.

28. See Glen O. Robinson, The Federal Communications Act: An Essay on Origins and Regulatory Purpose, in *A Legislative History of the Communications Act of 1934*, at 3, 5–6 (Max Paglin ed. 1989); Cox and Byrnes, supra note 26, at 30.

29. 47 U.S.C. § 153(10).

30. Id. § 203.

31. Id. §§ 201(b), 202(a).

32. Id. § 201(a).

33. Id. § 214.

34. Id. § 205.

35. Id. § 204.

36. Id. §§ 206–209.

37. See Amendment of Section 64.702, 72 FCC 2d 358, 389–390 (1979).

38. 47 U.S.C. § 222.

39. Id. § 223.

40. Id. § 225.

41. Id. § 228.

42. Id. § 229.

43. See id. § 152(b).

44. For more recent struggles with that dividing line, see, e.g., AT&T Corp. v. Iowa Utilities Bd., 119 S. Ct. 721 (1999) (rejecting the argument that FCC rules implementing the local competition provisions of the 1996 Telecommunications Act relate to local—rather

than interstate—communications and are thus beyond federal authority); Inter-Carrier Compensation for ISP-Bound Traffic, CC Docket Nos. 96–98, 99–68 (rel. Feb. 26, 1999).

45. 282 U.S. 133, 148–149 (1930); see National Association of Regulatory Utility Commissioners v. FCC, 737 F.2d 1095 (D.C. Cir. 1984) (discussing *Smith*), cert. denied, 496 U.S. 127 (1985). In *Smith*, the Supreme Court reviewed a district court decision adjudicating the legality of Illinois Bell's Chicago pay phone rates. The Court explained that the lower tribunal had erred in including all of Illinois Bell's Chicago property in its rate base. "The separation of the intrastate and interstate property, revenue and expenses of the Company," it explained, "is essential to the appropriate recognition of the competent governmental authority in each field of regulation." 282 U.S. at 148.

46. Smith, 282 U.S. at 148–151.

47. See National Association of Regulatory Utility Commissioners v. FCC, 737 F.2d at 1104 n.3. Where the local carrier was not affiliated with AT&T, AT&T remitted to it the amounts necessary to recover its allocated interstate costs, including a return on investment. See Access Charge Reform, 12 FCC Rcd 15982, 15990–15991 (1997).

48. Before the mid-1970s, one could place ordinary long-distance telephone calls only through AT&T. MCI filed tariffs for its own service in 1974; the D.C. Circuit twice reversed FCC rulings that would have shut that competition down. See MCI Telecommunications Corp. v. FCC, 580 F.2d 590 (D. C. Cir.), cert. denied, 439 U.S. 980 (1978); MCI Telecommunications Corp. v. FCC, 561 F.2d 365 (D. C. Cir. 1977), cert. denied, 434 U.S. 1040 (1978).

49. These were referred to as ENFIA (Exchange Network Facilities for Interstate Access) payments. See ENFIA Agreement, 43 Fed. Reg. 59,131 (1978); Access Charge Reform, 12 FCC Rcd 15982, 15991 (1997).

50. MTS & WATS Market Structure, 93 F.C.C.2d 241, on reconsid., 97 F.C.C.2d 682 (1983), further reconsid., 97 F.C.C.2d 834, aff'd in relevant part, 737 F.2d 1095 (D.C. Cir. 1984), cert. denied, 496 U.S. 127 (1985).

51. See id. at 1109; Federal-State Joint Board on Universal Service, 12 FCC Rcd 8776, 8890–8892 (1997), appeal pending, Texas Office of Public Utility Counsel v. FCC, No. 97-60421 (5th Cir.). In addition, in 1985, the commission established the Lifeline and Link Up programs, designed to make telephone service affordable for low-income consumers. Subscribers eligible for Lifeline need not pay the federal subscriber line charge and certain intrastate end user charges; until 1996, the federal portion of Lifeline was funded through a charge assessed on interexchange carriers. Linkup pays a portion of eligible subscribers' installation charges and was funded, before 1996, by an expense adjustment allocating its costs to the interstate jurisdiction. See Federal-State Joint Board on Universal Service, 12 FCC Rcd at 8952–8960.

52. See Rural Telephone Coalition v. FCC, 838 F.2d 1307, 1311–1312 (D.C. Cir. 1988); NARUC v. FCC, 737 F.2d at 1129–1130.

53. See Access Charge reform, 12 FCC Rcd 15982, 15992–15993 (1997).

54. See id.

55. Regulatory and Policy Problems Presented by the Interdependence of Computer and Communications Services and Facilities, Notice of Proposed Rulemaking, 7 F.C.C. 2d 11, 13 (1966).

56. Amendment of Section 64.702 of the Commission's Rules and Regulations (Computer II), 77 F.C.C. 2d 384, 419, recon., 84 F.C.C. 2d 50 (1980), further recon., 88 F.C.C. 2d 512 (1981), aff'd sub nom. Computer and Communications Industry Association v. FCC, 693 F.2d 198 (D.C. Cir. 1982), cert. denied, 461 U.S. 938 (1983).

57. See id.

58. See id. at 434.

59. Id. at 417–430.

60. Id. at 419–420.

61. Id. at 420.

62. 47 C.F.R. § 64.702(a).

63. Computer II, 77 FCC 2d at 420–421.

64. The agency reasoned that enhanced services involve "communications and data processing technologies . . . intertwined so thoroughly as to produce a form different from any explicitly recognized in the Communications Act of 1934," and that enhanced service providers were not "common carriers" within the meaning of the act. Id. at 430–432.

65. Id. at 428.

66. See id. at 423–428.

67. See id. at 461–475; see also Amendment of Section 64.702, 2 FCC Rcd 3072 (1987) (Computer III), vacated, California v. FCC, 905 F.2d 1217 (9th Cir. 1990), on remand, Bell Operating Company Safeguards and Tier I Local Exchange Company Safeguards, 6 FCC RCd 7571 (1991), vacated in part, California v. FCC, 39 F.3d 919 (9th Cir. 1994), cert. denied, 115 S. Ct. 1427 (1995).

68. MTS and WATS Market Structure, 97 F.C.C. 2d 682, 711 (1983), on further reconsid., 97 F.C.C.2d 834, aff'd in relevant part sub nom. NARUC v. FCC, 737 F.2d 1095 (1984), cert. denied, 469 U.S. 127 (1985).

69. See id. at 715.

70. See NARUC v. FCC, 737 F.2d 1095, 1130–1136 (1984), cert. denied, 469 U.S. 127 (1985).

71. See 47 U.S.C. § 153(20), (43). These categories originated in the 1982 Modification of Final Judgment (MFJ) ending the antitrust suit between the U.S. government and AT&T. See United States v. American Telephone & Telegraph Co., 552 F. Supp. 131, 226–232 (D.D.C. 1982), aff'd sub nom. Maryland v. United States, 460 U.S. 1001 (1983); Federal-State Joint Board on Universal Service, 13 FCC Rcd 11501, 11514, 11521–11522 (1998) (*Report to Congress on Universal Service*). The legislative history does not reveal why the drafters preferred this terminology.

72. 47 U.S.C. § 153(43).

73. Id. § 153(20).

74. *Report to Congress on Universal Service*, 13 FCC Rcd at 11511.

75. See 47 U.S.C. § 254(b)(4), (e); Joint Explanatory Statement of the Committee on Conference (H.R. Rep. No. 458, 104th Cong., 2d Sess.) 131.

76. See Access Charge Reform, 12 FCC Rcd 15982, 15998–16001 (1997).

77. See 47 U.S.C. § 254(d). The statute requires all common carrier providers of "telecommunications services," as defined in 47 U.S.C. § 153(46), to contribute, and authorizes the FCC to require contributions from other interstate telecommunications providers.

78. The purposes of high-cost support are contested. When the FCC first created an explicit Universal Service Fund in 1983, it characterized its universal service policymaking as seeking to avoid situations in which the price of local telephone service "cause[s] a significant number of local exchange service subscribers to cancel that service." See MTS and WATS Market Structure, Third Report and Order, 93 F.C.C.2d 241, 266 (1983), aff'd in relevant part sub nom. NARUC v. FCC, 737 F.2d 1095 (D.C. Cir. 1984), cert. denied, 496 U.S. 127 (1985). This suggests that subsidies in high-cost areas should be high enough to prevent rural users from dropping off the network, but need not be so high as to equalize rates in urban and rural areas.

The Telecommunications Act of 1996, though, asserts a broader goal, legislating the principle that universal service support should give rural consumers telecommunications services at rates comparable to those charged in urban areas. 47 U.S.C. § 254(b)(3). Policymakers in Europe also appear to treat geographical equality of rates as an independent universal service goal. See, e.g., Barbara Bardski and John Taylor, "Understanding Universal Service: A European Perspective" (1998), at 5 (in the early stages of network diffusion, it is a central universal service objective that telecommunications services be available at uniform prices throughout the country).

It is not clear, though, why it should be desirable for government to equalize rural and urban telecommunications costs, to the extent that unequal costs are consistent with high telephone penetration in high-cost areas. A wide variety of goods and services, after all, have different costs in different parts of the country. Achieving this goal requires a higher level of subsidies than would be necessary if government sought to enable high penetration without more.

79. More precisely, they paid .0305 percent of those revenues to fund the high-cost program together with the Lifeline and Linkup programs. Proposed Fourth Quarter 1998 Universal Service Contribution Factors Announced, CC Docket No. 96-45 (rel. Aug. 18, 1998), http://www.fcc.gov/Bureaus/Common_Carrier/Public_Notices/1998/da981649.html. About 78 percent of that money will go to the high-cost program and about 22 percent to the low-income programs. Id.

80. See supra note 51.

81. For the second quarter of 1999, the Universal Service Administrative Company estimated $433 million demand (excluding administrative overhead) for the high-cost program, amounting to 49 percent of all Universal Service Fund expenses. The schools and libraries fund was projected to make up 36 percent and the Lifeline and Linkup programs 14 percent. See Proposed Second Quarter 1999 Universal Service Contribution Factors, CC Docket No. 96-45 (rel. Mar. 4, 1999), http://www.fcc.gov/Daily_Releases/Daily_Business/1999/db990305/da990455.wp.

82. 47 U.S.C. § 254(c)(1); see also Federal-State Joint Board on Universal Service, 12 FCC Rcd 8776, 8822 (1997), appeal pending, Texas Office of Public Utility Counsel v. FCC, No. 97-60421 (5th Cir.). The FCC has interpreted section 254(c)(3), though, to allow support of other services in connection with the Schools and Libraries program. See Federal-State Joint Board on Universal Service, 12 FCC Rcd at 9009–9011.

83. 47 U.S.C. § 254(c)(1).

84. See Federal-State Joint Board on Universal Service, 12 FCC Rcd at 8809. But see supra note 82.

85. Federal-State Joint Board on Universal Service (Report to Congress), 13 FCC Rcd 11501 (1998).

86. See Federal-State Joint Board on Universal Service, 12 FCC Rcd 8776, 9010–9012, 9179–9181 (1997), appeal pending sub nom. Texas Office of Public Utility Counsel v. FCC, No. 97-60421 (5th Cir.); see also Amendment of the Commission's Rules and Policies Governing Pole Attachments, 13 FCC Rcd 6777, 6795 (1998).

87. See *Report to Congress on Universal Service*, 13 FCC Rcd at 11515–11516.

88. The gist of their argument was that a service should be deemed both telecommunications and information service if it involved both transmission and manipulation of information. Such a "hybrid" service, Senators Stevens and Burns argued, should be subject to all Title II obligations, including those relating to universal service. See Letter from Senators Conrad Burns and Ted Stevens to William E. Kennard, Chairman, Federal Communications Commission (Jan. 26, 1998), at 1–7; *Report to Congress on Universal Service*, 13 FCC Rcd at 11517–11519.

89. See Letter from Senators Conrad Burns and Ted Stevens to William E. Kennard, Chairman, Federal Communications Commission (Jan. 26, 1998), at 7–12. It is useful to remember that the main function of the Universal Service Fund today is to make possible the provision of low-cost telephone service in rural and other high-cost areas, a function to which one would expect Senators Stevens and Burns, who hail from Alaska and Montana, respectively, to be sensitive. See supra note 78 and accompanying text.

90. Departments of Commerce, Justice, and State, the Judiciary, and Related Agencies Appropriations Act, 1998, Pub. L. No. 105-119, 111 Stat. 2440, 2521–2522, § 623.

91. *Report to Congress on Universal Service*, supra note 85.

92. Id. at 11536–11540.

93. Id. at 11532–11536.

94. Id. at 11543.

95. Id.; see 47 U.S.C. § 153(46), 254(d).

96. *Report to Congress on Universal Service*, 13 FCC Rcd at 11543. If the user is reaching her ISP over a dial-up telephone connection, then the telephone company is providing her with telecommunications, but that service is wholly distinct from the Internet Telephony functionality. Id. at 11523 n. 187.

97. Id. at 11541–11542 and n.177, 11544.

98. Id. at 11508.

99. Id. at 11503–11504.

100. Id. at 11548–11549.

101. Id. at 11543–11544.

102. See id. at 11623–11624 (dissenting statement of Commissioner Furchgott-Roth).

103. Or imagine technology that sets up an Internet Telephony call from a person's computer to a corporate call center when that person clicks on a button on the corporation's Web page; whether the call is characterized as computer-to-phone or computer-to-computer will depend on the fortuitous consideration of whether the IP gateway serving the call is on- or off-site.

104. These examples are Mike Nelson's.

105. 47 U.S.C. § 153(43).

106. The genius of *Computer II* was the recognition that it is difficult to disentangle communications and computing functionality and that therefore, at least where the provider does not own transmission facilities, "offerings . . . combining communications and computing components" should be treated as unitary services and exempted from regulation. See *Report to Congress on Universal Service*, 13 FCC Rcd at 11530. This approach had salutary effects, yet it has its limits: "It is plain, for example, that an incumbent local exchange carrier cannot escape Title II regulation of its residential local exchange service simply by packaging that service with voice mail." Id.

107. See Implementation of the Non-Accounting Safeguards of Sections 271 and 272, Report and Order, 11 FCC Rcd 21905, 21955–21958 (1996) (Non-Accounting Safeguards Order) (in general, services involving protocol processing fall within 47 U.S.C. § 153(20)'s definition of "information service," because they offer "a capability for . . . transforming [and] processing . . . information via telecommunications"), on recon.., 12 FCC Rcd 2297, aff'd sub nom. Bell Atlantic Tel. Cos. v. FCC, 131 F.3d 1044 (D.C. Cir. 1977).

108. See Deployment of Wireline Services Offering Advanced Telecommunications Capacity, CC Docket No. 98-147 (Aug. 7, 1998), at ¶ 35 n. 57 (Section 706 Order and NPRM); *Report to Congress on Universal Service*, at 11526 and n. 106; Non-Accounting Safeguards Order, 11 FCC Rcd at 21958; see also Amendment of Section 64.702, Report and Order, Phase II, 2 FCC Rcd 3072, 3081–3082 (1987), on recon., 3 FCC Rcd 1150 (1988), 4 FCC Rcd 5927 (1989), vacated sub nom. California v. FCC, 905 F.2d 1217 (9th Cir. 1990).

109. I am indebted to Stagg Newman for his emphasis of this point.

110. David S. Isenberg, Dawn of the Stupid Network, http://www.isen.com/papers/Dawnstupid.html. "All that matters is that the bits sent by your machine are received by my machine, and vice versa." Id.

111. See id.

112. See Independent Data Communications Manufacturers' Association, 10 FCC Rcd 13717 (1995), and cases cited in Section 706 Order and NPRM, at ¶ 35 n. 56 and accompanying text.

113. *Report to Congress on Universal Service*, 13 FCC Rcd at 11537–11539.

114. Universal service contributions are calculated as a percentage of end user revenues. See 47 CFR §§ 54.706, .709.

115. There are surely good arguments that we should not increase the cost of Internet service in order to subsidize telephone service. See, e.g., Michael Riordan, "Conundrums for Telecommunications Policy," Remarks to the National Economists Club, Washington, D.C., May 28, 1998, at 14–15.

116. See Computer II, 77 F.C.C.2d at 419–420; 47 U.S.C. § 153(20), (43), (46).

117. The OSI model was developed by the International Standards Organization to provide a common design framework for communications networks. While the specific protocols developed as part of the OSI model were not widely adopted (and particular implementations may not follow the model rigorously), the concepts underlying the model are dominant in the computing world. The National Research Council followed a similar approach in devising its open data network architecture: a conceptual model that incorporates a bearer service layer (sitting on top of the "network technology substrate"), a transport layer, a middleware layer, and an application layer. See National Research Council, *Realizing the Information Future* 47–51 (1994).

118. See Newton, *Newton's Telecom Dictionary* 519–520 (14th ed. 1998).

119. See id.

120. See id.

121. See supra text following note 2.

122. I owe this point to Stagg Newman.

123. As the 1996 act put it, a firm offers information services "via telecommunications." 47 U.S.C. § 153(20).

124. See supra text at notes 104–106.

125. See supra notes 107–109 and accompanying text.

126. The FCC in the *Report to Congress on Universal Service* took this approach when it mused about the possibility of requiring only "the actual facilities owners . . . to contribute to universal service mechanisms on the revenues they receive. It is facilities owners that, in a real sense, provide the crucial telecommunications inputs underlying Internet service. If universal service contribution obligations, in the context of the Internet backbone, were based on facilities ownership rather than on end-user revenues, then firms purchasing capacity from the facilities owners would still contribute indirectly, through prices that recover the facilities owners' contributions. This matter deserves further consideration." *Report to Congress on Universal Service*, 13 FCC Rcd at 11535–11536.

127. A facilities-based approach, however, would not be appropriate in connection with all Title II obligations. Most important, one could not sensibly apply a facilities-based approach to the tariffing rules carried over from railroad regulation. Similarly, one could not apply a facilities-based approach to the requirement that carriers safeguard customer privacy.

128. See supra text accompanying note 78.

129. In suggesting this approach, I am assuming that facilities owners would in fact be able to pass on their costs. To the extent that they could not—so that the obligation would weigh heavily on facilities owners but only lightly on lessors—the proposal would have the effect of singling out a particular industry segment without policy justification and would be rather more problematic.

130. To illustrate that convergence, a working group of the European Telecommunications Standards Institute, developing standards for computer-to-phone IP telephony, is considering an approach under which E.164 telephone numbers with a special country code would correspond to Internet addresses. See e-mail from Marvin Sirbu to the telecomreg mailing list, Sept. 3, 1998 (on file with author).

131. But see Riordan, supra n., at 14–15 (requiring Internet providers to pay universal service fees to sustain high telephone penetration "is exactly backwards"). Indeed, to the extent that high-cost subsidies today are too high (because they are designed to equalize the prices of telecommunications services in rural and urban areas without regard to whether less-subsidized rural prices would be a threat to telephone penetration; see supra note 78), requiring IP-based services providers to contribute to those subsidies only makes a bad situation worse. On the other hand, universal service subsidies not only support voice telephony; a consumer can use the local loop made affordable by universal service support for Internet as well as circuit-switched telephony services.

132. See supra text following note 81.

133. See supra note 78.

134. See 47 CFR §§ 54.706, 709.

135. See Kevin Werbach, How to Price a Bit, *Release* 1.0 (June 1998), at 1 (the "cost to send a bit of data across the Internet . . . is surprisingly complex. Networks involve a mix of fixed and variable investments, and pricing requires assumptions about demand levels, competition and usage patterns").

136. See Erik Kreifeldt, NFOEC '98: DWDM Hot Topic, But Not Magic Bullet, (Sept. 17, 1998) http://news.fiberopticsonline.com/news-analysis/19980917–5443.html (dense wave division multiplexing).

137. See generally Operation of Unlicensed NII Devices in the 5 GHz Frequency Range, 12 FCC Rcd 1576 (1997), recon., 13 FCC Rcd 14355 (1998).

138. I have not so far, in this chapter, addressed the legal constraints on these approaches. Any solution the FCC adopts, absent statutory amendment, would have to be consistent with 47 U.S.C. § 254(d), which mandates that "every telecommunications carrier providing interstate telecommunications services" contribute to universal service mechanisms "on an equitable and nondiscriminatory basis." A facilities-based approach would be vul-

nerable to the objection that it did not require "every" carrier to contribute. Alternatively, one might argue that under this approach, non-facilities-based carriers would contribute (albeit indirectly) through the prices they paid for transmission, since those prices would reflect the facilities-based carriers' direct payments. Indeed, if the statute were read to impose an inflexible requirement that all carriers contribute directly, the current approach would not comply, since it is only the provision of telecommunications to end users that triggers the payment obligation. A carrier that does not serve end users is not required to contribute today.

The approach described here might also be vulnerable to the argument that the FCC has no authority to impose payment obligations on facilities-based information service providers. Here, though, the *Report to Congress on Universal Service* provides the answer: Such a firm should be deemed to be providing telecommunications to itself, and thus falls within the FCC's authority to require "any . . . provider of interstate telecommunications . . . to contribute to the preservation and advancement of universal service if the public interest so requires." 47 U.S.C. § 254(d); see *Report to Congress on Universal Service*, 13 FCC Rcd at 11534–11535.

139. The Fifth Circuit is now considering whether the USF contribution obligation (or any part of it) is inconsistent with the constitutional command (U.S. Constitution, Art. 1, sec. 7, cl. 1) that "all bills for raising Revenue shall originate in the House of Representatives." Texas Office of Public Utility Counsel v. FCC, No. 97-60421 (5th Cir.). It would be incongruous, though, if the FCC were found to have overstepped constitutional boundaries merely by following Congress's direction to refashion existing implicit subsidies into explicit ones.

140. See supra text accompanying note 84.

141. See Francois Bar and Annemarie M. Riis, "From Welfare to Innovation: Toward A New Rationale for Universal Service" 14 (1998).

142. See generally Barbara Esbin, "Internet Over Cable: Defining the Future in Terms of the Past," OPP Working Paper No. 30 (Aug. 1998).

143. See supra notes 8–11 and accompanying text.

144. See Federal-State Joint Board on Universal Service, Report and Order, 12 FCC Rcd 8776, 8784 (1997), appeal pending sub nom., Texas Office of Public Utility Counsel v. FCC, No. 97-60421 (5th Cir.).

145. See supra text preceding note 75.

146. See id.

147. See Federal-State Joint Board on Universal Service, Report and Order, 12 FCC Rcd 8776, 8785 (1997) (Universal Service Order), appeal pending sub nom., Texas Office of Public Utility Counsel v. FCC, No. 97-60421 (5th Cir.).

148. See Access Charge Reform, First Report and Order, 12 FCC Rcd at 15986–15987, 15915–16004; supra note 76 and accompanying text.

149. See supra notes 68–70 and accompanying text.

150. Access Charge Reform (Notice of Proposed Rulemaking), 11 FCC Rcd 21354, 21480 (1996) (footnote omitted). The agency confirmed this tentative conclusion in its Access Charge Reform Order. 12 FCC Rcd 15982, 16133 (1997), aff'd, Southwest Bell Tel. Co. v. FCC, No. 97-2618 (8th Cir. Aug. 19, 1998).

151. Access Charge Reform, 12 FCC Rcd 15982, 15986 (1997), aff'd, Southwest Bell Tel. Co. v. FCC, No. 97-2618 (8th Cir. Aug. 19, 1998).

152. See Kevin Werbach, *Digital Tornado: The Internet and Telecommunications Policy* 62–63 (1997), http://www.fcc.gov/Bureaus/OPP/working_papers/oppwp30.pdf.

153. See id. at 58–61.

154. See Implementation of Local Competition, 11 FCC Rcd 15499, 15905, 16024–16026 (1996) (Local Competition Order).

155. See Werbach, supra note 152, at 58–63.

156. Local exchange carriers have asserted that Internet traffic commonly gives rise to congestion at the telephone switch serving the ISP. See id. at 58. A local exchange carrier switch cannot simultaneously support connections for all users of the switch. Id. Rather, there is one call path through the switch for every four to eight users. Because calls by users to ISPs tend to be longer than voice calls, but still—like all calls on the circuit-switched public telephone network—tie up an end-to-end call path for the duration of the call, local exchange carriers claim that heavy Internet usage will increasingly lead to situations in which all available paths through the switch are in use and additional calls seeking a call path through the switch will be blocked. See id. at 58–60.
ISPs, however, sharply dispute the extent to which switch congestion is a serious problem. See id. at 60. A study commissioned by the Internet Access Coalition concludes that incidents of congestion have been localized, are easily corrected, and are primarily attributable to inadequate planning and inefficient engineering by the local exchange carriers. Id. The FCC-chartered Network Reliability and Interoperability Council takes the view that Internet-related congestion is primarily a provisioning issue, best handled by close coordination between carriers and ISPs. See id. at 60–61.

157. See generally Local Competition Order, 11 FCC Rcd at 16028–16029 (discussing peak and nonpeak pricing plans for reciprocal compensation).

158. The question whether ISPs impose uncompensated costs on the local exchange is different from the question whether they impose uncompensated costs on local exchange carriers. In the Access Charge Reform Order, the FCC found insufficient evidence that local exchange carriers suffered losses by virtue of Internet use. Access Charge Reform Order, 12 FCC Rcd 15982, 16133–16134 (1997), aff'd, Southwest Bell Telephone Co. v. FCC, No. 97-2618 (8th Cir. Aug. 19, 1998). It noted that the carriers received revenue not only from ISPs' connections to the local exchange, but also from consumers' purchases of second lines and ISPs' purchases of leased lines to provision their internal networks. Moreover, the popularity of the Internet generated revenue through subscriptions to incumbent local exchange carriers' own Internet access services. Id. These considerations, though, suggest that uncompensated costs in one area are balanced by monopoly profits in another. They do not speak to whether the rates paid by ISPs are related to the costs they impose (much less to whether either the profits local exchange carriers earn or the costs they incur are passed on to the rate-paying public).

159. See id. ("commenters point out [that] many of the characteristics of ISP traffic (such as large numbers of incoming calls to Internet Service Providers) may be shared by other classes of business customers").

160. The FCC made this clear in GTE Telephone Operating Cos., CC Docket No. 98-79 (rel. Oct. 30, 1998), at ¶¶ 22–26 (GTE ADSL Tariff Approval).

161. That traffic is sometimes stored on ISP computers along the way, but storage (in a Web cache, Usenet news feed, or mail queue) is simply an intermediate step in a larger journey. Inter-Carrier Compensation for ISP-Bound Traffic, CC Docket Nos. 96–98, 99–68 (rel. Feb. 26, 1999), at ¶¶ 12–13. "The Commission analyzes the totality of the communication when determining [its] jurisdictional nature." Id. at ¶ 13.

162. The "key to [federal] jurisdiction" is the interstate movement of communications traffic. BellSouth Corp., 7 FCC Rcd 1619, 1621 (1992) (quoting New York Telephone Co. v. FCC, 631 F.2d 1059, 1066 (2d Cir. 1980)). In characterizing a service as interstate or intrastate, thus, we look to the nature of the traffic: "the actual uses to which the property is put." Smith v. Illinois Bell Telephone Co., 282 U.S. 133, 151 (1930); see also, e.g., California v. FCC, 567 F.2d 84, 86 (D.C. Cir. 1977) (the regulatory characterization depends on "the nature of the communications that pass through the facilities"); MTS and WATS Market Structure, 97 F.C.C.2d 682, 713 n. 58 (1983) (MTS and WATS Market Structure Reconsideration Order), on further reconsid., 97 F.C.C.2d 834, aff'd in relevant part sub nom. NARUC v. FCC, 737 F.2d 1095 (1984), cert. denied, 469 U.S. 1227 (1985).

In important respects, Internet access traffic is best characterized as jurisdictionally mixed. Not all ISP services are necessarily interstate; some users may make such limited use of the Internet that they never interact with data bits that have crossed, or will cross, a state line. It is impossible, however, to identify those users, or to separate them out, by examining Internet traffic; packet-switched networks by their nature are less amenable than circuit-switched networks to such partition. The status of the traffic as jurisdictionally mixed gives the FCC some discretion over its jurisdictional and separations treatment. See Southwestern Bell Telephone Co. v. FCC, No. 97-2618 (8th Cir. Aug. 19, 1998), at 40–41.

163. Both basic and enhanced service providers were "users of access service," in that they "obtained local exchange service or facilities which are used . . . for the purpose of completing interstate calls." MTS and WATS Market Structure Reconsideration Order, 97 F.C.C.2d at 711. The FCC's initial order defined "access service" to include "services and facilities . . . provided for the origination or termination of any interstate or foreign enhanced service." MTS and WATS Market Structure, 93 F.C.C.2d 241, 344 (emphasis added), on reconsid., 97 F.C.C.2d 682 (1983), 97 F.C.C.2d 834, aff'd in relevant part sub nom. NARUC v. FCC, 737 F.2d 1095 (1984), cert. denied, 469 U.S. 1227 (1985); see supra note 68 and accompanying text.

164. MTS and WATS Market Structure Reconsideration Order, 97 F.C.C.2d at 715. See generally GTE ADSL Tariff Approval, at ¶¶ 7, 21.

165. But see Inter-Carrier Compensation for ISP-Bound Traffic, CC Docket Nos. 96-98, and 99-68 (rel. Feb. 26, 1999), at ¶¶ 28–30 (though traffic passing from an end user to an originating local exchange carrier (LEC), to a second local exchange carrier, to an ISP bound for the Internet, is largely jurisdictionally interstate, and any inter-LEC compensation in connection with that traffic should be governed by a federal rule, the best rule would simply effectuate negotiated agreements between the carriers).

166. See Kevin Werbach, *Digital Tornado: The Internet and Telecommunications Policy* 72 (1997), http://www.fcc.gov/Bureaus/OPP/working_papers/oppwp30.pdf.

167. See Fact Sheet: No Consumer Per-Minute Charges to Access ISPs (February 1999), http://www.fcc.gov/Bureaus/Common_Carrier/Factsheets/nominute.html.

168. 47 U.S.C. § 271 provides that a Bell operating company may provide in-region long-distance service only when it satisfies a fourteen-point checklist demonstrating that it has opened its local market to competition. So far, the FCC has rejected every such petition filed with it, finding that the checklist was not yet satisfied. The process has been highly complex, and highly contentious.

References

Chapter 2

Braden, R., ed. 1997. *Resource ReSerVation Protocol (RSVP)—Version 1 Functional Specification.* Available online: ftp://ds.internic.net/rfc/rfc2205.txt.

Computer Science and Telecommunications Board. 1994. *Realizing the Information Future: The Internet and Beyond.* Washington, D.C.: National Academy Press.

Computer Science and Telecommunications Board. 1996. *The Unpredictable Certainty: Information Infrastructure Through 2000.* Washington, D.C.: National Academy Press.

McKnight, L., and J. Bailey, eds. 1997. *Internet Economics.* Cambridge, Mass.: MIT Press.

Werbach, K. 1997. "Digital Tornado: The Internet and Telecommunications Policy." Office of Plans and Policy, Working Paper 29, Federal Communications Commission.

Wroclawski, J. 1997. "Specification of the Controlled-load Network Element Service." Internet RFC 2211. Available at: ftp://ds.internic.net/rfc/rfc2211.txt.

Chapter 3

Brown, S., and D. Sibley. 1986. *The Theory of Utility Pricing.* Cambridge: Cambridge University Press.

Coll, S. 1986. *The Deal of the Century.* New York: Atheneum.

de Sola Pool, I. 1977. *The Social Impact of the Telephone.* Cambridge, Mass.: MIT Press.

de Sola Pool, I. 1990. *Technologies Without Barriers.* Cambridge, Mass.: Harvard University Press.

Drake, W. J., and E. M. Noam. 1997. "The WTO Deal on Basic Telecommunications. Big Bang or Little Whimper?" *Telecommunications Policy,* *21*(9–10), 799–818.

References

Frieden, R. M. 1997. "The Impact of Call-back and Arbitrage on the Accounting Rate Reqime." *Telecommunications Policy, 21*(9–10), 819–827.

Kahn, A. E. 1989. *The Economics of Regulation.* Cambridge, MA: MIT Press.

Kuhn, T. 1996. *The Structure of Scientific Revolutions.* Chicago: University of Chicago Press.

Lynch, D. C., and M. T. Rose. 1993. *Internet System Handbook.* Reading, Mass.: Addison-Wesley.

McGarty, T. P. 1990. *Alternative Networking Architectures: Pricing, Policy, and Competition, Information Infrastructures for the 1990s.* Cambridge, Mass.: John F. Kennedy School of Government, Harvard University, November.

McGarty, T. P. 1991a. "Information Architectures and Infrastructures: Value Creation and Transfer." Paper presented at the Telecommunications Policy Research Conference, September.

McGarty, T. P. 1991b. "Alternative Networking Architectures." In B. Kahin, ed., *Building Information Infrastructure.* New York: McGraw-Hill.

McGarty, T. P. 1991c. "Communications Networks: A Morphological and Taxonomical Approach." Paper presented at the Private Networks and Public Policy Conference, Columbia University, October.

McGarty, T. P. 1992a. "Wireless Communications Economics." Paper presented at the Advanced Telecommunications Institute Policy Chapter Meeting, Carnegie Mellon University, February.

McGarty, T. P. 1992b. "Communications Network Morphological and Taxonomical Policy Implications." Paper presented at the Telecommunications Policy Research Conference, Solomon's Island, Md., September.

McGarty, T. P. 1995. *From High End User to New User: A New Internet Paradigm.* New York: McGraw-Hill.

McGarty, T. P. 1996a. "Disaggregation of Telecommunications." Paper presented at the CITI Conference on the Impact of Cybercommunications on Telecommunications, Columbia University, March.

McGarty, T. P. 1996b. "The Economic Viability of Wireless Local Loop and Its Impact on Universal Service." Paper presented at the CITI Conference on Universal Service, Columbia University, March.

McGarty, T. P. 1997. "Competition in the Local Exchange Market: An Economic and Antitrust Perspective." *Federal Communications Law Journal.*

McGarty, T. P., and G. J. Clancey. 1983. "Cable Based Metro Area Networks." *IEEE Journal on Selected Areas in Communications, 1*(5), 816–831.

McKnight, L. W., and J. P. Bailey, eds. 1997. *Internet Economics.* Cambridge, Mass.: MIT Press.

References

Neuman, W. R., L. W. McKnight, and R. J. Solomon. 1997. *The Gordian Knot: Political Gridlock on the Information Highway.* Cambridge, Mass.: MIT Press.

Office of Economic Cooperation and Development. 19••. *Information Infrastructure and Pricing: The Internet.* Paris: OECD.

Posner, R. A. 1976. *Antitrust Law.* Chicago: University of Chicago Press.

Posner, R. A. 1983. *The Economics of Justice.* Cambridge, Mass.: Harvard University Press.

Posner, R. A. 1992. *Economic Analysis of Law.* Boston: Little, Brown.

Spulber, D. F. 1990. *Regulation and Markets.* Cambridge, Mass.: MIT Press.

Temin, Peter. 1989. *The Fall of the Bell System: A Study in Prices and Politics.* Cambridge, Mass.: Cambridge University Press.

Chapter 4

Clark, D. 1995. "Interoperation, Open Interfaces, and Protocol Architecture." Mimeo. Laboratory of Computer Science, Massachusetts Institute of Technology.

Coase, R. 1937. "The Nature of the Firm." *Economica, 4,* 1–44.

Grossman, S., and O. Hart, 1986. "The Costs and Benefits of Ownership: A Theory of Vertical and Lateral Integration." *Journal of Political Economy, 94,* 691–719.

Katz, M. 1989. "Vertical Contractual Relations." In R. Schmalensee and R. Willig, eds., *Handbook of Industrial Organization.* Amsterdam: Elsevier Science.

Kavassalis, P., T. Lee, and J. Bailey. 1997. "Sustaining a Vertically Disintegrated Network Through a Bearer Service Market." Draft mimeo.

Krattenmaker, T., and S. Salop. 1986. "Anticompetitive Exclusion: Raising Rivals' Costs to Achieve Power over Price." *Yale Law Journal, 96,* 209–293.

National Research Council. 1994. *Realizing the Information Future and Beyond.* Washington, D.C.: National Academy Press.

Perry, M. 1989. "Vertical Integration: Determinants and Effects." In R. Schmalensee and R. Willig, eds., *Handbook of Industrial Organization.* Amsterdam: Elsevier Science.

Riordan, M., and S. Salop. 1995. "Evaluating Vertical Mergers: A Post-Chicago Approach." *Antitrust Law Journal, 63,* 513.

Srinagesh, P., and J. Gong. 1996. "The Economics of Layered Networks." In L. McKnight and J. Bailey, eds., *Internet Economics.* Cambridge, Mass.: MIT Press.

Williamson, O. 1987. *Markets and Hierarchies: Analysis and Antitrust Implications.* New York: Free Press.

Chapter 5

Clark, D. 1998. "A Taxonomy of Internet Telephony Applications." In D. Waterman and J. K. Mackie-Mason, eds., *Telephony, the Internet and the Media: Selected Papers from the 1997 Telecommunications Policy Research Conference.* Mahwah, N.J.: Erlbaum.

Computer Science and Telecommunications Board. 1994. *Realizing the Information Future: The Internet and Beyond.* Washington, D.C.: National Academy Press.

Computer Science and Telecommunications Board. 1996. *The Unpredictable Certainty: Information Infrastructure Through 2000.* Washington, D.C.: National Academy Press.

Esbin, Barbara. 1998. "Internet over Cable: Defining the Future in Terms of the Past." Working Paper 30. Washington, D.C.: FCC Office of Plans and Policy.

Gong, J., and P. Shrinagesh. 1997. "The Economics of Layered Networks." In L. McKnight and J. Bailey, eds., *Internet Economics.* Cambridge, Mass.: MIT Press.

Kavassalis, P., T. Y. Lee, and J. P. Bailey. 1998. "Sustaining a Vertically Disintegrated Network Through a Bearer Service Market." In E. Bohlin and S. L. Levin, eds., *Telecommunications Transformation: Technology, Strategy, and Policy.* Washington, D.C.: IOS Press.

NTIA. 1998. Filing before FCC by NTIA concerning Section 706 of the Telecommunications Act of 1996. Available at: http://www.ntia.doc.gov/ntiahome/fccfilings/sec706.htm.

Tennenhouse, D., B. Lampson, S. Gillett, and S. Klein. 1996. "Virtual Infrastructure: Putting Information Infrastructure on the Technology Curve." *Computer Networks and ISDN Systems,* pp. 1769–1790.

Chapter 6

Bailey, J. P., and L. W. McKnight. 1995. "Internet Economics: What Happens When Constituencies Collide." In *Proceedings of INET'95.* Internet Society.

Claffy, K., H. W. Braun, and G. Polyzos. 1994. "Long-Term Traffic Aspects of the NSFNET." In *Proceedings of INET'93.* Internet Society.

Hough, R. W. 1970. "Future Data Traffic Volume." *Computer,* September–October, pp. 6–12.

Kahin, B., ed. 1995. *Public Access to the Internet.* Cambridge, Mass.: MIT Press.

McKnight, L. W., P. Vaaler, and R. Katz. 2001. *Creative Destruction: Business Survival Strategies in the Global Internet Economy.* Cambridge, Mass.: MIT Press.

Mutooni, P. K. 1997. "Telecommunications @ Crossroads: The Transition from a Voice-Centric to a Data-Centric Communication Network." Master's thesis, Massachusetts Institute of Technology.

Noll, A. M. 1991. "Voice vs. Data: An Estimate of Future Broadband Traffic." *IEEE Communications Magazine,* June, pp. 22–29, 78.

References

Noll, A. M. 1996. "CyberNetwork Technology: Issues and Uncertainties." *Communications of the ACM, 39*(12), 27–31.

O'Shea, D., ed. 1996. "Voice and Data: Riding in Tandem on ATM." *Telephony*, March 11, pp. 41–47.

Wilson, C., ed. 1992. "The Changing Face of the CO Switch." *Telephony*, April 13, pp. 21–28.

Chapter 7

Antonelli, C. "The Diffusion of Information Technology and the Demand for Telecommunications Services." *Telecommunications Policy, 13*(5), 255–264.

Apostolidis, K., L. Merakos, and Xie-Hao. 1993. "A Reservation Protocol for Packet Voice and Data Integration in Unidirectional Bus Networks." *IEEE Transactions on Communications, 41*, 478–485.

Bane, W. S. Bradley, and D. Collis. 1997. "The Converging Worlds of Telecommunications, Computing, and Entertainment." Unpublished manuscript, Harvard University.

Branden, R., et al. 1997. *RFC 2205: Resource ReSerVation Protocol—Version 1 Functional Specification.* Available online: ftp://ds.internic.net/rfc/rfc2205.txt.

David, P., and J. Bunn. 1988. "The Economics of Gateway Technologies and Network Evolution." *Information Economics and Policy, 3*, 165–202.

Fisher, J. C., and R. H. Pry. 1971. "A Simple Substitution Model of Technological Change." *Technological Forecasting and Social Change, 3*, 75–88.

Griliches, Z. 1957. "Hybrid Corn: An Exploration in the Economics of Technological Change." *Econometrica, 4*(25), 501–522.

Handley, M. 1997. "An Examination of MBone Performance." *UCL and ISI Research Report*, January 10. Available at: http://northeast.isi.edu/~mjh/articles.html.

Hilgemeier, M. 1997. "Internet Growth." Available at: http://www.isbremen.de/~mhi/inetgrow.htm.

Lotter, M. 1992. "Network Working Group Request for Comments 1296: Internet Growth." SRI International. January. Available at: http://www.nw.com/zone/rfc1296.txt.

McKnight, L. 1997. "Internet Telephony and Open Communications Policy." Paper presented to the Impact of the Internet on Communications Policy, Harvard University, December.

Mehta, S. 1998. "Bells Seek Advanced Networks as Entry into Long Distance." *Wall Street Journal*, February 19.

Mueller, M. 1996. *Universal Service.* Cambridge, Mass.: MIT Press.

Mutooni, P. 1997. "Telecommunications @ Crossroads: The Transition from a Voice-Centric to a Data-Centric Communications Network." Master's thesis, Massachusetts Institute of Technology.

References

Neuman, W. R., L. McKnight, and R. J. Soloman. 1997. *The Gordian Knot: Political Gridlock on the Information Highway.* Cambridge, Mass.: MIT Press.

Noam, E. 1987. "The Public Telecommunications Network: A Concept in Transition." *Journal of Communications, 37*(1), 30–48.

Rockström, A., and B. Zdebel. 1998. "A Network Strategy for Survival." *IEEE Communications Magazine,* January.

Rogers, E. 1995. *Diffusion of Innovations.* New York: Free Press.

Werbach, K. 1997. "Digital Tornado: The Internet and Telecommunications Policy." NTIS PB97 161905. Working article, Federal Communications Commission.

Chapter 8

America's Carriers Telecommunication Association. 1996. "Petition for Declaratory Ruling, Special Relief, and Institution of Rulemaking Against Vocaltec, Inc.; Internet Telephone Company; Third Planet Publishing, Inc.; Camelot Corporation; Quarterdeck Corporation; and Other Providers of Non-tariffed, and Uncertified Interexchange Telecommunications Services."

Bailey, J. P., and L. W. McKnight. 1997. "Scalable Internet Interconnection Agreements and Integrated Services." In B. Kahin and J. H. Keller, eds., *Coordinating the Internet.* Cambridge, Mass.: MIT Press.

Boardwatch Magazine Directory of Internet Service Providers. 1997 Winter.

European Commission Directorate-General for Competition. 1997. *Notice by the Commission concerning the Status of Voice on the Internet Under Directive 90/388/EEC,* OJ C 140. July 5. http://www.europa.eu.int/en/comm/dg04/lawliber/en/97c140.htm.

Federal Communications Commission. 1980. *Amendment of Sec. 64.702 of the Commission's Rules and Regulations.* Final Decision, 77 FCC 2d 78b.

Federal Communications Commission. 1996. *Access Charge Reform, Price Cap Performance Review for Local Exchange Carriers, Transport Rate Structure and Pricing and Usage of the Public Switched Network by Information Service and Internet Access Providers.* CC Docket Nos. 96-262, 94-1, 91-213, and 96-263. *Notice of Proposed Rulemaking, Third Report and Other and Notice of Inquiry,* FCC 96-488 (Access Reform NPRM). December 24.

Federal Communications Commission. 1997a. *Federal-State Board on Universal Service,* CC Docket No. 96-45, First Report and Order, FCC 97-157 (Universal Service Order). May 8.

Federal Communications Commission. 1997b. *Price Cap Performance Review for Local Exchange Carriers and Access Charge Reform,* CC Docket Nos. 94-1 and 96-262, Fourth Report and Order in CC Docket No. 94-1 and Second Report and Order in CC Docket No. 96-262, FCC 97-159 (Access Reform Second Report and Order). May 16.

Federal Communications Commission. 1997c. *Commission Reforms Interstate Access Charge System.* Report No. CC 97-23. May 7.

References

FIND/SVP. 1996. *Home Use of the Internet and Commercial Online Services*. Available at: http://etrg.findsvp.com/financial/homeuse.html.

Forrester Research Telecom Strategies Group. 1996. *Sizing Internet Service*. August.

Leida, B. 1998. "A Cost Model of Internet Service Providers: Implications for Internet Telephony and Yield management." Master's thesis, Massachusetts Institute of Technology.

McKnight, L. W., and J. P. Bailey, eds. 1997. *Internet Economics*. Cambridge, Mass.: MIT Press.

McKnight, L. W., P. Vaaler, and R. Katz, eds. 2001. *Creative Destruction: Business Survival Strategies in the Global Internet Economy*. Cambridge, Mass.: MIT Press.

Morgan Stanley (Technology/New Media). 1996. *The Internet Report*. Available at: http://www.ms.com.

Neuman, W. R., L. McKnight, and R. J. Solomon 1997. *The Gordian Knot: Political Gridlock on the Information Highway*. Cambridge, Mass.: MIT Press.

Paschalidis, I., P. Kavassalis, and J. N. Tsitsiklis. 1997. "Efficient Resource Allocation and Yield Management in Internet Services." In *Internet Telephony Consortium Year-End Report*.

Short, K. I. 1997. "Towards Integrated Intranet Services: Modeling the Costs of Corporate IP Telephony." Master's thesis, Massachusetts Institute of Technology.

Students of the MIT Telecommunications Modeling and Policy Analysis Seminar. 1996. *A Cost Model of Internet Telephony for Regulatory Decision Making, In the Matter of "The Provision of Interstate and International Interexchange Telecommunications Service via the 'Internet' by Non-Tariffed, Uncertified Entities."* TPP91. MIT. Available at: http://itel.mit.edu/docs/ACTA/TPP91.htm.

Werbach, K. 1997. *Digital Tornado: The Internet and Telecommunications Policy*. OPP Working Paper No. 29, Federal Communications Commission Office of Plans and Policy.

Chapter 9

ADSL Forum. 1997. *ADSL Forum System Reference Model*. TR-001. N.P.: ADSL Forum.

Bill, H. 1998. "Home Network." *PC Magazine, 17*, 209.

Clark, D. 1997. "A Taxonomy of Internet Telephony Applications." In *Proceedings of the 25th TPRC*, October.

Federal Communications Commission. 1997. "NPRM: Deployment of Wireline Services Offering Advanced Telecommunications Capability." CC 98-147, August 8.

Freed, L. 1998. "Networks Made Easy." *PC Magazine*, September 8.

Fryxell, D. 1998. "Analysis of ATM/ADSL Architectures for a Public Broadband Network from an Economic and Public Policy Perspective." Paper presented at the Internet Telephony Consortium Meeting, Helsinki, Finland, June.

References

Hatfield Associates. 1997. Hatfield Model Release 3.1.

Hawley, G. 1997. "System Considerations for the Use of xDSL Technology for Data Access." *IEEE Communications Magazine*, March.

Holliday, C. R. 1997. "The Residential Gateway." *IEEE Spectrum, 34,* 29–31.

Huber, P. 1997. "Local Exchange Competition under the 1996 Telecom Act: Red-Lining the Local Residential Customer." November 4.

Humphrey, M., and J. Freeman. 1997. "How xDSL Supports Broadband Services to the Home." *IEEE Network,* January–February.

Leida, B. 1998. "A Cost Model for Internet Service Providers: Implications for Internet Telephony and Yield Management." Master's thesis, Massachusetts Institute of Technology.

Morgan, S. 1998. "The Internet and the Local Telephone Network: Conflicts and Opportunities." *IEEE Communications Magazine,* January.

Niccolai, J. 1998. "Vendor Groups to Ease Home Networking." *Infoworld,* June 29, p. 68.

Ohr, S., and R. Boyd-Merritt. 1998. "Wireless-Network Debate Hits Home." *EE Times,* March 9.

Okubo, S., et al. 1997. "ITU-T Standardization of Audiovisual Communication Systems in ATM and LAN Environments." *IEEE JSAC, 15,* 965–982.

Thom, G. A. 1996. "H.323: The Multimedia Communications Standard for Local Area Networks." *IEEE Communications Magazine, 34,* 52–56.

Turner, J. S. "Design of an Integrated Services Packet Network." *IEEE JSAC, SAC 4,* 1373–1380.

Wanichkorn, K., and M. Sirbu. 1998. "The Economics of Premises Internet Telephony." Working Paper, Carnegie Mellon University. June.

Chapter 10

Cisco Systems. 1998. "Packet Voice Networking Solution Guide." Cisco Seminar Series. May.

Clark, D. "A Taxonomy of Internet Telephony Applications." Paper presented at the Telecommunications Policy Research Conference. September 27–29.

Federal Communications Commission. 1998. *Report to Congress.* CC Docket No. 96-45. April 10.

Lande, J., and T. Waldon. 1997. *"Reference Book of Rates, Price Indices, and Household Expenditures for Telephone Service.* Washington, D.C.: Industry Analysis Division, Common Carrier Bureau, FCC.

References

Leida, B. 1997. "A Cost Model of Internet Service Providers: Implications for Internet Telephony and Yield management." Master's thesis, Massachusetts Institute of Technology. 1997.

Leida, B., and L. McKnight. "Internet Telephony: Costs, Pricing, and Policy." Paper presented at the Telecommunications Policy Research Conference. September 27–29.

Meir, E., et al. 2000. "The Next Generation." *Business Communications Review*, January, pp. 38–42.

Rigney, S. 1999. "PBX Meets the LAN." *PC Magazine*, Nov. 24.

Sears, A. P. Mutooni, R. Cheng, and others. 1996. "A Cost Model of Internet Telephony for Regulatory Decision Making." FCC Comment, May.

Selsius Systems. 1998. "A Fundamental Shift in Telephony Networks." White Paper. March 1.

Short, K. 1997. "Towards Integrated Intranet Services: Modeling the Costs of Corporate IP Telephony." Master's thesis, Massachusetts Institute of Technology.

Chapter 11

de Sola Pool, I. 1977. *The Social Impact of the Telephone*. Cambridge, Mass.: MIT Press.

de Sola Pool, I. 1990. *Technologies Without Barriers*. Cambridge, Mass.: Harvard University Press.

Kahn, A. E. 1989. *The Economics of Regulation*. Cambridge, Mass.: MIT Press.

Lehr, W., and L. McKnight. 1998. "Next Generation Internet Bandwidth Markets." *Communications and Strategies*, October.

Lynch, D. C., and M. T. Rose. 1993. *Internet System Handbook*. Reading, Mass.: Addison-Wesley.

McGarty, T. P. 1990. *Alternative Networking Architectures; Pricing, Policy, and Competition, Information Infrastructures for the 1990s*. Cambridge, Mass.: John F. Kennedy School of Government, Harvard University.

McGarty, T. P. 1991a. "Information Architectures and Infrastructures: Value Creation and Transfer." Paper presented at the Nineteenth Annual Telecommunications Research Conference, Solomon's Island Md.

McGarty, T. P. 1991b. "Alternative Networking Architectures." In B. Kahin, ed., *Building Information Infrastructure*. New York: McGraw-Hill.

McGarty, T. P. 1991c. "Communications Networks: A Morphological and Taxonomical Approach." Paper presented at the Private Networks and Public Policy Conference, Columbia University, New York, October.

References

McGarty, T. P. 1992a. "Wireless Communications Economics." Paper presented at the Advanced Telecommunications Institute Policy Chapter, Carnegie Mellon University, Pittsburgh, Pa., February.

McGarty, T. P. 1992b. "Communications Network Morphological and Taxonomical Policy Implications." Paper presented at the Telecommunications Policy Research Conference, Solomon's Island, Md.

McGarty, T. P. 1992c. Architectures et Structures de L'Information, Reseaux, No 56, pp. 119–156, Paris (December).

McGarty, T. P. 1993a. "Economic Structural Analysis of Wireless Communications Systems." Paper presented at the Advanced Telecommunications Institute Policy Chapter, Carnegie Mellon University, Pittsburgh, Pa., February.

McGarty, T. P. 1993b. "Spectrum Allocation Alternatives; Industrial: Policy versus Fiscal Policy." Paper presented at the Universal Personal Communications Symposium, MIT, March.

McGarty, T. P. 1993c. "Wireless Access to the Local Loop." Paper presented at the MIT Universal Personal Communications Symposium, March.

McGarty, T. P. 1993d. "Access to the Local Loop: Options, Evolution and Policy Implications." Paper presented at Infrastructures in Massachusetts, Kennedy School of Government, Harvard University, March.

McGarty, T. P. 1993e. "Internet Architectural and Policy Implications." Paper presented at Public Access to the Internet, Kennedy School of Government, Harvard University, May.

McGarty, T. P. 1993f. "Access Policy and the Changing Telecommunications Infrastructures." Paper presented at Telecommunications Policy Research Conference, Solomon's Island, Md., September.

McGarty, T. P. 1994. "Wireless Architectural Alternatives: Current Economic Valuations Versus Broadband Options." Paper presented at Gilder Conjectures, Solomon's Island, Md., September.

McGarty, T. P. 1995. *From High End User to New User: A New Internet Paradigm.* New York: McGraw-Hill.

McGarty, T. P. 1996. "Disaggregation of Telecommunications." Paper presented at Columbia University CITI Conference on the Impact of Cybercommunications on Telecommunications, March.

McGarty, T. P. 1997. "Competition in the Local Exchange Market: An Economic and Antitrust Perspective." *Federal Communications Law Journal*, submitted and to be published.

McGarty, T. P. 1999. "IP Telecommunications QoS (Quality of Service): Is Service Quality a Sustainable Metric?" Paper presented at the MIT ITC Conference, Telcom Italia, L'Aquila, Italy, June.

McGary, T. P., and G. J. Clancey. 1983. "Cable Based Metro Area Networks." *IEEE Journal on Selected Areas in Communication, 1*, 816–831.

References

McGarty, T. P., and J. Davidson. 1997. "Comparative Deregulation of Far Eastern Telecommunications Markets: Economic Incentives and International Competitive Strategies." Arlington, Va.: TPRC.

Posner, R. A. 1976. *Antitrust Law*. Chicago: University of Chicago Press.

Posner, R. A. 1983. *The Economics of Justice*. Cambridge, Mass.: Harvard University Press.

Posner, R. A. 1992. *Economic Analysis of Law*. Boston: Little, Brown.

Spulber, D. F. 1990. *Regulation and Markets*. Cambridge, Mass.: MIT Press.

About the Authors

David D. Clark is a senior research scientist at the MIT Laboratory for Computer Science. Since the mid-1970s, he has been leading the development of the Internet; from 1981 to 1989 he acted as chief protocol architect in this development and chaired the Internet Activities Board. Recent activities include extensions to the Internet to support real-time traffic, explicit allocation of service, pricing and related economic and policy issues surrounding the Internet, such as local-loop deployment. His new activities focus on the architecture of the Internet in the post-PC era. He has also worked on computer and communications security. Clark is chairman of the Computer Science and Telecommunications Board of the National Research Council and has contributed to a number of studies on the societal and policy impact of computer communications. He received his Ph.D. from MIT.

Daniel Fryxell is a Ph.D. candidate at Carnegie Mellon University. His research interests are in economic, technical, and policy aspects of local access networks offering advanced telecommunications capability. His dissertation is a study of broadband networks integrating data and voice over asymmetric digital subscriber lines and cable modem platforms. He received an M.S. and a B.S. from the Technical University of Lisbon, Portugal.

Sharon Eisner Gillett is the executive director of the MIT Internet and Telecoms Convergence Consortium and a research associate at the

MIT Center for Technology, Policy and Industrial Development. She is the author of numerous articles about the Internet and telecommunications. From 1982–1992, she developed computer networking software for BBN Communications Corporation and Thinking Machines Corporation. She received her M.B.A. and M.S. from MIT and her A.B. from Harvard-Radcliffe.

William Lehr, an economist and industry consultant, is a research associate in the Center for Technology, Policy and Industrial Development, at MIT and associate director of the MIT Internet and Telecoms Convergence Consortium. He is also an associate research scholar on the faculty of Columbia University's Graduate School of Business and a research associate at the Columbia Institute of Tele-Information. His academic research focuses on the industrial economics, competitive strategy, and public policy implications of the Internet and computer technology. He has published numerous articles in scholarly journals on such topics as Internet pricing, industry structure, and regulatory policy, and he speaks regularly at academic and industry research conferences in the United States and abroad.

In addition to his academic research, Lehr provides litigation, economic, and business strategy consulting services for firms in the information technology industries. He has advised information technology companies on strategic marketing, pricing, financial planning, and competitive strategy and has prepared expert witness testimony for both private litigation and for regulatory proceedings before the Federal Communications Commission and numerous state commissions. Lehr holds a Ph.D. from Stanford, an M.B.A. from the Wharton Graduate School, and M.S.E., B.S., and B.A. degrees from the University of Pennsylvania.

Brett Leida was a graduate student who worked with the Internet Telephony Consortium at MIT. He received his M.S. from MIT in the technology and policy and the electrical engineering programs. He is currently working in the optical networking industry with Sycamore Networks.

Terrence P. McGarty is a member of the steering committee of the MIT Internet and Telecoms Convergence Consortium and CEO of the

Telmarc Group. He is also CEO of Zephyr Telecommunications, an international record carrier, and was chairman of COMAV, a competitive local exchange carrier.

Lee W. McKnight is associate professor of international communication and director of the Edward R. Murrow Center at the Fletcher School of Law and Diplomacy at Tufts University. He is a visiting scholar at the MIT Center for Technology, Policy, and Industrial Development and the founder and former principal investigator of the MIT Internet and Telecoms Convergence Consortium, previously known as the Internet Telephony Consortium. He is the president of Marengo Research, an international consultancy. He is the author, co-author, or co-editor of many books and articles on information and communication technology, economics, and policy. Lee holds a B.A. from Tufts University, an M.A. from Johns Hopkins University, and a Ph.D. from MIT.

Philip Mutooni is a manager at iBasis, Inc. iBasis is a leader in advanced Internet-based communications services for international carriers and other service providers. Prior to joining iBasis, Mutooni was a cofounder of IP. Fusion Technologies, a spin-off from the Internet Telephony Consortium at MIT. He has also been a researcher at MIT's Internet Telephony Consortium and Laboratory for Computer Science. He holds two degrees from MIT and has a bachelor's degree from the University of Rochester.

Husham Sharifi has been the cofounder of or contributor to Internet start-ups in web hosting, networking, and Internet incubation. He has been a consultant for the Strategic Planning Unit of the International Telecommunication Union in Geneva. Husham has authored ITU report and conference papers in the Internet field. He was a research assistant in the MIT Internet and Telecoms Convergence Consortium, where he additionally founded the xDSL Group (based in MIT). Husham, a member of the engineering honor fraternity Sigma Xi, holds a B.S. from the University of California at San Diego and two M.S. degrees from MIT.

Marc S. Shuster a management consultant, holds a B.S. and an M. Eng. degree from MIT. While a researcher at MIT's Research Program on

Communication Policy (RPCP), he prepared a thesis on demand and adoption models of technological innovations in the nascent Internet telephony industry and presented his research to the International Telecommunication Society's Twelfth Biennial Conference.

Marvin Sirbu holds a joint appointment as professor of engineering and public policy, industrial administration, and electrical and computer engineering at Carnegie Mellon University. His work is concerned with how new communications technology affects public regulation and corporate decision making and, conversely, how public policy influences the development of new information technologies. He received his S.B., M.S., and Sc.D degrees from MIT and was a faculty member at its Sloan School of Management before moving to Carnegie Mellon.

David Tennenhouse an Intel vice president and director of research, is one of the pioneers of asynchronous transfer mode networking, active networks, software radio, and desktop media processing. Before Intel, and the Defense Advanced Research Projects Agency, he held appointments in MIT's Department of Electrical Engineering and Computer Science and in the Sloan School of Management. He received his B.A.Sc. and M.A.Sc. degrees from the University of Toronto and the Ph.D. at the University of Cambridge.

Kanchana Wanichkorn is a Ph.D. candidate in the Department of Engineering and Public Policy and an M.S. candidate in the Department of Electrical and Computer Engineering at Carnegie Mellon University. Her research interests are in the areas of economic and policy issues related to voice over IP and IP-based broadband networks. Her dissertation is a study of broadband fixed wireless networks offering integrated voice and data services. She received an M.S. and an M.A. from the University of Michigan and a B.S. from the University of Minnesota.

Jonathan Weinberg is a professor at Wayne State University Law School in Detroit, Michigan. He has also clerked for Judge Ruth Bader Ginsburg and Justice Thurgood Marshall, studied Japanese communications law as a visiting scholar at the University of Tokyo, and was an associate at the Washington, D.C., law firm of Shea & Gardner. He has been a scholar in residence at the Federal Communications Commission, where he worked on Internet-related matters, and a professor in residence at the Justice Department. He is currently a visiting scholar at Cardozo Law School's Howard M. Squadron Program in Law, Media and Society and co-chair of the Internet Corporation for Assigned Names and Numbers's Working Group C on new global top-level domains.

Index